The International Dictionary of

MARKETING

The International Dictionary of

MARKETING

over 2,000 professional
terms & techniques

DANIEL YADIN

**KOGAN
PAGE**

First published in 2002

Apart from any fair dealing for the purposes of research or private study, or criticism or review, as permitted under the Copyright, Designs and Patents Act 1988, this publication may only be reproduced, stored or transmitted, in any form or by any means, with the prior permission in writing of the publishers, or in the case of reprographic reproduction in accordance with the terms and licences issued by the CLA. Enquiries concerning reproduction outside these terms should be sent to the publishers at the undermentioned addresses:

Kogan Page Limited
120 Pentonville Road
London N1 9JN
UK

Kogan Page US
22 Broad Street
Milford CT 06460
USA

© Daniel Yadin, 2002

The right of Daniel Yadin to be identified as the author of this work has been asserted by him in accordance with the Copyright, Designs and Patents Act 1988.

British Library Cataloguing in Publication Data

A CIP record for this book is available from the British Library.

ISBN 0 7494 3532 1

Typeset by JS Typesetting, Wellingborough, Northants
Printed and bound in Great Britain by Creative Print and Design (Wales), Ebbw Vale

Contents

Introduction: a practical guide for marketers

The only duty a writer has is to defend the language. If language is corrupted, thought is corrupted.

W H Auden

You will find this Dictionary very practical, with text designed as a guide on a day-to-day level. It can help you in two ways. First, it uses language that people actually speak, and helps to make clearer much of the jargon used in marketing. Two examples: you read in a marketing magazine about FMCG; but the author, assuming that everybody knows what this means, fails to explain it. The Dictionary comes to your aid. In a marketing textbook, you come across a term that the author uses and discusses, but which you still cannot fully appreciate. The Dictionary may help to resolve this.

Second, on an even more pragmatic level, it explains marketing practices and procedures. You may, for example, be interested in how the monitoring of Web site hits is carried out. The Dictionary comes to the rescue by explaining ABC// electronic monitoring. Or, you may be undecided whether to use litho or flexography for a catalogue or brochure. The Dictionary helps you to make up your mind, and to understand what your printer is saying.

Value for time and effort

In an ordinary dictionary, you usually find little but definitions. Here, you find a more encyclopedic approach, and good value for your time and effort. The Dictionary includes clear explanations, observation and comment, plus guidelines and advice based on practical experience. For example:

Video News Release   *Broadcast communications, Editorial, Public relations*
A corporate or product news item, prepared and edited before submission to television stations; popularly referred to as **VNR**. Current wisdom on VNRs is that, on a busy news day a VNR can get an item on air mainly because it is already in the can; that is, complete and ready for transmission. However, mere submission of a VNR will not guarantee airtime. . .

1

References and associations

In addition to marketing concepts, tools and techniques, the Dictionary abounds with appropriate references, associations and cross-references. These are designed to help you extend and amplify your knowledge and understanding of marketing practice. Associations include: Advertising; Artwork; Brand management; Business; Campaigns; Communications; Composition; Consumer behaviour; Controls and legislation; Copywriting; Corporate; Creative; Desktop publishing; Distribution; E-commerce; Economics; Editorial; E-marketing; Graphics; Information technology; Internet; Media; Merchandising; Organizations; Packaging; Paper; Photography; Planning; Print; Public relations; Publishing; Radio; Retailing; Sales; Television; Typography; Video; Web sites; Word-processing.

Associations and connotations

Each entry heading is shown in bold, followed by associations and connotations in italics. Associations are the contexts in which the term or concept is used or associated. This does not signify that each association is exclusive to that entry. For example:

Deadline   *Advertising, Public relations, Publishing*
The date or time planned and set for the completion of a job, or for the submission of copy to a newspaper, magazine or printer.

(This indicates that a deadline procedure is in common use in advertising, PR and publishing. However, it is not exclusive to these activities. It is also used in project management, building, and a wide range of business and professional work.)

Spike   *Editorial, Newsroom practice, Press media, Public relations, Publishing*
Used as a verb, this means to kill a story with no possibility of reinstatement. The term comes from pre-computer times, when editors used a piece of desk-furniture, a spike, to collect non-viable stories for disposal. . .

(The term is used in press media newsrooms, by editors and journalists, though not normally in public relations practice. However, PR executives need to be aware of what could happen to their news stories if they are inappropriate to the media to which they are sent.)

Technical guidelines

Many entries are accompanied by guidelines on how techniques are used. Often there will be more than one definition for the same term. For example:

Filler *Desktop publishing, Editorial, Print, Publishing*
A piece of copy or an illustration inserted on a page to fill up a column; an editorial technique used before the days of DTP and computerized typesetting. Today, an editor can often juggle page elements on the screen so that fillers are unnecessary. However, a filler often makes a page easier on the eye than it would be with a strictly clinical layout. To enjoy some really delightful fillers, read the *New Yorker*.

Filler *Paper, Paper-making*
A material, usually a white mineral substance such as china clay, titanium dioxide or calcium carbonate. When added to the material from which the paper is made, it increases its opacity, improves its flatness, and imparts a smoother surface to the finished product.

Body copy in bold

In many entries, the text is interspersed with words in bold. This is meant to highlight them and call them to your attention. They do not indicate cross-references.

Essential repetition

Some definitions appear in more than one place, sometimes repeating the same copy. This is deliberate, because it allows explanations to be presented complete and self-contained.

Spelling and language

Although this Dictionary is meant for international consumption, it has been written and produced in the UK. It follows that the spellings used are those found in Queen's English. Some spellings may differ from spelling conventions used in US English. This is because Americans, perhaps wisely, have deliberately simplified their language; whereas the British have not, despite encroachments from Hollywood. You will, of course, find the usual differences: colour for color, analyse for analyze, and so on. All language used here is Queen's English, which is used by much of the English-speaking world, including Commonwealth countries. Appendix 1 lists over 200 differences between Queen's English and US English.

Errors and omissions

Any *lapsus calami* or error of fact and procedure is mine. It would be unfair, and ignoble, to blame anyone else. On the other hand, if you find errors or omissions, don't just sit there and fume. Contact me via the publisher, and suggest corrections and additions. Since marketing and its technology are in constant change, there are bound also to be changes to the Dictionary over time. In return, I will acknowledge all contributions used in the next edition. You may then join gurus David Ogilvy, Martyn P Davis and Rosser Reeves, whose thought I admire and have mentioned several times in these pages.

Intellectual honesty

Marketing transcends questions of gender, age and creed. In most normal market economies, half of the market is male, half female. It is a poor marketer who either wastefully amalgamates the two, or throws away half her market, in the name of political correctness. It is an even poorer marketer who will allow himself to be bullied by pressure groups pushing political correctness. Unelected and unappointed, except by themselves, pressure groups have no mandate for controlling individual, private or public behaviour or thought. However, they do have a covert agenda for securing and enhancing their own political power. Stalin probably had a word for it.

Throughout this book, for the sake of brevity, simplicity and style, 'he' is used to include 'she', and vice versa. Man, so to speak, embraces woman. Besides, he/she, h-she, s-he and similar idiocies are not Queen's English. What is more, they look gauche on the page and offend a reader's intellect. In the words of my bank, in its terms and conditions, 'Words importing a gender shall include all genders'. Can one be more intellectually honest than that?

Aa

A *Communications, Information technology*

A character used in many computer operating systems, denoting a disk drive in the system. Where a computer has several disk drives, alphabetical characters are used to differentiate them. The floppy disk is usually given A:; a second floppy disk, B:; the hard disk, C:; and any others, from D: onwards. Copy, graphics, data and other material are rendered portable by the use of floppy and Zip disks. Sending copy to a printer, for example, may be carried out in this way; or downloaded via a telephone line.

AA *Advertising organizations*

A common abbreviation for the Advertising Association in the United Kingdom.

AAA *Advertising organizations*

The American Advertising Association.

AAAA *Advertising organizations*

The American Association of Advertising Agencies. Web site: www.commercepark.com/AAAA/index.html.

ABC *Media research and planning*

Initials used by newspaper and magazine publishers to indicate that their circulations have been independently audited by the **Audit Bureau of Circulations**. This does not refer to audits of newspaper of magazine readership, which is entirely different.
See Audit Bureau of Circulations.

A, B, C1, C2, D, E *Planning and research*

Social grade classification of target audiences, used by marketing planners. This is a simple and practical system for differentiating target groups. It is pragmatic, in the marketing sense, not the political.

Social grades used in UK marketing communications:

Grade		Members	Approx % of UK population
A	Upper middle class	Top businessmen; other leaders; key opinion-formers	2.7%
B	Middle class	Senior executives; managers	15.2%

C1	Lower middle class	White-collar, white-blouse office workers	24.1%
C2	Skilled working class	Blue-collar factory workers	27.1%
D	Working class	Semi- and unskilled manual workers	17.8%
E	Lowest level of subsistence	Poor pensioners; disabled; casual workers	13.1%

Identification of consumer needs and wants, UK socio-economic groups:

Class   Needs and wants:

A   Status-conferring products and services of high quality, eg investments, private schools, luxury travel and travel services; five-star hotels and cruises; expensive leisure activities; special interests, eg fine arts, music, wine and antiques.
B   Products and services with cachet, conferring aspirant status; banking, investment, insurance and life assurance; weekend breaks; three- and four-star hotels; good restaurants, night-clubs.
C1   Products and services of above-average quality, conferring aspirant status; above-average-quality foreign holidays, fashion products, personal and domestic possessions; restaurants of slightly above-average quality; take-away meals; convenience foods; efficient kitchens; improving quality of home decor. Popular sports activities.
C2   Average-quality products and services; mass-produced fashion and personal products; packaged holidays; convenience and fast foods; DIY products and personal effort in home improvements. Popular sports activities.
D   Economy-emphasized products and services; fast foods; above-average, routine consumption of fish and chips; packaged holidays and holiday camps. DIY activities. Much time and money spent on popular sports and leisure activities.
E   Product purchases of the most basic kind, heavily angled towards the best economic value. Occasional use of services, especially those most economically priced.
See Socio-economic grades.

Above the line   *Advertising campaign planning*
The metaphorical, horizontal line drawn by advertising planners, to differentiate between those media that allow agency commission, and those that do not.

Above the line:
cinema
outdoor
press
radio
television

The line: _____

Below the line:

advertising gifts
body media (T-shirts, hats etc)
direct mail
exhibitions
mini media
packaging
point-of-sale material
print
public relations
retail display and merchandising
sales promotion
sponsorship

Abrasion resistance   *Paper, Print*
The resistance of a printing ink to removal by rubbing and scratching.

Absolute placement   *Desktop publishing*
The exact position on a page where a line of copy is to start; the position the corner of a graphic element is to be anchored to.
See Origin.

Absorbency   *Paper, Print*
The extent to which a paper will take up and hold a liquid. This is important in litho printing, in which both water and oil-based inks are used.

Absorption   *Print*
The first stage of drying of an ink when printed on porous material.

Absorption   *Marketing planning*
The allocation of the costs of marketing a product or service, so that they are absorbed in the final calculation. These include fixed costs, such as rent and business tax, and variable costs such as raw materials and delivery.

Absorption pricing   *Marketing planning*
The calculation of all costs to be taken into account when marketing a product, in order to determine a viable price for it. The technique used covers the entire cost of marketing a product or service, so that the selling price also covers everything.

Accelerator   *Marketing*
A situation in the marketing of consumer products. A small change in the demand for a product can lead to a big change in the demand for the systems and machinery for producing it. This in turn can lead to changes in the retail price of the product.

Access
Information technology

To find or go to an area of computer memory or auxiliary storage for storing or retrieving information. When you have retrieved an application program or file from a disk, you are said to have **accessed** it.

Accordion fold
Print

Also called a concertina fold. A leaflet folded like the bellows of a piano accordion. All sides are available for printing. Sometimes lack of copy, or of imagination, results in the reverse side remaining unprinted. This may be deliberate when the intention is to have the recipient pull out the concertina into a single sheet.

Account
Advertising, PR and marketing agency administration

Another name for a client organization whose advertising, PR or marketing business is being handled by its agency. Also applied to a department of a client organization that supplies the business on which the agency produces campaigns. In sales administration, this is the term used for an invoice.

Account executive
Advertising, PR and marketing agency personnel

An executive responsible for the day-to-day management of a client's business within an agency. This person 'handles the account'; in other words looks after the client's day-to-day business within the agency. In actual practice, the account executive is also responsible for bringing in the business, and ensuring that the client remains loyal to the agency. The account executive represents the agency to the client and, ideally, the client to the agency.

At its most basic, this position is akin to a ballboy on a tennis court. At its most sophisticated, businesslike and practical, a person responsible for the planning, organization supervision, implementation and analysis of clients' campaigns. This executive, however, is expected to sell the agency's services, as well as provide advice and expertise. Sometimes called an **account manager**.

Account group
Advertising, PR and marketing agency administration

A division of an agency, often under a board director, responsible for handling a number of accounts. Sometimes a group is set up as a profit centre within the agency.

Accreditation
Business

When a company is appointed to act on behalf of a client organization as its agent, it is said to be accredited. Advertising agencies, by contrast, are actually principals in contracts undertaken for clients, and therefore are not agents in the usually accepted and legal sense.

Acetate
Artwork, Production

Transparent plastic sheeting used for underlays in the creation of artwork. Also used for the protection of layouts and finished artwork. The acetate overlay enables you to examine the artwork underneath without accidentally putting beery thumb-marks on it. It also discourages clients from making amendments to the artwork itself in marker or ballpoint pen. Artwork, after all, is expensive to produce.

Achromatic lens   *Photography*
A lens design using different elements to bring different colours of the spectrum to a common focus. **Chromatic aberration** is the inability of a lens to bring all the colour components of light to a single point of focus. White light can be split into seven main colour components in a spectrum. As each component enters a lens, it is refracted – bent – to a different degree. The red constituent comes to focus at the rear of a film plane, the blue closest to the lens; green falls roughly between the two. In an exposure, a single lens may produce colour fringes, particularly around highlights. By using an achromatic lens, different colours are brought into focus at the film plane. An achromatic lens doublet comprises two types of glass, each with a different refractive index – the ability to bend light. A two-element achromatic lens brings only two colours to the same focal point, usually blue and green. The third colour, red, is already correctly focused.

Acid-free   *Paper, Print*
Paper that does not contain free acid. During manufacture, precautions are taken to eliminate active acid in the furnish. This helps to increase the life of the finished paper.
See Furnish.

Acknowledgement   *Business administration*
The written or spoken expression of thanks to an individual or organization, for the use of their material. Acknowledgements are used in advertising and public relations material where attribution is required.

ACORN   *Marketing planning, Marketing research*
Acronym for **A Classification Of Residential Neighbourhoods**. A research system that classifies people according to where they live. Some years ago, it dawned on a certain bright research team that the places people choose to live are directly related to their spending power. Of course, the fact had been staring everybody in the face for centuries, but these particularly fertile and disciplined minds saw its commercial potential. ACORN is now an indispensable part of marketing planning and practice.

Acrobat   *Information technology, Marketing communications, Print*
A commercial software program for viewing and editing portable document formats (PDFs). The **Acrobat distiller** is the program within Acrobat used for generating PDFs from PostScript files; the **Acrobat reader** is the program used for viewing PDFs.

Acronym   *Business, Language, Marketing, Promotion*
The initials of a group of words put together to form a separate, identifying word. Acronyms are differentiated from initials, in that they are capable of being

pronounced like a word. NATO, for example, is formed from North American Treaty Organization. Certain familiar logos may also qualify as acronyms. A good example is **3M**, formed from the words Minnesota Mining and Manufacturing Corporation; it is used in all the company's marketing communications.

Across the network *Media*
In media scheduling, specifying that an advertiser's commercials shall be transmitted simultaneously throughout a named network.

Activity sampling *Marketing research, Research*
In attempting to evaluate a particular activity in a specified target audience, the audience is observed using a range of discontinuous tests. The tests enable the researcher to estimate and quantify the incidence of the activity.

Adaptation *Art direction*
A press advertisement or piece of print in one size or shape when modified to another size or shape. This is usually referred to as an **adapt**. Adaptation of the creative concept for a press advertisement is routinely made for other media, such as posters and point-of-sale material.

Ad-click *Advertising, Internet*
A term denoting that an advertisement on a Web site has been clicked by a visiting Internet surfer. Clicks are counted and totalled, giving some quantitative value to the advertisement and, by implication, to the Web site.

Ad Council *Advertising organizations*
The common abbreviation for **The Advertising Council of the USA**. A private corporation conducting public service advertising campaigns.

Added value *Business, Marketing*
Augmenting and increasing the value of a product, service or business activity, by adding services and features to the actual product, and promoting them with the product. Guarantees, warranties, free delivery and support services are good current examples of this. In manufacturing, value can be added to materials by processing and handling. Envelopes, diaries, keyrings and pens can be overprinted with company logos and campaign slogans. Lumps of iron can be turned into swords, and timber into furniture, by expert labour and a good deal of sweat.

Address *Information technology*
A location in computer memory or auxiliary storage.

Address line *Advertising, Creative*
That part of an advertisement, brochure, leaflet, Web site or other promotional material containing the address of the advertiser. This is usually, but not always,

the address to which a coupon or reply card should be returned. Be careful to specify which is which. In a coupon or reply card, another valid address line is the one filled in by the enquirer when requesting information or ordering a product. Do not confuse the two, or you may confuse the recipient.

Ad hoc *Advertising, Business, Marketing*

An over-used, and sometimes misused, Latin phrase, taken to mean a 'one-off'. Its real meaning is 'for this particular purpose', or 'special'. In marketing and advertising, an ad hoc campaign is one created and run as a one-off or short-term effort; to respond to a competitive attack, for example, or a temporary downturn in a market.

Ad hoc survey *Research*

A one-off research survey on a specific topic.

Admark *Advertising, Controls, Web sites*

An opt-in scheme in the UK, allowing member advertisers and publishers to promote their support for legal, decent, honest and truthful advertising. This is done by displaying the Admark icon on their paid-for advertisements, and by providing information about the scheme on their Web sites.

The growth of the Internet, and consequent emergence of online advertising, has led to the need for a 'safe harbour' scheme that tells consumers who has pledged to follow advertising's rules. The Admark scheme is the result.

Admark was developed by the Committee of Advertising Practice (CAP), the UK industry body that writes and enforces the British Codes of Advertising and Sales Promotion (the Codes). It has been welcomed by the Advertising Standards Authority, the independent body that administers the Codes.

Administered prices *Marketing*

Another word for retail price maintenance. It refers to the fixing of prices within an industry, designed to eliminate price differences at the point of sale. In the UK, RPM was prohibited in 1963; however, certain products still display this characteristic.

Adobe Illustrator *Information technology, Marketing communications, Studio work*

Commercial vector image creation and editing software. This is one of the many graphical applications collectively termed 'drawing' programs.

Adobe PhotoShop *Information technology, Marketing communications, Studio work*

Commercial software for raster image creation, editing and format translation. This is one of the many graphical applications collectively termed 'painting' programs. Painting applications work by manipulating the values of pixels.

Adoption of innovation *Marketing*
Consumers taking up a new product or service fall into three main categories. In marketing jargon, innovators are those who try or buy on or near launch day. The next group of consumers to do this are termed **early adopters**, followed chronologically by early and late majority buyers. Last to adopt the innovation are usually called **laggards**, though this does not demean their value as customers.

Adshel *Outdoor advertising*
A roadside poster illuminated from within a transparent or translucent shell. Usually sited in high streets, shopping precincts and other busy locations. Popularly used at main road passenger bus shelters, rail and bus stations. Adshel is also the poster contractor's trade name.

ADSL *Internet communications*
Initials for **Asymmetric Digital Subscriber Line**. A system for super-fast access for home Net users. It allows access at between 10 and 40 times normal speeds using a standard telephone line. It is usually described as '**always on**'.
See ISDN.

Advance *Authorship, Publishing*
Money paid to a writer or artist in advance of publication of their work. This sum is offset against any royalties that the work may produce.

Advert *Advertising terminology*
A corrupt form of the word **advertisement**, used by amateurs; professionals use either 'ad' or 'advertisement'.

Advertisement *Advertising*
A paid-for promotional announcement. This applies both to press and broadcast media; though, strangely, not to printed literature or direct mail. It is gradually being adopted universally to advertising on the Internet; initially, banners were the only form of advertising to quality for the term.

Advertisement department *Advertising, Publishing*
In newspaper, magazine and poster publishing, and broadcast media, this is the department dedicated to the promoting and selling of advertising space and airtime.

Advertisement manager *Advertising, Publishing*
A senior executive managing an advertisement department, responsible to an advertisement director. This is usually a sales manager, who not only controls the sales staff of the department but is also an experienced salesperson. Often, the advertisement manager also commissions advertising and other material promoting his publication, poster sites, radio or TV station as an advertising medium. Do not confuse this term with **advertising manager**, who is an entirely different animal and works within an advertiser's organization.

Advertisement rate card   *Media*
A tariff booklet, leaflet or card showing the costs of advertisement space or airtime. The card also usually contains terms of business, and mechanical production details.

Advertisement wrap   *Advertising, Outdoor advertising*
Advertisements placed on windows of vehicles and buildings, so that the image appears on the outer side while remaining see-though from the inside. Vehicle wrap includes images on taxis, buses, trams and trains; building wrap, images on buildings, roadside shelters and so on. The first full wrap building project was on four sides of the Panasonic building in Paris in 1998. Several different designs have now been wrapped on this building.

Advertising   *Marketing communications techniques*
Many people have attempted to define and describe this difficult subject. The answer depends on who you are, and also what your investment is. Here are a few concepts to be going on with:

- For advertisers, it is presenting the most persuasive message to the right prospective customers for the product or service, at the lowest possible cost. This is the official IPA definition.
- For marketers, it is an economical communication system, aimed at achieving fast payoff of marketing investment.
- For agency account management, it is a means of reaching and influencing a chosen group of people quickly and cost-effectively.
- For academics, it is a specialized form of communication used in marketing, to influence choice and buying decisions.
- For creatives, it is a highly skilled creative trade, demanding imagination and creative flair of an extremely high order.
- For everybody else: it is paid-for, non-personal, promotional communications through mass media.

If you have a single definition that describes advertising to perfection, dear reader, please send it, care of the publisher of this book. You will get proper credit for it in the next edition; possibly achieve a degree of immortality as well.
See Public relations.

Advertising agency   *Advertising business*
A specialist business dedicated to researching, planning, producing and placing advertising campaigns and material for its clients. The original advertising agents were freelance representatives selling advertising space for newspapers in the 19th century. Demand by advertisers for extra services, such as design and copywriting, compelled the agents to supply them. Since nobody can serve two opposing masters, agents' loyalties shifted from publisher to advertiser. Today, advertising agencies serve their clients as independent specialists; they are not 'agents' in the legal sense, but principals. Agency services include:

- copywriting for press, print and broadcast media;
- design;
- direct marketing services and activities;
- exhibition design, booking and implementation;
- marketing planning and services;
- media planning and buying;
- photography;
- print;
- production;
- researching and planning advertising campaigns;
- sales promotion;
- Web site creation.

Some agencies concentrate on single specialist activities, such as creative services. *See* À la carte agency.

Advertising appropriation *Advertising planning*
An allocation of money for advertising activities. Advertising departments can usually work this out for themselves, but most substantial advertisers have agencies to do it for them. An appropriation may cover part of an advertising campaign, such as expenditure on press or television, or the whole of it including print and direct mail.

Advertising Association *Advertising representative organizations*
The Association, formed in 1926, is a federation of 26 trade associations, representing advertisers, agencies, the media and support services. It speaks for all sides of an industry with an annual worth of over £14 billion*. Its constituent bodies include:

AMCO	Association of Media & Communications Specialists
BMRA	British Market Research Association
BPIF	British Printing Industries Federation
CAA	Cinema Advertising Association
CAM	Communication Advertising & Marketing Education Foundation
CRCA	Commercial Radio Companies Association
DMA	Direct Marketing Association (UK) Ltd
DPA	Directory & Database Publishers Association
DSA	Direct Selling Association
IAA	International Advertising Association – UK Chapter
IPA	Institute of Practitioners in Advertising
ISBA	Incorporated Society of British Advertisers

*At 1 January 2000

ISP	Institute of Sales Promotion
ITV	ITV Network Ltd
MOTA	Mail Order Traders' Association
MRS	Market Research Society
MS	Marketing Society
NPA	Newspaper Publishers Association Ltd
NS	Newspaper Society
OAA	Outdoor Advertising Association of Great Britain Ltd
PAGB	Proprietary Association of Great Britain
PPA	Periodical Publishers Association
PRCA	Public Relations Consultants Association
RM	Royal Mail
SCBG	Satellite and Cable Broadcasters' Group
SNPA	Scottish Newspaper Publishers Association

Other member organizations:

BSkyB
BT – Yellow Pages
Channel Four Television
GMTV

The Association is a non-profit-making company, limited by guarantee. It is funded by a combination of subscriptions, donations and revenue-raising activities such as seminars and publications. Its remit is 'to promote and protect the rights, responsibilities and role of advertising' in the UK. It is also committed to upholding the freedom to advertise in the UK. This is in line with Article 10 of the European Convention of Human Rights, which recognizes commercial freedom of speech as a right, together with political and artistic freedoms of speech.

The organization exists to provide a coordinated service in the interests of its wider membership; that is, the individual companies that make up this large, diverse and competitive business. It is also concerned with the mutual interests of the business as a whole. It operates in a complementary way with the vested interests of its members who have specific roles for their individual sectors.

The Association speaks as 'the common voice' on:

- promoting public understanding of, and respect for, commercial communication and its role in promoting competition, innovation and economic and social progress in society;
- upholding standards and the principle of self-regulation;
- providing information, research and statistics about the advertising business;
- combating unjustified restrictions and outright bans on commercial communication for freely and legally available products or services.

The Association operates a number of departments and activities, including:

- communications;
- food advertising unit;
- information centre;
- self-regulation;
- seminars;
- statistical and other publications;
- statistical services;
- Web site, www.adassoc.org.uk.

Advertising campaign
Advertising

The planning, creation, administration and implementation of specific advertising activities for the fulfilment of specific marketing objectives. Sometimes advertising campaigns are carried out as stand-alone activities; more often they are part of a wider plan, which could include sales promotion, corporate identity, public and industrial relations activities.

Advertising manager
Advertising administration

A manager or executive within an advertiser's organization, with specific responsibility for the management of the organization's advertising. This may sound tautological. However, this job is often confused with that of advertisement manager – an entirely different animal with an entirely different job.

The advertising manager is responsible for buying advertising on behalf of his company, whereas the advertisement manager's job is selling it on behalf of his publisher. He, or she, runs the advertising department of the company; hires and fires the staff; plans and implements its advertising effort; calculates and prepares the budgets for the approval of the company's directors; appoints, briefs and liaises with advertising agencies and evaluates their output; commissions work from creatives, photographers, printers and exhibition contractors. In some organizations, the advertising manager is called marketing services manager; sometimes publicity manager, particularly when he is also responsible for public relations.

Advertising medium
Media

The advertising business comprises two main streams of activity: the message and the medium. A medium is any means of communication that enables an advertiser to convey his message to target audiences. Hence, the press is a medium. So are television, radio, exhibitions, cinema, posters, taxi-cab doors, bus and train interiors, direct mail, directories, catalogues and the Internet. The plural of the word is media, often used, and abused, as a singular.

Advertising package
Media

When advertisement space is bought in groups of insertions rather than single spaces, these are termed packages. The same applies to airtime, particularly radio, where spots are almost always bought in packages.

Advertising rates *Media*

The cost of advertisement space and airtime, as shown in publishers' and television and radio station rate cards.

Advertising research *Marketing research*

This activity includes:

- pre-campaign research;
- concept research;
- copy testing;
- media research;
- mid-campaign research;
- motivational research;
- post-campaign research;
- tracking studies.

Pre-campaign research

To determine the likely effect of advertising effort before any serious money is spent on it. Includes research into:

- brand share;
- consumer behaviour;
- product use.

Concept research

Determining the most motivating copy themes and platforms before the creative specialists get to work on building the campaign.

Copy testing

The use of panels of consumers to assess press advertisement copy and visuals, TV and radio scripts and other creative effort. This takes place, of course, before any money is spent on production proper. The results either confirm the creative team's judgement, or indicate how it can be modified to achieve the best chance of success. Or scrapped.

Media research

a. Evaluating the circulations or audiences of media during the media planning stage of a campaign.

b. A form of research in which readers, listeners and viewers are studied. The objective is to find out who has seen or heard the advertising, and how many of them there are; then to evaluate their response to it.

Mid-campaign research

Quizzing and discussing with panels of readers, listeners or viewers, while a campaign is in progress. Often, depending on the research brief, this is done by interviewing consumers in the street or in panels. For business-to-business campaigns, it is sometimes done by telephoning respondents during office hours.

Motivational research
Seeks out the motives of people in relation to their behaviour. For example, why mothers buy toothpaste; why executives buy certain types of car.

Post-campaign research
As mid-campaign research, but after a campaign has ended. Useful for comparing the results with pre-campaign and mid-campaign findings. Later, for matching the money spent on the campaign with the product sales anticipated and actually achieved.

Tracking studies
Usually carried out before a campaign breaks, then again after the campaign has finished. It seeks to compare the awareness of the brand at both ends of the research; the take-up of the product; consumers' declared intention to try the brand compared with the actual take-up; their knowledge of what the product is, and what it does; awareness of the advertising, or selected features of it.

There is a problem here. Although advertising does make marketing run, it is not the only measure that does. Sales force effort, public relations, sales promotion, distribution and other marketing tools also influence the progress of marketing campaigns and their results. Tracking studies are usually injected with control features, so that they are able to indicate with more accuracy the value of the advertising effort.

Advertising space   *Media*
Commercially run newspapers and magazines devote some of their pages to advertising. The revenue from this advertising space helps to pay their overheads and make a profit for shareholders. From the advertiser's point of view, the value of advertising space depends on the ability of the publication to reach and influence closely defined target audiences.

Advertising Standards Authority   *Advertising controls*
This is the independent organization that polices and regulates the advertising industry. It was set up by the industry itself to protect the public from misleading and offensive advertising, and to protect the industry from unwanted legislation. It also administers and enforces the British Codes of Advertising and Sales Promotion (*qv*).

According to their own statement, the Advertising Standards Authority promotes and enforces the highest standards in all non-broadcast advertisements in the UK. The Authority's responsibility, and its Codes, cover:

- advertisement promotions;
- advertisements and promotions covered by the Cigarette Code;
- advertisements in newspapers and magazines;

- advertisements in non-broadcast electronic media such as computer games;
- advertising on the Internet;
- advertorial;
- aerial advertising;
- brochures, leaflets, circulars, mailings, catalogues and other printed publications containing advertising;
- cinema and video commercials;
- facsimile transmissions containing advertising or promotional material;
- mailing lists, except for business-to-business;
- posters, transport and other outdoor advertising;
- sales promotions;
- viewdata services.

The Codes do not apply to broadcast commercials, which are the responsibility of the Independent Television Commission and the Radio Authority. The Authority acts independently of both the government and the advertising industry. It operates in the public interest, and in cooperation with the whole of the industry, by ensuring that everyone who commissions, prepares, places and publishes advertisements observes the British Codes of Advertising and Sales Promotion. Together, the Codes require that advertisements and sales promotions should be:

- in line with the principles of fair competition generally accepted in business;
- legal, decent, honest and truthful;
- prepared with a sense of responsibility to consumers and society.

The Codes are devised by the Committee of Advertising Practice. CAP members include advertising, sales promotion and media businesses. The CAP provides a free and confidential copy advice service for the industry.

If an advertisement or promotion breaks the Codes, advertisers are asked to amend or withdraw it. If they choose not to comply, a number of sanctions are available:

- **Adverse publicity**. The ASA's monthly reports contain details of complaint adjudications. These include the names of the advertisers, agencies and media involved. The reports are circulated to the media, government agencies, the advertising industry, consumer bodies and the public. Published cases receive extensive media coverage, and are also available through a fully searchable database on the ASA's Web site.
- **Refusal of further advertising space**. Media can be asked to enforce their standard terms of business, which require compliance with the Codes. They may decide to refuse further space to advertisers until the advertisement has been amended.
- **Poster pre-clearance**. Posters that are the subject of upheld complaints on grounds of taste, decency and social responsibility may be subject to a compulsory two-year vetting procedure through the CAP Copy Advice team.

- **Removal of trade incentives**. Advertisers and their agencies may jeopardize their membership of trade and professional organizations. This could result in the loss of financial and other trading benefits.
- **Legal proceedings**. Ultimately, the ASA can refer a misleading advertisement to the Office of Fair Trading. The OFT can obtain an injunction to prevent advertisers using the same or similar claims in future advertisements.
- **Repeat offenders**. Most advertisers who have complaints upheld by the ASA agree to remove their advertisements or make the required changes. However, there are companies that persistently break the Codes, and a special procedure is used to deal with them.

Of the offenders dealt with since the procedure was set up, virtually all gave assurances that they would improve. One was referred to the Office of Fair Trading under the Control of Misleading Advertisements (Amendment) Regulations 2000 – the ASA's legal backstop. This company subsequently agreed to amend its advertising.

Once an offending company is identified, an assessment of its track record is made. This determines the type of commitment the ASA needs to ensure the offender will bring future advertising in line with the Codes.

Sometimes a reminder about the Copy Advice service, and a commitment to take advice more often, is enough. In other cases, the ASA may insist on an undertaking to pre-vet future advertising. However, this happens only in the most serious cases.

After a commitment has been given, the ASA monitors the company's advertising for a time, to ensure that it is keeping to its assurances. However, the best way for this process to be avoided is for advertisers to observe the Codes in the first place, and maintain confidence in the system.

Mail order and sales promotions complaints
As part of its role in administering the British Codes of Advertising and Sales Promotion, the ASA investigates complaints from consumers about the non-receipt of goods, refunds and sales promotion offers. The advertisers need to be aware that the Codes require that the delivery date for mail order transactions should be no more than 30 days unless otherwise indicated in the advertisement. If there is a delay in the fulfilment of an order and the customer wishes to be reimbursed, the advertiser must provide a full refund. If unwanted mail order goods are returned undamaged within seven working days, the advertiser must send a full refund to the customer.

Direct marketing list and database complaints
The British Codes of Advertising and Sales Promotion regulate the use of personal information for direct marketing purposes. The direct marketing rules cover the obtaining, compiling, processing, management and use of personal information for the purpose of marketing products and services to the public through targeted and personalized mail. All complaints are investigated on the understanding that

previous direct requests by the complainants to the advertisers have proved unsuccessful. It is often not possible, however, to establish whether this is so.
See Radio Authority, Independent Television Commission, British Codes of Advertising and Sales Promotion, CAP.

Advertising strategy
Advertising planning
The planning of an advertising campaign, complete in all its aspects, designed to fulfil a marketing brief.

Advertorial
Media
A term combining advertising and editorial. An advertisement written and designed to look like an editorial. Popular with advertisers in the past, and usually highly effective in terms of response, this is today allowed only when headed by the words 'Advertisement', 'Advertisement feature' or similar phrase. This is because the media fear that their readers will be fooled into believing that such advertisements really are editorial, and that products and services promoted in this way are endorsed by the editor and publisher. The Advertising Standards Authority polices this policy and regulates the advertisers accordingly.

Aerial advertising
Media
Advertising displayed from aircraft, airships or balloons. Two of the best-known vehicles are the airships carrying the logos and slogans Dunlop and Fuji Film. Aeroplanes trailing banners and streamers are also used, though not now over urban areas. This is often to be seen at seaside resorts, where aircraft trail their banners along the shoreline several hundred metres out to sea. Hot-air balloons often display the logos of their sponsors. Some balloons are even designed to represent sponsors' packaging; balloons representing bottles of Coke and Pepsi, and cans of Virgin Cola, can be seen at rallies, for example.

Aerosol
Packaging
A word used to describe a metal container, pressurized inside, which dispenses its contents in the form of a fine liquid spray. Pressing on its actuator, usually at the top of the container, releases the contents into the atmosphere. This definition is only partly true; the spray itself is the aerosol, not the container.

After-sales service
Customer relationship management
To fulfil the terms of a purchase contract, a supplier may be obliged to maintain a product in full working order after its sale to a customer. Many suppliers also offer technical advice and support following a sale; usually by telephone or over the Internet. This is good customer relations, with a view to long-term loyalty and further sales in the course of time.

Agency audit
Marketing, advertising and PR business
Checks are often made by clients into their agencies' and consultants' performance and business practice. Such audits can cover not only the efficiency and cost-effectiveness of agencies, but their probity as well. Clients may feel entitled to

examine the invoices of agencies' suppliers, such as media, creative and production, and the mark-ups made in their own invoices. Agencies and consultancies have the option of refusing to submit to audits, but clients have the whip hand, and may be powerful enough to take their business elsewhere.

Agent
Advertising, Business, Marketing

In the usually-accepted sense of the term, an individual or organization representing others, with their verbal or written consent. However, in the case of advertising and marketing agencies, the word agent is a convention, rather than legal terminology. An advertising agency is actually a principal in business transactions. Even though an agency works for and carries out work and purchases for its clients, media, creative and production for example, these transactions are made as principals in the contracts, not as agents. Separate contracts are drawn up between the agency and its clients for these activities. In cases of client default, as when an advertiser goes into liquidation, suppliers have no recourse to clients for payment. The agency has to pay up.

AIDA
Advertising creativity

An acronym for **Attention**, **Interest**, **Desire**, **Action**. An important communication discipline employed in creating advertisements and print. Advertising is not an art form: it is part of the tough business of competitive marketing communications. A discipline for creating those communications effectively is therefore vital. This may sound academic, possibly a little naïve, but it's simple common sense.

Those of us in the marketing communications business know that the arena we work in is not the supermarket, the chainstore or the showroom. It is not even the press advertisement, the TV or radio commercial. Nor yet the leaflet, brochure or poster. It is the human mind. It is here that we get the reactions to marketing communications, advertising, public relations and sales promotion messages we create and deliver. It is where the action that produces a sale begins to take place.

AIDA is a discipline of progressive steps in the process of promoting a product, a service or an idea. It is an intellectual tool that helps you to achieve the levels of understanding you need to write sales-winning copy and produce motivating visuals and dynamic illustrations. It also provides you with the levels of understanding you want your target reader to achieve so that you achieve the response you want.

As every successful salesman knows:

A First, you must seize your reader's, viewer's or listener's **ATTENTION**.

I You must then tell him something important that appeals to his self-**INTEREST**.

D You must arouse a strong **DESIRE** to try or buy your product; or send for your literature; or make an enquiry; or ask for a sales representative to call. Or all these things at different times. Your primary objective at this stage is get a decision in favour of your proposition, product or brand.

A Finally, you must urge your potential customer to take the **ACTION** you want.

This action must be in line with your marketing plans. For this reason alone, it is essential to plan your AIDA before you begin writing and designing any marketing communication. Why do we need this carefully structured thinking? Because *they don't want to read it, look at it or hear it.* Your job, of course, is to entice and seduce them into reading, viewing and listening to your promotional material – and with enthusiasm!
See Conviction.

Aided recall
Advertising research

A multiple-choice interviewing technique during which interviewees choose responses to questions from a list.

AIR
Media, Research

Average issue readership.

Airbrush
Artwork, Production

A studio tool for retouching and illustration work. Basically a spray gun, powered by compressed air. The operator directs a fine spray of coloured ink or paint on to the artwork or photoprint being prepared or retouched. In plate-making, an airbrush is used with an abrasive-like pumice to remove spots and other unwanted areas from the metal.

Air date
Radio, Television

The date on which a radio or TV commercial is broadcast.

Air-dried
Paper, Print

Paper dried slowly in a warm current of air, or over skeleton drum dryers, not by conventional drying cylinders.

Airtime
Radio, Television

The amount of time during which radio or TV entertainment or advertising is allocated or actually transmitted.

Aisle
Retailing

In supermarkets, the display cabinets, often called gondolas, contain products for sale. The passages between the gondolas are the aisles.

À la carte agency
Advertising business

An advertising or marketing specialist company offering one particular aspect of service, eg creative services, is termed **à la carte**. This is in contrast to full service marketing and advertising agencies, whose services include media planning and buying, marketing, public relations and sales promotion.

Alignment
Artwork, Desktop publishing, Production, Typography

The positioning of type or graphics on a page, so that the horizontals and verticals are accurate.

Alpha testing   *Marketing, Product research*
A technique for assessing the potential success of a product or service, done within
the company or marketing organization rather than in the marketplace.

Alterations   *Artwork, Desktop publishing, Type, Typography, Word-processing*
Amendments made to text after proofing. Sometimes called **corrections**. Where
the typesetter makes a mistake, he pays for the alteration. Where the originator or
author makes the mistakes, these are called **author's corrections**, and the author
pays. Bearing in mind that it often costs £50 or more to amend a proof by even a
comma, copywriters and authors beware.
See Corrections.

Alternative currencies   *Marketing*
Formats in which goods can be exchanged without resorting to actual money.
These include trading stamps and redemption coupons, Air Miles and loyalty or
reward scheme points. Most of these are based on the amount of money previously
spent by the customer, accumulated by her, and later exchanged for discounts or
gifts.

AMA   *Marketing organizations*
The American Marketing Association.

Amid matter   *Media buying*
An instruction to a media buyer to place an advertisement in a position surrounded
by or adjacent to editorial. Sometimes termed **within matter**.

Ampersand   *Desktop publishing, Typesetting, Typography*
The typographic short-form symbol for the word 'and' – &.

Analysis   *Research*
The reduction of complex data into smaller and simpler elements, capable of being
understood or worked more easily. An annual marketing plan, for example, may
be expressed in diagrams and charts of various kinds, so that finance and physical
tasks can be allocated more effectively.

Anamorphic scan   *Artwork, Computer graphics, Studio work*
Scanning a piece of artwork so that the width and height are not enlarged or
reduced in proportion. The image is modified to produce an image taller and
narrower, or shorter and fatter, than the original.

Angle   *Editorial, Journalism, Public relations*
The main basis and thrust of a story, giving it its identity and character. Journalists,
and writers working in public relations, strive to find or create an angle for a story,
especially where it does not constitute actual news. Human interest is often used
as an angle in a story, representing a benefit, crisis or predicament presented from
an individual human perspective.

Angle *Film, Photography, Television*

The camera's view of a photographic shot; high angle, low angle, and so on. The term is used to describe the act of facing a camera in a particular direction.

Anilox *Print technology*

In flexographic printing, the etched or knurled steel roller, which transfers ink to the printing substrate. The anilox surface is a regular pattern of cells.
See Flexography.

Animatic *Advertising, Film, Television commercials, Video*

A pre-production technique, in which a commercial is presented to the client without incurring the mega-pound expense of an actual production. A sequence of illustrations is prepared, showing the progress of the commercial, and shot on a video camera.

The illustrations usually follow the script and storyboard (*qv*). The client can then see what the commercial will look like, more or less. Sometimes, audiotape is employed for any accompanying music and sound effects. Many producers dislike animatics, since they do not present the full production values of the real thing. However, some advertisers with a spark of imagination like them, if only because they also save money.
See Storyboard.

Animation *Artwork, Film, Television*

A technique for film-making, using individual frames photographed on film. These are drawn by hand or generated by computer. When projected at 24 or 25 frames per second, the effect on screen is an optical illusion of movement. The human eye and brain cannot resolve the individual frames projected at speed, and therefore blends them into smooth and seamless action. *Snow White and the Seven Dwarfs* was the first major commercial animation production.
See Cell.

Annual *Media, Publishing*

A publication issued once a year. Annuals vary from yearbooks published by academic, learned and special-interest groups, to reference books and directories. Marketing industry annuals include the *Marketing Manager's Yearbook*, *Advertiser's Annual* (the 'Blue Book') and *The Creative Handbook*.

Annual report and accounts *Business, Corporate communications, Public relations*

A document issued by an organization showing its performance during the year in question. There is a legal requirement to produce the financial information; most companies also give corporate performance data, and projections for future performance. Many organizations create their annual reports with promotion in mind, and consider them part of their public relations effort. Many annual reports are lavishly illustrated in full colour, mainly to appeal to current and future shareholders and investors. Some companies also issue special versions of their annual reports for employees, in the interests of good industrial relations.

Anonymous testing   *Marketing research, Product research*
A form of competitive product testing in which different products of similar character are evaluated anonymously. This usually takes the form of anonymous or blank packaging. The idea is that the testing panel is able to assess all products being tested based on their differences and similarities.

Ansoff matrix   *Marketing planning*
A format used when considering the relationship between marketing strategies and a company's general business strategy. It is expressed as a diagrammatic box of four cells, highlighting market penetration and development, product development and diversification. This allows consideration of the various permutations that can exist in new and existing markets, and new and existing products.

Answer print   *Television commercials, post-production*
A check print of a commercial after colour grading (*qv*). Release prints are produced when the director approves the answer print.

Antique   *Paper, Print*
A high-quality, opaque, bulky paper grade, with a rough surface finish. It is made as deckle or straight edged, in various colours, laid or wove. It is characteristically an excellent printing surface; often used for expensive print, such as corporate literature.
See Laid, Wove.

'A' paper sizes   *Print, Production*
The international standard for paper sizes. The basic unit of this standard is the square metre, dubbed A0. The sizes then run in descending order, corresponding to the way the paper is folded or cut. All the folded sizes have the same proportions, 1:1.414. Curiously, the higher the A number, the smaller the paper size. For example:

Sheet size	Millimetres
A0	841 × 1,189
A1	594 × 841
A2	420 × 594
A3	297 × 420
A4	210 × 297
A5	148 × 210
A6	105 × 148
A7	74 × 105
A8	52 × 74

See Paper sizes.

Aperture *Photography, Reprographics*

Also termed a **stop**. The size of a lens diaphragm opening, through which light enters a camera to reach the film. Apertures are usually given in a series, preceded by the initial *f*; for example, f1.8, f2, f2.8, f4, f5.6, and so on. These figures, given equal illumination, give inverse degrees of exposure in geometrical progression. The higher the figure, the smaller the aperture. Thus, f2 admits more light than f4. The figure f2 also indicates that the diameter of the aperture is half the focal length of the lens.

Apochromatic *Photography, Reprographics*

A photographic, colour-corrected lens, which focuses blue, green and red in the same plane.

Appeal *Marketing communications, Product marketing*

The quality of a promotional message designed to satisfy the customer's needs, wants or aspirations. Careful research is needed before committing such ideas to creative treatment. The same applies to the concept, creation and marketing of a product, especially its packaging.

Application *Communications technology, Information technology*

A computing task to be carried out on data, using appropriate software. An application program is a specific set of instructions dedicated to operating the computer in carrying out the application. Often, these programs are given incomprehensible names. '*Word*' seems a reasonable name for a word-processing application program; '*WordPerfect*' is even better. However, '*PowerPoint*' and '*Access*' could apply to anything. Application software is different from operating software, which controls the environment of a computer, or controls server or network operations.

Application service provider *E-commerce, Information technology,*
Internet activity

A company specializing in the management and delivery of software applications from a data centre, to client users across a wide area network. This can best be described as 'software delivered as a service'. Client organizations can rent access to the software through Web technology, rather than own it, for ad hoc, monthly or pay-as-you-go fees. The main benefits to clients are:

- appropriate cost savings;
- minimum use of the client's own IT resources;
- predictable future costs;
- reduced initial investment;
- reduction in implementation times and associated problems;
- the possibility of fast up-grading and up-scaling.

Appreciation *Business, Marketing*
The rise in value of a business asset. This can apply to a company's capital
equipment as well as to its products, its marketing track record and its goodwill.
The more successful a company gets in marketing its products and services, the
greater the appreciation of its various assets.

Appropriation *Advertising*
The allocation of money for marketing activity. This includes its various individual
elements, such as advertising, public relations, sales promotion and other parts of
the marketing mix. The term is commonly applied to advertising budgets.

APR *Advertising, Business, Marketing*
Annual Percentage Rate. A figure given by banks and commercial companies, in
relation to interest rates charged on financial transactions. In UK law, this figure
must be quoted in such statements, and in the advertising of products and services
where finance is offered.

APR *Communications technology, Information technology,*
Print, Studio work
Automatic Picture Replacement. A low-resolution picture is placed in the file when
the page is RIPping. The RIP substitutes the low-resolution picture for the
corresponding high-resolution one.
See Raster Image Processing.

Arbitrary budgeting *Advertising finance*
The calculation of an advertising budget without taking into account the specific
objectives, costs, risks and prospects of the campaign to be carried out. This
haphazard method is still used by companies under autocratic management. The
strange thing is, where there is outstanding flair and business judgement within
such management, arbitrary budgeting sometimes works; but it needs luck as well.

Architecture *Business communications, E-commerce,*
Information technology, Marketing communications
Usually refers to the design or organization of a computer's central processing unit;
often, to the hardware and logical organization of a complete computer system.
This is always an important consideration in the selection of computers for
marketing and other business communications. In these cases, a computer's
architecture needs to support multiple, complex operations, vast amounts of data,
often conveyed over long distances to huge numbers of recipients.

Area composition *E-commerce, Information technology, Internet activity,*
Studio work, Web page design
The composition of Web pages, so that as many elements as possible are in place,
to reduce or eliminate page make-up.

Art   *Studio work*
Any visual element, whether photograph, illustration, drawing, lettering, graph, chart or pictogram.
See Artwork.

Art buyer   *Studio personnel*
A manager or executive responsible for commissioning and buying artwork, photography, retouching and other art speciality work.

Art director   *Studio personnel*
Currently, the term applies to an art design specialist responsible for producing or adapting creative ideas in visual form. The idea may start as a marketing or advertising brief, a piece of copy, or an original piece of thinking by the art director. Years ago, this job was called commercial artist. As the salaries went up, so did the job title. The next title was visualizer. Again, the money and the status rose, and art director was the result. The work itself has changed but little, although the technology has changed a great deal. An art director is not necessarily a member of a board of directors, though many art directors skilled at administration do become creative directors.

Artificial obsolescence   *Business, Marketing strategy, Product management*
A technique for inducing consumers to buy the next generation of a product or service. The existing product is superseded by making changes in design, increasing some of the essential or useful features, or simply changing the colour. The existing product is rendered out of date, or unfashionable, and the only thing the consumer can reasonable do is buy the new one. This technique can be observed at work in the marketing of computers, cars, insurance, fashion, food and toys.

Art paper   *Print, Production*
Paper stock coated with china clay or similar substance, given a smooth surface for printing of the highest quality. Traditionally, art paper refers to wood-free, coated papers with a highly polished surface; and to matt coated stock. The better the surface presented to the printing plate, the higher the quality of the finished product.

Artwork   *Artwork, Print, Production, Studio work*
Original material prepared for reproduction in print, at pre-film stage. The basis of artwork is graphics, illustrations and photography. 'Complete artwork', 'artwork ready for camera', and 'camera-ready artwork' includes typeset text. It implies complete material ready for making film and printing plates. At this stage, it also implies that no more material is to be added.

ASA   *Photography*
Acronym: **American Standards Association**. A universally accepted measure of light-sensitivity of photographic film; the 'speed' rating of film stock. The higher the ASA figure, the 'faster' the film-speed, and the greater its sensitivity to light.

The speed of film stock determines the aperture of the lens and exposure time. For example, in bright light, a fast film needs less exposure; a slow film needs more. If you are filming in low light conditions, an auditorium or a cave perhaps, you will need film stock with a high ASA rating, and probably a wider lens aperture. Maybe a slower shutter-speed as well. If you are filming at Le Mans, and need to capture fast-moving vehicles as they go by on the track, you will definitely need fast film and high shutter-speeds. On the other hand, if you are covering a garden party on a brilliantly sunny day, and are aiming for sharp portraits, consider a slower film, wider apertures and slower shutter-speeds. Advice: there's a vast literature on photography and photographic materials.
See Film speed, ISO.

ASBOF *Advertising controls*
Acronym: **Advertising Standards Board of Finance**. An arm of the UK Advertising Standards Authority, dedicated to raising funds for the running of the Authority's activities. It does this by imposing a levy on display advertising in the press and other non-broadcast media.

Ascender *Desktop publishing, Typography*
In type, the part of a lower case character rising above the 'x' height. The characters affected are b, d, h, k and l.
See Descender.

ASCII *Information technology*
Acronym: the **American Standard Code for Information Interchange**. A computer code that assigns a binary number to each alpha-numeric character. It does the same with non-printing characters used for controlling printers and other communication devices. **ASCII** text means straight text without formatting, the common basis of e-mail communications.

'A' series *Paper sizes, Print*
The international ISO range of sizes for paper and board.

ASP *E-commerce, Information technology, Internet activity*
Application Service Provider (*qv*).

Aspect ratio *Desktop publishing, Print, Production, Television, Typography*
The vertical to horizontal ratio of a TV screen or sheet of paper. The domestic TV screen ratio is 3:4; that is, 3 high to 4 wide. Some of the new wide screens are ratio 3:7 or the current European 9:16; others have an even greater aspect ratio.

Aspiration level *Research*
The height to which consumers are judged to aspire when considering the purchase of a product or service. The aspiration is bound up in the ownership of the product, rather than its purchase. Sometimes the aspiration can be tapped by featuring the

price of a product, such as an expensive car. Parking such a car outside your house may help to give you the status or prestige you aspire to.

Asset rich families   *Campaign planning, Marketing research*
A group in Experian's financial classification system, Financial Strategy Segments (FSS). Built on **MOSAIC** and **Pixel** segmentation systems, FSS classifies the UK population by 7 broad groups and 31 financial types, covering the full financial spectrum. The complete list of groups is:

- asset rich families;
- equity accumulation;
- grey lifestyles;
- money worth managing;
- parental dependency;
- small time borrowing;
- welfare borderline.

See Financial Strategy Segments.

Asymmetric Digital Subscriber Line   *Internet communications*
A system for high-speed access for home Net users. It allows access at between 10 and 40 times normal speeds using a standard telephone line. Usually referred to by its initials **ADSL**.

Atmosphere   *Media*
Sometimes called **editorial climate** or **entertainment climate**. The environment of print or broadcast medium being evaluated as a suitable vehicle for advertising. Thus, the *Daily Telegraph* has a different 'atmosphere' from the *Sun*; and Channel 4 from Channel 5. The differences are most marked among commercial radio channels.

Atmosphere   *Retailing*
The deliberate deployment of furniture, lighting, decor and other elements within a store so that they impact in a pre-planned way on customers. This can be related to the character of the store, or to the character of its customers. Some atmospheres are designed to hurry customers through the store and through the checkout; others can encourage customers to browse and buy more products while they are doing it. Such techniques can even influence customers in the quality and price of the products they buy.

Attachment   *Communications, Information technology*
A file transferred together with an e-mail message. It can be of any type, such as text, graphics, advertisement, print file, picture, spreadsheet, slide-show, movie or animation. *Caveat*: computer viruses and worms are transferred in attachments; anti-virus protection is therefore essential, at both ends of the transmission.

Attention span
Media, Research

The length of time an individual will concentrate on a particular subject. Research may reveal how long a reader can be induced to concentrate on a particular advertisement in a newspaper. Television soap operas seem to suggest that the attention span of viewers is very short. The average length of a scene, particularly among the Australian soaps, is about 45 seconds.

Attention value
Advertising research

If it is to have any impact, a press advertisement needs to attract and hold the attention of the reader. The extent to which an advertisement can do this can be quantified. A technique known as **The Starch Model**, devised in the USA by Daniel Starch, measures the effectiveness of advertisements using a structured checklist. From this, the actual page traffic of readers, and the effectiveness of advertisements, can be calculated.

Attitude
Consumer behaviour, Marketing research

The mental standpoint of individuals on a subject, object, concept or proposition. This can reflect positive or negative thinking on that subject, and may indicate the action or reaction that may follow. It may also indicate a state of indifference in customers' minds towards a subject or proposition.

Attitude research
Marketing research

Research into individual attitudes towards an organization and its products. This is often done by group discussions under the direction of trained specialists. Focus groups are a current popular method of revealing attitudes to organizations, products and services, and to political concepts.

Attributes
Marketing

Product features and consumer benefits are not the same. This is because the motives of producer and customer are different. From the producer's point of view, sales may be paramount, and products designed with appropriate attributes or features to achieve this. The consumer, on the other hand, is usually looking for benefits, personal, family or corporate. To encourage purchase, the producer must therefore concentrate on benefits to the consumer, and ensure that the product's attributes help to fulfil this objective.

Attributes
Desktop publishing, Typography

The variations in the character of typefaces. These include regular, medium, light, heavy, bold, semi-bold, extra bold, ultra, extended, narrow, condensed, italic and bold italic.

Attrition process
Marketing

The loyalty of a customer to a company, product or service may be gradually worn away by competitive activity, especially when the competition's offerings are more appealing, attractive or cost-effective. The process of attrition can also occur under pressure from competitors' advertising and sales promotion. Stages in consumer life cycle often influence loyalty, as with cars, fashion, travel, holidays and leisure pursuits.

Audience flow   *Media, Research*
During a television transmission, the extent to which the viewing audience increases or decreases.

Audience research   *Media research*
A form of advertising research for campaign planning. It is usually concerned with investigating the characteristics of print and broadcast media, mainly for audience statistics. For print media, circulation, readership, demographics, costs and production data. For broadcast media, quality, quantity, demographics, lifestyle and costs; production costs are considered separately.

Audiences   *Marketing, Media*
Groups of individuals selected by marketers as targets for products and promotional campaigns. This choice is usually refined by the ability of audiences to respond in the way the marketer requires. Thus, audiences in social grade A may be prime targets for Rolls-Royce; grades D and E may not be. This distinction influences the marketer's selection of media used for reaching specified target audiences.
See ACORN.

Audio   *Advertising, Cinema and television commercials*
Advertising writers' jargon for the sound or dialogue column of a script or storyboard.
See Video.

Audio-visual   *Presentations*
A combination of sound and vision techniques used in presentations. These include:

■ CD and CD ROM output;
■ computer-generated images and sound;
■ film;
■ music;
■ sound effects;
■ sound tracks;
■ transparencies;
■ videos.

Audio-visual sales aids   *In-store merchandising, Sales presentations*
Techniques and equipment used by retailers and sales personnel for demonstrating products and services. In-store sales aids usually comprise stand-alone video units, demonstrating products on sale in the store, using endless video loops. This enables

the demos to run non-stop throughout the day. A/V sales aids also enable sales departments to demonstrate products and services at remote locations. In the case of fork-lift trucks and other heavy equipment, it may be uneconomical, undesirable or impossible to take the equipment to the potential customer. It would be more practical for sales staff to take a video and use it to demonstrate the product; or have the video delivered ahead of a sales call.

Audit Bureau of Circulations *Media research and planning*
An independent organization dedicated to auditing the circulation figures of newspapers and magazines. The figures issued by the bureau accurately represent the number of copies actually sold. It also monitors exhibition attendance.

The certificates of circulation issued by the bureau are trusted by media owners, advertisers and agencies, and used as a true basis for comparison among media competing for advertising money. Circulation should not be confused with readership.

The ABC was founded in 1931 as a non-profit organization, by the forerunner of the Incorporated Society of British Advertisers (ISBA) (*qv*). This was done in response to concern shown by advertisers and publishers about false represent-ations and claims made by some unscrupulous publishers.

Since then, the publicity industry has recognized the ABC as the UK's only independent system for confirming the circulation credibility of the press. The ABC claims to be the country's only independent system for the validation of circulation and exhibition attendance data. It ensures that its members' figures are accurate, objective and comparable. In this way, it helps media owners and buyers in the effective selling and buying of advertising space. Today, the ABC is run by a full-time staff, governed by a general council of permanent and elected members, representing advertisers, agencies and publishers.

The ABC Council has 28 seats. The five permanent representatives comprise the chief executives of the Institute of Practitioners in Advertising, the ISBA, the Periodical Proprietors' Association, the Newspaper Society and the Newspaper Publishers' Association. The remaining seats are split between representatives of media-owner and media-buyer member companies, elected every two years.

ABC's staff include inspectors and auditors, responsible for certifying audit returns. They visit publishers' offices to check that the audit rules and procedures are adhered to, and to provide circulation advice to existing and potential members.

The ABC has three main divisions: the Consumer Press Division, the Business-to-Business Press Division and Verified Free Distribution (VFD). The ABC's Consumer Press Division administers national newspapers, paid-for regional newspapers, consumer magazines and specialist journals, international and world regional newspapers. The Business-to-Business Division administers business magazines, annual publications and directories; and exhibitions, for which the validation of audited attendance is carried out.
See Circulation, Controlled circulation, Penetration, Profile, Rate card, Reader, Readership, Television rating points, Verified Free Distribution.

Augmentation *Marketing planning*

Adding extra features or benefits to a product or service, which do not actually form part of the product itself, to increase its appeal or attractiveness. Such measures include after-sales service, guarantees and warranties, free installation and online support.

Autocue *Conferences, Presentations, Television*

A prompting system used by presenters and speakers. On a public platform, this comprises two small transparent glass or plastic screens either side of the speaker. The speaker's text is projected on both screens simultaneously, a few lines at a time, and invisible to the audience. The text is scrolled up by an operator out of sight of the audience. This enables the speaker to read and voice the speech without constantly resorting to notes on the lectern. The speaker can turn to right and left, seemingly looking at the audience, but actually looking at the autocue. In television studios, the autocue is a monitor screen mounted on the camera dolly next to the camera in front of the presenter. The text is displayed a few lines at a time, and scrolled up at the presenter's speaking pace.

Availability *Media planning*

Where advertising space in a newspaper or magazine is free for booking into, it is said to be available. The same applies to advertising slots in broadcasting airtime. The dates and times of publication and transmission need to be specified.

Average cost pricing *Marketing planning*

A procedure for calculating the average cost of a product or service, based on its price across the whole product range.

Average frequency *Media planning*

A technique for calculating the average number of opportunities for audience viewing of a television commercial, or radio listening audience. This is based on the gross cumulative audience divided by the net cumulative; or, gross reach over net reach. In radio audience research, weekly reach is defined as the number in thousands, or as a percentage, of the UK/area adult population who listen to a station for at least five minutes in the course of an average week.

Average issue readership *Media planning*

A technique for calculating the number of people who read an average issue of a publication. Circulation is based on an entirely different system.
See ABC.

Awareness *Marketing communications techniques*

A prerequisite for establishing brands and other concepts in a marketplace. Advertising, sales promotion and public relations techniques are used for placing a brand or corporate name in the minds of appropriate target audiences. Research is used to measure the effectiveness of such campaigns; sales or enquiry figures show similar results, based, as always, on the objectives. As an example, First Direct launched its UK home banking services with a substantial advertising campaign. Awareness in its target markets went from 0 per cent to 37 per cent in the first five days, and to 58 per cent after four months.

Bb

B2B   *Advertising, Marketing, Public relations, Sales promotion*
Advertising and editorial jargon for **business-to-business** (*qv*).

BACC   *Television advertising*
The Broadcast Advertising Clearance Centre in London.

Backbone   *Print*
Also termed a **spine**. The back of a bound publication connecting the two covers.

Back checks   *Research quality control*
A routine for following up research interviews, so that the extent to which instructions have been followed can be evaluated.

Back cover   *Advertising, Media buying*
The final page of a newspaper or magazine. These pages almost always cost more than the inside pages of the same publication. This is based on the school of thought which states that readers give more attention to the back cover than other pages. However, another school states that a magazine can as easily fall face up as face down. Publications also usually charge higher rates for inside front and back covers. You will, of course, be well advised to find independent research on the subject, or conduct your own, before investing your company's money on cover advertising.

Background   *Marketing brief*
Information about a company, organization, product, service or individual, which helps those being briefed to understand the current situation. This is one of the building blocks of efficient marketing campaign planning effort, and part of the evaluation routine summarized by the mantra:

Where are we now?
How did we get here?
Where do we want to be?
How do we get there?

Background   *Advertising campaigns*
Elements of an advertising or brochure layout taking a subsidiary role in its visual presentation. These can be colour, white space, tints or textures. Their function is

to highlight the important elements in the layout, especially those that need to seize attention and encourage action. In television commercials, backgrounds include images, colour, sound effects and music. In radio commercials, backing tracks, music and sound effects. *Caveat*: in radio commercials, sometimes the high audio volume of the music and sound effects can destroy the advertising message. Unfortunately, this has become a popular technique. Production teams seem not to realize that not every listener possesses expensive hi-fi equipment. Many ordinary listeners listen routinely to what marketing guru Martyn P Davis calls 'grotty little trannies' – cheap little radios. This is yet another case for insisting that art and production personnel undergo marketing training before being briefed to create advertising and public relations material.

Backing track *Music, Radio, Television, Video*
Background sounds accompanying audio-visual presentations. These include harmonies, orchestral and instrumental effects, singers and sound effects.

Backing up *Print*
Printing the reverse side of a sheet already printed on one side.

Back lining *Print*
A paper or fabric lining stuck to the backbone or spine of a publication such as a booklet or book. This helps to stiffen the cover, giving it a more substantial feel, and greater durability.

Back matter *Print*
Pages following the main text of a printed document, containing appendix, glossary, index and other reference material.

Back projection *Cinema and television commercials*
A technique in which live action may be shot, with a moving background taken separately. For example, a car with its occupants in conversation, seen apparently travelling along a road. In fact, the car is stationary in the studio, with a film projected on to a translucent screen behind or at the side of them. The whole set-up is shot simultaneously, giving the illusion of a moving car seen from the inside.

Back-up *Computing, Desktop publishing, Information technology*
Data or work done on a computer, copied to external or auxiliary storage. This can be retrieved if the original is lost, damaged or corrupted.

Bad break *Composition, Copywriting, Desktop publishing, Typesetting, Typography*
Starting a typeset page with a **widow** (*qv*), or ending a paragraph with one.

Bad debt *Business*
A customer who defaults on the settlement of an invoice. Also used to describe a company that goes out of business with unsettled debts. In financial accounting,

money lost in this way is described as a bad debt, which will eventually be 'written off' – completely abandoned.

Balance   *Advertising design, Art, Creative, Desktop publishing, Typography*

The relationship between elements in a layout. Balance aims at achieving a comfortable relationship between copy, graphics, illustrations and photographs. Balance is also applied to the overall look of a printed page. You can usually see when a layout is unbalanced. Sometimes, a reader may not easily see why it is unbalanced, and the effect may be disturbing. If you are aiming for this reaction, all well and good; but deterrence is not what advertisers usually want in pursuing a sale.

Balanced scorecard   *Business, Marketing planning*

A technique for achieving continuing business success, created by Dr David Norton, President of Renaissance Worldwide, and colleagues. It helps organizations to translate business strategy and vision into operational objectives, measures and strategy. The technique is designed to align all an organization's resources and energies, by ensuring that every single individual, department and team see a direct link between what they do and overall corporate goals.

Balloon   *Artwork, Desktop publishing, Typography*

The area containing speech in a newspaper or magazine cartoon. Sometimes used to good promotional effect in printed literature.

Banded pack   *Packaging, Retailing*

Two products physically banded together and offered at a single price; normally less than the price of two individual items when bought separately. This is usually promoted in-store, in advertising and print as a **special offer**.

Bangtail   *Advertising, Marketing, Print*

A type of wallet envelope, incorporating an additional, perforated flap extending from its normal flap or its back panel. The flap usually features a special offer, which can be accessed by tearing it off, filling in personal details and posting it back to the advertiser. This technique is often used by credit card companies.

Bank   *Paper*

A range of lightweight papers usually used for stationery, office copiers and computer printers. The substance of such papers is usually below 60 grams per square metre (60 g/m^2 or gsm). Heavier substance papers, above 60 g/m^2, generally used for letterheads and correspondence, are known as bond (*qv*).

Banner   *Artwork, Desktop publishing, Editorial, Typography*

A main headline. In newspaper and magazine publishing, the term banner headline means one running across the full page width, or most of its width. The term is also used in brochure design.

Banner *Internet advertising, Web site design*

A brief message or advertisement inserted into a Web page, linked to the advertiser's own Web site.

BARB *Television audience research*

Acronym for the **Broadcasters Audience Research Board**. The Board commissions research into audience ratings for independent television and the BBC. BARB's purpose is to provide ratings, forming an acceptable basis for comparison for buyers and sellers of television advertising. Advertising agencies and TV contractors negotiate on the basis of these ratings. BARB also provides much other data, but for advertising agencies and TV contractors, this particular basis cannot be obtained by any other means. The current basis is *consolidated ratings* – the live audience viewing a programme, plus those who record a programme and view it within seven days.

For the television contractors, it is important to see how well their transmission schedules are doing, in comparison with the BBC. The BBC uses the information for the same purpose. It also gives the programme-makers an indication of how well a production is doing. It may also suggest a good time to screen a particular programme.

BARB was set up in 1980 by the BBC and ITCA (now ITVA), and began operations in August 1981. Its function was to provide a single system for TV audience research in the UK.

The ITV audience research system was operated by JICTAR – the Joint Industry Committee for Television Advertising Research (since superseded by BARB). The system consisted of electronic meters attached to the televisions of a representative sample of viewing audience. The meters recorded when the televisions were switched on and off, and which channels were being viewed. Every week, each householder had to remove from the meter the tape that carried the information, and post it to the researchers.

In addition, a questionnaire had to be completed by the householder. This indicated the number of people viewing each programme. This was posted to the researchers week by week. The system was not always reliable, since it depended on complete and consistent questionnaires.

The BBC used a daily survey to obtain recall of programmes viewed the previous day. From this survey, the size and make-up of the audience to each programme was calculated.

JICTAR was concerned with minute-by-minute viewing, because of the need to know how many people were watching commercials. The IBA (now called ITC, Independent Television Commission), carried out a small audience appreciation survey.

The move towards a joint system was stimulated by the 1977 Annan Report on the future of broadcasting. This recommended a *combined* audience measurement system. This would eliminate the argument about which audience size information was correct. Resources could then be released to enable more attention to be directed to research on the reactions of audiences to the *content* of programmes.

The BBC and ITCA (now ITVA) designed a system to provide a common database, to meet the needs of all interested parties, offering acceptable reliability and cost. By 1980, they had announced the formation of BARB to manage the joint research programme.

Currently, the BBC and ITVA are sole and equal shareholders in BARB Ltd. The company's board comprises representatives of both, under an independent chairman. The organization operates through a committee system. The work of BARB devolves into two areas: audience measurement and audience appreciation. A management committee and technical sub-committee control these activities. The ITV companies, the BBC and various interested parties serve on the committees.

On the audience measurement committee, the IPA (Institute of Practitioners in Advertising) represents the advertising agencies. The IPA is also represented on the main board. The ISBA (Incorporated Society of British Advertisers) represents the advertisers. As users of television advertising, they have a direct interest in the way audiences are measured. For this reason, they have an equal voice with the shareholders on the committees.

The ITC is represented on the audience appreciation side; it too has an equal voice with the shareholders. Channel 4, Welsh Channel 4 and the satellite broadcasters are subscribers, and represented on appropriate committees.

In August 1991, a new seven-year BARB service was begun. BARB has allocated the work to two research contractors: RSMB Television Research, a joint subsidiary of Millward Brown, and RSL (Research Services Ltd). These are responsible for all survey and fieldwork, including the recruitment and operation of the audience panels.

The data supply and processing contracts are operated by AGB (UK) – Audits of Great Britain – which has awesome computing and number-crunching power. It services the panel-homes. It maintains the meters, retrieves the data, edits the data supply and the data-processing output. The edited data is provided to subscribers electronically, with minimal paperwork. The amount of data supplied each time could equal a fair-sized encyclopedia if committed to paper.

See IPA, ISBA, ITC, ITVA.

Bar code   *Marketing research, Retailing*

A pattern of vertical lines printed on a product, pack or printed material. Its function is to identify the product precisely. The information in the bars, in the form of 13 numbers, (10 in the USA), includes the price, date of purchase, point of sale, country of origin and manufacturer. To retrieve the information, the bar code is scanned and processed by computer.

Until recently, there seemed to be little compatibility among the various systems used in Europe. However, like many electronic techniques we now use in marketing, industry standards are being applied. We may have total compatibility by the end of the 21st century.

Base-line *Desktop publishing, Typography*
An invisible horizontal line on which the bases of alphabetical and some numerical characters sit. Characters g, j, p, q and y fall below the base-line. In some fonts, the figures 3, 5, 7 and 9 fall below.
See Ascender, Descender.

Basing-point pricing *Retailing*
A costing system used by multiple retailers such as supermarkets. The retail price of a product is calculated to include manufacture, packaging and storage. It must also include the cost of transportation from the points of manufacture and storage to the points of sale. Each storage location is given a base price, to which a variable cost is added for transportation. This ensures that retail prices can be rendered nationally as well as regionally, if that is the retailer's policy.

Battered type *Artwork, Desktop publishing, Print, Typesetting, Typography*
A typeset character with a blemish. This term is a relic of the days when type was set in metal. Occasionally a character emerged imperfect from the typesetting machine. Usually, this was detected only at proof stage, and the proof-reader would make appropriate marks to have the battered character replaced. Today, imperfect characters are rarer, but proof-readers still need to be vigilant.

BCU *Filming, Television*
Initials in a script, indicating a camera instruction, **Big close-up**. For example, a face filling the screen, ear to ear.

BDMA *Marketing organizations*
British Direct Marketing Association. An organization representing advertisers, agencies and suppliers in the direct marketing industry.

Behavioural science *Research*
A range of disciplines applied to and focusing on the behaviour of humans. This is usually studied from the point of view of economics, psychology, sociology, anthropology, geography and history. Each discipline varies in the way it studies human behaviour, the aspects of behaviour with which it is concerned and the concepts it uses. Moreover, their units of analysis are different. They are, however, not totally mutually exclusive. As knowledge within the disciplines increases, areas of overlap are more evident. This is of immense value to marketing business, especially where the various study disciplines contribute to each other's findings.

Behaviour segmentation *Marketing planning*
A technique for grouping consumers based on their relationship to the product being marketed. As examples: their knowledge or understanding of the product, their reasons for buying it, and the rate at which they use it.

Below the line   *Marketing jargon*
A metaphorical, invisible, horizontal line dividing various marketing communications media. By convention, those media granting commission to advertising
agencies are above the line; the rest are below it.

Above the line:
cinema
outdoor
press
radio
television

The line: _____

Below the line:
advertising gifts
body media (T-shirts, hats etc)
direct mail
exhibitions
mini media
packaging
point-of-sale material
print
public relations
retail display and merchandising
sales promotion
sponsorship

Benchmarking   *Business, Customer relationship management, Research*
A standard of performance, quality or excellence against which all similar activity
is judged, evaluated and measured. This was a key management concept of the
late 1990s, and continues to be discussed and developed. For example, for an
increasing number of organizations it is one of the key concepts of **customer
relationship management** strategy (CRM). They invest heavily in technology to
help them formulate and implement CRM strategy.

While many companies are good at formulating the strategy, they find it difficult
to implement. In essence, CRM combines marketing, campaign management, sales
and service functions, with technology to help implement it. To fulfil the aims of
its strategy effectively and efficiently, a company needs to take the *comprehensive*
approach to CRM. However, many companies treat marketing, campaign management, sales and service as separate functions, each with its own separate pools of
customer information. Consequently, under these circumstances, it is difficult,
sometimes impossible, to fulfil CRM objectives and measure results. Setting up
and implementing a comprehensive benchmarking system helps to overcome this
difficulty. It also lets a company know how well it is doing in relation to its direct
competitors and others within its industry.

Best before *Date coding, Packaging, Product management, Retailing*
A phrase printed on a product pack, followed by a date. In current practice, this form of date coding indicates the time limit by which the contents should be sold. However, it is a source of confusion. In theory, date coding is a measure designed to ensure that the customer receives the product in a reasonably fresh condition, or at least in good condition. In practice, it covers the producer and retailer against accusations of negligence. 'Use by' is another date code used in retail packaging. In reality, products sold in packs can often be safely used months or even years after the 'best before' date.

Sometimes, packs bear the phrase 'Display until' followed by a date. This indicates more clearly what is meant – that the retailer should display the product on his shelves until the date shown, after which it should be removed. Moreover, some packs bear both 'Best before' and 'Display until'

One UK national retailing chain currently throws into even greater confusion the system just described. Its customer care department states that 'Best before' means that the contents of the pack should be *used or eaten* before the date shown. This means that the responsibility is on the customer rather than the retailer.

This entire scenario is not only confusing to the purchaser, but sloppy retailing and marketing practice. Until there is an industry standard for this type of chaotic labelling, confusion will continue.
See Use by.

Bias *Marketing research, Statistics*
In statistical practice, errors arising as a result of the use of unrepresentative samples. Also applies to the way the sampling is handled by the company doing the research.

Bid price *Business transactions, Stock market*
The price a customer is prepared to pay for a product, service or company shares.

Bill *Business, Outdoor advertising*
In popular use, another term for an invoice, but not normally used in UK business practice. Usually also used in restaurants, except in the USA and countries under US influence, where the term *check* is used. Sometimes erroneously used instead of billboard (*qv*).

Billboard *Outdoor advertising*
A US term for a **poster**, now rather unnecessarily being adopted in Europe. In the UK, properly used, billboard should refer to very large posters.

Billing *Advertising agency practice*
Originally used to denote the gross value of an agency's media purchases. Now more often used to express the total value of an agency's business. Confusion can be avoided by asking for the precise definition of the term when discussing the topic.

Bi-metal plate   *Print, Production*
A technique used in litho print production. A plate used for long print runs, in which the printing image base is copper or brass, and the non-printing area aluminium, stainless steel or chromium.

Bin   *Retailing*
In a retail outlet, a container for displaying products, usually specially discounted offers or loss leaders (*qv*). Sometimes called a dump-bin. Sited at the end of a supermarket gondola, or in an aisle, a bin is designed to encourage shoppers to pick up a product in passing.

Binding   *Print finishing*
Techniques for joining pages of newspapers, magazines, brochures and books, carried out in the finishing department. Materials used in binding include glue, stitching, staples, board, plastics and fabrics.

Bingo card   *Magazine and directory publishing*
Also called a **reader enquiry card**. An enquiry card inserted or bound into a publication, which makes it easy for readers to send for information. It displays a matrix of key numbers or letters, which match those in the editorial or advertising pages of the publication. The return postage on the card is usually pre-paid by the publisher. Many publishers do not offer this free facility to readers, on the grounds that if the readers want the information badly enough, they will pay the postage.

Bit   *Computing, Information technology*
In computer jargon, the smallest unit of electronic information. A contraction of **BI**nary digi**T**.
See Byte.

Bit-mapping   *Computing, Information technology*
In computer typesetting, the characters and their shapes are stored digitally as 'dots' in the computer's memory. When retrieved from the computer's bit-map for printing, they are reproduced as dots.

.biz   *E-commerce, Internet activity*
A top-level domain name for business. Strictly speaking, .biz domain names are only for those intending to use their domain names for 'bona fide business or commercial use'. The registry for .biz defines this as:

> The bona fide use or bona fide intent to use the domain name or any content, software, materials, graphics or other information thereon, to permit Internet users to access one or more host computers through the domain name server:
>
> 1. to exchange goods, services or property of any kind;
> 2. in the ordinary course of trade or business; or,
> 3. to facilitate 1 or 2 above.

The registry for .biz has explicitly excluded from the definition those using or intending to use the domain exclusively for personal, non-commercial purposes, or exclusively for the expression of non-commercial ideas, eg trademarksarerubbish.biz. Domain name speculation is also explicitly excluded from the definition.

Black   *Print*
The colour used with the subtractive primaries yellow, magenta and cyan in four-colour printing. Its main function is to give depth to the other colours, and provide degrees of light, shade and emphasis.
See all these, and Process colours.

Black   *Television, Video*
When the screen is showing neither pictures nor 'snow' it is said to be showing 'black'. In post-production jargon, '**Going to black**' means inserting a section of black in the tape. Most commercially produced videos, training videos for example, start with about 20 seconds of black.

Black and white   *Artwork, Print*
Originals or reproductions in black only, as distinct from multicolour. Usually abbreviated to B&W. However, see the various caveats on abbreviations and initials elsewhere in this dictionary.

Black economy   *Business*
A covert economic system, operated by individuals and organizations for the main purpose of evading tax. This usually involves trading for cash, or by barter or other cashless method; often the employment of casual labour paid for in cash. Some of these activities are inherently criminal, as well as flouting taxation, Customs & Excise and employment law.

Black printer   *Print*
A black printing plate, used in colour reproduction for increasing the contrast of neutral tones and detail.

Blade coated   *Paper*
Paper coated by a process in which a freshly applied wet coating is smoothed, and the excess removed, by a thin, flexible metal blade. This produces an excellent surface suitable for high quality printing.

Blank   *Artwork, Film and television animation*
In animation, a cell without a drawing. This device is used to keep the number of cell layers constant during a sequence of animation photography.

Blanket   *Print*
A rubber-coated roller used on offset litho and some flexographic presses. This to prevent undue wear on the printing plate, paper being abrasive. The blanket takes

up the image from the printing plate and transfers it to the paper or other surface to be printed. There is no contact between printing plate and paper.
See Dry offset, Litho, Offset.

Blanket coverage   *Advertising*

Advertising, with the objective of getting as much coverage as possible, and without a pre-determined target audience. This is a useful technique where a target audience is unknown, or cannot be defined precisely. Many advertisers reduce the expense, and the risk of wastage, by using small advertisements, often carrying a **key** code (*qv*).

Blanket to blanket   *Print*

An offset litho printing press in which two blanket cylinders act as opposing impression cylinders. This allows both sides of a web or sheet to be printed simultaneously – a technique termed **perfecting**.

Bleed   *Artwork, Creative, Print, Production*

An illustration that prints beyond the trim edge of the paper. This brings the image right to the edge after trimming; no margin is visible.

Blind advertisement   *Advertising*

An advertisement in which the name of the advertiser is missing. If the advertiser chooses to remain anonymous, as in much recruitment advertising, the agency or recruitment specialist will feature its own name instead, or use a box number.

Blind embossing   *Print, Production*

An image raised up on paper or board above the common surface, but not printed. In embossing technique, the paper is pushed up from the back, by a die or other mechanical device, to create an image.
See Die stamping, Embossing, Relief printing, Thermography.

Blind image   *Print*

In litho printing, an image that has lost its ink receptivity, and fails to print adequately or at all.

Blind product testing   *Marketing research, Product research*

Testing various aspects, benefits or features of a product without revealing its name to the respondents.

Blink testing   *Marketing research, Retail research*

Tests on consumers involving the counting of the number of times they blink in a specified time. The tests are designed to reveal the level of concentration, arousal, interest or apathy in certain pre-determined circumstances. First used in the USA to gauge the level of concentration and interest of shoppers in supermarkets to products displayed on shelves. It was found that shoppers' blink-rates usually went down while they were cruising along the aisles. The rate usually rose sharply when approaching or standing at the checkouts.

Blister pack   *Packaging, Point-of-sale display, Retailing*
A product mounted on board, with transparent plastic shrunk tightly on to it. The blister effect not only protects the product from damage when the pack is handled; it helps to display the product to good effect.

Block   *Computing, Desktop publishing, Word-processing*
A group of characters or words treated as a single unit.

Block   *Letterpress printing, Process engraving*
An illustration, line or tone, etched into a metal or plastic plate. Once created in this way, plates can be moulded or cast in metal or plastic, or reproduced electrolytically. Blocks are usually mounted on wood or plastic, to bring them up to type height for printing. This technology is now little used in Europe, because of the cumbersomeness of the materials involved and the continuing popularity of litho printing. It is still used in less technologically driven countries.

Blocking out   *Artwork, Plate-making, Production*
See Masking.

Blow-up   *Artwork, Photography*
An enlargement of a photo negative or photoprint.

Blueprint   *Print, Production*
A photoprint made from stripped-up negatives or positives. This is used as a proof to check the position of image elements. The technique is frequently used in litho printing and photo-engraving.

Board   *Paper, Paper-making, Print*
Material used in printing and packaging, heavier and stiffer than paper and in various weights or thicknesses. The substance at which paper becomes board varies greatly among manufacturers. It can vary from as low as 180 g/m² to as high as 250 g/m². Board is extensively used for brochure covers, as well as for packaging.

Body   *Print*
A term used in ink technology, describing the viscosity or consistency of an ink. An ink with too much body, for example, is too stiff.

Body copy   *Copywriting, Desktop publishing, Typography, Word-processing*
The small type text of an advertisement, brochure, leaflet or editorial. Most advertisement body copy, and that for printed literature, is set in sizes under 12pt. Copy over 12pt, usually headlines, is referred to as display copy.

Bodyline capacity *Typesetting, Typography*
The number of lines on a page to be printed.

Body type *Copywriting, Desktop publishing, Typography, Word-processing*
Printing type smaller than 12pt. Also termed **text type**. Body type is used for the main part of a piece of copy, as distinct from its heading.

BOGOFF *Retailing, Sales promotion*
A slightly vulgar, but effective acronym for **Buy One Get One For Free**. A measure undertaken by marketers and retailers for increasing the sales of a product for a limited period. Also expressed as BOGOF and B1G1F.

Boiler-plate *Copywriting, Desktop publishing, Direct mail*
A piece of copy stored as a standard unit. Different parts of this can be rearranged and combined with new copy to produce new documents, such as personalized direct mail letters. Compare this term with *template* and *macro*.

Bold *Desktop publishing, Typography, Word-processing*
Also termed **boldface**. Heavier versions of regular type, with thicker strokes and curves. Bold is usually used for headings and sub-headings, and for emphasis in body copy. Also termed **heavy**.

Bond *Paper, Print*
A range of high quality paper generally used for letterheads, correspondence and expensive-looking mailshots. The substance of such papers is usually over 60 grams per square metre (60 g/m^2 or gsm). Lighter substance papers, below 60 g/m^2, used for copying and computer printing, are known as **bank** (*qv*).

Bonding *Print, Production*
Another term for **gluing**, where two materials are joined together permanently, usually by an adhesive.

Bonding *Business, Exporting, Importing*
The warehousing, under Customs & Excise guard, of imported goods, which have yet to have duty paid on them. They are held until the duty is paid, or the goods re-exported.

Bonus pack *Retailing*
A product pack at the point of sale, containing more than the normal quantity of product but sold at the normal price. This is always promoted on the pack, usually as an advertisement display.

Booklet *Advertising, Creative, Print*
A piece of promotional print designed and bound in the form of a book. The term is usually applied to such a format of 24 pages or more. Below that number of pages, it is usually termed a **brochure**.

Book token *Retailing*
A gift coupon or voucher, paid for by a customer at the point of sale. This can be exchanged by the recipient for a book having the same value. It can also be used as part-payment for a book, the rest made up in cash or by credit, debit or store card. Tokens can be obtained also for other merchandise, such as clothes, and for holidays and fitness centre activity.

Book value *Accounting, Business*
The value of a company asset as recorded in the company's accounts. This is often different from its **market value**.

Boom *Film and television, Photography*
A trolley-mounted jib, at the end of which is a microphone. Its design and mechanism allows it to be moved about silently, following the actors during a take. The boom operator is referred to as the **boom swinger**.

Booth *Advertising, Exhibitions*
Another term for an exhibition stand or shell.

Booting up *Computing, Information technology*
Starting up a computer, during which operating software is automatically loaded from the computer's hard disk. Most computers do this internally when being switched on. Nowadays, few if any computers are routinely booted from floppy disks. In the event of a 'crash' or a 'freeze', a computer can use **rescue disks**, prepared in advance.

Border *Design, Artwork, Desktop publishing, Print,*
Production, Typography
A simple or complex rule, or a decorated one, positioned round type and illustrated matter on a printed page.

Boston Matrix *Marketing planning, Product portfolio planning*
A tool for evaluating a company's product portfolio, devised by the Boston Consulting Group. The technique is expressed as a diagram in the form of a box with four compartments – a four-cell matrix. Each compartment shows the progress of a product in its life cycle, and its contribution to the health and profitability of the portfolio as a whole. It enables marketing and product management teams to assess the performance of products, their likely potential, and their destiny. It provides an insight into the relative importance of individual products in the portfolio. It also offers a view of the problems and opportunities likely to be encountered, and clues for the organization's policy for future investment and divestment.

The usefulness of the matrix can be expressed as follows. In high-growth markets, there are usually opportunities for all the contenders to gain market share. On the other hand, in markets where growth is low, the only way to increase market share is by seducing customers away from the competition. In view of this, the matrix helps to indicate the direction in which the company should be approaching business threats and opportunities, and the allocation of its resources to meet them.

Marketing and product teams use such fairly simple, linear concepts as aids to decision-making. A product portfolio involves a balance of products and services, opportunities and risks. Naturally, they also take into account such vital business considerations as return on investment, individual and overall profitability.

An explanation of the terms used in the Matrix:

■ *Problem child* – a product with high growth, low market share. Prospects are good, but possibly under-performing. May need high investment to reach its full profit potential; this could be a drain on the portfolio.

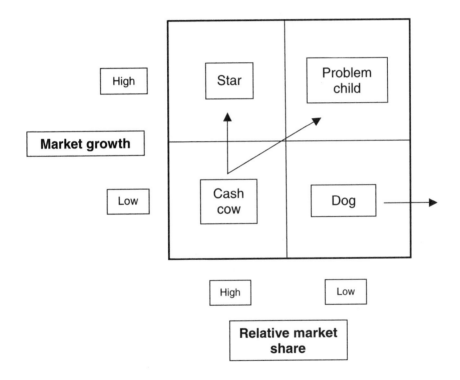

THE BOSTON MATRIX

In ideal product portfolio management, the aim is to use cash surpluses generated by cash cows for investment in the rising stars, and in selected problem children. Dogs are thrown out when no longer productive.

- *Star* – product with high growth, high market share. May need high levels of funding.
- *Cash cow* – product with low growth, high market share. Could be the main source of funds for the problem children and stars in the portfolio.
- *Dog* – a low growth, low market share product. Dubious performance. May qualify for removal from the portfolio.

Bounce flash   *Photography, Reprographics*

Electronic flash, reflected from a surface before it reaches the subject. This gives a soft, even light, with minimal shadow.

Boutique   *Marketing communications services*

An advertising services company offering a particular speciality, rather than a full range of services. For example, creative services without media planning and buying. Companies offering specialist media planning and buying services only, and not creative or production, are known as **media independents** (*qv*).

Box   *Advertising, Artwork, Desktop publishing, Print, Typography,*
                                                          Word-processing

A rule border round a piece of copy, isolating it from other matter on a printed page.

Bracketing   *Photography, Reprographics*

A technique for ensuring correct exposure when conditions are difficult. It comprises taking shots at twice and half the indicated exposure.

BRAD   *Advertising, Media, Media buying*

British Rate and Data: a monthly media directory compendium giving advertising rates, circulation figures and mechanical data for British print and broadcast media, plus cinema and e-zines. The directory is published by EMAP Communications; www.intellagencia.com. The publisher's *BRADbase* service offers this data online to subscribers. European counterparts include ***Tarif Media*** in France and ***Media Daten*** in Germany. In the USA, the counterpart is ***SRDS***, the ***Standard Rate and Data Service***.

Brand   *Advertising, Marketing, Marketing communications*

Defined simply and narrowly, the proprietary name of a product, along with the personality and visual identity given to it by its creator and owner.

Brand awareness   *Brand management, Marketing, Marketing research*

The percentage or proportion of consumers who, in a research operation, recognize a particular brand.

Branded products   *Marketing, Retailing*

Products marketed and offered for sale under a proprietary rather than a generic name. In developed countries such as in Europe and the USA, such products are safeguarded by legislation against pirating and **passing off** (*qv*). Pursuing pirates in the courts is another matter, which may be both costly and long drawn-out.

Brand equity   *Marketing planning, Product planning*

The values, assets, properties and perceptions of a product, service or idea, assigned to it and promoted by its creator. This term also applies to the responsibilities and liabilities linked to the brand.

Many brand operators state that this embraces such elements as the awareness of its name in the marketplace, customer loyalty to the brand, its perceived quality, its logos and trademarks. Others extend this to the ability of the brand to differentiate itself from its competitors. It can also include the corporate identity and image of its owner's organization.

Brand image   *Brand management, Creative, Media, Marketing,*
Marketing research

Generally speaking, this expresses the *total personality* of a company or product. It is this, rather than any trivial technical differences, which determines a product's position in the market. Brand **identity** is concerned with how a company *presents* the brand to its market. Brand **image** is how that market *perceives* the brand identity.
See Branding, Positioning.

Branding   *Creative, Media, Marketing, Marketing planning,*
Marketing research

The use of techniques by which a company, organization or product distinguishes itself from others. This is how it expresses its identity and function in its markets. In current marketing thinking, branding is the process of identifying and differentiating a product or service, and establishing its uniqueness. In practice, it is much more than that.

Branding is part of the process of being sensitive to how customers perceive your product or company. You use branding to send signals to customers at whom you have aimed the product, and who will benefit from possessing or using it.

Branding operations provide the following advantages:

- The product is more easily remembered and identified.
- It provides strong links between advertising and other forms of promotion; for example, public relations, sales promotion, sponsorship and packaging.
- It provides a bridge between the different media, such as press, television, radio and created media; and between campaigns.
- A brand has promotional value. Customer benefits can be associated with it.
- New products can be introduced more easily under a well-established, respected brand name. This applies equally to existing markets as to new ones. Heinz, Coke, Cadbury and Canon are obvious examples
- Heinz doesn't have to start from the beginning and introduce itself when launching a new packaged product. Canon operates in several different

markets, such as televisions and video recorders, cameras and office copiers. The brand name helps to bridge the gap.

- A manufacturer in one sector of the market can enter another sector with a different brand. Virgin, for example, now operates an airline, a railway and a pensions and investment company.
- Branding and positioning affect the messages aimed at existing and potential customers.
- UK supermarket chains such as Sainsbury, Safeway and Tesco offer their own labels at lower prices. This is in direct competition with the established brands they stock. The aim is to divert customer attention from the major brands into the retailers' own, without seriously affecting sales of the established brands.

The essential elements of successful branding:

- differentiation;
- identity;
- uniqueness.

Differentiation
Making absolutely clear the distinction between one's own product and all others.

Identity
The establishment, firmly and unambiguously, of the identity of the product, service, idea or company, and its distinct personality.

Uniqueness
In advertising, public relations, sales promotion and packaging, the taking of a strong position with statements only *you* can make about your product, service or company and statements no competitor can say, or dares say, or bothers to say, about theirs.

Clear, unambiguous branding offers a number of advantages:

- It establishes your identity and that of your product.
- It establishes, and can enhance, your reputation for high quality.
- It establishes and demonstrates a responsible attitude towards your market.
- It encourages lasting memorability in your company's markets, and elsewhere.

Brand leader   *Marketing, Product management*
An organization, brand or product holding the highest individual share within a market.

Brand loyalty   *Creative, Media, Marketing, Research*
Allegiance by customers to a particular brand. This varies a great deal, and can be complicated by swings of buying patterns by brand-loyal groups. Research, particularly rolling research, can determine the fads, fancies and swings, so that

marketers can decide on their marketing and advertising investment programmes with minimum risk.

Consumer loyalty to a particular product or service can be fickle. According to a Royal Mail advertisement in 1999, it costs six times more to get a new customer than it does to maintain an existing one. It follows that the marketer's aim should be to establish such a good relationship with customers that they stay loyal to his product. This brand loyalty is a valuable corporate asset, and should be pursued over a long term. Brand loyalty, and the marketing appeals made to achieve it, can be emotional, or based on physical advantages such as taste, price or design.

Brand manager   *Marketing, Product management*
Also termed **product manager**. A manager or executive responsible for the conduct of a product or brand in its markets. Duties include everything from the translation and implementation of the initial marketing brief for the brand, to the day-to-day running of the team handling brand affairs; from packaging to the pursuit of profitability objectives and plans for future development. Close liaison with other managers and departments is usually required; especially sales.

Brand personality   *Marketing, Product management*
The creation and maintenance of qualities and attributes that give a product or brand its identity, uniqueness and differentiation. It is the 'badge' by which consumers recognize the brand, and often those that help them towards buying decisions. High-quality, excellent value for money, fashionable styling, international availability, good after-sales service and support are some elements of brand personality.

Brand positioning   *Marketing, Product management*
The creation, maintenance and development of the concept of a brand, in the minds of its customers, vis-à-vis that of its competitors. Some motor vehicle brands, for example, may be perceived as good value for money. Others may be seen as expensive, have never been anything else, and are never likely to be. Individual brands of margarine, virtually identical in composition, can be perceived by positioning in different ways: slimming, health-promoting, ideal for baking, convenient because easy to spread, indistinguishable from butter, and so on.

Brand property   *Advertising, Brand management*
Images, sounds, slogans, colours and other physical elements designed to carry a brand's imagery over from one advertising medium to another, one campaign to the next. The IBM logo is always blue, whatever the visual medium; hence the company has acquired the nickname Big Blue. Duracell batteries are copper-coloured, and the visuals are accompanied in television commercials by a distinctive sound effect. In its radio advertising, the sound effect is used so that it represents, and is linked to, the visual imagery of the television commercials and full-colour press advertisements. Music from the opera *Lakmé* is closely linked to British Airways, and may be considered its brand property.

Brand recognition *Advertising, Marketing planning, Sales promotion*
The ability of a brand to achieve, in its markets, the level of pre-planned recognition and awareness.

Brand reinforcement *Advertising, Marketing, Sales promotion*
Promotional messages channelled through a variety of media, designed to bind existing consumers even tighter and more positively to a brand.

Brand share *Advertising, Marketing planning*
Statistics, in terms of cash or sales volume, showing what percentage share a product has achieved in its markets in a given period. It should be borne in mind that sales turnover and quantity volume are not the same. Turnover is expressed as money; sales volume as units. From this it is possible to calculate the cost of a sale, and whether it is cost-effective or not.

Breadth of range *Product management, Product portfolio, Retailing*
In product portfolio management, breadth of range expresses the range of different products produced by a manufacturer. In retailing and wholesaling, it is the number and variety of different products stocked for sale in a particular store or group of stores.

Break *Cinema, Radio, Television*
A pause during news and entertainment programming, in which advertising is inserted. Usually termed a **commercial break**. Usually, but not always, at a natural break point in the programming.

Breakdown *Business planning, Marketing planning*
Separation of the individual elements in a business, marketing, marketing communications or other plan, showing individual costs, timings, projected sales and profits, and so on.

Breakdown *Cinema and television commercials*
A schedule used in the filming of entertainment and commercials, prepared by an assistant director. It shows actors, sets, props and other items for each scene. It also indicates whether the shot is to simulate day or night, interior or exterior. It is essential to have a comprehensive breakdown available in the hands of all concerned in the shooting of a commercial, if only so that nothing is forgotten on the day. This is particularly important when a production extends to two or three days. Sending a messenger across town for a forgotten light bulb costs a fortune in lost production time.

Break-even *Business, Marketing planning*
The point in a planned enterprise or campaign, at which investment or expenditure in the project and the income gained from it are equal. Simply stated, the point at which the project becomes commercial viable. Traditionally, the time-frame

allocated for this process was in the region of five years. More recently, the time-frame allowed has become shorter and shorter; it is now 18 months or less. Under this kind of regime, a product may be abandoned if turnover and profits do not rise rapidly from the start. Marketers often look for ultra-quick profits, rather than long-term prosperity, however bad this may be for the consuming public.

Break-even analysis   *Business, Marketing planning*
A technique designed to evaluate the performance of a product in its markets, and to calculate the relationship between revenue and costs. From this it should be possible to decide on the viability of a product, and its future in a company's product portfolio.

Break for colour   *Artwork, Print, Production*
In artwork and composition for print, a technique for separating the elements to be printed in different colours.

Brief   *Marketing, Marketing communications*
A set of instructions for the preparation and implementation of a marketing campaign or project. Ideally they should be complete with background, research findings, objectives, statistics, costs and campaign execution details.

Brightness   *Photography, Reprographics*
Light reflected by the subject to be photographed.

Brightness   *Paper, Print*
The brilliance or reflectance of a paper.

British Codes of Advertising and Sales Promotion   *Advertising controls*
A compendium of rules by which the British advertising industry has agreed that the majority of advertisements it produces should be regulated. It is under the general supervision of the **Advertising Standards Authority**.

Radio and television advertisements are not covered by this code. They are covered by similar codes operated by the Radio Authority (*qv*) and the Independent Television Commission (*qv*).

The BCASP establishes a standard against which advertisements and sales promotion may be assessed. It is a guide to those concerned with commissioning, creating and publishing advertisements and sales promotion activities. It is also available to those who believe they may have reason to question what an advertisement says or shows. In this capacity, it helps to protect the public against misleading and offensive advertising.

The Committee for Advertising Practice is the self-regulatory body that devises and enforces the Codes. CAP's members include organizations that represent the advertising, sales promotion and media businesses:

Advertising Association
Association of Household Distributors

Association of Media and Communications Specialists
Broadcast Advertising Clearance Centre
Cinema Advertising Association
Council of Outdoor Specialists
Direct Mail Services Standards Board
Direct Marketing Association (UK)
Direct Selling Association
Incorporated Society of British Advertisers
Institute of Practitioners in Advertising
Institute of Sales Promotion
Mail Order Traders' Association
Mailing Preference Service
Newspaper Publishers' Association
Newspaper Society
Outdoor Advertising Association
Periodical Publishers' Association
Proprietary Association of Great Britain
Royal Mail
Scottish Daily Newspaper Society
Scottish Newspaper Publishers' Association

In the opening pages of a previous version of the Codes, the Committee outlined the essence of good advertising practice as follows:

- All advertisements should be legal, decent, honest and truthful.
- All advertisements should be prepared with a sense of responsibility both to the consumer and to society.
- All advertisements should conform to the principles of fair competition generally accepted in business.

No marketer can fail to support these worthwhile sentiments.

British Council   *Government agency*
A government agency with responsibility for promoting the UK. Its remit includes the promotion of British products, investment possibilities, exports, trading advantages, trade missions and visits, countryside, tourism, cultural and ethical values, and other major features of British life and commerce. The service is available to British exporters and supports an international network.

Broadcasting Act 1990   *Controls*
See CRCA, ITVA, Radio Authority.

Broadsheet   *Media, Print, Production*
A paper size used in newspaper and magazine printing. The trimmed page size is about 600 mm high × 380 mm wide, depending on the printing house. *The Times*,

Daily Telegraph and *Independent* are broadsheets. British daily newspapers, the *Daily Express* and *Sun* are tabloids (*qv*).

Brochure *Advertising, Creative, Print*

A piece of promotional print designed and bound in the form of a book. The term is usually applied to such a format up to 24 pages. Above that number of pages, it is usually termed a booklet. Brochures are often written, designed and produced with high quality in mind, so that their form and content reflect well on the organization represented in them.

Broken lot *Retailing, Wholesaling*

A quantity of goods smaller than that usually offered for sale; often when part of a larger consignment is broken up into smaller lots. This can happen when some of the original consignment is damaged in transit.

Broker *Business*

An independent individual who brings sellers and buyers together, acting as agent but not actually handling the products or services being negotiated. The essence of a broker's trade is her independence, and the impartiality of her advice. If a broker is tied to a single supplier, and offers only that supplier's products or services, she is called a representative. This should be made clear at the start of every transaction. It is worth noting that advertising agents are neither agents nor brokers. The term **agent** is a relic of the time when advertising agents were actually sales agents for publications they represented. Today, agents are principals in contracts entered into both with clients and with media.

Bromide *Photography, Reprographics*

A photoprint on silver-bromide coated paper. This technique is disappearing into photographic history, since more modern materials and techniques are now used. However, the terminology lingers on. To achieve different degrees of photographic image contrast, papers of different 'hardness' are still used.
See Photograph.

Bronzing *Print, Production*

A technique for achieving a bronze effect in a printed item. This comprises printing first with a sizing ink, then applying bronze powder while the ink is still wet, to produce a metallic lustre.

Brown goods *Marketing, Retailing*

Marketing jargon. Certain consumer durables, usually those purchased infrequently, with high unit cost, such as domestic furniture, storage units and carpets. This term is used to distinguish them from **white goods** (*qv*).

Brush coated *Paper*

A coated paper produced by coating a web with slip. This is distributed and smoothed by brushes, some stationary and others oscillating across the web. An excellent paper for high quality printing.

B series *Paper*

An international ISO range of sizes for paper and board, generally used for posters, wall-charts and so on. The ratio of the sides of A and B series papers is $1:\sqrt{2}$.

Sheet size	Millimetres
B0	1,000 × 1,414
B1	707 × 1,000
B2	500 × 707
B3	353 × 500
B4	250 × 353
B5	176 × 250

BSI *Product development, Quality control*

The British Standards Institute.

Bucket shop *Retailing*

A vulgar term for an outlet offering heavily discounted products and services, such as holidays, air fares and computer peripherals.

Budget *Advertising, Business, Marketing*

Money allocated to future business or marketing operations or campaigns over a fixed time-frame. Where appropriate, this is divided into constituent parts of the operation, taking into account all future expenditure needed to fulfil the objectives.

Budget *Cinema and television commercials*

A financial breakdown of estimated costs for producing a commercial. In addition to the personnel and materials for a shoot found in the breakdown (*qv*), other items must appear. These include travelling time; meals per day; first aid kit; preparation costs; portable lavatories, if shooting on location.

Bug *Computing, Information technology*

An error in a computer program. Correcting errors in computer software is called **de-bugging**.

Built-in obsolescence *Business, Manufacturing, Marketing*

Also termed **planned obsolescence**. A situation in which the working life of a product is limited by forward planning at concept stage. This forces the purchaser to decide, in the course of time, whether to continue to use the product until it actually breaks down, or buy a new one. Obsolescence is usually driven along by the introduction of frequent changes in the design of the same product, or by the introduction of completely new ones at short intervals. This phenomenon can be observed in the marketing of computers, mobile telephones, televisions, videos and cars. In the case of computer software, new products are often incompatible with older computers.

Bulk   *Paper*
The substance and feel of a printing paper.

Bulk breaking   *Reselling, Retailing, Wholesaling*
The purchasing of bulk quantities of goods, then reselling them in smaller quantities to other buyers. Supermarkets do this with commodities such as vegetables. The wholesaler benefits from the savings to be made when buying in quantity; the retailer does the same, to a lesser or greater extent. The end-customer may hardly benefit at all.

Bulk discounts   *Advertising, Retailing, Wholesaling*
Discounts offered when large quantities of a product or service are purchased. Advertising space and airtime are usually offered in this way, in the form of frequency and volume discounts (*qv*).

Bullet   *Copywriting, Desktop publishing, Print, Typesetting, Typography*
Symbol placed in front of lines of copy, for drawing attention to the text. Symbols vary, but the most popular are small, solid discs, squares and diamonds. The use of bullets enables the writer to use extreme terseness where appropriate, without regard to the niceties of grammar and syntax. Bullets help to convey information without wasting words. For examples, see **Branding**.

Bulletin   *Advertising, Publishing*
A publication, such as a newsletter, issued periodically, usually containing news and reviews of interest to recipients. Normally distributed by post, but increasingly now by e-mail.

Bulletin board   *Internet communications*
The electronic equivalent of a message board, accessed via the Internet. Contributors leave their observations, questions, queries and answers on the board, and read and reply to those left by others.

Burn   *Print, Production*
A popular term used in plate-making, particularly in the USA, for the photographic exposure of printing plates.

Burst   *Advertising*
An intense advertising effort concentrated into a short time-frame. A useful technique for a product launch or relaunch. Applies to press, broadcast and direct mail advertising, particularly when all three are coordinated.

Business format franchise   *Franchising*
The operator of a franchise, the franchisee, virtually rents a product concept from its owner, the franchisor. A franchise in business format enables the franchisee to benefit from a complete franchise package, which might include warranties, guarantees, after-sales service arrangements, online support, product literature and access to databases.

Business gift   *Advertising*
A gift from an advertiser, usually to existing and potential customers, carrying a promotional message, campaign slogan or company logo. Cheaper items are often sent through the post; more expensive ones usually handed over by salespeople during meetings with clients or prospects. Pens, diaries, keyrings and desk-furniture are common items of business giftware.

Business press   *Advertising, Publishing*
Media aimed at and read by the business community. For advertising media planning purposes, publications are usually grouped in business categories. For example, the marketing-related press includes, *Campaign, Marketing, Marketing Week, Media Week* and *PR Week* (the UK), and *Advertising Age* (USA).

Business reply service   *Advertising, Direct mail, Marketing*
A service offered by post offices in Europe, the USA and many industrialized countries. This entitles an advertiser to pay postage and handling charges on reply cards and coupons; recipients pay nothing. This marketing technique is designed to encourage enquirers and potential customers to reply to advertisements.

Business-to-business   *Advertising, Marketing, Public relations*
A situation in which a manufacturer or service supplier promotes and markets to other businesses, rather than to the general public. Thus, for example, the manufacturers of car electrics, computer chips or printing inks supply components and materials for the manufacturing activities of other companies. Also, popularly referred to as **B2B**.

Business-to-business advertising   *Advertising*
Advertising aimed at selected markets within the business community, rather than at consumers or the general public. This applies to any products or services that are purchased or used by businesses, including components, capital equipment, specialized services, and some classes of insurance and finance.

Business-to-business marketing   *Marketing*
Marketing of products and services among businesses and corporations, which does not use wholesale and retail channels of distribution. Sales effort in business-to-business marketing is usually carried out by specialists, such as sales engineers and technical representatives.

Bus sides *Outdoor advertising*

Horizontal advertising space on the sides of buses, usually below or between the rows of windows.

Buyer readiness *Product management*

Consumers can be categorized in terms of how close they may be to making a decision to buy, or to an actual purchase. Stages of consumer readiness range from initial awareness, interest and decision, to action.

Buyer-seller relationship *Marketing planning, Product management*

The character and quality of the relationship between buyer and seller, in terms of their social and economic interaction.

Buyer's market *Business, Marketing*

A negotiating position where there is more product on the market than customer capacity or ability to purchase. This situation can occur in a variety of fields of endeavour, including manufacturing, recruitment, finance, insurance, travel and academia.

Buying centre *Marketing planning, Product management*

A central unit within an organization, responsible for the purchase of commodities for the organization as a whole. A single buying centre, for example, may purchase fabrics for a clothes manufacturer or national reseller; or citrus fruits for a national supermarket chain. However, companies marketing on a regional basis may have buying centres in each region, responsible for purchases based on local demand, culture or taste.

Buying classes *Marketing planning*

In planning a marketing campaign aimed at corporations, the marketing team need to take into account customers' buying decisions and how they are arrived at. First-time buying is usually a complicated process, often demanding decisions from a variety of executives; for example, chief executive, finance director, production director, personnel director and administration manager. Repeat purchasing of the same product is much easier; modified re-purchasing, where the product has changed, may call for a new sales pitch by the seller.

Buying matrix *Company purchasing management*

A simple spreadsheet-like technique to help decision-making, enabling buyers to compare products, specifications and prices. These can then be more easily matched to the company's requirements.

Buying syndicate *Marketing, Retailing*

A group of like-minded people or businesses, collaborating to obtain the best possible terms for purchases. This technique enables small businesses, such as individual grocery outlets and other retailers, to trade on nearly the same terms as giant supermarkets. This has been known to work well on a consumer level. Some years ago, a Japanese housewife, disgusted with the poor quality and high price of groceries in her locality, formed a small cooperative purchasing group of neighbours, friends and relatives. Although this was purely private, and not intended to go beyond a few families, it eventually expanded into a huge national discount buying syndicate. Purchasing power is always with the people, if only they would seize it.

B/W or B&W   *Artwork, Creative, Desktop publishing, Print, Production*
Initials for **black and white** usually, but not always wisely, used in written instructions. It is prudent to spell out such instructions and descriptions, if only to avoid confusion and unnecessary expense and time-loss when initials are misunderstood.

Byline   *Editorial, Public relations, Publishing*
A line in a newspaper or magazine above a report, column or feature, giving the name of the writer. It shows who the piece is 'by'.

By-product   *Business, Manufacturing, Marketing*
A secondary product or service, produced as the result of the manufacture of a primary one. Lanolin, for example, is a by-product of the wool industry, and marketed as a separate product; it is popularly used in cosmetics.

Byte   *Computing, Information technology*
A group of eight bits of electronic data; a unit of digital information.
See Bit.

Cc

CA *Consumer organizations*
The Consumers' Association (*qv*) in the UK.

Cable television *Television*
Television transmissions distributed to consumers via cable. In the UK, a number of companies are operating cable television, and offering other services such as Internet access and telephone services. With this system, it is possible to target distinctive market segments, and individual subscribers.

CAD/CAM *Computer graphics, Design*
A combination of computer-aided design and computer-aided manufacture. This term is usually used to express graphic output, both on-screen and printed.

Calender *Paper, Paper-making, Print, Production*
A metal roller used in paper-making.

Calendering *Paper, Paper-making, Print, Production*
During paper-making, passing paper through a series of calenders to condition it for printing. The surface of the paper can be made smoother by calendering, which is cheaper than coating it.

Caliper *Paper*
The thickness of paper, usually expressed in thousands of an inch or fractions of a millimetre.

Call-back *Marketing research*
That part of a research programme in which a researcher pays a second call on a respondent, having failed to make contact during the first call. This applies to personal fieldwork and to research conducted by telephone.

Call cycle *Sales management*
The planned frequency and regularity with which a sales executive calls on clients or customers. Often this is determined by computer at the sales support office, for the sake of efficient coverage of sales territories.

Callout *Artwork, Desktop publishing, Typography, Word-processing*
Depends on which software manual you are using. Usually describes a caption to
an illustration, in which the copy is connected to the illustration by a thin rule. In
some desktop publishing and word-processing software, callout describes a box
in which copy is inserted. Often, the callout is not a box proper, but single or
double rules above and below the copy. Or at the sides.

Call rate *Sales management*
The number of contacts made by a sales executive in the field, in a pre-planned
time-frame.

Camcorder *Television, Video*
A video camera that has a tape cassette built in.
See U-Matic, VHS.

Camera-ready *Artwork, Print, Production*
Finished artwork, ready for the process camera. All the elements are in position
with a high degree of accuracy. Printing plates are then made from the film. In the
case of computer-to-plate technology, the artwork image is exposed direct to
printing plates.
See Copy date.

Campaign *Marketing, Marketing communications, Planning operations*
A carefully and meticulously worked-out scheme aimed at fulfilling marketing
objectives. This can include every stage of marketing planning and implementation, from the initial concept for a product or service, to the follow-up carried
out after the close of the scheme. It can include all elements of the marketing and
promotional mixes: product creation, branding, packaging, distribution, advertising, direct mail, telesales, public relations, sales promotion, e-commerce
techniques, customer relationship management and after-sales service.

Cancellation *Media planning and buying*
Cancellation of media bookings. All media have deadlines by which bookings may
be cancelled without penalty. The lead time varies with the individual publication.
For example, with some national newspapers, the cancellation deadline can be as
short as three days. With national magazines, especially those carrying full-colour
advertising, cancellation dates can be a long as four months preceding publication.

Canned presentation *Sales technique*
A pre-written sales pitch used by salespeople during sales presentations. Almost
always used by telesales staff when cold calling potential customers by phone.
Sometimes the rigid delivery of these scripts is painfully obvious during sales calls.
They are useful for training staff new to a company or a product, but post-training
supervision often does not include humanizing canned presentations as the
salespeople get used to them.

Canvass *Marketing research, Sales technique*
To seek out, contact and interview a potential respondent or group of people. This term can apply either to research, or to selling by telephone or in the field. A person doing such work is a canvasser. Where the contact is made without prior arrangement, and uninvited by the respondent, this is termed cold canvassing.

CAP *Controls*
The Committee of Advertising Practice. The Committee responsible for the preparation, amendment and enforcement of the British Codes of Advertising and Sales Promotion (*qv*).
See Advertising Standards Authority, British Codes of Advertising and Sales Promotion, CRCA, Independent Television Commission, ITVA, Radio Authority.

Capital *Business, Economics*
Accumulated wealth, especially where this is used for investment or manufacturing production. Also applied to the stock with which a company or person contributes or enters into a business.

Capital *Creative, Desktop publishing, Typography, Word-processing*
The capital letters in an alphabet or a type font.
See Caps, Lower case, Upper case.

Capital goods *Business, Manufacture*
The popular term for equipment, machinery or plant used for the production of commodities, directed towards the consumer, industry and commerce.

Caps *Composition, Desktop publishing, Typesetting, Typography, Word-processing*
A common diminutive for capital letters. Caps and small caps are two sizes of capital letters made in one size of type, commonly used in most roman typefaces.
See Capitals, Lower case, Upper case.

Caption *Artwork, Creative, Print*
Copy attached to a halftone or other illustration, describing or explaining what is being shown. Captions are usually positioned underneath a picture; they can be anywhere, as long as you make sure they do relate to the picture and are closely attached to it.

Caption *Film, Television*
Usually written **CAPT** in the left-hand column of a script. More accurately, a caption board. A board containing an illustration to be shot, usually in the studio. Often used to make animatics (*qv*).

Captive audience *Advertising*
An audience assembled in one place for a length of time, and unlikely to leave before that time is up. Thus, it can be exposed to advertising messages without

interruption. A cinema or theatre performance, or a conference, has a virtually captive audience. Some individuals may leave, and some return, but the audience as a whole stays put until the end.

Captive market *Marketing*
Where there is only one supplier of a commodity, and its customers have no choice but to purchase from it, the market is said to be captive. In the UK, this used to be the case with telephone and postal services, and some utilities.

Cardboard *Packaging, Print*
The amateur term for **board**.

Caret mark *Print, Proof-reading*
A reader's mark, ∧, used for correcting typescripts and proofs. A caret marked in the text shows where additional copy, eg a letter, phrase or sentence, should be inserted. This is matched by a similar mark in the margin, plus the additional copy to be inserted.

Carlill vs The Carbolic Smoke Ball Company *Advertising, Consumer law*
An early leading case in UK advertising litigation and consumer protection. Mrs Carlill saw an advertisement, bought the product and used it as prescribed. She contracted influenza within two weeks, and successfully sued the advertiser.

Carrier *Distribution, Telephone service provision*
A company supplying distribution, haulage or delivery services is termed a carrier. In the UK, British Telecom, and its competitors supplying telephone communication lines and services, are termed carriers.

Carry-through *Broadcast media*
Where radio or television commercial scheduling goes over into a higher-rated programming time segment, and a higher advertising rate applies, this is termed carry-through. The higher rate applied is the carry-through rate.

Cartel *Business, Marketing*
Conspiratorial price-fixing by a number of suppliers for a particular commodity. This may be seen, for example, in the supply of petrol (gasoline). In the UK, the Competition Act 1998, which came into force on 1 March 2000, prohibits anti-competitive agreements and the abuse of a dominant position in the market. Information is on www.oft.gov.uk.

Carton *Packaging*
A container, usually of tough, thin board, but sometimes completely or partially of plastic. Its main purposes are to allow the supplier to ship the contents in predetermined quantities; and to protect them in transit.

Cartridge *Paper, Print*

A tough, uncoated, matt paper with a slightly rough surface. It is popular for use in litho printing.

Cartridge *Radio*

A tape cassette containing a jingle, station announcement or commercial. Usually referred to as a **cart**.

Cartridge *Photography, Reprographics*

A light-proof metal or plastic holder for photographic film, particularly sizes 126 and 110.

Case *Print, Typography*

When letterpress was in its heyday, and type composition done by hand, compositors stored type in cabinets in the composing room. Each drawer in the cabinet was termed a case. The upper case housed the capital letters; the lower case, the small letters. Capitals came to be called upper case; small letters, lower case. These terms are in widespread use today in English-speaking countries.

Case *Export, Import, Packaging, Retailing, Wholesaling*

Another term for a crate or box. In importing and exporting practice, crates and cases are entirely or mostly of wood, to afford maximum protection in transit for the contents. In retailing, a case is usually of board, and contains a set number of product units, such as tins of shoe polish, bars of soap or aerosols of hair spray. Wine is sold by the case, rather than the box or crate.

Case history *Briefing, Research*

The origin, progress and development of a marketing, advertising or other operation, or a campaign, giving facts and figures and other important information, in a document produced for that purpose. Case histories are usually incorporated in documents relating to product re-launches, for example, to help in decision-making.

Case studies *Education, Training*

Case histories written or adapted for academic study. Students are usually briefed and asked questions on a case, leaving them to devise their own conclusions, solutions, outcomes and predictions.

Cash and carry *Retailing, Wholesaling*

A distribution operation where a wholesaler sells stock for cash, and does not deliver. Retailers, caterers, and sometimes members of the public, collect using their own transport. Discounts offered by the wholesaler usually make this worthwhile for customers. This often makes it somewhat easier for small traders to compete with supermarkets.

Cash discount   *Retailing, Wholesaling*
A worthwhile cut in price offered to retailers and consumers, to encourage them
to pay cash for commodities, rather than ask for credit.

Cash flow   *Business, Distribution, Marketing*
The amount of money lying between revenue and expenditure during the course
of day-to-day or week-by-week business operations. Cash flow rates can affect a
company's marketing operations, especially where its products are fast-moving
consumer goods. Retail advertising is especially vulnerable to variations in cash
flow.

Cash on delivery   *Advertising, Business, Direct marketing,*
                                                               Distribution
A distribution system by which goods are advertised, but paid for only when
delivered. This works both ways to protect buyer and seller. The seller does not
receive payment unless and until the goods are delivered. Although the goods have
been ordered in advance by the buyer, she holds on to her money until the goods
turn up, and the seller's obligation has been discharged satisfactorily. Usually
abbreviated to **COD**.

Cassette   *Photography, Reprographics*
A light-proof container for 35 mm film.

Cast off   *Desktop publishing, Typography*
To calculate the amount of type space – type area – which will be taken by
typescript copy when set in a given typeface and size. Older typographers may
still do this with slide-rule or calculator. Computer typesetting, however, has
rendered this technique and, sadly, those who practise it, obsolete. Type is now
usually infinitely scaleable, and can be composed and adjusted on screen to fit the
space allotted to it.

Catalogue   *Direct marketing, Distribution, Marketing*
A brochure, booklet or book showing products on offer, often in full-colour, with
their descriptions, and usually with prices. Terms of business are usually given.
Many catalogues contain order forms, so that intending purchasers can place
orders by post or fax. Modern catalogue practice also encourages customers to
order by telephone, paying immediately by credit card. A business-to-business
catalogue may not feature prices in the body of the text, but may have a separate
price list inserted. This is because such a catalogue may have a long and active
sales life, during which time prices may change, but not products. In this case, it
is more economical for the supplier to reprint a price list than a catalogue.

Catch-line   *Journalism, Public relations*
Also termed a **tag-line**. A word placed at the head of a news item, feature or article,
and at the top left-hand corner of continuation pages. On a proof, it serves as a

temporary headline. This is done to identify the piece as concisely as possible; essential when several hundred pieces are passing through a newsroom at the same time. It is also a handy, colloquial way of referring to a piece when discussing it at meetings and on the telephone.

Caveat emptor *Business, Consumer activity*

Latin for 'Let the buyer beware'. The implication is that the law does not protect the consumer from making bad deals. In the UK, numerous acts of parliament have gone a long way towards protecting consumers from fraud and other trickery, making such activities criminal offences. But the consumer is still individually responsible for careful and prudent purchasing.

CAVIAR *Audience research*

Acronym for **Cinema and Video Industry Audience Research**. Operated in the UK by an independent marketing research company, it conducts research into cinema-going audiences for the Cinema Advertising Association.

CCTV *Social control, Surveillance, Television*

See Closed circuit television.

Ceefax *Broadcasting*

A free public information service provided by the British Broadcasting Corporation (BBC) via its television networks. On television sets equipped to receive it, Ceefax can be accessed by pressing the text key when viewing BBC1 and BBC2 channels.

UK commercial television channels provide a similar service. On independent commercial television Channels 3 and 4, the service is called **Teletext**; on Channel 5, it is called **5 Text**.

Cell *Film production*

In film animation, a single frame in a sequence of frames, drawn on clear acetate. Each cell is different and progressive, so that when the finished sequence is shot and run through a projector, the illusion of movement is created. In film animation, there are normally 24 frames for every second of movement. Think of the people who animated Tom and Jerry, and genuflect. The word is a corrupt abbreviation of celluloid, on which early animators used to work.

See Animation.

Cell *Print*

On a gravure printing cylinder, one of the myriad, minute impressions or pits that hold the ink.

Cell *Computer spreadsheeting, Market forecasting and planning*

A rectangle containing a single unit of information.

Census *Direct marketing, Social control*
A national population count, carried out by governments. In the UK, this is carried out every 10 years, to determine demographic data. From time to time, various other censuses are carried out, including data on distribution, production and property.

Central Office of Information *Government agency, Marketing*
A government agency with responsibility for distributing information on the UK, including manufacturers, their products and services, via offices in foreign countries.

Centred *Desktop publishing, Typography, Word-processing*
Type positioned in the centre of a page, column or ruled box.

Centre spread *Print*
The true centre of a newspaper or magazine. Both pages face each other, carry consecutive page numbers, and are printed by the same plate. In the USA, these are known as centerfolds. Publishers claim that advertisers benefit from its central position, and therefore charge premium advertising rates for it.

Certificate of attendance *Exhibitions, Research*
An auditing system operated by the Audit Bureau of Circulations (*qv*), requiring registered members to show proof of public attendance at exhibitions. It also requires accurate information for certification purposes.

Certificate of insertion *Publishing*
Confirmation that a loose insert in a newspaper or magazine has actually been inserted and distributed in the publication. The publisher or printer issues this to the advertiser.

Certificate of origin *International trade*
A certificate issued by an exporter, showing the origin of goods being exported. Often used by governments and importers to restrict the importation of goods of inappropriate political origin.

Certificate of transmission *Radio, Television*
Confirmation issued by a broadcasting station that a commercial has actually gone out on air. It contains air-date, time, channel, airtime and other relevant information.

CGI *Television, Video*
Initials for **computer-generated images**.

Chainstore *Retailing*
One store in a group owned by a single company or individual. Each store in the group will carry a range of merchandise appropriate to demand in its own area, plus any national brands enjoying a good level of sales.

Channel *Distribution*
A short name for a channel of distribution. Channels include wholesalers, retailers, mail order and the Internet. Channel selection involves a mix of the routes through which suppliers serve their customers.

Channel *Broadcasting*
A term indicating a radio or television broadcasting station.

Character *Desktop publishing, Typography, Word-processing*
A single typeset letter of the alphabet. Often also used to refer to punctuation marks, letter-spaces and, sometimes, numerals. Numerals, however, are a separate case.
See Monotype, Nought, Null, Proof, Proof-reader, Proof-reader's marks, Quote.

Character count *Desktop publishing, Typography, Word-processing*
The number of characters and spaces in a piece of copy.

Character merchandising *Marketing, Retailing*
Retail merchandising using popular characters from television or cinema. Such characters include Teletubbies, Paddington Bear, Thomas the Tank Engine, Noddy, Ninja Turtles, Batman, The Lion King, the Muppets and The Simpsons.

Charge account *Finance, Retailing*
A facility offered to regular customers by a store. The customer is invoiced monthly, and expected to pay promptly.

Charge card *Finance, Retailing*
A payment facility offered by a store in the form of a purchase card, which is presented when buying goods at the store. The customer is sent a statement each month. This works in a fashion similar to a credit card; customers are required to pay by a certain date, after which they are charged interest.

Chart *Presentations, Research analysis*
A diagram based on arithmetical interpretation of research figures. This serves to present figures for judgement and comparison, help discussion, highlight certain facts and findings. Several forms of chart exist, including curves, histograms, pie charts and bar charts, all of which can be designed to appear in three dimensions.

Chartered Institute of Marketing *Marketing organizations*
Formed in the UK in 1911 as the Sales Managers Association and incorporated 10 years later, its range of activities expanded steadily to include other aspects of marketing. In 1961, the name was changed to the Institute of Marketing and Sales Management. In 1968, with the sales management accepted as part of the overall marketing function, it became the Institute of Marketing.

In 1975, the Royal College of Arms gave authority to use the motto 'The World is our Market'. Ten years later in 1985 the new Institute logo was adopted with the message 'Marketing Means Business'.

Marketing education has always been a key Institute activity, the first Certificate examinations being held in 1928. The range of qualifications now includes the Diploma and Certificate in Marketing, and the Certificate in Sales Management. The Diploma is widely accepted by the University Business Schools, as an academic qualification for entry to post-graduate courses leading to MBA awards. In 1965, the Institute funded the creation of the first Chair of Marketing, at the University of Lancaster. Today the UK has 38 Professors of Marketing.

In 1975, Fellows of the Institute established the Guild of Marketors that two years later became the Worshipful Company of Marketors. It is now helping to spread the understanding of marketing within the City of London.

Originally based in London, the Institute moved in 1971 to its present nine-acre site at Moor Hall, Cookham. This move provided the environment and space for the organization's expanding operations, including the development of residential training. Major investments in 1980, 1987 and 1988 resulted in the construction of one of Europe's most prestigious purpose-built residential training facilities. It incorporates a new, much enlarged library and information centre, and additional accommodation to house the expanding education, membership and marketing consultancy operations.

The trend towards greater professionalism in marketing was given a major boost in 1980, when the Institute decreed that all future membership would be by qualification. By 1984, the fast-changing UK and international environment brought a new phase in the Institute's development, and the redefinition of its strategic objectives:

- to extend awareness of effective marketing as the vital factor in business success and national prosperity, and stimulate enhanced marketing performances in the UK;
- to raise the calibre and effectiveness of people involved in marketing through professional education and executive training programmes;
- to develop the Institute as the professional body in the UK and international marketing, setting professional standards of conduct, providing the necessary services for its members, representing the interests of marketing and the people employed in it, and operating the Institute as the umbrella body for other specialist organizations;
- to operate appropriate commercial activities in support of these objectives, and the future development and financial viability of the Institute.

Checklist *Business, Management, Research*

A list of tasks to be done, conditions to be met or objectives to be fulfilled. Often compiled as an aide memoire, but more usually as a tool for carrying out work with efficiency, leaving nothing undone. A variety of listing techniques are used;

alphabetical, for example, or numerical. When writers use this technique for planning books and newspaper features, or business executives for report and proposal writing, such a list is termed a **synopsis**.

Checkout *Retailing*
A US word for a till or cash register, usually applied to the payment point in a supermarket or self-service shop.

Chroma *Artwork, Print*
A colour print made without an intermediate negative.

Chromatic aberration *Photography, Reprographics*
The inability of a lens to bring light of all colours to a common focus point.

Circular *Direct marketing, Mailings, Sales promotion*
Printed literature delivered to a pre-defined target audience. This term usually applies to promotional pieces delivered door-to-door. Many circulars, though not all, are written and designed to appeal to residents with similar disposable incomes, identified by the districts in which they live.
See ACORN.

Circulation *Advertising, Media, Publishing*
The number of copies actually *sold* of each issue of a publication. Do not confuse this term with **readership** (*qv*).
See ABC, Controlled circulation, Rate card, Readership, Verified Free Distribution.

Classified *Press advertising*
Newspaper and magazine advertising sold by the line, rather than by the page unit. Copy is set in caps and lower case, and no illustrations or logos are allowed.
   A variation of this format is **semi-display classified**, sold by the single-column-centimetre. In this case, simple illustrations, headlines and logos are often allowed. In the USA, this is called **classified display**, and sold by the column inch.
See Display.

Cleaning *Databases, Direct marketing, Mailings*
Various methods of making mailing lists more efficient. To optimize a mailing list, it is necessary to eliminate duplication, remove names and addresses of those who have died or 'gone away', revise data on those who have been promoted, changed jobs, job titles, companies and addresses. Failure to do this periodically can result in a list's becoming more and more outdated, less and less efficient, and costing more and more to run.

Clearance sale *Retailing*
A simple technique for clearing out goods at the end of a season, or when such goods become unfashionable. Sales are announced in local media.

Click-through rate *E-business, E-commerce, Internet activity*
The number of visitors who click and land on a Web site or Web page. *Caveat*: there is currently no reliable, independent, international auditing process for click-through traffic. At the time of writing this edition of the Dictionary, there is only the Web site owner's word to be had.

Client *Business*
Among the professions, of which marketing is one, another term for a customer. This sounds more sophisticated than the more ordinary word **customer**, which is usually used in retailing. Referring to a customer as a client often implies substantial fees.

Clip *Film, Video*
Also called a library shot. An existing shot or sequence abstracted from an existing film, and used on its own for another production. In radio, this is called a sound bite.

Clipping *Media services, Public relations*
The physical cutting out of an editorial item from a newspaper or magazine. The companies that do this commercially are called press-cutting or clipping agencies. In the UK, Romeike and Newsclip are two such agencies.

Closed circuit television *Social control, Surveillance, Television*
Closed circuit television (CCTV). An installation comprising television cameras positioned at strategic points in public places or stores, so that the public can be observed on monitors in a central control room. Used extensively by police and local government, and in retail and wholesale outlets, shopping malls and sports grounds, it is a measure adopted to help prevent theft, street crime and vandalism. In January 2000, the UK *Independent* newspaper reported the installation of CCTV cameras on housing estates, in town and city centres, along beach-fronts, in universities, outside pubs and overlooking car parks and streets in England and Wales. The UK Home Office estimates that there are at least a million cameras on the streets and shopping centres of the UK. In London, it is estimated that anybody moving around the capital is caught on camera at least 300 times a day.

Closing technique *Sales techniques*
Towards the end of a salesperson's sales pitch, a technique for encouraging or inducing the potential customer to buy the product, secure an order or sign a contract. This is probably the most crucial moment of the pitch, except perhaps for the opening moments. It takes a good deal of training and practice to achieve this, though many companies fail to equip their sales staff with such techniques.

Cluster *Research*
A group of respondents who agree in principle on a pre-determined topic being researched.

Cluster sample *Research*
A group of respondents selected geographically by locality.

Coarse screen *Print, Production*
A halftone screen that has a smaller number of dots per square centimetre or square inch. Each dot is correspondingly larger. While all halftone printing is a compromise, coarse screen is recognized as the optimum technique for printing on coarse materials such as newsprint. The better or smoother the surface to be printed, the finer the screen can be; that is, smaller dots, and more of them to the square centimetre or square inch.

COD *Business, Direct marketing, Distribution*
Initials for **cash on delivery** (*qv*). This should never be pronounced 'cod'.

Coding *Marketing, Media, Press advertising, Print*
The use of letters and numbers as keys to identifying the origin of coupons and reply cards. It is important that replies be traced and attributed accurately, so that the media and account planners can evaluate the cost-effectiveness of the media and printed literature used.

Cognition *Behavioural science, Buyer behaviour*
Mental processes that enable humans to give meaning to their environment and experiences. They are of most importance during learning and perception.
See Cognitive dissonance.

Cognitive dissonance *Buyer behaviour, Marketing*
There is a widely held theory that a person's attitudes tend to be consistent. The actions of an individual are therefore held to be consistent. However, in making a decision to purchase a product, for example, this is not always the case. A person often experiences inner conflict, in which she needs to weigh positives, negatives and alternatives relating both to the product and the purchase. This is said to produce cognitive dissonance. The psychological discomfort generated by cognitive dissonance may produce irrational and unpredictable buying decisions. The opposite is **cognitive consonance**.

COI *Government agency, Marketing*
Initials for **Central Office of Information**, a UK government information, publicity and propaganda agency (*qv*).

Cold calling *Sales technique*
A field technique involving visits to prospective customers by sales staff without an appointment. Also called cold canvassing.
See Canvass.

Cold mailing   *Marketing, Sales*
A mailing technique using a new or refurbished database, to solicit new business.
The mailing equivalent of cold calling.

Collar retailing   *Sales promotion*
A paper or plastic collar designed to fit over the neck of a bottle. Offers, competitions, give-aways and other promotional material are printed on the collar.

Collateral   *Advertising, Marketing*
Promotional activities in support of main press and broadcast advertising campaigns.
These can include printed literature, direct mail, exhibitions, give-aways and
Internet activity.

Collateral   *Finance*
Physical assets, such as property, pledged as a guarantee for the repayment of
loaned money.

Collating   *Bindery practice, Finishing, Print, Production*
Assembling pages of a piece of printed literature in the correct order before
binding.

Colour bars   *Print*
Small rectangles in four-colour process printing colours, yellow, magenta, cyan
and black. These enable the printer and production team to check the density
of the colours on the printed page; and also to a limited extent the registration
of the colours being printed, though this is done more accurately by **register
marks** (*qv*). The same check scheme appears on wet proofs (*qv*), and on **Crom-
alins** (*qv*).

Colour bars   *Television*
The test signal for television cameras; a series of vertical colour bars on screen.

Colour display   *Computing, Information technology*
A colour video display unit (VDU); a multicoloured screen.

Colour filter   *Photography, Reprographics*
A tinted glass disk attached to the front of a camera lens. Its function is to change
the colour values of the light reaching the film. The tints vary widely, according
to the modification the photographer wants. A red filter, for example, will produce
spectacular sky and cloud effects. A yellow filter is often used to correct flesh
tones.

Colour grading   *Film, Television, Video*
A laboratory procedure in which the colour values of the master footage are
adjusted for consistency.

Colour negative   *Photography*
A type of photographic film producing the colour image in negative form. Used for making photoprints.

Colour reversal   *Photography*
A type of photographic film that produces the colour image in positive form. Used for making photographic transparencies.

Colour separations   *Photography, Print, Production*
An electronic-photographic technique for preparing printing plates from full-colour originals. The process transmutes the full-colour image into the four component colours used in process printing: yellow, magenta, cyan and black. This in turn produces either a set of printing plates, or a set of photographic negatives, one per colour, from which plates are made. Each plate prints only one of these colours. In the purely photographic technique, optical colour filters are used. Each filter produces the colour values for a single printing plate.
See Screen angle.

Colour supplement   *Publishing*
A full-colour magazine sold with a newspaper and included in the **cover price** (*qv*). Most weekend newspapers in the UK and the USA include colour supplements. In the UK, some mid-week newspapers carry colour supplements.

Colour temperature   *Photography, Reprographics*
The measurement of a light source in terms of its colour quality. Its colour temperature is expressed in **degrees Kelvin**.

Column   *Artwork, Desktop publishing, Typography, Word-processing*
A block of text and other copy set vertically on the screen or printed page. The unit of horizontal measurement of the column is its width. You describe the type area of a column on a page as follows: an area of copy 20 cm high and one column wide is described as '20 cm by 1 column', or '20 column centimetres'. The same type area over several columns is described thus: '10 cm by 2 columns'. The height is always given first.

For advertising media planning in the UK and the European Union (EU), type area is measured in column-centimetres. In the USA, column height is measured in inches, type area in column-inches.

Column rules   *Desktop publishing, Typography*
Thin, solid rules, usually 1pt, separating columns of copy in newspapers, magazines, catalogues and other publications.

Comb binding   *Finishing, Print, Production*
Binding together pages of a document or printed literature, using plastic strip shaped like a comb. Wire spiral is also used for this binding method.

Combine   *Block-making, Print, Production*
In letterpress printing, a physical combination of halftone and line techniques in
the same printing block. Usually termed a **line and tone combine**.

Command   *Computing, Information technology*
An instruction in computer language, in the form of a character string or an alpha-
numeric mix of letters and numbers.

Commando selling   *Marketing, Product management, Sales operations*
Also called **blitz selling**. An intensive and often aggressive field selling effort, using
a specially constituted sales force. An organization's regular sales force may be
supplemented by a freelance specialist team assembled for a particular operation
or period. Often used in product launches and re-launches, and when a product is
under competitive attack.

Commercial   *Film, Television, Video*
Shorthand for a televised, videoed or filmed commercial advertisement.
See Still, Voice-over.

Commercial break   *Radio, Television*
A break during news and entertainment programming, in which advertising is
inserted. Usually, simply called a **break**.

Commission   *Advertising*
Reward in the form of a percentage discount, paid to advertising agencies for
placing advertising space and airtime bookings on behalf of clients. In former
times, 15 per cent was the accepted norm; sometimes 10 per cent. Today, following
de-regulation, agency commission is negotiable.

Commission   *Freelance services*
To sub-contract a job to an outside specialist, such as a copywriter, photographer,
artist or researcher.

Communication mix   *Marketing communications*
In a promotional campaign, the various elements of communication combined to
achieve a pre-determined marketing objective. Each campaign may have a
different mix, possibly a different target audience. The elements of the mix include
advertising, public relations, sales promotion, direct mail and corporate communications.

Communication objectives   *Marketing, Marketing communications*
Pre-determined results to be achieved by marketing campaigns using marketing
communications techniques. This embodies a set of criteria against which a
campaign can be judged once it is running and after its completion. Objectives
can include enquiry and sales levels to be achieved, consumer awareness levels,

customer, supplier and shareholder confidence, and coverage by the media. From the marketer's point of view, the most effective objectives, and the results obtained from them, are those that can be measured using established research techniques.

Company profile   *Briefing, Business, Marketing planning*
A detailed description of a business or organization. Detail may include the history of the company from its inception; its directors and their backgrounds; its financial set-up, turnover and profitability over time; its marketing history and current market share, assets and liabilities, products, services and employees. There should be enough detail in a profile to enable management, their suppliers, shareholders and customers, to compare the organization with others.

Comparative advertising   *Advertising creative technique*
In advertising copy, highlighting direct comparisons between a company's products and services and competitors. Naturally this is usually done when one's own comes off best. In the UK, codes of practice allow comparative advertising only when the comparisons are based on fact. Disparagement, also known as **knocking copy**, is not allowed; penalties and punishments follow breaches of the codes. Similar arrangements exist in mainland Europe and the USA.
See Advertising Standards Authority, Independent Television Commission, Radio Authority.

Comparative media   *Advertising, Marketing communications*
A compilation of media facts and figures, enabling media planners to compare one medium with another. This is an important technique in evaluating media cost-effectiveness. Each publication or broadcast medium is assessed on its ability to reach a pre-determined target audience with maximum penetration and minimum cost.

Comparison shopping   *Marketing, Marketing research, Retailing*
Investigation by a retailer or retail group, into the in-store or merchandising techniques of its competitors. Individual shoppers are assigned to note such detail as prices, special offers, loss leaders, shelving arrangements and changes, and report back to their sponsors. This enables them to study, evaluate and compare brands against each other, and estimate the value of brand loyalty.

Comparison testing   *Marketing, Marketing research*
A technique for investigating, comparing and evaluating brands, products and services in relation to each other. This is best achieved by commissioning an independent research organization with no connection with manufacturer, distributor or marketing specialist or any intermediary.

Compatibility   *Computer networking, Computer peripherals, Computing*
When one machine can use the same software, data and components as another without modification it is said to be compatible.

Competition *Business, Marketing*
Businesses in a market in active confrontation for commercial advantage. The act of competing for a market or market share is normal in all normal business activity. In terms of competitive activity, markets are structured in the following way:

- **Pure competition**. A large number of companies marketing identical products and services.
- **Monopolistic competition**. Several large companies, each offering a unique marketing mix.
- **Oligopoly**. A small number of large companies dominating sales in a particular industry.
- **Monopoly**. A single company marketing a particular product or service.

Competitions *Sales promotion*
Consumer marketing activity designed to revive flagging sales, or respond to competitive attack. In the USA, the terminology is **consumer contests**. The public is asked to compete for prizes by testing their skills and provide solutions or answers to questions. There is usually a tie-breaker, a device for ensuring outright winners. Proof of purchase is often required.

Many newspapers and magazines run competitions sponsored by advertisers or companies mentioned in editorials. Proof of purchase in this case is usually the entry coupon itself. Competitions and prize draws are tightly controlled by legislation and voluntary controls.
See Advertising Standards Authority, British Codes of Advertising and Sales Promotion.

Competitive advantage *Business, Marketing*
Efforts by an organization to gain greater advantage over its competitors in the same market. Techniques vary, but they usually include the offer and promotion of extra products, benefits, warranty, services, support and competitive claims (*qv*).

Competitive claims *Advertising, Business*
A set of benefits offered by a manufacturer, supplier or organization, seeking to convince customers to take a decision to purchase from it, rather than from the competition. In the UK, and most of mainland Europe, these claims must, by law, be based on fact and capable of substantiation.

Competitive edge *Business, Marketing*
A situation in which an organization has, or seeks to have, a major commercial advantage over its direct competitors.

Competitive pitching *Advertising, Business, Marketing*
Competing for business, based on unique advantages offered by the organization doing the pitch. This may involve advantages in added value, quality, price, service, support or timing; or all these together.

Competitive pricing *Marketing, Retailing*
Essentially, lower-than-normal prices, sometimes accompanied by inducements. Sometimes offered to loyal customers or frequent purchasers as an incentive to remain loyal to a supplier, product or service. Popular among insurance and software companies, carpet retailers and supermarkets.

Competitive strategy *Marketing*
The planning and working through of a long-term policy, with the objective of overtaking the competition, and maintaining a company's competitive position in an industry. To fulfil this objective, all the tools of the marketing mix are used.

Competitor *Business, Marketing*
A company or individual that competes for trade with one's own company, product or service, and usually with others in the same industry or business arena.

Complementary demand *Business, Marketing*
The demand for a particular product or service prompting demand for another, generally related to it. For example: Oral-B and Sensodyne, both brands marketing toothpaste and toothbrushes. Kodak markets film and cameras.

Composition *Desktop publishing, Print, Typography, Word-processing*
Originally meant setting metal type, either by hand or machine. It still means this, even though computers have now largely taken over composition. One of the most useful advances computers have brought to composition is automatic hyphenation, justification and page formatting. The person composing the type is a **compositor**, though sometimes a **DTP operator**.
See Make-up, Mark-up.

Computer graphics *Computing*
Any graphic created and generated on a computer, and which can be processed, modified and stored electronically: drawings, graphs and charts, for example.

Computer to plate *Print, Production*
Also known by its initials, **CTP**. A production technique in which printing plates are imaged direct from a digital file, rather than from film. At a time when printers and their customers demand shorter lead times, increased productivity and reasonable costs, CTP helps to achieve these objectives. There are a number of other substantial advantages. After a plate has been produced, the production data can be archived by the system's software. This can be retrieved at any time, and another copy made of the plate. With some CTP production systems, the operator can view the layout of the plate, and the design and colour of the image requested in a preview file displayed on screen.

Concept *Advertising, Creative teamwork, Marketing communications*
A basic design for an advertisement, leaflet, brochure or other marketing communications tool. The concept expresses the promotional ideas behind the design, as

much as highlighting elements of its physical appearance. After the concept has been approved by management, the creative team proceeds to develop the concept into a campaign.

Concept testing *Manufacturing, Marketing, Product management*
The first stage in the evaluation of an idea or concept for a product. A focus group or panel of potential customers is introduced to the idea, under the guidance of an experienced researcher. The discussion, and the panel's reactions to the concept, are monitored, recorded and analysed by the research and product management teams. The results may determine whether the concept is worthy of development, or should be abandoned.

Concept testing *Marketing communications*
A similar procedure is carried out in the testing of advertising, public relations, sales promotion and other marketing communications ideas. A variety of copy and designs are usually presented to the panel for discussion and reaction.

Concertina fold *Print finishing*
Sometimes called an accordion fold. A page or leaflet with two parallel folds, which open like the bellows of an accordion.

Condensed *Composition, Desktop publishing, Typesetting,*
Typography
A tall or narrow version of a roman or standard typeface. Often used for headlines and body copy in narrow pages or columns where horizontal space is at a premium. Condensed type is more difficult to read than regular type, particularly where the italic version is used; it should therefore be used in moderation.
See Extended.

Conjoint analysis *Marketing, Marketing research*
A comparison technique designed to reveal features and benefits of products and services most likely to influence purchasing decisions. Product attributes are evaluated and weighed against each other in each case.

Consideration *Business, Contract law*
An essential part of a legally binding contract. The other two essentials are offer and acceptance. Consideration usually refers to the financial value of the goods or services named in the contract. It can also refer to a thing given or done as equivalent by a person to whom a promise is made.
   There is an appropriate anecdote about a man who sees another drowning in a river. The man on the bank offers to save the man in the water, and asks what he would give in exchange for being saved. The drowning man proposes giving his daughter in marriage. The other, agreeing, pulls him from the water. The following day, the saver turns up at the other's house, demanding his reward. 'No way,' says the saved man. 'But you accepted my offer!' says the saver. 'Let that be a lesson

to you,' replies the saved one. 'Past consideration is no consideration.' Readers would be well advised to consult a lawyer before conducting marketing business along these lines.

Conspicuous consumption   *Economic theory, Marketing theory*

A US economist, Thorstein Veblen, uncovered a strong emotional element in the motives behind the purchase of products. According to his theory, most products tend to be bought as much for approval by others as for strictly practical purposes. Thus, the car you buy, and park outside your house, has as much to do with impressing neighbours, friends and relatives, as with safety and comfort. The same applies to choices in fashion, food, wine, holidays and, to some extent, social contact. It further applies to the display of evidence of charitable donations. In the UK, the wearing of a poppy long before and after 11 November, for example, is visible evidence of conspicuous compassion. So is the display of red plastic hemispheres on car radiators, and maintaining them there long after a 'red nose day' charitable event.

Consumer   *Marketing, Research*

A buyer or user of a product or service. This is not a straightforward, watertight definition, however. Children, for example, are consumers of household and other products, but do not usually buy them. However, they can heavily influence purchases made by the parent or householder, and much advertising is aimed at them for this purpose.

Another, more complex example: in medical and pharmaceutical marketing, the manufacturer promotes his product both to the general practitioner and the pharmacist. However, the GP does not buy the product, and does not usually handle it; he merely prescribes it for the patient. The patient is the end-user of the medication, but has no influence over its selection. The patient takes the prescription to a pharmacist, who dispenses it, as prescribed, from his stock. Under the UK National Health Service, the government pays the pharmacist part of the cost, the patient paying the rest. Pensioners, and some patients with chronic conditions, consume medications but pay nothing.

Although the manufacturer may promote the product to the pharmaceutical profession, the pharmacist has no choice but to supply the product specified by the GP. Confused? You should be.

In consumer and business-to-business marketing communications, the tableau of decision-makers includes:

- identifiers;
- influencers;
- specifiers;
- deciders;
- buyers;
- end-users;
- gatekeepers.

Industrial consumers are not normally referred to as such, but that is what they are in the final analysis. The chain of influence and decision-making is fairly straightforward, however, bearing in mind the decision-makers in the previous paragraph.

Consumer advertising

Advertising, Marketing,
Marketing communications

Advertising activities aimed at the general public, as distinct from business-to-business, trade and technical and industrial markets. Consumer advertising uses consumer media – television, press, radio and cinema; also outdoor advertising, sales promotion and mass mailing, when supporting mainstream consumer campaigns.

Consumer behaviour

Marketing techniques

In a marketing context, the observation of the decision-making, purchasing patterns and habits of the general public. Behavioural science is increasingly used in the service of marketing, in the sense that consumer behaviour can be analysed and predicted. Group consumer behaviour can be more easily predicted than individual behaviour.

Consumer benefits

Advertising, Marketing,
Marketing communications

The presentation of product functions and features so that they are represented in terms of what they can do for the consumer. This is the true value to the consumer of a product or service.

In marketing communications such as advertising and sales promotion, consumer benefits are sometimes presented as a promise of advantages or delights to come. Insurance is a case in point. Kodak has for decades promoted its film range not on a platform solely of technical excellence, but of memories preserved for years to come. Thus, using Kodak film on unrepeatable occasions such as birthdays or weddings, and viewing it at a future time, justifies the purchase. The appeal is emotional rather than technical. Charles Revson of Revlon used to say that although he sold bottles of scented fluid, what his customers were buying was hope. I have paraphrased here, obviously. Product features are what a product does or how it performs in a technical sense. The technical features of a product or service must be capable of supporting the benefits, and the advertiser is legally obliged to tell the truth about both.

Consumer credit

Finance, Marketing, Retailing

To encourage or help consumers to purchase a product or service, an offer of credit by a supplier. This is done either through a finance house, or by credit cards such as Visa or Mastercard. A **store card** or **charge card** is also a credit card, provided that it gives the user a period of credit, either free or subject to interest, or both. A **debit card** is not a credit card, since it is the equivalent of a cheque (check), and is therefore subject to different terms and conditions.

Consumer durables *Marketing*

Consumer products that are bought infrequently and have a long life in use. These include furniture, carpets, refrigerators, televisions and motor vehicles.

Consumer group *Marketing, Marketing research*

A classification of consumers, based on particular characteristics or criteria. These include demographics, psychographics, lifestyle, buying power and disposable income.

Consumerism *Marketing*

Organized activity, mainly by pressure groups, aimed at improving and safeguarding consumer interests. Many of these efforts are covertly political; appropriate caution needs to be exercised by marketers.

Consumer needs and wants *Advertising, Marketing, Marketing research*

Needs refers to the basics of human function and need, and is a fundamental of marketing practice. Wants refers to the desire to acquire, whether rational and pragmatic or irrational and emotional. Sometimes needs and wants appear interchangeable, and can change with time. Thus, a television is now a need, having once been a want; a car is a now a need; foreign holidays, a want, but sometimes treated as a need. Marketing and advertising techniques should be tailored both to needs and wants, with the usual cautions about research findings.

Consumer orientation *Business, Marketing*

A company philosophy that actively takes its consumers or customers as the basis for its long-term development. Consumer satisfaction is here seen as the prime motivation for its management and workers, from chairman to floor staff. In such a company, marketing, competitive positioning, returns on investment, product and corporate growth are focused and depend directly on it.

Consumer panels *Marketing research*

Groups of ordinary consumers set up and organized to offer views on products and services they have purchased. Their opinions, purchasing patterns and habits are evaluated by professional researchers reporting to research organizations or marketing teams.

Consumer preference *Marketing research*

A research technique in which relative strengths of consumer preference for products and services are analysed statistically. This offers marketers clues to the likely success of their own products and services in the marketplace.

Consumer press *Marketing, Media*

Journals and magazines usually bought for and read by the general public. The consumer press is highly segmented, with magazines targeted at wide and narrow consumer interests. For example, there is a segment aimed at women as a whole, with sub-segments such as singles, marrieds, the young, the very young, the old and so on. There is a vast range of magazines produced for consumers with common interests. These include sports, model aircraft, travel and animal care; medical conditions such as diabetes; intellectual pursuits such as books and films. The range is too wide for the inclusion of everything here; consult *British Rate and Data* (UK), *Standard Rate and Data Service* (USA), *Tarif Media* (France), *Media Daten* (Germany) and similar publications.

Consumer prices   *Marketing, Retailing*
The generally accepted range of prices charged at retail level for consumer products. The concept can loosely be applied also to consumer services.

Consumer products   *Marketing, Retailing*
Products produced for and aimed at individual consumers. Those produced for business and corporate use are loosely termed industrial goods or products.

Consumer protection   *Legislation, Marketing, Retailing*
Legal instruments and codes of practice used in the marketing of consumer goods and services. In the UK, consumer protection measures have infiltrated almost every area of commercial life and trading practice. The volume increases every year.

Consumer purchasing power   *Marketing*
Another way of saying disposable income. This is the money a consumer has left after statutory and other obligations have been met. These include income tax, national insurance, mortgage, loan repayment, credit agreements, alimony and child support.

Consumer research   *Marketing research, Research*
Research into the habits, motives, attitudes and patterns of behaviour of individuals and groups of consumers. Mostly applied to the purchase of goods and services, but also to political and cultural matters.

Consumers' Association   *Consumer organizations*
A UK watchdog organization. A registered charity, set up in 1950, with a current membership of about 680,000, and headquarters in London. Its publications include *Which?*, *Gardening Which?*, *Holiday Which?*, *Drug and Therapeutics Bulletin*, *Health Which?* and *Legal Services*. The total subscriptions to CA products are about 970,000.

Consumer satisfaction   *Marketing, Marketing research*
Ideally, consumer products and services are marketed with consumer satisfaction as an objective. Directing marketing activity towards consumer satisfaction is one way of encouraging brand loyalty; whether targeted at consumer needs or wants (*qv*). Long-term loyalty is a basic aim of all marketing effort. Measuring and evaluating it accurately is another matter, though techniques do exist for this.

Consumption *Marketing*
The quantity of a product used by a group of individuals or organizations over a period of time, and the rate at which it is used.

Contact print *Photography*
A photographic print made when the negative or positive is in intimate contact with the photographic paper. The contact is direct between emulsion and emulsion; that is, both light-sensitive surfaces. Colloquially termed **contacts**.

Contact report *Client account handling*
A structured report written by an account manager after meeting with a client. It should cover:

- the date of the meeting;
- time;
- venue;
- names of those present;
- summary of matters discussed;
- decisions taken;
- action required;
- names or initials of those responsible for taking the action;
- circulation list;
- date of the next meeting.

The report should be printed and copies circulated quickly to all who attended the meeting, plus any others affected by the matters discussed and action agreed. A copy of the report should be filed in a Facts Book, the permanent record of such meetings.

Contact screen *Artwork, Photography, Plate-making*
A halftone screen on film or glass, consisting of ruled lines laid out in a pattern to produce halftone dots. The screen is positioned in intimate contact with the receiving film or plate; emulsion to emulsion for the sharpest definition.
See Halftone.

Contest *Sales promotion*
The US term for a **competition** (*qv*).

Continuity *Advertising, Film, Marketing, Video*
In advertising and marketing, the consistent use of an attribute, illustration, phrase or other brand property throughout a campaign or series of campaigns.

Continuity *Film, Video*
A consistent succession of content in scenes that appear to follow one another without a break. Often the shooting of a scene is distantly spaced over time. However, a man wearing a dark blue shirt, seen entering a doorway, should not be seen emerging from it on the other side in a white shirt.

Continuous research *Advertising, Marketing,*
Marketing communications

A research technique used in monitoring the performance of campaigns, before, during and afterwards. Often used between campaigns on a regular basis or at regular intervals. Also termed rolling research.

Continuous tone *Artwork, Photography, Plate-making*

In original photographs, the colours and shades are reproduced from black to white, in a seamless range of tones. Because the tones are continuous right across the range, this manifestation is referred to as continuous tone. Technically, it is an image in which tonal gradation is produced by changes in density.
See Halftone, Contrast.

Con-tob *Classified advertising*

A popular UK abbreviation in trade and recruitment classifieds, indicating that a business is confectioner, tobacconist and newsagent. Sometimes expressed as **con-tob-news**.

Contra *Business, Marketing communications, Media*

A deal struck between two media, in which each carries promotion material for the other, without money changing hands. Thus, a radio station may carry a promotion for a newspaper, and the paper carry the radio station's promotion. Similar bartering takes place in other business dealings; in this case, goods and services are involved.

Contract *Advertising, Business, Marketing, Public relations*

An agreement, usually between two parties, for the supply of goods, services or work. To be legally binding and enforceable, it must have three essentials: offer, acceptance, and a specified price, called 'consideration'. It can also be an accepted promise to do or not to do something specified. A legal contract need not be in writing. However, in advertising and marketing business, in which large sums of money are usually involved, it is prudent to have everything in writing.

A **contract of service** is an agreement between an advertiser and an advertising agency, or a client and a public relations agency. This usually stipulates conditions of service, including fees, method of working together, personnel involved, method of remuneration, conditions of assignment of copyright, and the agreed notice of contract termination.

Contrast *Artwork, Photography, Plate-making, Television*

Although photographically produced material is continuous in tone, there is a degree of separation between tones. If there were not, you would see just a blur of coloured mud on the print, rather than the proper image. Contrast, therefore, is the ability of the photographic material to separate the degrees of light and shade in an image, so that it is intelligible. The same applies to electronically produced images on screen.

Contribution analysis *Product management*
A technique for establishing the difference between the selling price of a product and its variable production costs. It should then be possible to establish its contribution to fixed costs and profits.

Controlled circulation *Media planning, Publishing*
A publication that circulates to a pre-selected target audience is described as having controlled circulation. Many professional, trade and specialist publications are distributed using this system. The main commercial characteristic is that they are free to the reader.

Circulation is determined by the precise description of the category of reader. The qualification system is common to all controlled circulation magazines.

Marketing Week, for example, circulates to the marketing and advertising industry. To receive your free copy, you must first fill in, date and sign a reader application card. The personal details you are asked for are:

- company address;
- company name;
- county;
- initials;
- personal title;
- postcode;
- surname;
- telephone number;
- town.

You are then asked for two main items of information. First, your company's main area of business, including:

- agencies;
- consultancies;
- manufacturing;
- media owner;
- services.

This is followed by:

- the number of full-time employees in your company;
- your responsibility for part/all of your company's marketing/advertising expenditure;
- your involvement in any marketing/sales/promotion activities in Europe;
- your involvement in decisions on recruitment advertising;
- your involvement in your company's selection or purchase of various products and services;

- if you are with a client company/consultancy, your company's total marketing/ advertising spend;
- if you are with an advertising agency, your company's approximate billings.

The application must be signed and dated. If you fail to complete *any* of these sections, including signature and date, the publisher will send the card back to you for completion.

The publisher then considers your application, and decides if you really do qualify for a free 'subscription'. If you do qualify, you get the publication free for a year, after which you will be asked to fill in a further application. If you don't qualify, you can still get the publication, but you'll have to pay for it, and the publisher will tell you how much it costs.

The whole point of this procedure is that the circulation is audited by an independent third party, such as the ABC (*qv*). That is how advertisers know they are getting the utmost value for that part of their budgets spent with controlled circulation publications.

See ABC, Circulation, Rate card, Readership, Verified Free Distribution.

Control question   *Marketing research*

A technique used in the compilation of research questionnaires, designed to check the validity of the respondent's answers to other questions.

Controls   *Advertising, Marketing, Marketing communications,*
Product management

The number of legal instruments, parliamentary acts, orders and regulations applying to marketing is constantly increasing, being updated, augmented and amended. There are also local laws and by-laws to be taken into account. The laws on contract, negligence, libel and intellectual property also need to be checked and observed. Not surprisingly, the Advertising Standards Authority advises that businesses have primary responsibility for ensuring that everything they do is legal.

The European Union, in addition, imposes its own laws, decrees, directives and regulations, some of which supersede, replace or overlay UK law. For this reason, the reader of this Dictionary is recommended to check, and check again, when planning marketing operations. Here is a taster, a mere 179 laws British marketers have to live with:

Accommodation Agencies Act 1963; Administration of Justice Act 1985; Adoption Act 1976; Agriculture (Safety, Health and Welfare Provisions) Act 1956; Alcoholic Liquor Duties Act 1979; Architects Act 1997; Banking Act 1987; Banking Act 1987 (Advertisements) Regulations (1988) as amended; Betting and Gaming Duties Act 1981; Betting Gaming and Lotteries Acts 1963–1985; Bingo Act 1992; Bread and Flour Regulations 1995; British Telecommunications Act 1981; Broadcasting Acts 1990 and 1996; Building Societies Act 1986; Business Advertisements (Disclosure) Order 1997; Business Names Act 1985; Cancer Act 1939; Charities Act 1992 and Regulations; Children Act 1989; Children and Young

Persons (Harmful Publications) Act 1995; Children and Young Persons Acts 1933 and 1963; Civil Aviation Act 1982; Civil Aviation (Air Travel Organizers' Licensing) Regulations 1995 as amended; Civil Aviation (Aerial Advertising) Regulations 1995; Cocoa and Chocolate Products Regulations 1976; Coffee and Coffee Products Regulations 1978; Companies Act 1985; Competition Acts 1980 and 1998; Condensed Milk and Dried Milk Regulations 1997; Conduct of Employment Agencies and Employment Businesses Regulations 1976; Consumer Credit Act 1974; Consumer Credit (Advertisements) Regulations 1989; Consumer Credit (Exempt Advertisements) Order 1985; Consumer Protection Act 1987 and the Code of Practice for Traders on Price Indications; Consumer Transactions (Restrictions on Statements) Order 1976 as amended; Control of Misleading Advertisements Regulations 1988; Control of Pesticides Regulations 1986 as amended; Copyright Designs and Patents Act 1988; Cosmetics Products (Safety) Regulations 1996 as amended; Crossbows Act 1987; Customs and Excise Management Act 1979; Data Protection Act 1984; Data Protection Act 1998; Defamation Act 1952; Defamation Act 1996; Dentists Act 1984; Deregulation and Contracting Out Act 1994; Deregulation (Betting and Bingo Advertising etc) Order 1997; Deregulation (Casinos) Order 1999; Disability Discrimination Act 1995; Education Act 1996; Employment Agencies Act 1973; Endangered Species (Import and Export) Act 1976 as amended; Energy Act 1976; Estate Agents Act 1979; European Communities Act 1972; Fair Trading Act 1973; Finance Act 1981; Financial Services Act 1986; Financial Services Act 1986 (Investment Advertisements) (Exemptions) Orders 1995–97; Firearms Act 1968 as amended; Fireworks (Safety) Regulations 1997; Flavourings in Food Regulations 1992; Food Labelling Regulations 1984 and 1996 as amended; Food Safety Act 1990 and Regulations; Food Intended for Use in Energy Restricted Diets for Weight Reduction Regulations 1997; Forgery and Counterfeiting Act 1981; Friendly Societies Act 1974 and 1992; Gaming Act 1968 as amended; General Optical Council (Rules on Publicity) Order of Council 1985; Geneva Convention Act 1957 as amended; Hallmarking Act 1973; Hearing Aid Council Act 1968; Hearing Aid Council (Amendment) Act 1989; HIV Testing Kits and Services Regulations 1992; Honey Regulations 1976; Human Organ Transplant Act 1989; Human Rights Act 1998; Income and Corporation Taxes Act 1988; Indecent Displays (Control) Act 1981; Industrial and Provident Societies Act 1965; Infant Formula and Follow-on Formula Regulations 1995; Insurance Brokers (Registration) Act 1997; Insurance Brokers Registration Council (Code of Conduct) Approval Order 1994; Insurance Companies Act 1982; Insurance Companies Regulations 1994; Jam and Similar Products Regulations 1981; Knives Act 1997; Licensing Act 1964; Local Government Act 1992; Local Government (Miscellaneous Provisions) Act 1982; London Cab Acts 1968 and 1973; London County Council (General Powers) Act 1938; Lotteries and Amusements Act 1976 and amendments; Mail Order Transactions (Information) Order 1976; Malicious Communications Act 1988; Marine etc Broadcasting (Offences) Act 1967; Meat Products and Spreadable Fish Products Regulations 1984; Medicines Act 1968; Medicines (Advertising of Medicinal Products) Regulations 1975 and 1975 (No 2); Medicines (Advertising) Regulations

1994 as amended; Medicines (Advertising and Monitoring of Advertising) Amendment Regulations 1999; Medicines for Human Use (Marketing Authorizations) Regulations 1994; Medicines (Monitoring of Advertising) Regulations 1994; Metropolitan Streets Act 1867; Milk and Milk Products (Protection of Designations) Regulations 1990; Misrepresentation Act 1967; Mock Auctions Act 1961; Motor Cars (Driving Instruction) Regulations 1989 as amended; National Lottery etc Act 1993 as amended; National Lottery Regulations 1994; Natural Mineral Water Regulations 1984; Nightwear (Safety) Regulations 1985 as amended; Nurses Agencies Act 1957; Nurses Midwives and Health Visitors Act 1997; Obscene Publications Act 1959; Olympic Symbol etc (Protection) Act 1995; Opticians Act 1989 and Regulations; Organic Products Regulations 1992 as amended; Package Travel, Package Holidays and Package Tours Regulations 1992 as amended; Passenger Car Fuel Consumption Order 1983 as amended; Personal Pension Schemes (Advertisements) Regulations 1990; Post Office Act 1953; Prevention of Corruption Acts 1889–1916; Price Indications (Method of Payment) Regulations 1991; Price Marking Order 1991 as amended; Private Hire Vehicles (London) Act 1998; Professions Supplementary to Medicine Act 1991; Property Misdescriptions Act 1991; Protection of Children Act 1978; Protection of Children (Tobacco) Act 1986; Race Relations Act 1976; Registered Designs Act 1949; Registered Homes Act 1984; Rent Act 1977; Representation of the People Act 1983; Restriction of Offensive Weapons Act 1959 as amended; Restriction on Agreements (Estate Agents) Order 1970; Restrictive Trade Practices Act 1976; Road Traffic Act 1988; Sale of Goods Act 1979; Sex Discrimination Acts 1975 and 1986; Social Security Act 1986; Solicitors Act 1974; Specified Sugar Products Regulations 1976; Spreadable Fats (Marketing Standards) Regulations 1995; Sunday Entertainments Act 1932; Sunday Observance Act 1780; Sunday Theatre Act 1972; Sunday Trading Act 1994; Supply of Goods and Services Act 1982; Surrogacy Arrangements Act 1985; Tattooing of Minors Act 1969; Telecommunications Act 1984; Telecommunications Apparatus (Advertisements) Order 1985 as amended; Telecommunications Apparatus (Marking and Labelling) Order 1985 as amended; Telecommunications (Data Protection and Privacy) (Direct Marketing) Regulations 1998 as amended; Textile Products (Indications of Fibre Content) Regulations 1986; Thefts Acts 1968 and 1978; Timeshare Act 1992; Timeshare Regulations 1997; Torts (Interference with Goods) Act 1977; Trade Descriptions Act 1968; Trade Descriptions (Sealskin Goods) (Information) Order 1980; Trade Marks Act 1994; Trade Union and Labour Relations (Consolidation) Act 1992; Trading Schemes Act 1996; Trading Schemes Regulations 1997; Trading Stamps Act 1964; Unfair Contract Terms Act 1977; Unfair Terms in Consumer Contracts Regulations 1994; Unsolicited Goods and Services Act 1971 as amended in 1975; Vagrancy Act 1824; Venereal Disease Act 1917; Veterinary Surgeons Act 1966; Weights and Measures Act 1985; Wildlife and Countryside Act 1981; Wireless Telegraphy Act 1949

See Advertising Standards Authority, Independent Television Commission, Radio Authority.

Convenience foods *Retailing*

Also called fast foods. Complete dishes, prepared in advance and pre-packed, which need only heating and serving. Sometimes a minimal amount of cooking is required.

Convenience store *Retailing*

In the UK, also termed a **corner shop**. A shop, often a family business, usually in a residential neighbourhood, stocking a great variety of commodities, from food and cigarettes to books and small items of hardware. Such a shop is open seven days a week, from very early to very late; hence the term convenience.

Converging verticals *Photography, Reprographics*

An optical effect produced when a camera lens is directed away from a parallel position. Verticals appear to converge and meet in the distance.

Conversion *Marketing, Sales*

The turning of an enquiry or response to an advertisement, or advertising campaign, into a sale. This is usually done during a follow-up by a salesperson or telephone call, or when the enquirer has been encouraged or persuaded to visit a retail outlet. The calculated extent of such conversions is termed conversion rate.

Conviction *Creative*

Part of the communication discipline, AIDCA, Attention, Interest, Desire, Conviction, Action. Its aim is to attract the attention and hold the interest of potential customers; get a decision in favour of your brand; and get the action you want. Essentially, you need to convince your reader, viewer or listener that:

- You have attracted her attention for a good reason.
- What you are telling her is *truly* in her self-interest.
- Your promise and benefits help her to fulfil an unsatisfied need.
- The desire you arouse will lead to that fulfilment.
- The action you are asking for will lead to it.
- That when she has taken it, her life will be improved – in terms of that unsatisfied need:
  - in her business life;
  - in her domestic life;
  - in her social life;
  - in her personal life;
- You are offering this certainty on a reliable and permanent basis.

See AIDA.

Cooperative *Retailing*

A group of retailers, having set up a wholesaling or buying operation for its members, and benefiting from economies of scale. This measure enables participating individual retailers to compete with supermarkets. Some groups have their own brand name, such as Spar and Wavy Line, displayed on store facias and product packaging.

Cooperative advertising *Advertising, Marketing, Retailing*

Advertising campaigns created and paid for by individual companies acting as a group. Also, where a national advertiser collaborates with local retailers or distributors. In this case, the national advertiser supplies the locals with pre-produced advertising material for use in local media. Either the cost is shouldered entirely by the national advertiser, or shared with the locals. Often the cost of the space and airtime is the responsibility of the local outlets.

Cooperative marketing *Marketing, Retailing*

A scheme in which different companies in the same business collaborate to increase market activity for all participants in the scheme. Each participating company contributes money for advertising and public relations, and the product is promoted in generic terms. In the year 2000, for example, a cooperative campaign to promote fish ran on television and in the press. In former decades, milk was promoted by the Milk Marketing Board. This was heavily overlaid with politics, ran on a compulsory quota system, and was widely loathed by dairy farmers. However, it worked well and kept milk prices stable.

Copy *Advertising, Copywriting, Editorial, Public relations*

The text of a manuscript or typescript.

Copy *Print*

All the material to be printed in a newspaper, magazine, brochure or leaflet; including text, illustrations, graphics, halftones, ornaments and borders.
See Hard copy, Manuscript, Print, Typescript.

Copy briefing *Advertising, Creative team work*

Structured instructions to a copywriter or creative team, setting out in detail the requirements of a campaign or piece of promotional material. The work done by the team is based on the briefing, and evaluated against it. Not only is it vital that the team understands the purpose of the campaign, it must also understand the psychological and promotional values to be used. The mechanics of the campaign are also given in the briefing.

A good creative briefing not only ensures that the work will be done effectively, appropriately and efficiently. It enables the copywriter and the team to present their creative work with confidence. It also protects the creative team against unreasonable objections by account management (who would have produced the briefing in the first place).

Copy claims *Advertising, Consumer protection, Creative work*
Statements made in printed or broadcast media, describing the functions, benefits, values or merits of a product or service, or of a particular aspect of it. For example, claiming that a washing powder will make clothes smell as fresh as on the day they were bought; or that a hi-fi system will reproduce orchestral sounds with the utmost purity, clarity and fidelity; or that a financial consultation will guarantee profitable investment.

In the UK, and increasingly in mainland Europe, every claim in advertising copy must be technically accurate and capable of substantiation. In Advertising Standards Authority terms, it must be legal, decent, honest and truthful. Misleading the consumer with spurious claims is a criminal offence. For the range of laws relating to this, *see also* Controls.
See Advertising Standards Authority.

Copy date *Advertising production, Editorial, Public Relations*
The deadline by which the publisher must receive advertising or editorial copy. This usually also means copy ready for camera.
See Camera-ready.

Copy platform *Advertising, Creative work, Marketing communications*
The main concept or theme of an advertising campaign or other material. A copy platform can be adapted in various ways, to suit the requirements of the media being used. A single platform can be tailored for advertisements, television and radio commercials, posters, brochures and sales presentations.

Copyright *Creative, Intellectual property*
The exclusive legal right to create, produce, perform or reproduce an original work, whether written or designed. The Copyright, Designs and Patents Act 1988 sets out the rights of creators of original material. Under the Act, copyright belongs to the creator for 70 years from the date of his or her death. A photographer now owns the copyright both of a negative and any print produced from it. In the Act, the concept of intellectual property is introduced. In a film or video, for example, the creator is entitled to a credit, and is protected against any alteration to the work that may detract from it.
See Controls.

Copy testing *Advertising, Marketing communications*
A technique for testing the viability, comprehension, impact, branding quality and potential response of copy used in advertising. This is usually done using focus groups or consumer panels, under the supervision of a researcher.

Copywriter *Advertising, Creative personnel, Marketing communications,*
Public relations
A writer specializing in creating concepts and writing advertising or other copy for marketing communications. Often also applied to a writer involved in public relations work, including news releases and house journals.

Core strategy   *Business, Marketing planning*
The main elements of a marketing mix on which planning operations are based. Core strategy, and any changes in it, will affect all marketing operations, especially marketing communications. Complete reviews should be carried out periodically, and always after a change in the core strategy for a product or service.

Corporate advertising   *Advertising, Corporate strategy and planning,*
Marketing communications
Advertisement techniques designed to create, develop and maintain a company's image and reputation in its markets. Emphasis is on the company, rather than its products and services, though these may be part of the corporate message and presentation. All media are used in corporate advertising. Corporate campaigns are at their most effective when media and message are coordinated, and combined with publicity activities. This needs careful control, especially when a number of outside specialists are employed.

Corporate affairs   *Media relations, Publicity, Public relations*
Also termed **public affairs**. Public relations activities conducted by a company, corporation or organization at corporate level. These are aimed at, or relate to, other corporations, local and national government, foreign governments, the military, the company's shareholders and supporters. Sometimes also at foreign corporations, particularly customers and suppliers, at highest management levels. Some public affairs activity may be aimed at or relate to pressure groups, especially where such groups interfere with or disrupt a company's operations.

Corporate culture   *Business, Public relations*
The values, attitudes, beliefs, conduct and practices of an organization, and the way it does day-to-day business. This inevitably carries over into the organization's wider sphere of activity and influence. An organization's corporate culture is often reflected in its mission statement (*qv*).

Corporate identity   *Advertising, Business, Marketing, Public relations*
The tools and techniques through which an organization projects its personality and represents itself in the marketplace. Everything is carefully tailored to affect the way in which it is perceived. In ordinary circumstances, corporate identity is bound up in physical elements with which the organization allows itself to be identified. The most common are corporate logo and house colour, of which some of the best examples are Coca-Cola, IBM, *The Economist*, Virgin, McDonald's and UPS. The UPS logo is a masterpiece of design; gold and brown convey service, quality and reliability, with the quiet confidence and competence one expects from true professionals.

Other physical elements used to convey corporate identity include advertising, letterheads, staff uniforms, printed literature, vehicles, showroom design and product packaging. Less tangible, but equally important, is an organization's public relations programme, promoting both the physical and the philosophical sides of its activities and personality. This includes customer care and after-sales service.

Corporate image *Advertising, Business, Marketing, Public relations*
How an organization is perceived by its public and market is its corporate image. Ideally, it is the effect produced by its corporate identity programme; the reverse side, if you like, of its corporate identity. If the corporate identity programme works as planned, it will influence and colour how the organization is judged by its customers when it comes to making decisions to buy. Image is all-important, for example, when an investor is considering buying shares in the company; possibly also when buying baked beans. Investors are, after all, ordinary consumers who watch television, listen to radio, read the press and purchase everyday products.

Corrections *Artwork, Desktop publishing, Typography,*
Word-processing
Amendments made to text after proofing. Sometimes called **alterations**. Where the typesetter makes a mistake, he pays for the alteration. Where the originator or author makes the mistakes, these are called **author's corrections**, and the author pays. *Caveat*: it often costs up to £50 to amend a proof, by even as little as a comma.
See Alterations.

Correlation *Marketing research*
The quantitative or qualitative relationship between two sets of research data; for example, family size and disposable income, or car ownership and credit card use.

Corridor traffic *Exhibitions*
Also termed **aisle traffic**. The flow of visitors at an exhibition along a particular aisle and past a particular exhibitor's stand. At established exhibitions, such as the Ideal Home, this traffic can be anticipated, based on that of previous years. This helps the exhibition stand sales and marketing team to determine the price of each stand.

Corrugated fibreboard *Packaging, Paper*
Board comprising sheets of fluted paper, stuck to a flat sheet or several sheets. The fluting provides strength in one direction, flexibility in the other, and enhanced protection for the contents of a package.

Cost analysis *Business, Marketing planning*
A technique for calculating the risk in the launch, re-launch or development of a product or service. It involves the assembly of all cost data involved in the operation, and putting them through a rigorous test against the expected benefits and profits.

Cost centre *Business, Marketing planning*
An accounting technique where the costs of marketing a particular product are assigned to that product. The product is the cost centre. On the other side of the operation, the product is also the profit centre.

Cost-effectiveness
Business, Marketing

The degree to which a business project meets its financial objectives. Whether this is actually the case is a matter of business judgement, as much as an accounting calculation. This is because many marketers take unacceptable risks when planning or developing products and services. A 5 per cent risk of failure, for example, might be acceptable to many marketers, while a 75 per cent risk would be unacceptable. Other marketers may consider taking a 75 per cent risk, or higher; perfectly acceptable if they could gain an edge in the market. This is why many products fail within months of launch.

Cost per enquiry
Advertising, Marketing, Sales promotion

The cost of an enquiry from an advertising campaign or, more usually, from a single advertisement in a campaign. It is usually calculated as an average of all enquiries received in a pre-determined timescale.

Cost per thousand
Media planning

Also termed CPM, **cost per mille**. A technique providing a common base for comparing the circulation of publications. In calculating CPM circulation, the cost of an advertising unit is divided by the number of copies sold expressed in thousands. In the case of CPM readership, this does not use copies *sold*, but copies *read*, which can be substantially higher. An advertising unit is usually a display unit, such as a page, half-page or quarter-page.

Cost profile
Marketing planning

The basis of calculating the total cost of a product to be marketed, in which all elements of the marketing mix are taken into account.

Coupon
Advertising, Creative, Sales promotion

A response element in a press advertisement, brochure or catalogue page. Its main function is to give the customer or reader an opportunity to send for information, a sales call, a demonstration or a product. The coupon should be designed so that readers can fill in their requirements and personal details, then cut the coupon from the page and post it (mail it) to the advertiser.

At first sight, this is quite a simple response device for building-in to an advertisement. In practice, it is usually the reason why the advertisement was created in the first place. Yet it is often so badly and inefficiently done, I'm not surprised that some advertisers are convinced that their advertising doesn't work.

David Ogilvy states that, to get the best results from coupons, you should write and design them like mini-advertisements. Excellent advice. Give every coupon a motivating headline, with a promise or a benefit in it. Include a couple of lines of motivating body copy.

You need to show the reader what the product looks like; it needn't take up much space – a thumbnail illustration will do. Even a tiny illustration can increase the response by a worthwhile amount. Then ask for action. How many coupons have you seen in the last three months that actually follow this important creative discipline?

Another problem with coupons is the information advertisers expect to get from them. When you decide to include a coupon in an advertisement, you should also estimate its value to your database. Any database is only as effective as the information it contains. Therefore, when using coupons to build a database, you need to consider the importance of the information you are asking your respondents for.

Coupon offer   *Advertising, Creative, Sales promotion*
A coupon offering a discount on the price of a product, or some other benefit. When a product is being introduced or promoted, a coupon or voucher offering consumers a discount can encourage them to try the product. It can lead to long-term brand loyalty.

Coverage   *Advertising*
The percentage of a market or target audience likely to see an advertisement or advertising campaign.

Cover date   *Advertising, Publishing*
The date shown on the cover of a publication. Often, particularly in the case of full-colour monthlies, the publication is on the street well in advance of the cover date. It sometimes means, for example, that the April issue of a magazine is available on the first of March. Don't forget that advertising copy dates are always correspondingly early.
See Issue date.

Cover price   *Publishing*
The retail price of a newspaper or magazine; the price printed on the cover or first outside page.

CPT   *Media planning*
Initials for **cost per thousand**. The cost to the advertiser of reaching a thousand members of the target audience he is aiming at. This is one of the generally accepted bases for comparing one publication with others in the same field. Also termed CPM, **cost per mille**.

CRCA   *Radio*
Commercial Radio Companies Association. In the UK, the trade association for independent commercial radio companies. It is voluntary, non-profit-making, incorporated as a company limited by guarantee; formed by the first radio companies when independent radio began in 1973. Formerly called AIRC, Association of Independent Radio Companies.
    CRCA enjoys the support of the radio industry; all but a handful of stations are members. It is funded by the subscriptions of its member radio companies, which share the cost of CRCA in proportion to their shares in the industry's broadcasting revenue.

CRCA's affairs are managed by a board of eight directors: the Association's chairman and six other non-executive directors elected annually. In addition, one executive director, the director and chief executive, who manages the eight-person directorate.

Industry forum: the CRCA board meets five times a year. There are also two general meetings of all member companies: the AGM in January and the Annual Congress in June or July.

Reporting to the board are six standing committees: copyright, finance and general purposes, marketing, programming, research, and technical matters. There are also a number of specialist sub-committees.

Representations: since 1984, CRCA has been active in representations to government, the Radio Authority (*qv*) and other bodies. CRCA had a significant input into the 1987 Green Paper, 'Radio: Choices and Opportunities', to the 1990 Broadcasting Act, which substantially de-regulated independent radio, and to the BBC Charter Review.

Copyright: CRCA's Copyright Committee negotiates on behalf of members with the principal music copyright bodies, the Performing Rights Society, the Mechanical Copyright Protection Society, and Phonographic Performance Ltd. With the aid of consultants, the Committee monitors copyright developments outside the UK, and lobbies European institutions and bodies such as the World Intellectual Property Organization.

Marketing: CRCA's Marketing Committee is the focal point for liaison between radio companies, national sales houses and the Radio Advertising Bureau.

Audience research: radio audience research is conducted by RAJAR – Radio Joint Audience Research Ltd (*qv*). RAJAR is jointly owned by CRCA and the BBC, but all broadcasters contract with it direct. CRCA's Research Committee monitors the performance of RAJAR on behalf of CRCA members, and formulates independent sector research policy that, after approval by the CRCA board, is taken forward to the various RAJAR committees by CRCA representatives, who are all members of the Research Committee.

Copy clearance: the Radio Authority's Code, and almost 60 acts of parliament, determine what can and cannot be said in radio advertisements. To protect advertisers and broadcasting stations, a central script clearance system is operated by the Broadcast Advertising Clearance Centre, on a basis agreed by CRCA. All stations contribute to the cost, and the Radio Authority collects the fees.

Information and involvement: CRCA is the prime source of up-to-date information about all aspects of independent radio. Members' requirements have priority and, in addition to swift response to enquiries, regular guidance. Enquiries are handled from the media, advertisers and agencies, financial analysts, other researchers, and people seeking careers in radio.

Programming: CRCA's Programming Committee liaises with the Radio Authority over programming issues, and develops network projects, which provide attractive programming and additional revenues for member stations.

New members: new radio companies are eligible to join CRCA as soon as they are granted a licence by the Radio Authority. There is a small joining fee, and no further subscription is due until the company begins broadcasting. After that, members' subscriptions relate direct to broadcasting revenue. The smallest companies – often those that find CRCA most valuable – therefore pay least.

Creative department   *Advertising, Design, Public relations*
The department of an advertising or PR agency or consultancy devoted to producing concepts, copy and designs from marketing, advertising and PR briefings. Ideally, copywriters and art directors work as creative teams, with the objective of achieving the best results. In many agencies they work in isolation, though usually the results are just as good. Evaluating their work is not only a matter of comparing it with the brief they receive; it can also be seen in enquiries, orders and sales achieved.

Creative group   *Advertising, Design, Public relations*
A team of agency creatives working on an account or group of accounts, under the supervision of a creative director or manager. This method of working often resolves problems of conflicting client interests within an agency.

Creative hotshop   *Advertising, Design, Public relations*
A company, team or unit specializing in creative work, usually for print media and promotional literature. Such companies do not plan, buy or handle media.

Creative strategy   *Advertising, Marketing, Public relations*
The overall objective of an advertising or PR campaign, based on a marketing brief. The interpretation of the objective is converted into advertising or PR campaigns or material by the creative department, based on the creative values demanded by the brief.

Credibility   *Advertising, Public relations*
The degree to which claims made by an advertiser are accepted and believed by the target audiences at which campaigns are aimed. This should not be confused with credulity. People have been well educated by television, and can usually distinguish between true and exaggerated or misleading claims. If an advertiser persists with misleading claims penalties, and usually prosecution, follow. The true penalty, however, is applied by the public, who turn to other advertisers' products, often permanently.
See Advertising Standards Authority, ITC, Radio Authority.

Credit   *Artwork, Film and video, Publishing*
A reference, usually a line of copy, showing the name of the individual or organization responsible for creating or supplying the material. The material to which it applies can be text, a graphic, a halftone illustration, photograph or artwork.

Credit note *Business, Retailing*

A document, usually a letter or standardized form, issued by a supplier to a customer. Its function is the acknowledgement and correction of an overpayment by the customer. Either the money is held by the supplier against future purchases, or added to the customer's account.

Credit sale *Business, Retailing*

A sale using a credit arrangement. In short-term credit, as with low-cost consumer durables, the customer acquires the ownership of the goods at the time of the sale. With hire-purchase, the supplier or credit house owns the goods until the final payment.

Crisis management *Media relations, Public relations*

Techniques for identifying, investigating and analysing potential crises likely to affect a company or industry group. Plans are drawn up to handle, manage or cope with crises as they occur. Constant updating is required to ensure the effectiveness of crisis management.
See Issues management.

Crisis management planning *Business, Corporate communications,*
Public relations

The creation of a detailed plan designed to cope with a variety of crises and issues likely to arise in future business activity. This is often seen as a function of public relations, but is actually a management responsibility. A whole range of 'unpredict-able' critical scenarios can in fact be foreseen in a basic crisis management plan. Strikes, production and distribution problems, and their consequences, can be anticipated and planned for; the same for fire, flood, property damage and poor weather. There is a mass of software on the market available for this purpose. Public relations can present these situations in ways that minimize the severity of the problems and their consequences, and help the organization recover quickly.

Critical path analysis *Business, Marketing planning,*
Project management

An organizational planning technique using diagrams, showing clear paths for resolving complex project activities. It breaks down an entire project into easily defined moves, and gives timing guides for each one. The 'path' is an unbroken line from the beginning of a project to its end, with individual activities shown leading from it. The path is termed critical because any deviation from it may result in running over time, increased cost and lower quality. A critical path analysis can be presented also in text-only form, with moves and timings given in columns.

CRM *Business, Internet business activity,*
Marketing

Initials for **customer relationship management** (*qv*) and **customer relationship marketing**.

Cromalin *Print, Production*
A proprietary dry proofing system, using coloured toners rather than inks. This is DuPont's brand name for their process. 3M and Kodak also market dry proofing systems.
See Press proof, Proof, Wet on wet.

Crop *Artwork, Photography, Reprographics*
To trim an illustration, transparency or photoprint. This is done physically on the drawing board, or electronically on computer screen. The objective is to cut off unwanted parts of the photograph, such as dustbins standing outside the front entrance of your new office or factory; or to improve the shape of the print; or to make it fit a column width. Basic cropping can sometimes be done during photography, but this usually needs to be finished in the darkroom or studio.

Cross-head *Copywriting, Creative, Desktop publishing, Editing,*
Typography, Word-processing
A type of subhead (*qv*).

Cross-over testing *Advertising, Media, Research*
Split run comparison testing of different advertisements, in different publications. The advertisements are initially inserted in the selected publications, then transposed in subsequent editions of the same publications.

Cross-track site *Outdoor advertising*
A poster site across a railway line, parallel with a platform and facing the passengers.

Crown *Outdoor advertising*
A poster size, 500 mm × 381 mm (20 in × 15 in), the basic dimension unit for larger-size posters. Larger posters, however, do not comprise sheets of crown size, but are scaled up from this dimensional basic unit.
See Double crown.

CRT *Computing, Television*
Cathode ray tube. A fancy name for a computer screen or television monitor. This is a proper technical term used by manufacturers of oscilloscopes and early television equipment. Nowadays, in the mouths of end-users, it sounds a bit 19th century-ish, and pretentious. VDU (video display unit) is not much better. **Computer screen** is the term now generally used.

CTP *Print, Production*
Initials for **computer to plate** (*qv*).

Cumulative reach *Advertising, Media research*
The total number of readers, viewers or listeners aware of a press advertisement or broadcast commercial in a fixed period.
See Reach.

Current demand   *Business, Economics, Marketing*
The ability and readiness of consumers for a product or service to purchase, and to pay the current market price.

Cursor   *Computing, Desktop publishing, Word-processing*
A flashing vertical or horizontal bar, rectangle or graphic device on a computer screen. This marks the current working position on-screen, and the place where text will be inserted when you type. You can move it by using the keyboard or mouse.

Custom-built   *Manufacturing, Marketing*
The US term for **tailor-made**. A product or service made or adapted to a specific-ation provided by a customer.

Customer   *Marketing, Retailing, Sales*
One of the parties to a legally binding contract to purchase goods or services. This is the pedantic definition. In popular terms, a customer is an organization or individual making a purchase. It is also used to refer to one considering a purchase, or being approached to make a purchase. Any person walking into a shop is usually referred to as a customer, whether she makes a purchase or not. This may sound confusing, but all these terms are in current use. The use of the word consumer may be less precise, but it includes the ultimate user, who may not have made the purchase. Be cautious.

Customer care   *Marketing, Retailing*
Ideally, a corporate concept that encourages staff, from chairman to floor staff, to consider the customer in every thought, procedure and action. This has developed into CRM, **customer relationship management** (*qv*), stimulated partly by the rise of marketing potential and activity on the Internet.

Customer profiling   *Marketing, Marketing research, Retailing*
Classification into groups of a company's customers, using categories broad enough for comparison with each other. From this, it should be possible to describe individual customers by their purchases, demographics, lifestyles and so on. Thus, owners of cars, property, dishwashers, bank accounts and mortgages, can be cross-matched with age, occupation, profession, disposable income, and a liking for expensive restaurants and foreign holidays. In the UK, due regard needs to be taken of the Data Protection Act.

Customer records   *Customer care, Customer service,*
Marketing research, Retailing
Individual records of a company's customers. These cover the usual name, address and other basic demographic data; plus detailed information on enquiries, orders and purchases, with dates and locations; satisfaction or dissatisfaction with products and services. Due regard needs to be taken of the UK Data Protection Act.

Customer relationship management   *Business, E-commerce, Internet*
marketing activity, Marketing

Usually abbreviated to **CRM**. A concept of the mid-1990s. A CRM company, Impiric, has produced the following definition:

> An ongoing process for maximizing customer value over time, through the application of a mix of integrated customer management tools and techniques. CRM covers the strategy and process of co-ordinating all points of contact with customers by integrating people, process and technology from the customer point of view, resulting in longer-term customer value, profitability and loyalty.*

CRM did not spring fully armed from the brow of Zeus. It has evolved from a number of working concepts: after-sales service, customer care, enterprise relationship marketing, customer relationship marketing and so on. It began to dawn on marketers that the cost of making a sale from a new customer was six times more than getting an existing one to buy something. This was finally confirmed by a Royal Mail survey in 1999.

Marketers now know that information technology can produce some stunningly effective database marketing; and that they actually have access to individual customers! It gives them the ability to capture, manipulate and use information about consumers – particularly their own.

Essentially, CRM is the deployment of a variety of related marketing tools, techniques and activities. It is dedicated to the identification of named individual consumers; creating a commercial relationship with them; managing the relationship for their mutual benefit, and company profitability, over a long period.

Customer service department   *Marketing, Retailing*

Formerly known as the company customer complaints department, it deals with issues of customer satisfaction as well as day-to-day complaints. It is often a company's most frequent and active interface with its customers, having a vital public relations job to do. For this reason, special training is advised for customer service staff.

Cut-out   *Artwork*

A photograph or illustration with the background cut away.

Cut pricing   *Retailing*

A retailing technique for stimulating trade and increasing store turnover; usually a temporary measure. Shoppers are, in theory, induced by lower prices to purchase more products, or purchase more frequently. Tactics, timing and pricing need to be carefully calculated, since consumers who normally buy small quantities do this either out of habit or need. You may not, for example, persuade consumers to buy more toothpaste than they may habitually use. People already cleaning their teeth

---

*Thanks to Tess Harris, former Chairman of the Chartered Institute of Marketing, Central London.

three times a day will not be stimulated by cut pricing into doing it four times. If they do buy more toothpaste at reduced prices, it will have to be stored at home; future purchases may be smaller as a result. Unless cut pricing is applied to fast-moving or speedily used consumer goods, it may fail; the retailer's gain in turnover may be lost in lower profits. Supermarkets frequently use **loss leaders** (*qv*) during slack periods, or when new products have not taken off as rapidly as predicted.

Cutting copy   *Film, Video*
The first version of a film or television commercial, or of an entertainment film, video or documentary.

Cyan   *Advertising, Print*
One of the subtractive primary colours used in four-colour process printing. The others are magenta, yellow and black.
See Black, Cromalin, CYMK, Magenta, Pantone, Primary colours, Process colours, Yellow.

Cyclical trade   *Marketing, Product management, Retailing, Sales*
Upturns and downturns in the sales movement of products and services. These often follow global or national economic booms and recessions. Careful and expert study and analysis of such movements over a long period may help with production and sales forecasting.

CYMK   *Print*
The four colours used in four-colour process printing: cyan, magenta, yellow and black. The initial K us used to denote black, presumably to avoid confusion with blue and brown.
See Primary colours.

Cynicism   *Marketing philosophy*
A marketing concept stating that the function of creativity in marketing is to arrest the customer's mind long enough to extract money from it. All business techniques are designed to move money from one person's pocket to another's without resorting to violence.

Dd

DAGMAR *Advertising planning, Advertising research, Marketing planning*
An acronym used in marketing and advertising planning and practice: **Defining Advertising Goals for Measured Advertising Results**. This popular concept was developed for advertising modelling in a 1961 book, and academic papers, by Russell Colley. It is still valid and respected, mainly because it is based on common sense, and because it works. The main thrust of the concept is that 'all commercial communications that weigh on the ultimate objective of a sale must carry a prospect through four levels of understanding'. The 'prospect' is the prospective customer for a product or service. The four criteria applied to making a successful sale to the future customer are that he must:

- first be aware of the existence of a brand or company;
- have a comprehension of what the product is and what it will do for him;
- arrive at a mental suspicion or conviction to buy the product;
- stir himself to action.

The usefulness of this model lies in its orientation towards the future customer's needs and desires. It also enables the product's marketing and advertising teams to prepare a research programme for forthcoming promotional campaigns, and research them pre-, mid- and post-campaign.

Bearing in mind that there are several distinct categories of prospect and customer, and that some will not purchase immediately, the model has limitations. As you will find elsewhere in this Dictionary, customers fall into three basic types: new customers, existing customers and brand-switchers. Advertising messages to these types need to be different in each case. A single message to all categories will almost certainly be deficient, ineffective or wasteful, or all three. Consider the following:

New customers
Never used or heard of the brand
Basic message: try it; you may like it
Technique: attractive demonstrations, endorsements, inducements, discounts

Existing customers
Already use the brand
Basic message: use more of it
Technique: attractive ideas for increased product use

Brand-switchers
Habitually use another brand
Message: you will like this brand; it will do more for you than the one you are using
Technique: attractive demonstrations of customer satisfaction, endorsements, inducements, discounts

Dampening system   *Print technology*
On litho presses, the mechanism for transferring dampening solution to the plate during printing.

Damping   *Paper, Print technology*
The process of applying water to the printing plate on a litho press. The term applies also to the application of moisture to paper in preparation for a subsequent process, such as **supercalendering**.

Dandy roll   *Marketing communications, Paper manufacture*
A roll or cylinder at the wet end of a paper-making machine, in contact with the upper surface of the forming paper web. The roll is covered with a woven wire, which makes wove or laid effects on the paper texture. It often carries a design for a watermark, such as a brand, logo or trademark. In high quality papers, such as *Conqueror* or *Distinction*, the watermark is the manufacturer's own brand. Otherwise, it can be a brand name, design or logo commissioned by a client, used as an in-built marketing communication.

Data   *Computing, Research, Statistics*
A collection of facts and figures. In computing, data is used for the electronic processing and manipulation of the collected material, and its conversion into useful information. In statistics, data are based on research and manipulated for analysis. Any space here devoted to whether data is a singular, plural or collective noun is futile.

Data analysis   *Computing, Marketing, Research*
The collation and study of facts and figures in a data file, whether on computer or paper. In marketing, one objective of such study is to enable marketing or product management teams to weigh up the strengths, weaknesses, opportunities and threats to their products, services or brands before committing money to campaigns.

Database *Computing, Information technology, Marketing research*
A computer file containing information and facts on a specific subject, eg customers' names, job titles, addresses and other useful stuff. Usually organized for fast access, retrieval and manipulation. In information handling, database usually refers to a bibliographic file; a statistical file is usually referred to as a **databank**.

Data capture *Computing*
Data downloaded into a computer from another source, for storage, processing and manipulation.

Date coding *Packaging, Retailing*
A technique for marking dates on consumer packaging. Coding usually indicates the latest date by which a product may be displayed, sold, used or eaten.
See Best before.

Data-sheet *Marketing, Product management*
A document prepared by a marketing or product management department, showing the performance record of a product or service in terms of enquiries, orders, sales and profits. Other data can be included, eg market share.

DC *Media planning and buying*
Initials for a double column in a newspaper or magazine, indicated in advertisement rate cards and space orders. When booking media insertions, it is always best to avoid initials and spell out the requirements in full. Confusion can arise when using initials; DC, for example, also stands for double crown, a poster size.

Deadline *Advertising, Public relations, Publishing*
The date or time planned and set for the completion of a job, or for the submission of copy to a newspaper, magazine or printer.

Dead matter *Advertising, Print media, Publishing*
Any creative, production, proofed or printed material superseded by more up-to-date or advanced material. To avoid expensive and time-wasting confusion, dead matter is best removed and archived until the job is completed and paid for. After that, it can be destroyed.

Dealer *Distribution, Retailing*
A term imported from the USA; usually applied to a seller and distributor of products in business-to-business transactions; but increasingly used in consumer retailing. In the same way, 'shop' is becoming 'store'; words like mall and precinct are gaining ground. In marketing jargon, retailer and retail outlet are synonymous.

Dealer aids *Product management, Retailing, Sales force activity*
A wide range of material, usually printed, supplied by manufacturers to retailers, to help in persuading consumers to buy at the point of sale. Material includes:

banners, brochures, dump-bins, leaflets, leaflet dispensers, mobiles, posters, shelf pelmets, showcards, stickers, wire baskets and cages. Cheaper items are often supplied free; often, retailers are asked to share the cost with the supplier. In-store video material is popular for selling cars, furniture, white goods and other expensive products.

Dealer audit   *Product management, Research, Retailing*
Regular research into sales at retail outlets. This is designed to reveal ongoing data on sales by product, price, sales volume, stock, dates and times over a specified period. It enables product management teams to compare one period or season with another, one area with another, one brand with another, the effectiveness of brand promotions, and other essentials for successful brand and product management.

Dealer incentive   *Product management, Retailing*
An inducement by manufacturers and suppliers to retailers, to encourage them to stock and sell a product, and to promote it actively. This can vary from extra discounts and freebies, to foreign holidays.

Debit card   *Banking, Retailing*
A plastic card issued by a bank or other financial institution. It enables a customer to buy goods and services, without using cash, from businesses that accept the card. Using electronic funds transfer (EFT), a participating retailer debits the customer's bank account direct. In the case of HSBC (Hong Kong and Shanghai Banking Corporation) for example, its cards can be used to withdraw cash from its self-service machines in the UK, machines operated by certain other financial institutions in the UK and from all HSBC Group self-service machines abroad. Its debit cards can also be used in card-operated machines with retailers and other suppliers, and/or as a cheque guarantee (in the UK only), and/or as a cheque guarantee. If a customer issues a cheque in the UK using a debit card, HSBC guarantees to pay the cheque if the amount of the cheque does not exceed the limit shown on the card.

When withdrawing cash from machines, the customer needs to key in a personal identification number (PIN), which the bank supplies. Cash withdrawals in the UK are normally debited from a customer's bank account on the same day, or the next working day.

Debris   *Print*
Paper dust that finds it way on to a litho printing plate or offset blanket. If allowed to accumulate, debris can smudge or otherwise damage the printed image while the press is rolling.

De-bug   *Computing*
Computer software programs often contain errors, known as bugs. De-bugging is the art of seeking, identifying and eliminating bugs. Computers are excellent pieces

of equipment, usually very reliable. It is very nearly always software that gives computers a bad reputation among end-users.

Deck *Copywriting*

A US term for copy, such as a subhead, between a headline and a section of body copy.

Deckle edge *Paper, Print*

An uneven, ragged or feathery edge usually found with hand-made paper, or machine-made paper simulating the hand-made sort. A **deckle** is the frame determining the width of a wet paper sheet as it comes off the wire of a paper-making machine.

Dedicated communication link *Electronic communication, Information technology*

Two or more sites linked by telecommunication lines for their sole use. For example, where an advertiser, advertising agency, pre-press house and printer are linked in a private, dedicated network. No other users have access to the links.

De-dupe *Databases, Direct marketing*

De-duplication. Removing duplicate data from a database or mailing list, to make it more efficient and effective. It is estimated that a dormant or unused database deteriorates at up to 10 per cent a month. The same applies to directory entries; a directory is out of date on the day it is published. It is estimated that the monthly deterioration of mailing lists is:

gone-aways	5%
deceased	2%
movers	7%
duplicates	8%

Deep-etched *Art, Print*

The treatment of a printing plate, in which some of the printing area is removed. This ultimately leaves areas of unprinted white space, usually for the brightest of highlights, for example.

Deep-etched plate *Print, Production*

In litho plate-making, a positive-working plate used for long runs, where the inked areas are slightly recessed below the surface.

Definition *Computers, Photography, Print, Television*

The sharpness or resolution of a photoprint or printed image, and its computer and television screen equivalent.
See Dot, Pixel, Resolution.

De-inking *Paper, Print*
The removal of ink and mechanical impurities from previously printed paper before it is recycled. This is necessary in order to preserve the integrity of the newly recycled paper and the purity of its colour.

Delayed response *Advertising, Direct marketing, Marketing*
The effect of an advertising or marketing campaign, where the expected response takes longer than planned for. A direct mailshot, for example, under normal conditions, may produce a response within three days. Weather, strikes, elections, holidays and other manifestations may delay the response.

Deliberate obsolescence *Marketing*
A technique for ensuring the uptake of an old product or service in a new guise. The technique often involves a re-launch together with appropriate promotional activity. Sometimes this is essential as a product approaches the zenith in its life cycle. Often, technical innovation forces manufacturers to re-launch. Sometimes, as with computer and telecoms marketing, rapid change in a highly competitive marketplace drives deliberate obsolescence. However, it is a disease that feeds on itself, and any gain disappears in the loss, especially to consumers.

Demographics *Campaign planning, Marketing research, Research, Statistics*
The division and classification of populations and target audiences, by age, sex, occupation, social status and other characteristics.

Demonstration *Exhibitions, Marketing, Retailing, Sales promotion*
Displaying a product and demonstrating its functions and benefits. Often done in retail outlets and at exhibitions, by live demonstrators or presenters, followed by encouragement to buy on the spot. Department stores, among others, often use continuous video demonstrations. Some are interactive, enabling customers to select particular features they would like to see; or colours. sizes, variations and prices.

Densitometer *Print*
An instrument for checking and measuring the colour and tone density of printing inks. This is used in proofing, and on print runs, to control inking levels.

Density *Photography, Plate-making, Print*
The depth, darkness or tonal value of a printed image, or part of an image.

Density *Typography*
The amount and tonal quality of a typeset area. Type set solid, and with minimal word- and letter-spacing can look very dense. Where it becomes actually unreadable, the term can also be a quality ascribed to the typographer who made it so.

Depreciation *Business, Marketing, Planning*

The loss in value of a piece of equipment or other asset during its working life, calculated over a period of time. The calculation is done as part of an accountancy technique, which sets the loss off against a company's tax bill. More important, it helps a marketing team to predict a product's future profits and losses; equipment inevitably needs to be replaced over time.

Depth interviewing *Marketing research, Research*

Low-key, informal interrogation of interviewees during one-to-one or group discussions. The researcher works to a pre-arranged plan with specific objectives. One of these is to elicit from the respondents information that may not emerge during straightforward interviewing.

Depth of field *Photography*

The area surrounding the true point of focus, where the image appears sharp. To produce a sharp image, a lens needs to be focused at a certain point in front of it. In front of and behind this point, the image continues sharp, depending on how far the subject is from the lens. Outside these areas, the image becomes blurred as it goes further and further out of focus. The area of acceptable sharpness on either side of the focal point is the depth of field.

Descender *Typography*

That part of a type character that descends below the base-line (*qv*); especially the lower case characters g, j, p, q and y. In some fonts, the figures 3, 5, 7 and 9 fall below the base-line. Some exotic and fancy typefaces have other descending characters, depending on the whim of the designer.
See Ascender.

Designer products *Business, Fashion, Marketing*

Usually, often deliberately, confused with exclusivity. In its honest and purest definition, a designer product is one designed exclusively for a manufacturer or distributor by a well-known and respected specialist. The product bears an exclusive label and an appropriately high price. The quantity produced is limited; the quality expected to be of the highest. In today's reality, however, products often are dubbed 'designer' when they are of indifferent and mediocre quality; and produced in huge numbers for mass-consumer markets.

Desk research *Marketing research, Research*

A form of research using existing information from the Web, company data and sources, directories, magazines and other published sources. This is not to say that desk research is inferior to field research. It is highly valued because of the speed with which it can be obtained. Often, desk research is a prelude to field research. Bear in mind that some forms of desk-research sources, such as directories, go out of date quickly; they are often so on the day they are published.

Developer   *Photography, Reprographics*
A chemical agent and process used for rendering photographic images visible
following exposure.

Developer   *Print*
In litho plate-making, the chemical material used for removing unexposed
photographic emulsion.

Diary research   *Marketing, Marketing research, Retailing*
A consumer research technique, in which groups of respondents record information day to day in an organized way, pre-determined by the research organization.
It is used to gather information on purchases of products and services, reading
habits, television viewing, radio listening and other daily or frequent consumer
activities.

Diazo   *Photography*
A non-silver-based coating and process for contact printing.

Die-cuttability   *Paper, Print*
An evaluation of the suitability of paper and board for die cutting (*qv*) into blanks
of a pre-planned design or shape.
See Blind embossing, Embossing.

Die cutting   *Packaging, Print*
The technique, using sharpened steel rules, for cutting printed sheets into shapes
for labels, mailshots, containers and boxes. This can be carried out either on rotary
or flat-bed machines. Rotary die cutting is usually carried out in line with printing.

Die stamping   *Print*
An intaglio printing process, using pressure, from lettering engraved into copper
or steel plates. The die is the engraved plate. The printed results are usually of
exceptionally high quality, density and sharpness.
See Blind embossing, Embossing, Thermography.

Differential pricing   *Marketing, Retailing*
A pricing policy in which the same product is sold to different groups of consumers
at different prices. Viking, a well-known international office supplies company,
uses differential pricing very successfully. Customers are classified according to
whether they are frequent or infrequent purchasers, and whether they buy high-
or low-value products. Using the Web, and several different catalogues, Viking is
able to target such customers by their purchasing track records with the company,
and price offerings accordingly. Differential pricing of products in Viking's
catalogues is made possible by the use of digital printing.

Diffusion transfer   *Photography, Plate-making*
A one-stop photographic processing system, such as Polaroid. This comprises a photographic emulsion on which a negative is produced, and a receiver sheet or plate on which a positive of the image is transferred during processing.

Digital   *Communications, Computing, Photography,*
Print, Radio, Television
Any data, image or calculation that can be accessed, processed and stored electronically, and later retrieved, processed and re-formed. The term describes the use of discrete pulses, signals or values to represent data in computer graphics, telecommunications systems, fax transmissions and word processors. Until recently, the term was mostly applied to the processing of images by computer. It is now current in radio and television transmission and reception, print and photography.
   A digital clock is one that shows the time by digits, rather than by the use of revolving hands.

Digital asset management   *Advertising, Art, Creative, Design, Writing*
The archiving and indexing of content for re-use in print or electronic media. This is now a common practice, as publishers recognize the long-term value of copyright material.

Digital image   *Computer graphics, Design, Information technology*
Any computer or photographic image that has been encoded electronically. This applies both to graphics and type.

Digital image processing   *Design, Graphics, Information technology,*
Marketing communications
A range of techniques used to generate, process and reproduce images by computer. Processing includes image enhancement and colour correction.

Digital printing   *Print processes*
The printing process in which an image is applied to the substrate direct from a digital file, rather than from film and plates. Information technology enables variable data to be included in a print run. This means that each sheet, page or publication on such a run can contain different information, depending on the content of the customer's database. In a catalogue, for example, different prices can be offered to customers, based on their frequency of purchase or loyalty to the advertiser.

Dimensional stability   *Paper, Print*
The ability of a paper to retain its proper shape and dimensions despite changes in moisture content. In a print shop or paper store, paper can come under the influence

of variations in the surrounding atmosphere. It can also be subject to variations in physical and mechanical stress during printing, especially at high speeds.

Diminishing returns *Business, Economics, Marketing*

A theory in economics, proposing that increasing the input of one factor, beyond a certain limit, may not produce a corresponding output of another. For example, increased investment in a product by, say, 10 per cent, may produce a return of 10 per cent or more. However, beyond a certain point, increased investment may actually produce a *diminished* return; further investment may eventually become uneconomical. In crude marketing terms, fishing in a lake may produce a good catch over a certain period. Beyond this, the fish caught will be smaller and leaner, and not worth the extra effort.

Directive *European law, Marketing*

In the European Union, a ruling binding on member states. It usually includes both the procedure to be adopted to meet the requirements of the directive, the results expected to be achieved by it, and the time-scale by which it must be implemented. One of the best-known, possibly anecdotal, EU directives concerns the growing and marketing of cucumbers. The directive requires all cucumbers marketed in the Union to be straight, not curved. How this is to be achieved, and what happens to cucumbers found to be curved, is not mentioned.

Direct mail *Advertising, Sales promotion*

A form of advertising or sales promotion in which selling is done by sending promotional material through post. In other words, selling by post. Do not confuse this with **mail order**, which is *buying* by post.

Director *Commercials, Film, Television, Video*

The individual in charge of turning a script into a production. He may write or participate in writing the script, and often supervises the editing.

Direct response *Direct marketing*

Advertising, and other promotional activities, in which a measurable response is obtained direct from the target audience. The media used includes press, television, radio, mail, telephone, fax, and the Internet. Direct marketing by Internet is now firmly established, especially in the USA, and increasingly in Europe.

Direct sales *Direct marketing, Distribution*

The sale of products and services direct from manufacturer to customer. No retailer, wholesaler, agent, broker or other intermediary is involved.

Direct to plate *Print, Production*

Also known as **computer to plate**, and **CTP**. A production technique in which printing plates are imaged direct from a digital file, rather than from film. At a time when printers and their customers demand shorter lead times, increased productivity and reasonable costs, CTP helps to achieve these objectives. There are a number of other substantial advantages. After a plate has been produced, the production data can be archived by the system's software. This can be retrieved at any time, and another copy made of the plate. With some CTP production systems, the operator can view the layout of the plate, and the design and colour of the image requested in a preview file displayed on screen.

Dirty proof *Print*
A press proof with a large number of errors. Where errors are the printer's, they are the printer's responsibility, and he pays for corrections. Where they are the author's, the author may be asked to pay. Typographical errors are termed **typos**; printers' textual errors are termed **literals**.

Discount house *Retailing*
A distributor of products conducting an actual or near cash and carry operation, with products substantially discounted. Such distributors are used by retailers, large companies with high turnaround of consumables. Products can range from grocery and catering products to office equipment. In return for low prices, the distributor may not offer credit or delivery services. Often, customers pay an annual membership subscription; in the UK, Costco and Makro are two discount houses operating in this way.

Discrimination testing *Marketing research*
A research procedure for providing qualitative and quantitative evidence of consumer differentiation for products and services.

Disparaging copy *Advertising*
Advertising copy that puts a competitor's product in a bad light by using unfavourable comparisons. This technique is frowned upon by self-respecting advertisers, who consider their own best points capable of selling a product, proposal or argument. It is also in breach of the British Codes of Advertising and Sales Promotion. These state that comparisons should be clear and fair, and that comparisons should not be selected in a way that gives the advertiser an artificial advantage. As to denigration, the Codes stipulate that advertisers should not unfairly attack or discredit other businesses or their products. The only acceptable use of another business's broken or defaced products in advertisements is in the illustration of comparative tests. The source, nature and results of these tests should be clear.
See Knocking copy.

Display *Press advertising*
Newspaper and magazine advertising sold and bought by the unit of a page. Units are fractions of a page, eg whole page, half, quarter, eighth, sixteenth and so on. Other units of press advertising are classified or straight paper-typeset lineage; and semi-display, which is a form of classified with bold type, borders, rules, logos

and, sometimes, colour. In Europe, semi-display advertising is sold by the column-centimetre. In the United States, it is called **display classified** and sold by the column-inch.

Display   *Retailing*
The display of merchandise within a store or showroom, or in display windows.
See Classified.

Display highlight   *Computer graphics, Desktop publishing, Typography,*
                                                                          Word-processing
An image on a computer screen highlighted to call attention to it. This is done by the use of bright bars or other areas, some of which flash or blink. In DTP and WP, highlighting is done by a procedure termed **dragging** (*qv*), used for taking items to different positions on screen.

Display outer   *Distribution, Retailing*
A bulk container for protecting products during transportation. Its other important function is the display of advertising, promotional or corporate messages. Smaller containers decorated in this way are used to display and dispense products at the point of sale, usually on counters and shelves.

Display packaging   *Retailing*
A technique for packaging single items at the point of sale, while also identifying and promoting the product. Lawnmowers, microwave ovens, electric drills and similar high-value items are often packaged in this way.

Display type   *Design, Typesetting, Typography*
Type sizes 14pt and larger. Used mainly for headlines in press advertisements and print. Smaller sizes are termed **body type**.

Dissolve   *Film, Slide presentations, Television, Video*
Also termed **cross-fade**. An optical technique giving gradual transition from one scene to another. When changing from one scene or shot to the next, the first is faded out at the same time as the second is faded in. With slide presentations, two or more projectors are used, the dissolves controlled by computer. In this way, a kind of animation can be achieved; this is slow, but it can be made to look very interesting.
See Fade, Wipe.

Distribute and print   *Print planning and buying, Production*
A production department instruction to forward a file electronically to a printer, then print the job at the point of delivery.

Distribution channels   *Distribution, Marketing, Retailing*
The various methods of getting products from where they are manufactured or stored, to the consumer or end-user. From farm gate to dinner plate, so to speak. Methods include wholesaling, retailing, direct marketing and mail order.

Distribution network   *Distribution, Retailing, Wholesaling*
A manufacturer's network of approved or authorized dealers. Networks are usually divided up among the dealers, locally, regionally and nationally, depending on the manufacturer's needs. Usually the dealers carry out all the basic functions of dealership, such as servicing, spares stock-holding and warranty operations.

Distributor   *Marketing, Retailing, Wholesaling*
A company dealing in one specified manufacturer's products, or a range of related products by several manufacturers. Car dealers, for example, acting as main distributors for specified automotive brands may also carry accessories related to those brands. Usually the distributor will have purchased the products for re-sale. rather than selling on commission.

Distributor brand   *Retailing, Wholesaling*
David Ogilvy once wrote that when they cut him open after death, they would find 'Own label' engraved on his heart.* Dedicated to manufacturers' national and international brands, he earned his living by promoting them. His reference was to retailers' own brands and labels, designed, produced and marketed by super-markets, department and chain stores, and others. Such brands are usually competitively priced, in direct competition with national brands, and usually occupy shelves adjacent to them. No real harm seems to come to either from this practice.

In the late 1990s Sainsbury, a UK national supermarket chain, introduced its own dark, sweet, carbonated drink in a red and gold can, branding it as 'Classic Cola'. It was sited in bays right next to Coke. Coca-Cola, irritated by this direct affront, decided to withdraw from the chain. However, after a few months Coke was back on the shelves. This seems to indicate that conflicting brands can co-exist profitably side by side. Curiously, during the hiatus, Sainsbury left empty the shelves formerly occupied by Coke, probably anticipating their return.

Doctor   *Flexography, Gravure, Print*
On gravure presses, a sprung, stainless steel blade pressed against the up-running surface of the engraved printing cylinder. This removes excess ink, and any foreign matter, before the image is transferred to the paper. The pressure of the blade is finely judged; too much, and the doctor could scrape away the surface of the cylinder – a costly error; too little, and the surplus ink may smudge the printed image. On flexographic presses, a steel blade or rubber roller is applied to an anilox roll, to control the amount of ink on the anilox.
See Anilox.

**Confessions of an Advertising Man*, Atheneum, New York, 1962.

Documentary *Cinema, Television, Video*
A presentation or programme made using facts obtained by research. Document-aries are used in public relations, often in the form of sponsored promotions and training programmes. Documentaries are sometimes described as 'the creative treatment of reality'. Techniques range from straight reporting to those used for fiction. In fact, all the cinematic techniques used for entertainment are used in documentaries, including: special visual effects, animation, cut-aways, voice-overs, fades, wipes and flashbacks.

Dog *Marketing planning*
In the Boston Matrix (*qv*), a product at the end of its productive marketing life, making no contribution either to the company's product portfolio or to its profits. The function of the Matrix technique is the estimation of the value of products during their life cycles. Products in the portfolio can then be treated appropriately, with effort devoted to maintaining or increasing their share of the market, retaining or dumping them. In theory, even a dog can be useful; for example, in helping maintain public awareness of a company in its marketplace. The value may be in the logo or packaging, rather than in the high competitiveness and profitability of the product itself. As always, this is a matter for the mature judgement of the marketing team.

Dolly *Film, Television, Video*
A hand-propelled trolley for a film or television camera, used in studios and on location. The dolly is equipped with devices to ensure smooth movement and action, and to prevent shake and shudder during camera operation.

Domain name *E-commerce, Internet, World Wide Web*
An individual, company or organization name used as an address for a Web site; eg www.cim.co.uk, used by the Chartered Institute of Marketing. 'CIM' is the identifying corporate part of the domain name. The whole address is usually termed a **URL, universal resource locator**. Of course, it could be called a Web site address, but this would be too easy and rob the technology of some of its mystique. Eventually, all URLs will be referred to in this way.

Domination *Advertising, Marketing, Sales promotion*
A technique for dominating the marketplace for a while, by a high concentration of advertising and sales promotion in a particular area of it. This calls for business courage and astuteness; with few exceptions, no product or service is likely to dominate its market forever. However, at the right time and with enough money, a product can increase its market share and frighten the competition, and stay in the lead until a competitor comes up with something similar.

Door to door *Sales force effort, Sales promotion*
A technique for selling consumer products and services cost-effectively in concentrated residential areas. The salespeople call on householders and make the sales pitch there and then on the doorstep. The technique is useful where a product

demonstration is called for, or where an explanation is necessary. Archetypal sales pitches are those for vacuum cleaners, encyclopedias and insurance policies. The same can be done in business areas where companies are tightly packed together; the City of London, for example. The high cost of door-to-door selling is offset by paying the salespeople low salaries and high commission. Sales promotion material is distributed in selected areas, using minimum effort to gain, hopefully, maximum sales. In the UK, legislation restricts door-to-door selling activity.

Dot *Plate-making, Print, Production*
The smallest reproducible element of a halftone (*qv*).
See Definition, Pixel, Resolution.

Dot for dot *Plate-making, Print, Production*
A technique for reproducing a halftone illustration from an image that has already been screened. For example, a picture of your chairman is needed for an advertisement. You have lost the most recent negative and prints, and the only suitable picture you have is one already published in your house magazine. You can't organize another photo-shoot, because the chairman is on holiday in the Caribbean. You cut out the chairman's picture from your house magazine, and have it reproduced on film, dot for dot, by your production house or plate-maker. Each dot on the magazine halftone is individually reproduced on the film. Usually, little quality is lost by this method. However, don't enlarge or reduce the image by more than 10 per cent, or serious loss of quality, as well as some bizarre distortions, may result. Before attempting this with colour halftones, consult your production house.
See Halftone.

Dot gain *Print, Production*
A printer's nightmare. In printing halftones (*qv*), dots may increase in size once deposited on the substrate, especially paper. This can produce a result different from the one planned by the creative and artwork teams, usually darker tones or colours.

There are two ways this can occur, often at the same time. First, the printed dot is absorbed into the paper and dries, or is 'cured', as a crust on the surface. The thickness of the crust, though microscopic, casts a minute shadow on the paper. Second, the portion of the printed dot below the surface of the substrate may bleed, or spread, giving a further increase in dot size. Multiplied up by the screen density, with up to 6,400 dots to the square centimetre, the printed result is different tones and colours from the ones planned for. Pre-press techniques should therefore take the effect of dot gain into account.

Dot gain can be controlled. In theory, FM screening (*qv*) should increase the problems of dot gain. The dots are smaller than those obtained by conventional screening. However, although distributed at random on the plate, all the FM dots have the same surface area. This means that the level of gain is the same throughout the range of tones. Corrections can be fed back to the scanner and the settings adjusted to compensate for dot gain.
See FM screening, Halftone.

Double bump   *Print*
The application of two layers of ink to an image, to achieve more intense colour or greater opacity.

Double column   *Editorial, Press advertising*
A double column in a newspaper or magazine, usually indicated in advertisement rate cards and space orders. Also referred to as DC. However, when booking media insertions, it is best to avoid initials and spell out the requirements in full. Confusion can arise when using initials; DC, for example, also stands for **double crown**, a poster size.

Double crown   *Outdoor advertising*
An ancient, but still-used, name for the basic size of paper used for posters. Crown is 500 cm high × 381 cm wide (20 in high × 15 in wide); and double crown 762 mm high × 508 mm wide (30 in × 20 in).

Double exposure   *Film, Photography, Video*
Superimposing one shot on another. In film and video photography, this is done either by winding the film or tape back and taking a second exposure, or in an optical printer or editing suite.

Double-page spread   *Advertising, Print, Publishing*
Two facing pages in the centre of a publication, magazine or brochure, usually printed on a single sheet. This gives somewhat more scope for design on the page, since the headline and illustration can be treated as a single unit, and do not need to be split into two separate sections. On two single, facing pages, the pages are often separated by a gutter in the centre. Splitting a headline sometimes results in uneven alignment on the spread, and can also read with a somewhat bizarre effect.
See Spread.

Download   *Computing, Information technology, Internet*
A technique used in Internet activities. The transfer of electronic data from one computer to another, or from a remote computer to a storage medium such as diskette or tape. Doing it the other way round is termed **uploading**.

Downmarket   *Marketing, Retailing*
A segment of a market in which prices, especially lowest prices, have greatest influence on buyer behaviour, decision-making and purchasing habits.

Down-stroke   *Typography*
In a type character, a heavy downward stroke. This is equivalent to the downward stroke of a pen when producing characters by hand.

Down time *Print*
Non-productive time when a printing press or paper-making machine is being cleaned or maintained. Printers and paper-makers earn their living only when their machines are rolling, and they like to keep it that way.

DPI *Information technology, Print*
Initials for **dots per inch**. When this term is used in the context of halftone, semitone and process printing, it refers to the density or frequency of dots within an image. The greater the number of dots per inch, the finer and sharper the printed image. DPI is also used in computer printer specifications.

DPS *Advertising, Print, Publishing*
Abbreviation for **double-page spread** (*qv*). There are caveats throughout the Dictionary on the dangers of using initials in media and production instructions.

Draft *Art, Creative, Desktop publishing, Publishing, Word-processing*
A piece of raw copy, which may be edited, amended, modified, added to; possibly even mutilated. A final draft is one on which all modifications and mutilations have been made, and is ready for typesetting. Used as a verb: to write or prepare a piece of copy, usually in the form of a typescript, ready for editing.

Dragging *Computing, Desktop publishing, Word-processing*
Highlighting characters, words, lines and blocks of type. These can then be deleted, moved or copied, or changed in style or attribution, eg from roman to italic.

Dragging is usually done by using a mouse to place the cursor at the start of the drag, holding down one of the buttons, then dragging up or down. Releasing the button stops the dragging. Most DTP and WP programs allow you to drag via the keyboard; however, mouse dragging is the simplest way of doing it.

Drip advertising *Advertising, Media planning and buying, Promotion,*
Sales promotion
A campaign using modest spaces over a long period. The idea is to insinuate a promotional message gently and steadily into the minds of target audiences, instead of bulldozing it. This technique is essential where continuity of message is needed. Educational campaigns are often conducted in this way; political ideas are often disseminated using this technique. It is a useful technique to consider where promotional budgets are modest.

Drive time *Advertising, Media buying, Radio advertising and broadcasting*
A period during weekdays when people are driving home from work. Main drive time is 4.30 pm to 7.30 pm. There is also a useful drive-time period between 7.30 am and 9 am. It is important to bear in mind that telephone numbers and Web site addresses are distracting, and difficult or impossible to absorb while driving. On the other hand, easy-to-remember words are useful, especially when constituting part of free telephone numbers and Web site addresses. The advertiser's objective,

of course, is to lodge messages in the targets' minds, so that they act on them after reaching their destinations.

Drum   *Distribution, Retailing*
A cylindrical package holding day-to-day household consumables such as corn-flour and cocoa, sweets or table salt. Open-top drums are often used in-store, containing a variety of small items displayed higgledy-piggledy to encourage impulse purchase. In this case, the drums are termed dump-bins. Larger drums are used for shipping bulk products such as cooking oil.

Dry goods   *Retailing*
Non-perishable products sold in wholesale and retail outlets.

Dry mounting   *Artwork*
Mounting a photoprint or illustration on to special board, using a heat-set adhesive. The technique is one of sandwiching an adhesive membrane between the print and the mounting board, and applying an electric iron to melt the adhesive. This often sets like concrete, and the only way to de-mount the print is to use a sharp knife. You may damage the print in the process. Given time, the adhesive will probably crack.

Because of the disadvantages, the technique is not much used now in the marketing communications industry. The current favourites are:

- *Cow Gum rubber solution*: a brilliant invention that allows you to reposition a print on the mounting board once you have laid it down. You can usually do this safely up to 10 minutes later. You can de-mount a print without damaging it, even years later by applying, sparingly and progressively, a solvent such as lighter fuel. You can also dampen the edges and back of the print with the solvent, and lift it off gently.
- *Spray mount*: a rubber-based adhesive applied from an aerosol can.
- *Tack-adhesive*: a method of coating the back of a print with small dots of light adhesive. As with Cow Gum, you can reposition the print for quite a while after mounting it. You may not always de-mount as easily as with a solvent; read the instructions on the pack.

Dry offset   *Print, Printing processes*
Also known as indirect letterpress. A letterpress process that uses the offset tech-nique, but using a relief plate. The image to be printed is first transferred to a rubber blanket cylinder, which in turn transfers it to the paper. Unlike conventional litho, no water fountain is used; hence 'dry'.
See Litho, Offset.

Dry proofing   *Pre-press, Print, Production*
Proofing a print job without using printing plates or a printing press. Several excellent methods of dry proofing are available, faster and more economical than

wet proofing. Du Pont's **Cromalin** being one of the popular techniques currently in use. Proofing is done by laying down toners on a special substrate, a coated paper dedicated to the purpose. Printers earn their living when their presses are rolling, and lose money when they are idle. Wet proofing – using a press for proofing – is slow, wasteful, expensive and unnecessary. It means shutting down a press for setting up the proofing. However, wet proofing can be done on a special proofing press, a cut-down version of the full-size production press.
See Cromalin, Progressive proof, Proof, Wet proof.

Dry run   *Commercials, Film, Television, Video*
A studio rehearsal, using a closed circuit system, or without a camera.

Dry transfer lettering   *Artwork, Creative, Studio techniques, Typography*
A hand-applied lettering system for the studio drawing board. In the absence of desktop publishing, it is quite good for headlining. It uses characters pre-printed on a sheet of translucent, coated paper. The individual characters are self-adhering. You position each character wherever you want it on the page – with precision – then rub it down with the blunt end of a pen, the back of a spoon, or a special instrument. You may find the spoon more effective than the special instrument.

The main disadvantage with this system is that you can't reposition the character once you have rubbed it down. If you have messed up the positioning, all you can do is scrape the letter off with a scalpel, or lift it off with self-adhesive tape and start again. Better still, give the job to a professional desktop publishing operator.

Dubbing   *Film, Television, Video*
The blending of speech, music and effects into a single sound track, and the adding of sound to mute film or videotape. Sound includes voice, music and sound-effects, and mixtures of these techniques. Dubbing also refers to the substitution of a foreign language dialogue or commentary for the original.

Dummy   *Creative, Design, Print*
An unprinted, preliminary version of a piece of print or packaging, with the design in place, folded to represent the finished article. Useful for discussions and presentations, where modifications might be made. Though dummies can look rough and ready, computer-aided design and desktop publishing enable a dummy to look almost as realistic as the printed piece. The use of standard colours, and correct paper grammage, can add realism, and production values, to the presentation.

Dump-bin   *Merchandising, Retailing, Sales promotion*
A large cardboard cylinder containing and displaying consumer products, sited in retail outlets where it will encourage rapid take-up by customers. The items are deliberately displayed higgledy-piggledy in the bin, to avoid any symmetry that might discourage customers from grabbing them when passing.

Duplicate *Artwork, Film, Video*
An exact copy of an original print, illustration, drawing, transparency, film, video and other production material. The popular abbreviation is **dupe**. The term is also applied to hot-metal printing, where printing blocks are duplicated by electro-typing or casting.

Duplication *Advertising, Media planning and buying*
The degree to which the circulation, readership or audience of one medium overlaps others. Duplication can be either negative or positive, depending on whether the media buyer wants lean or fat coverage of a particular geographical area or target audience.

Durables *Marketing, Retailing*
A term popularly applied to infrequently purchased, high-unit-cost products, such as washing machines, refrigerators and furniture. In consumer retailing, they are referred to as **consumer durables**; in business-to-business, **capital goods**.

Dustbin research *Marketing research*
A field research technique where panels of consumers are given containers in which they are asked to keep their discarded packages. The contents are collected at regular intervals, and analysed by researchers. This gives continuous information on purchasing frequency, stores, brands, prices and packaging. When the panels are scientifically selected, and carry out their functions conscientiously, the technique can produce very accurate research results. The findings can be related to advertising and other promotional effort.

DVD *Information technology, Video*
Initials for **digital versatile disc**, or **digital video disc**. A digital storage format capable of storing very substantial amounts of information, particularly for video and multimedia applications. At the time of writing this edition, the storage capacity of a 120 mm (5 in), single-sided, single layer DVD is 4.7 gigabytes. This represents about 133 minutes of video play.

DVE *Film, Video*
Initials for **digital video effects**, an instruction in film and video scripts. Visual effects include wipes, fades, dissolves, spirals, splits, stretches, blinds, boxing, chequerboarding, morphing, crawls, flashes, peeking, stripping and zooming.

Ee

Early adopters *Marketing*

One of the **adopter** categories used in product marketing. A term for consumers who take up a new product during one of its early life cycle stages. First to take up a new product are termed:

- innovators, the first 2.5 per cent of all adopters;
- early adopters are next (13.5 per cent);
- then early majority (34 per cent);
- late majority (34 per cent);
- finally, laggards (16 per cent).

These groups are usually also defined by demographics, including age, sex, location, education, occupation and social grade. These are generalized groupings, but when used as guidelines are usually accurate enough for marketers to make decisions on targeting for new or re-launched products.

Earpieces *Advertising, Media buying, Publishing*

Small advertising spaces on the front page of a newspaper, positioned either side of the main masthead. Mostly used in **broadsheets** (*qv*). They function usefully as reminders, and make offers which can be taken up immediately by using a highlighted telephone number, e-mail or Web site address.

E-commerce *Business, Communications, Internet, Marketing, Retailing*

Electronic commerce. Business transactions carried out via the Internet, using software that automates them. Typical of e-commerce activity is electronic shopping, including product selection, purchase, invoicing and payment. Financial transactions are made by credit card, for which a high level of security is necessary.

Economic life *Manufacturing, Marketing, Production*

The viable or profitable working life of a product, usually one of high unit cost, or a piece of capital or production equipment. Such equipment arrives at a point in time when it is no longer economically viable. Conditions for this can vary from unusually heavy maintenance costs and high cost of component replacement, to high insurance premiums; all of which can provide reasons for replacement. The cost of running equipment at the end of its economic life may be reflected in the price of the end-product.

Economic order level *Marketing, Re-selling, Retailing*
The point at which orders for the supply of a product for production, processing or re-sale is economically viable, and can produce a worthwhile profit for the supplier.

Economic pricing *Marketing*
The price of a product arrived at through taking into account every direct and indirect cost. This includes costs involved in conceiving it, designing, prototyping, manufacturing, warehousing, selling and distributing it. Also includes marketing activities and their administration; marketing communications such as advertising, packaging, public relations, sales promotion and after-sales service. All of which, of course, must be anticipated and planned for. A similar regime must be adopted when marketing a service.

Economies of scale *Economics, Manufacturing, Marketing, Production, Re-selling, Retailing*
A costing system based on the optimistic marketing philosophy that the more you buy of a product, the less it should cost. This usually works in practice, since market forces can compel a manufacturer to reduce the unit price of a product on a sliding scale. It depends on how much you buy at a particular time. Ideally, any savings made on these deals are passed on to the consumer, wholly or in part, through the distribution chain. In the world of aggressively competitive marketing, this usually happens. Sometimes it does not, and one of the companies in the chain keeps the savings. This may be legal, but it is certainly not noble. As it is said, in this life you do not get what you deserve; you get what you negotiate. The true price of consumer goods can be estimated when the retailing companies declare their seasonal sales.

Economy size *Packaging, Retailing*
An extra-large pack created for the purpose of stimulating or increasing demand for a product. The price of the pack is often pitched at that normally paid for a standard pack; or slightly higher. This is usually a temporary measure, sometimes also regional, where the brand is under competitive assault.

ECU *Film, Television, Video*
Extreme close-up. An instruction within a script. When you can see the individual hairs of an actor's eyelashes, it's an ECU.

Editing *Advertising, Copywriting, Creative, Editorial, Public relations*
Making changes to a piece of copy, augmenting, improving or condensing it; preparing it for press. In unskilled hands, this often means also mutilating it in the process. The term also includes adapting a piece of copy for different media. News releases often need considerable editing before appearing in a newspaper or magazine. Copy written for newspaper or house magazine editorial use would need to be completely rewritten for an advertisement or a piece of print on the same theme.

Editing *Film, Video*

Assembling and collating film or video material, manipulating, pacing and shaping it to create a finished presentation. This includes arranging the length of shots and cutting them precisely, so that the finished result portrays the facts and spirit of the script. The editor uses a high order of skill, experience and judgement in controlling the length and pace of each shot and scene, so that the finished film flows seamlessly from beginning to end. The editor strives to produce impact and rhythm not explicit in the written word or immediately apparent in the first prints or rushes.

Edition *Print, Publishing*

A specific issue of a publication, distributed at a specified place and time. The place and time are usually displayed on the front page, and generally also throughout the publication. For example, an edition of the *London Evening Standard* displays its date, time, edition, serial number and price on its front page. There is also a codeword for the time of day it is issued; for example, 'Mid-day', or 'Final'. Inside pages carry a running head showing the name of the publication, and page numbers. *Radio Times* publishes a number of regional editions, each displaying the name of the region alongside the information already mentioned.

Editor *Press, Print, Publishing, Radio, Television*

A professional responsible for preparing the work of others for publication or broadcasting. In press media, the editor has total responsibility for what is published; plus many other responsibilities such as hiring and firing.

Editor *Film, Video*

The professional responsible for collating filmed material, shaping it to form a presentation that portrays the facts and spirit of the script. Her skill in arranging the length of shots and precise cuts can produce impact, pace and rhythm not explicit in the script, or immediately apparent in the first prints.

Editorial *Publishing*

The text of a newspaper or magazine, news, features and comment, created and produced by its journalists. The term is sometimes used to describe leading articles written by the editor and her team, covering and commenting on major issues of the moment. The non-advertising content on television is usually referred to as **programming**.

Editorial advertising *Advertising*

Advertising written and designed to resemble editorial. Also termed advertisement promotions or advertorials. This is an effective marketing technique, especially when the advertorial is in the style of the publication in which it appears. There are certain rules governing this type of advertising. In particular, the British Codes of Advertising and Sales Promotion (BCASP) stipulate that advertorials should be designed and presented in such a way that it is clear that they are advertisements.

The words 'Advertisement Feature', or 'Advertisement' must appear at the head of the presentation. When considering creating an advertisement in the editorial style of a publication, it is prudent to get permission or approval from the editor; better still, get the advertisement director to get it for you.

Editorial mention *Press relations, Public relations*
Information on products, services and companies appearing in editorial, usually from copy or contact by public relations specialists. This is not a form of advertising (though that is what it eventually amounts to), but is entirely at the discretion of the editor. There is no guarantee when it will appear, or that it ever will. It will run only if the editor considers it a good story, or part of a story, of genuine and intense interest to readers.

Effective demand *Economics, Marketing*
The desire, readiness and financial ability of customers to acquire a product or service, and to pay the price asked for it.

Effects *Film, Radio, Video*
Sound-effects, such as traffic, ticking clocks, gunshots and storms. In scripts, this is usually abbreviated to **FX**. In film- and video-making, virtually all effects are added during the post-production stages.

Egyptian *Composition, Desktop publishing, Typesetting, Typography*
A range of slab serif typefaces, such as Cairo, Karnak, Rockwell, and the rather fancier Playbill and Ghost Town.

Electrostatic plates *Reprographics*
Plates for high speed laser printing, using zinc oxide, organic photo-conductor or cadmium sulphide coatings.

Elliptical dots *Pre-press, Print, Production*
Also termed **chain dots**. Elongated dots used in halftone photography, which give improved gradation of tones, particularly in middle tones and vignettes.

Em *Copywriting, Design, Printing, Typography*
A unit of measurement based on the space occupied by a capital M in the 12pt size of a typeface. The length of a line of type is often indicated by the number of ems it takes up. Line length is now also measured in millimetres; in the USA, in inches.

E-mail *Business, Communications, Information technology, Internet,*
Marketing communications
Shorthand for **electronic mail**: communication of messages and computer files between individual users' computers on the Internet, via an independent central computer – a **server**. While e-mail is no real substitute for letters and conventional correspondence, it has several characteristics specific to the computer age:

- It is immediate; though delays are frequent, often because of equipment problems.
- One message can be distributed to a large number of destinations at the same time. This facility is used constantly by companies engaged in the distribution of news releases.
- The medium encourages brevity; conventionally, e-mail messages are short and to the point.
- More complicated and sophisticated material, including graphics, can be electronically attached to it.
- It can be replied to, and the reply received, almost at once, which helps fast decision-making.

There is a downside to the speed made possible by e-mail; you can receive hundreds of e-mails every day, all of which may need to be considered and acted on. Parkinson's Law definitely rules here (the notion that work expands so as to fill the time available for its completion).

Embargo   *Editorial practice, Marketing communications,*
                                        Public relations, Publishing
A time constraint on the publication of information made available in a news release. In fact, it is more of a request by the organization issuing the release, than an order to be obeyed. An editor is not obliged to respect the request. But if he does not, he is unlikely to receive important news from the organization in future, possibly robbing him of a good and timely story. It is a matter of good relationships between an organization and its media contacts. The embargo consists of the word 'Embargo', or 'Embargoed until. . .' plus a date and time, printed at the top of a news release. It appears before the heading, in a position that cannot be overlooked.

Embargo   *Exporting, Importing, International trade*
A ban on goods being imported into a country; often for political reasons, or for the protection of that country's own products and industries. This usually amounts to the same thing. Embargoes can be initiated by governments of importing countries, or by those whose companies are doing the exporting.

Embossed finish   *Print*
Paper with a raised or depressed surface resembling cloth, wood, leather or other textures.

Embossing   *Print*
Impressing an image into paper or board from the back, to raise the image's surface. The raised image is printed. Where the raised impression is unprinted, this is termed **blind embossing**.
See Blind embossing, Die stamping, Relief printing, Thermography.

Em dash   *Copywriting, Design, Desktop publishing, Print, Typography*
A long printed dash, the width of an em. Do not confuse this with the hyphen, which is shorter and has a different semantic function.

Emotional appeal   *Advertising, Copywriting, Creative,*
Marketing communications
The basis of an advertising message having strong emotional character. Fund-raising advertising run by charitable organizations is often like this. Emotional appeals are often mixed with factual, logical and rational arguments, to make them more effective.

Emulsion side   *Photography*
The side of a film coated with silver halide emulsion. This should face the lens during exposure.

Emulsion side   *Plate-making, Pre-press, Print, Production, Publishing*
In plate-making practice, the side of a film in intimate contact with the plate. Publications accepting film rather than artwork may specify either **right reading emulsion side down**, or **right reading emulsion side up**, depending on their individual plate-making and production requirements. This means that, in both cases, the copy reproduces correctly on the press.

En   *Copywriting, Design, Desktop publishing, Print, Typography*
Half the width of an **em** (*qv*).

Enclosure   *Direct mail, Direct marketing, Mailshots*
An additional item enclosed as part of a mailshot. This may be a piece of print such as a brochure or reply card, a photoprint, a product sample or some other object in the envelope, in support of the main promotional item. The main item is often a sales letter.

Encoding   *Direct mail, Print*
Characters printed using ink containing iron, which can be recognized by magnetic ink character recognition systems (MICR). This is found on cheques (bank checks) and other security documents, and often on reply cards enclosed in mailshots, using the characters for keying.

En dash   *Copywriting, Design, Desktop publishing, Print,*
Typography
A short printed dash, the width of an en character.

Endorsement   *Advertising, Marketing communications, Public relations*
A statement by a personality or celebrity, showing a preference for a product or service being advertised or promoted. In press advertising and print, the endorsing celebrity is usually shown and named. In television advertising, the endorser is

often the main presenter, sometimes actually speaking the promotional copy, either to camera or as a voice-over. It follows that an endorsing celebrity should be known to the target audience, or at least famous for some activity connected with the product. Bear in mind that today, even with virtual saturation of news and gossip by the media, some members of the public may not recognize your endorser.

End user *Advertising, Marketing, Public relations*

The actual user of a product, as distinct from its purchaser or specifier. A computer system, for example, may be recommended or specified by a creative manager, approved by a managing director, signed off by an office manager and paid for by a finance director. When the machine arrives on your desk and you switch it on, you are the end user. Some markets are not nearly as straightforward as this. The pharmaceutical market, for example, is particularly complex. As a patient, you are the end user of a medicine, but you don't specify, approve or purchase it. The pharmacist stocks the product, but has no choice as to its distribution. The doctor does specify the product, but neither handles nor sells it. It follows that careful marketing planning is called for here, especially as far as the promotional message is concerned. Markets for products aimed at children are complicated, but in a different way. The child is the end user, and often specifies the product. The parent examines the product, determines its suitability, sometimes consults another parent, approves and pays.

Enlargement *Photography, Reprographics*

Popularly referred to as a **blow-up**. A print made from a negative, blown up to an unusually large size.

Enterprise zone *Business development*

A piece of land or real estate dedicated to the setting up and development of businesses. In the European Union, conditions applying to such zones are preferential, offered to entrepreneurs as inducements to transfer to the areas. The inducements include tax breaks, inexpensive or interest-free loans and other financial assistance, professional advice and business counselling. In the UK, such inducements come from local and national government, and from the European Union.

Equilibrium price *Marketing*

The price of a product arrived at when the demand for the product is the same as its supply. This does not usually last for long, and the price rises or falls in line with movement in the marketplace.

Escalator cards *Outdoor advertising*

On the London Underground and urban rail transportation systems throughout Europe, small advertising posters displayed on the walls of its escalators (moving stairs).

Esparto *Paper, Print*
A printing and writing paper made from, or containing substantial quantities of, esparto grass. This is a long-fibre material, giving excellent bulk to the paper, and a satisfying 'crackle'.

Established brand *Advertising, Marketing communications, Retailing*
A brand well enough known in its markets, and often elsewhere, that constant introduction and explanation is unnecessary. The best current examples include Coke, Pepsi, the BBC, CNN, Microsoft, Virgin, Jaguar, Rolls-Royce and Toyota.

Estimate *Advertising, Creative, Print, Production, Public relations*
The costing of a job, prepared in advance by a printer, production house, advertising agency, photographer or other supplier. Estimates are not normally binding; in the UK, quotations are, so be careful.
See Origination.

E-tailing *Business, Communications, Internet, Marketing, Retailing*
Electronic retailing. Retail transactions carried out via the Internet, using software that automates them. Typical e-commerce activities include electronic shopping, product selection, purchase, invoicing and payment. Financial transactions are made by credit card, store or debit card, for which a high level of security is necessary. Efficient though e-tailing may be, the downside is the physical delivery of the goods, which might not be as efficient.

Etching *Photoengraving, Plate-making, Pre-press, Print, Production*
Producing an image on a printing plate by chemical or electrolytic action.

Ethernet *Electronic communication, Information technology*
A proprietary local area network, together with its products and technical specifications. It was designed in collaboration with the Digital Equipment Corporation and Intel.

Ethical advertising *Advertising, Marketing communications, Pharmaceuticals*
Advertising by suppliers of medicines and other treatments prescribed exclusively by qualified medical practitioners. Such advertising is not aimed at the general public, but at clinicians, doctors and pharmacists. Pharmaceutical products marketed to the public are termed **proprietaries**. Both types of advertising are subject to their own licensing terms and codes of practice.

Eurodollar *Business, International trade*
The US dollar is described in this way when held by banks in Europe, or by European companies, or when used as a trading currency in Europe.

Excess demand *Economics, Manufacturing, Marketing*
A market condition in which demand for a product exceeds the ability of suppliers to produce it. In this climate, prices tend to rise.

Excess supply   *Economics, Manufacturing, Marketing*
The reverse market condition to excess demand, in which prices tend to fall.

Exchange rate   *Currency transactions, International marketing*
The level of value at which one country's currency can be exchanged for another. In today's volatile markets for currency and equities, the rate changes virtually every day. In the 1980s, the pound sterling hovered very narrowly around $2.40. At the time of writing this edition, it varies from $1.60 to $1.40. Some years ago, the value of the pound fell almost to a dollar. Vast fortunes have been made, and still can be made, from cashing in on the difference between exchange rates.

Exclusive   *Journalism, Media relations, Public relations*
A major news story or interview, offered exclusively to, or acquired exclusively by, a newspaper, magazine, television or radio station, is termed an **exclusive**. Among journalists this is also referred to as a **scoop**, especially where a newspaper or broadcast channel gets an exclusive after having pursued it aggressively. The terms apply also to photographic material.

Exhibition   *Advertising, Marketing communications*
A venue at which products and services or works of art are put on show, either for business transactions or inspection and enjoyment. They are popularly referred to as **shows**; in the USA, **expositions**.
   Exhibitions vary greatly, both in size and content. Mini-exhibitions, usually local or regional, are aimed at local business, trade and technical audiences. They are organized by companies specializing in such activities, and feature a small number of related exhibitors. Each exhibitor sends invitations to its customers, clients and prospects, together with free tickets; or gets the organizer to do it. Manufacturers, distributors and service suppliers often organize their own private mini-exhibitions, sending invitations to a highly focused list. At the other end of the scale, there are huge trade exhibitions, such as Hanover; and the Farnborough and Paris air shows. In the UK, exhibitions aimed at the general public include the Ideal Home Exhibition and the Motor Show.

Expanded   *Desktop publishing, Typesetting, Typography*
A type of a width greater than regular, standard or normal.

Expense-to-profit ratio   *Marketing planning*
The ratio of a company's expenditure on marketing operations to its profits from them.

Expense-to-sales ratio   *Marketing planning*
The ratio of marketing expenditure to revenue from sales. This is one of a company's financial measures for controlling its expenditure, aimed at achieving maximum profit from marketing operations. It also needs to employ techniques for calculating its expense-to-profit ratio.

Exploded view *Artwork, Computer-aided design, Design, Desktop publishing, Photography*
An illustration of an object, such as a piece of equipment, showing how its components relate to each other. The illustration is complete in itself, and in proper perspective, showing its components separated, usually 'floating', or with sections cut away to show what is underneath.

Exposure *Advertising, Marketing communications, Media, Propaganda, Public relations*
The amount of time to which readers, viewers and listeners are given opportunities to see and hear advertising, editorial and other messages. As an example, in the UK the Radio Authority has a number of standards for measuring audience exposure:

- *weekly reach* – the number in thousands or as a percentage of the UK/area adult population who listen to a station for at least five minutes in the course of an average week;
- *average hours* – the total hours of listening to a station during the course of a week:
  - per head, across the total adult population of the UK/area;
  - per listener, across all those listening to the station for at least five minutes;
- *total hours* – the overall number of hours of adult listening to a station in the UK/area in an average week;
- *share of listening* – the percentage of total listening time accounted for by a station in the UK/area in an average week.

Exposure *Photography, Plate-making, Reprographics*
In photographic processes, the step during which light produces an image on a light-sensitive coating. The term also refers to the amount of light allowed to reach the sensitive material.

Extended *Desktop publishing, Typesetting, Typography*
A wider version of a roman or standard typeface. Also termed **expanded**.
See Condensed.

Extended guarantee *Business, Distribution, Manufacturing, Marketing, Retailing*
An extra guarantee period, usually paid for by the customer, during which the terms of the original guarantee are honoured and can be enforced. If a customer wants an extended guarantee, the extension is usually added to the original at the time of purchase.

Extranet *Electronic communications, Information technology, Marketing communications*
An internal network available to specified external users. Extranets are used mainly for teleworking and data exchange among different organizations that wish

to keep the content private among members of the network. They also enable staff working away from the office to keep in touch with it and with each other. In marketing communications, extranets exist between advertisers and suppliers such as printers and research organizations, where the frequency and density of the traffic justifies the expense. Since extranets are essentially intranets connected to the public Internet, security measures are essential for protection against hackers and unauthorized users.

Ex-works   *Distribution, Manufacturing, Marketing*
The condition or status of a product as it leaves the factory. The ex-works price of a product is its basic price to customers, before distribution costs have been added. Other costs usually added include packaging, bulk crating, warehousing and insurance.

Eye-movement research   *Editorial, Press advertising, Research*
Laboratory techniques for determining the way readers look at newspaper and magazine pages, particularly advertising material. The reader taking part in the tests is seated in front of a page of advertising. A special camera records the amount of time the reader spends looking at various elements on the page, and the sequence in which this happens. The main problem with this research lies in the analysis and interpretation of the findings, and their subsequent application to advertisement design.

E-zine   *Corporate communications, Marketing communications,*
                                           Public relations, Publishing
An electronically distributed magazine. A magazine created and produced electronically, and distributed via the Internet or corporate intranet. Many house journals are produced and distributed in this way. The main advantages include fast distribution speed at low cost or virtually no cost; and that no printer is involved. Many company e-zines are produced in-house, either by company personnel or by outside specialists.

Ff

Face *Desktop publishing, Typesetting, Typography, Word-processing*
Shorthand term for **typeface** or alphabetical character; the name given to the
design of a particular typeface. Times Roman, for example, is a typeface. Sometimes the term is used to refer to a typographical family to which a typeface belongs.

Facia *Exhibitions, Retailing*
A banner or board above an advertiser's stand at an exhibition. Normally this
features only the exhibitor's name, logo and stand number; sometimes also the
theme of the stand and its campaign slogan. The term also applies to a display
board over a shop front.

Facility visits *Media relations, Public relations*
As a function of media relations, companies invite journalists to visit their
production, storage and distribution facilities. The objective is to give the visitors
enough information and help for them to produce features about the organization
visited. Usually, food and drink are provided, as well as photo opportunities.

Facing matter *Media planning and buying, Press advertising*
An instruction in a media purchase order to a publisher's advertisement department, to position an advertisement directly opposite a specified editorial page.
Some publishers accept this instruction without the firm guarantee of a particular
page. An insertion facing matter is usually more expensive than one placed 'run
of paper' – anywhere in the publication at the publisher's discretion.

Factor *Business*
A company that takes over the responsibility for settling the invoices of a client,
usually for a fee or a percentage of the value of the invoices. The factor undertakes
credit control, collects from the client's debtors, and also takes the risk. Some
factoring organizations pursue reluctant debtors into court.

Fade *Cinema, Television, Video*
Gradually fading out a picture, to end up with a black or blank screen.
See Dissolve, Wipe.

False claim *Advertising, Sales promotion*
A feature or benefit mentioned or described in an advertisement, which later
proves to be false or misleading. It can also apply to claims that are simply

inaccurate. Advertising of this kind is tightly regulated by the Advertising Standards Authority and the British Codes of Advertising and Sales Promotion (*qv*). Persistent breaches of the Codes can lead to the media's outlawing of the advertiser, and possible prosecution.

Family   *Desktop publishing, Typography, Word-processing*
A typeface (*qv*) with specific, identifiable characteristics running throughout its range. Members of the family have attributes related to the base design. Typographical attributes include: bold, semi-bold and demi-bold; condensed; expanded; extra bold; hairline; heavy; italic; light and extra light; medium; regular; roman; shadow and outline; thin; ultra.

Family brand   *Marketing*
A brand, identifying a range of products or services, usually expressed as a name, word, symbol, logo, graphic or trademark. Looking at the brand, a consumer or prospective customer should be able to identify immediately the family or parent company. In the mind of the observer, a strong family brand helps to transfer the attributes of the parent to the individual product. Attributes such as innovative design, reliability, high quality, long working life, excellent after-sales service, no-quibble guarantees and warranties, can be implied in this way. Companies successfully using the family brand approach include Dyson, Virgin, Sony, Canon, Bosch, the BBC and Hewlett-Packard.

Fast-moving consumer goods   *Marketing, Retailing*
Usually referred to as **FMCG**. Consumer products, mostly of low cost, which the consumer buys frequently and uses almost immediately. This includes the wide variety of high turnover household and other domestic products. The ordinary consumer seems not to care over-much about brands, being concerned more about price and availability. One exception is tobacco products, which, despite high price and adverse publicity, still retain a great deal of brand loyalty.

Fat face   *Desktop publishing, Typesetting, Typography, Word-processing*
A heavyweight version of a typeface, often with wide contrast in the visual weight of its thick and thin strokes. Sometimes used instead of the term **ultra**.
See Face, Font.

Fax Preference Service (FPS)   *Controls, Marketing*
The Fax Preference Service, set up in the UK by the Direct Marketing Association (UK) Limited (DMA), was originally formed in 1997. It was a voluntary self-regulatory mechanism to enable consumers to opt out of receiving unsolicited sales and marketing faxes at home.

Following the adoption of the Telecommunications Data Protection Directive by the European Parliament in 1997, the Department of Trade & Industry (DTI) and the Office of Telecommunications (OFTEL) entered into a public consultation period. This resulted in the Telecommunications (Data Protection and Privacy)

Regulations 1999. This came into force on 1 May 1999, and affects all tele- and fax-marketers in the UK.

In February 1999, OFTEL issued an invitation to tender for the Management of the Telephone and Fax Opt-out Schemes. The DMA was awarded the contract to run the Telephone Preference Service (TPS) and Fax Preference Service (FPS).

Under the Regulations it is unlawful to fax to individuals unless the faxing company has their prior consent. The term 'individual' in UK law includes consumers, sole traders and (except in Scotland), partnerships.

The FPS does, however, enable businesses to register, with a central service, their objection to receiving direct marketing faxes. Fax-marketing companies receive the fax numbers of businesses that have registered by subscribing to the FPS.

Feasibility study   *Marketing planning, Product development*
A research technique applied to the conception, creation and development of a product during the first stages of its life. Before any serious money is spent on commercialization, the product idea is subjected to rigorous tests: conceptual, academic, theoretical, technical, financial, economic, managerial and practical. Investing a little money at this early stage can prevent waste and loss of financial resources and management time and effort later, should the product not come up to expectations, or actually fail.

Feature   *Media, Press relations, Public relations, Publishing*
A newspaper or magazine story or editorial piece, somewhat longer than a report, often of substantial length. Some photographic material may be included. The writer will cover the subject material in some depth, and incorporate her own views, comments, reflections and predictions. The writer will usually be a journalist on the staff of the newspaper or magazine, or else a freelance engaged for the particular assignment. In press relations practice, the organization being written about, or its PR consultancy, usually offers the opportunity as an exclusive.

Feed   *Broadcasting, Radio, Television*
A live transmission from one broadcasting station relayed by land line or satellite to other stations for onward transmission. Often used to convey news or other unique events, where the receiving station has no personnel on the spot. A prior arrangement, and fee structure, is usually in existence.

Feedback   *Advertising, Communications, Public relations*
Information, opinion, views and reactions fed back to an organization by a target audience, following an outgoing communication. Original communications include advertising, house journals, brochures, telephone contact, conferences, meetings, seminars, discussion groups and Internet activity. Feedback is usually asked for by the communicating organization. The term is often used in reference to letters to a newspaper or magazine from its readers.

Field force *Marketing research, Opinion research*
A term sometimes used to define teams or researchers assigned to gather data from the public, either in the street, at the workplace or at home. Researchers are usually organized in teams, under a leader responsible to a research organization.

Field research *Marketing research, Opinion research*
Research conducted face to face with customers, prospects or the general public, in gathering primary data. This is different from desk research, which is done from published material, documents and other secondary data.

Field sales force *Sales activity*
Teams of salespeople assigned to sell products or services to the general public or businesses. They are organized by, and report to, a sales manager or director. Other sections of a company's sales organization sell by telephone from their offices, from home if they work regions or territories distant from the office, or are freelance.

Field selling *Sales activity*
Selling products and services by face-to-face contact with customers or prospects. This sales activity involves contacting and visiting people at home or the work-place.

File *Computing, Desktop publishing, Information technology,*
Word-processing
The name given to a unit or compilation of data stored under a single name.

Filler *Desktop publishing, Editorial, Print, Publishing*
A piece of copy or an illustration inserted on a page to fill up a column. This is an editorial technique, perfected before the days of DTP and computerized type-setting. Today, an editor can often juggle page elements on the screen so that fillers are unnecessary. However, a filler often makes a page easier on the eye than it would be with a clinical layout. To enjoy some really delightful fillers, read the *New Yorker*.

Filler *Paper, Paper-making*
A material, usually a white mineral substance such as china clay or calcium carbonate. Added to the raw material from which the paper is made, it increases its opacity, improves its flatness, and allows a smoother finish to the surface of the finished paper.

Film make-up *Artwork, Print, Production*
Assembling the elements of an editorial page, or an advertisement, ready for film-making and plate-making.

Film master *Artwork, Print, Production*
A complete, made-up positive of an editorial page or advertisement.

Film-setting *Pre-press, Print, Typesetting*
See Photo-setting.

Film speed *Photography, Reprographics*
A numerical expression of a film's sensitivity to light. The sensitivity of photographic film is usually known as its **speed rating**. Rating scales, adopted internationally, are set by the American Standards Association, International Standards Organization and the European Deutsche Industrie-Norm. Film speed is therefore usually designated by the initials **ASA**, **ISO** or **DIN**.

The higher the rating, the higher the film 'speed', and therefore the 'faster' the film stock. It follows that the faster the film speed, the shorter the exposure needed. This term should not be confused with **shutter-speed** (*qv*).
See ASA, ISO.

Filter *Artwork, Photography, Print, Production, Reprographics*
A transparent coloured glass, gelatin or plastic sheet placed in front of a camera lens. This has the effect of changing the colour and quality of the light reaching the film. In four-colour process film-making:

Blue filter   Green filter   Red filter   Yellow filter

give colour values for making the plate to print:

Yellow   Magenta   Cyan   Black

Filter question *Research*
In questionnaires used in marketing research and other surveys, a question designed to direct the procedure in a particular direction. For example, if a respondent replies 'no' when asked if he uses sugar, the researcher might ignore questions related to sugar and move on to another section. Alternatively, the respondent's reply may render him unsuitable for further questioning, and the researcher will terminate the interview.

Final edition *Newspaper publishing*
The final edition of the day, containing the latest news, financial and sport information and results.

Final proof *Advertising, Editorial, Print*
A final proof before going to press, showing that all agreed copy modifications and corrections, illustrations and colour grading have been made. No further changes are made at this stage, and the editor, client or advertiser is expected to sign a declaration that this is the approved final version.

Financial advertising   *Advertising, Financial marketing,*
                                             Media planning and buying

Advertising created and implemented by the financial institutions, including banks, insurance companies, unit trusts, investment trusts, building societies, independent brokers and other investment specialists. Most financial advertising is aimed at the general public, promoting consumer financial products such as life assurance, credit cards, mortgages and loans. Opportunities to invest via the Internet are increasing in number and variety, including online share trading systems and banking. At the business-to-business level, financial advertising includes notices of industrial and commercial loans, usually issued by the leading institution, and nearly always after the loan has been effected. These are usually inserted in the specialist business and financial press, and selected journals such as *The Economist*.

Financial Strategy Segments   *Campaign planning, Marketing research*

A classification system devised and marketed by the Experian information solutions company, a subsidiary of Great Universal Stores PLC.

Financial Strategy Segments (FSS) has been developed by combining two of Experian's established segmentation systems, **MOSAIC** and **Pixel**. *MOSAIC* is the UK's postcode-based consumer lifestyle classification system, used by companies in all industry sectors. It draws on a range of demographic, socio-economic and financial information to classify all local neighbourhoods (1.6 million unit postcodes) across the UK into one of 52 distinct lifestyle types.

Pixel is a high-resolution segmentation system, which assigns every adult in the UK to one of over 6,000 categories. It combines seven known pieces of information on every consumer (gender, age, length of residency, company directorships, shareholdings, property type, household composition) to arrive at a unique *Pixel* code.

By combining the *MOSAIC* and *Pixel* classification systems it is possible to assign every consumer in the UK to one of over 300,000 detailed segments. These reveal a wide range of information about the consumers, the households in which they live and key characteristics about the immediate neighbourhood.

By analysing the segments against a variety of data from Experian's internal lifestyle and financial databases, it is possible to quantify the propensity of consumers in every *MOSAIC/Pixel* segment in terms of their demographics, financial product holdings, financial behaviour and channel preferences. Responses to MORI's financial consumer tracking survey have been overlaid on the resulting classification to provide valuable additional information on the financial characteristics/behaviour patterns most commonly associated with the individuals in each segment.

The statistical technique known as clustering has been used to create clusters of consumers whose *MOSAIC/Pixel* codes display similar characteristics when analysed against the lifestyle and financial data. The cluster algorithm used to build FSS is proprietary to Experian, and based on over 25 years of research in the academic and commercial environment. The full range of FSS segments:

A	**MONEY WORTH MANAGING**	**Distribution of Adults**
A1	Aspirant Millionaires	0.6%
A2	Women with Wealth	1.0%
A3	Owner/Investors	1.3%
A4	Higher Rate Salariat	1.3%
B	**ASSET RICH FAMILIES**	
B5	Capital Gainers	1.0%
B6	Professional Heights	1.5%
B7	Wealth from the Land	3.2%
B8	Cusp of Retirement	2.2%
B9	Upscale Middle Agers	3.9%
B10	Ready for Retirement	6.5%
C	**GREY LIFESTYLES**	
C11	Equity Rich Elders	4.4%
C12	On Private Pensions	7.2%
C13	Greys Just Surviving	6.5%
C14	Subsisting Elders	3.2%
D	**WELFARE BORDERLINE**	
D15	Young Job-searchers	1.6%
D16	Transient Lifestyles	2.4%
D17	Lone Parents in Debt	1.0%
D18	Hardened Cash Payers	4.1%
D19	Cash Strapped Mums	4.3%
E	**SMALL TIME BORROWING**	
E20	Anxious Breadwinners	3.5%
E21	Aspiring Mid Market	6.7%
E22	Wives on a Budget	6.2%
E23	Prospering Flatmates	4.9%
F	**EQUITY ACCUMULATION**	
F24	Nest Forming Mothers	4.8%
F25	Juggling Home and Work	2.1%
F26	Women Flying High	2.4%
F27	Men Behaving Well	3.8%
F28	Urban Enterprise	3.1%
G	**PARENTAL DEPENDENCY**	
G29	Rich Kids at Home	1.4%
G30	Sons Still at Home	1.8%
G31	Girls Still at Home	2.1%

For more information: www.experian.com.

Fine grain *Photography, Reprographics*
Grain is the term applied to the tiny particles in photographic film emulsions. An image on film is composed of these particles. As with halftone screens, the smaller the particle size, the sharper the picture, the better and more effective the optical illusion. In conventional film photography, where the emulsion contains silver halides, the slower the film-speed the finer the grain. During chemical development, the process produces the latent photographic image by fixing the grain within the emulsion. With slow-speed film and correct development, the grain remains fine, and the image sharp. Incorrect development may cause the grain particles to bunch together, making them separately and annoyingly visible. Other types of emulsion, not containing silver, help to prevent this from happening.

Fine screen *Print*
Halftone screens finer than 120 lines per inch. Finer screen rulings, such as 200, 300 and above, are used for high quality colour reproduction in litho printing.

Finished artwork, finished art *Artwork, Print, Production, Studio work*
See Artwork.

Finished rough *Artwork, Creative, Print, Production*
See Visual.

Finishing *Packaging, Print, Production*
All stages in the production of print following the actual printing. These include collating, binding, cutting, creasing and scoring, folding, stitching, trimming, cutting and guillotining. The term could also extend to shrink-packaging, increasingly used instead of kraft paper or board packaging, and banding.

Firewall *Communications, Information technology, Internet*
A computer security measure for protection against hackers and others seeking to penetrate a company's server when connected to the Internet. It is designed to allow access only to certain users. A firewall can be sophisticated software, which checks the address of each user trying to access your server, and blocks unrecognized users. Or it can be hardware dedicated to preventing sensitive information from reaching a Web server.

Fisheye lens *Cinema, Photography, Video*
A camera lens with a wide angle of view, usually more than 60°. Distortion produced by such a lens is extreme, curving straight lines and exaggerating curved ones. This is best employed for special effects.

Fixed pitch *Desktop publishing, Typography, Word-processing*
A typeface with characters of equal width, and where the spaces between the characters are also of equal width. Internet browsers usually offer this facility.

Fixed spot *Media planning, Television advertising*

A television commercial transmitted during a particular programme break, at a pre-planned day and time. An additional charge is made by the contractor for this arrangement.

Fixing *Photography, Reprographics*

A darkroom technique for terminating, by chemical action, the development of a negative or print. A chemical solution – the fixer – removes unexposed silver halide particles, and renders the image stable and insensitive to further exposure to light.

Flag *Databases, Direct marketing, Mailing lists*

A marker applied to a specific entry in a database. Its function is to isolate the entry for when future selections are made. For example, if you are planning a mailing campaign aimed at red-headed accountants in Scotland aged 35–45, appropriate entries in your database would be flagged. You would then be able to mail these recipients only, with total accuracy and without waste.

Flagship brand *Marketing*

The most profitable, widely known or respected brand in a company's product portfolio. The company's good reputation for quality, reliability and service often rests on its flagship brand. It is therefore worth safeguarding, nurturing and developing.

Flash pack *Retailing*

A retail pack offered at a discounted price, on which the discount or reduction is printed as a highlight. There are two popular methods: featuring the price on a banner – a flash – in a corner on the front of the pack; or on a starburst or balloon in a convenient space, on in a space created for it.

Flat rate *Media planning and buying*

A single rate scheme for the purchase of press advertising space, radio or television airtime. Frequency, volume and other discounts are not taken into account.

Flexography *Print*

A relief printing process similar to letterpress, but using flexible rubber, neoprene or photo-polymer plates. It is in popular use for the printing of long-run newspapers and magazines. Popularly referred to as **flexo**.

Main characteristics

- Most modern flexography is rotary web-fed.
- It uses fast-drying, water-based inks.
- As with letterpress, the printing plates have a raised image. Ink is applied to the raised surface and transferred by pressure to the substrate – the paper, board or other material to be printed.

- Flexo plates are usually backed with thin metal sheet for strength and stability.
- Plates are exposed photographically and developed chemically.

Advantages of flexography

- High-speed web printing.
- A simple printing technique, economical for long runs.
- Compares favourably with photogravure on price and flexibility, especially in terms of shorter runs and special workings. However, photogravure may have the edge on quality.
- Can print difficult materials, eg cellophane, plastic film and metal foil.
- Can print curved surfaces.
- Prints four-colour process, or individual colours.
- Manual proofing is possible, though this is not cheap.
- Good quality can be achieved, using special mechanical techniques.

Disadvantages of flexography

- Print quality depends on the surface of the material being printed.
- Being flexible, the image carrier, the plate, can distort the printed image.
- Small type and fine-screen images may be difficult to print.
- Make-ready can be expensive; this is mitigated by the use of flexible, economical printing plates.

Optimum and economical uses of flexography

- newspapers;
- direct mail;
- packaging;
- long-run catalogues;
- books;
- wallpaper.

Flighting   *Advertising, Marketing communications*
The use of bursts of advertising, interspersed by periods of inactivity.

Flip-chart   *Presentations*
A large layout pad, fixed, clipped or ring-bound at the top. The presentation material is pre-mounted on the pages and flipped over during presentation. Flip-charts are popularly used during presentation of film and video storyboard material. They are also used as live material during lectures and other face-to-face presentations. They are often used in addition to, or instead of, white-boards and blackboards.

Floating *Press advertising*
A technique for allowing an advertisement of a fixed dimension to appear in publications with different column widths, without special adaptation. The advertisement is allowed to 'float' in a space, with white space round it.

Floating accent *Desktop publishing, Typesetting, Typography, Word-processing*
An accent sign that does not require its own separate space. It is already combined with a type character and prints with it as a single unit.

Fluff *Cinema and television commercials*
In the making of commercials, or any other production involving actors, a slip of the tongue in dialogue or commentary. This always results in a retake.

Flush left *Copywriting, Desktop publishing, Typography, Word-processing*
A technique for text alignment. Copy arranged in a straight vertical line on the left of a typescript or block of copy. The right-hand edge is unaligned and uneven.

Flush right *Copywriting, Desktop publishing, Typography, Word-processing*
In this case, the right-hand edge is vertically aligned, the left-hand edge uneven.

Flyer *Direct mail, Direct marketing*
A mailshot, usually comprising a single-sided or double-sided promotional leaflet. Flyers are also distributed by hand, door to door. They are sometimes also inserted in the pages of newspapers and magazines, and handed out at exhibitions and on street corners.

Flying paster *Pressroom techniques*
In web printing, an automatic pasting device, which splices a new paper web on to an expiring one, while the press is running. This is one of the more astonishing sights to be viewed in the pressroom. The paster mechanism operates quietly, smoothly and seamlessly while the press is running at top speed. Its efficiency ensures that the absolute minimum of copies is wasted. It is also very fast; blink, and you'll have missed it.

Flying splice *Pressroom techniques*
The term used to describe what happens when a new web is pasted on to an expiring one.

Fly posters *Outdoor advertising*
Posters placed illicitly on poster sites owned legitimately by advertisers or contractors; sometimes over existing, legitimate posters. They are also seen on unoccupied private property, including shop windows and doors. Often they advertise unlicensed local entertainments and leisure activities. By the time local authorities have been alerted to the problem, the advertised activity has come and gone, and so have the advertisers.

FM *Media planning, Print production*
Initials for **Facing matter**. An advertisement inserted facing editorial material in a newspaper or magazine. FM is stipulated in the space order, and usually costs more than **run-of-paper** insertions.

FM *Radio transmission standards*
Frequency modulation. A transmission technique, using the frequency range 88 to 108 mHz.

FMCG *Consumer marketing, Retailing*
Fast-moving consumer goods. A term applied to low-value domestic products purchased frequently by the general public; often over the counter, usually using cash. Such products are usually consumed immediately or soon after purchase. Brand loyalty to FMCG products is usually low, since the consumer has an extremely wide choice at the point of sale. If the product bought last time is not available, the consumer is likely to buy a competitive product of similar price and quality. Profound decision-making is not a factor here.

FM screening *Print, Production*
Frequency modulation screening. Also called **stochastic screening** and **random screening**. A form of halftone screening in which the distribution of dots is random. The effect is rather like the sand on sandpaper. The familiar rosette effect of conventional halftone screens is avoided.

Advocates of FM screening claim that printed results are sharper than with the conventional method. However, I have not found this to be the case; or rather, I haven't detected any difference on certain substrates. In one case the result was, if anything, slightly fuzzier than the same image printed on identical paper using a conventional halftone. However, FM screening techniques continue to improve. In the meantime, continue to exercise intellectual honesty in evaluating production techniques.
See Dot gain, Halftone.

Focal length *Photography, Pre-press, Reprographics*
The distance from the centre of a lens to the image of an object at infinity. At the same image size, the distance from copy to image is four times the focal length of the lens. A change in focal length affects both image size and depth of field (the area of sharpness round the point of true focus). As an example, a 135 mm telephoto lens gives a greater image size than does a 28 mm wide-angle lens. However, the depth of field of a lens at a given aperture and focusing distance is also affected by focal length. With a constant aperture and focusing distance, the shorter the focal length the greater the depth of field. What's more, the greater the focal length of a lens, the less its angle of view. As the focal length increases, so does the minimum focusing distance. These optical balances and compromises affect hand-held cameras – still, video and film – and the large repro cameras used in pre-press studios.
See f-stops.

Focal plane   *Photography, Reprographics*
The plane at which light entering a lens forms a sharp image. A **focal plane shutter** is a camera shutter system situated as close as possible to its focal plane.

Foil   *Advertising, Packaging, Print*
Thin metal film used for packaging perishable products. Also used for plastic film processed to look like metal. The outer surface of the film is suitable for printing. Sometimes also used for advertising pages in magazines, and foil blocking for printed literature.

Foil blocking   *Print, Production*
A technique for applying metal foil decoratively to paper and board, using adhesives, pressure and heat.

Folio   *Print, Publishing*
An historical term for a page number, still widely used in book publishing.

Following matter   *Media planning, Press advertising*
A media buying instruction to place an advertisement immediately following a piece of editorial. As with all such **preferred positions**, a premium is paid by the advertiser.

Font   *Desktop publishing, Typesetting, Typography, Word-processing*
The complete range of one size and visual weight of a typeface. This includes upper and lower case characters, small caps, accents and accented characters, punctuation, numerals, fractions and symbols. Also termed a **fount**. Both terms reflect the history of printing, much of which was carried out in churches or on church property. The real origin of font is probably French: *fonte*, from *fondre*, meaning found; or old French, *fondre*, meaning to use a foundry.
See Face, Typeface.

Foot   *Print*
The unprinted margin at the foot of a page.

Footage   *Cinema, Photography*
The running length of a piece of film, usually timed in seconds. Footage is frequently inserted into news reports, showing, for example, incidents and interviews shot at a previous time and place. 35 mm film runs at 24 frames a second. Be careful: television pictures are transmitted at 25 frames a second, which can get out of phase with the running speed of film footage. This can cause unwanted or bizarre effects, such as flicker or black bars moving up the screen. With film and video, the wheels of a moving car, at certain speeds, look as though they are revolving backwards. This is because they are out of phase with the frame speed.
See FPS, Frame.

Format *Art direction*

The size, shape and appearance of a designed page, and its subsequently printed version.

Format *Computing, Desktop publishing, Word-processing*

Instructions to a computer for determining the size, shape and appearance of material on screen. This affects what is subsequently reproduced.

Form letter *Business, Direct mail, Direct marketing*

A letter with a fixed text, including phrases, paragraphs and messages, aimed at a particular market or group of customers. The names and addresses of individual recipients are **matched in**, so that each appears to receive an individual letter. Some of the detail in the letter can also be changed, to suit individual recipients; the main elements of the letter, however, are standard. Also termed a **standard letter**.

Forty-eight sheet *Outdoor advertising, Print, Production*

A large poster, size 20 ft high × 10 ft wide, 6.1 m × 3 m.

Fount *Desktop publishing, Typesetting, Typography, Word-processing*

Also termed a **font**. The complete range of one size and visual weight of a type face. This includes upper and lower case characters, small caps, accents and accented characters, punctuation, numerals, fractions and symbols. Both names reflect the history of printing, much of which was carried out in churches or on church property. The real origin of font is probably French: *fonte*, from *fondre*, meaning found; or old French, *fondre*, to use a foundry.
See Face, Typeface.

Four-colour process *Print*

An economical colour printing system, using only four colours to represent virtually the whole visible colour spectrum. This means that, using only yellow, cyan, magenta and black, you can print virtually any colour range. The system is economical because the printing inks are standard throughout the industry, manufactured and sold in vast quantities.

Four-colour scan *Pre-press, Print*

A set of film positives, made from a full-colour transparency or photoprint by electronic scanning.

Four-colour set *Pre-press, Print*

A set of film and printing plates, one for each of the colours to be printed. In four-colour process printing, the colours used are **yellow, magenta, cyan** and **black**, usually designated **YMCK**. The letter K is used presumably to avoid confusion with blue.

Four Ps   *Marketing planning, Marketing theory*
In the **marketing mix**, a simple way of expressing the main factors influencing marketing decisions. They are **product, price, place** and **promotion**:

- product – the concept, design, character, action and viability of a product;
- price – pricing systems appropriate to the market for a product;
- place – channels of distribution for a product;
- promotion – advertising, sales promotion, public relations and other promotional tools.

In reality, there are many more elements bearing on marketing operations. The marketing mix is mainly about the combination and allocation of resources, intellectual, physical and financial effort, put into marketing planning and campaigns. The range of elements in the marketing mix depends on who you are talking to or reading on the subject. Some marketing academics, including Professor Neil Borden of the Harvard Business School, offer 12 elements in a marketing mix:

- advertising;
- after-sales service;
- branding;
- distribution channels;
- marketing research, fact-finding and analysis;
- packaging;
- personal selling;
- physical handling;
- pricing;
- product planning;
- promotion;
- retail display.

Four-sheet   *Outdoor advertising*
A poster size, 40 in wide × 60 in deep, 101.6 cm × 152.4 cm. This is equivalent to four double crown posters, each 20 in × 30 in, 50.8 cm × 76.2 cm.

FPS   *Cinema, Television, Video*
Frames per second. In the UK, television images are screened at 25 frames per second. The international standard for 35 mm film is 24 frames per second.
See Footage, Frame.

Frame   *Cinema, Photography, Television, Video*
Each individual picture in a length of film; an individual picture in a sequence, or the space it occupies. In filming, each picture is shot as an individual frame, at 24 frames a second. The sequence is projected on to a screen at 24 frames a second, giving the illusion of movement.

Film used for television in the UK is scanned at 25 frames a second, to match the transmission frame speed. This difference is virtually undetectable on screen. However, if you are running conventional film on television at 24 frames per second, this needs some adjustment, otherwise the frames appear to creep slowly up the screen, one after another.

One oddity of the FPS technique can be seen on screen, when the wheels of cars seem to revolve backwards while the car is moving forwards. This happens when the projection speed and the speed of the wheels are out of phase. In television transmissions and on video, while the wheels are revolving at under 25 revolutions per second, they appear to move in the same direction as the car. At exactly 25 rps, the wheels appear stationary. At more than 25 rps, the wheels appear to revolve backwards. Bizarre. No one has yet succeeded in curing this unwanted effect, though someone is probably working on it right now.

See FPS, Freeze-frame, Opticals, Shot, Still.

Freephone
Direct marketing, Direct response

A free telephone service used in British press, outdoor and broadcast advertising, and direct mail. This is a facility offered by BT (formerly British Telecom, the national telephone communications company) to advertisers to encourage consumers to respond or order by telephone. The customer's call is paid for by the advertiser. The customer dials 100, and asks for the advertiser's Freephone 'number'. This is not actually a number but a word, which can be the advertiser's company name, brand name or any word she chooses.

This response technique is certainly better than trying to get consumers to remember a telephone *number*, especially a long one. Today, telephone numbers can be 12 digits or longer. Can you mentally grasp such a number when sitting in your car listening to the radio, or when watching television? The Freephone *word*, however, when carefully selected, can be recalled hours later, when you are at the office or at home, and in a position to respond.

Mobile telephones make the response process much easier and faster. *Caveat*: do not use your mobile phone while driving; you could wind up in court, or on a marble slab.

At the time of preparing this edition, there is still some confusion about what the service is called. BT seems unsure about it. I telephoned them several times for a definitive answer to the question 'What is the difference between Freephone and the 0800 service?' The operators, the Business Customer Service and the Business Sales Department could not provide an answer. They all felt that the two services were the same, but were not certain. I was shunted from department to department for almost two hours, and still had no firm answer. *Moral*: check the facts and the service names before you promote a free-to-customer telephone response service in your advertisements.

Freepost
Direct marketing response technique

A free postal address service operated by the UK Post Office, used by advertisers to encourage consumers to respond or order by post (mail). The return postage is paid for by the advertiser. It is popularly used in press, outdoor and broadcast advertising and direct mail campaigns.

Freesheet *Newspaper and magazine publishing*
A newspaper distributed free of charge to households and offices. The cost of publishing and distribution is covered by advertising revenue. Most freesheets are heavy on advertising and light on editorial; sometimes in a ratio of 90:10. In London, an excellent free daily newspaper, *Metro*, is available at London Underground stations, Mondays to Fridays. Free magazines are handed out, usually on Mondays, at Underground stations in central London; the majority of advertising in this case is for staff recruitment.

Freeze-frame *Cinema and television commercials, Video*
Holding the same frame on screen, producing the effect of a still image. In filming, this is done by printing the same frame for as many seconds as required to hold the image, at the rate of 24 frames per second (fps). With television and video, the same frame is scanned for the required time at 25 fps. Freeze-frames are sometimes used at the end of a commercial to allow time for a change to another commercial, or to get back to programming.
See Shot.

Frequency *Publishing*
The number of times in a week, month, quarter or year, in which a publication appears.

Frequency discounts *Advertising, Distribution, Marketing, Media buying, Purchasing*
Discounts given by a supplier based on the frequency with which a product or service is purchased. This can be crudely expressed as 'The more often you buy, the less it costs'. Advertising media buyers expect discounts on frequency of insertion in the press, and on frequency of spots on television and radio.
See Quantity discounts.

Front matter *Print, Publishing*
Pages at the front of a printed document, containing the title, contents and introductory material.

f-stops *Photography, Reprographics*
Also termed **f numbers**. Fixed positions used for setting lens apertures, designated by the initial *f*. In hand-held cameras, the stops are usually 1.8, 2.8, 4, 5.6, 8, 11, 16 and 22. Oddly, the greater the f-stop number, the smaller the aperture. This is because each time the aperture decreases, the amount of light reaching the film is halved. Apertures are varied to control exposure and depth of field (the area of sharpness round the point of true focus). The initial 'f' is the symbol for the mathematical formula relating lens aperture to exposure.
See Focal length.

FTP *Communications, Information technology*
Initials for **file transfer protocol**. A technique for transferring files between computers via the Internet.

Fudge *Newspaper and magazine publishing*
A technique for introducing new or late editorial copy into a newspaper or magazine while the press is running. Sometimes called **stop press**, except that the press is not actually stopped, but is running at high speed. The equipment for doing this is called a **fudge box**.

Fulfilment *Direct marketing, Direct response*
The physical delivery of goods to a customer who has ordered them by telephone, fax, advertisement, coupon or the Internet. Many advertisers sub-contract this service to specialist companies.

Full out *Composition, Desktop publishing, Print, Production, Typesetting,*
Typography, Word-processing
An instruction to the DTP operator or compositor, to set the copy without indents, across the full measure of a column or page. It is also termed **fully justified** setting. The left and right edges of the typeset copy are straight and vertical. In the wrong hands, this technique sometimes involves a good deal of uneven word-spacing and much hyphenation. Sometimes, rivers of white within the text may stream down the page or column. Often the software used is to blame for these unpleasant and distracting effects, but the responsibility lies with the operator and typographer. *See* Justified, Measure, Ragged right, Range.

Full-plate *Photography*
Also termed whole-plate. A large negative or photoprint measuring 8 in × 6 in, 202 mm × 152 mm.

Full-service advertising agency *Advertising services*
Advertising agencies come in all sizes and capabilities. Some specialize in individual aspects of client service, such as creative or media. Others, usually the largest, offer a full range of services, including creative, graphic design, packaging design, media planning and buying, corporate communications, print, marketing, marketing research, public relations, media relations and sales promotion. Some full-service agencies have branches or associates in many of the world's commercial centres, and offer an international service. The main advantages here are integration of services and extensive local knowledge of markets, politics and legislation. Selecting an agency is an exacting and sometimes difficult procedure. There are, however, three main considerations:

- whether you need an agency;
- what you need from an agency;
- what a particular agency can give you to enable you to fulfil your organization's objectives.

Following through from the first consideration, you need to consider alternatives. For example, whether a number of specialist suppliers can give you the service you need. These include:

- artwork specialists;
- design services;
- freelance copywriters, art directors and designers;
- media specialists;
- photographers;
- pre-press houses;
- printers.

When considering this route, you need to bear in mind that everything needs to be organized and coordinated by a manager within your own organization. This means selecting the right person for the job; someone promoted sideways from the packing and dispatch department will not do. It needs an experienced specialist. This manager may need an assistant. You need to have office and communication facilities laid on, and a budget for running the department.

If this is unsuitable, or does not meet your short- and long-term requirements, an agency may be a viable alternative. In this case you need to test and verify its expertise and experience in at least its:

- ability to avoid conflict over competitive accounts;
- ability to handle your business;
- client experience, history and track record;
- communications capability, expertise and track record;
- creative ability and track record;
- full service capability and facilities;
- knowledge of media, local, national and international, especially the new media;
- management, and its compatibility with your organization;
- marketing, experience and track record;
- research competence and experience, including its specialist contacts and resources;
- specialist expertise and experience;
- staff, and its ability fully to meet your needs;
- terms of business.

In addition, you need to examine its track record in such detail as:

- campaign planning;
- client service, stability and retention;
- copy control;
- financial stability and history;
- international marketing, especially its overseas branches and associates;
- production control.

Furnish *Paper*

The mix of various materials blended into the stock or raw materials from which paper and board are made. The main constituents are wood or other pulps, sizing materials, fillers, dyes and various additives. The character of a paper, determined by its furnish, often influences its choice by a designer or print buyer for a print job.

See Acid-free.

FVO *Advertising, Cinema, Radio, Television, Video*

Abbreviation for **female voice-over**. This is the disembodied voice that speaks while the screen is showing live action, animation, stills or black.

See Voice-over.

FX *Cinema and television commercials, Video*

In a script, the abbreviation for picture-effects. Sound-effects are usually abbreviated to **SFX**.

Gg

Gable end *Outdoor advertising*
A poster site situated on the external end wall of a building such as a store or house.

Galley proofs *Desktop publishing, Print, Typography*
One form in which typeset copy is presented for proof-reading.
See Galleys.

Galleys *Desktop publishing, Print, Typography*
Popular short-form for galley proofs. Proofs of typeset copy before it is made up for printing. Usually set in columns or blocks of type. In letterpress printing, a galley is a metal tray in which columns of metal type are stored before making up into pages.

Gatefold *Paper, Print*
A technique for folding a printed leaflet so that it opens like a gate. A leaflet bound into a magazine, for example, can be folded so that it fits neatly into the magazine with no protruding edges. This enables the designer to use all pages of the leaflet, with its inside pages presented as a continuous double or triple page.

Gatekeeper *Business, Customer contact, Direct marketing,*
Marketing
An executive or secretary whose job is to intercept promotional material aimed at a more senior member of staff. The gatekeeper may shred it or drop it into a waste-paper basket, or otherwise dispose of it, instead of handing it to the boss. In the case of telephone calls, the contact terminates with the gatekeeper. An intelligent gatekeeper, of course, should be able to assess the value of a promotional contact, and decide whether or not to pass it on to the boss.

Gateway *E-marketing, Information technology,*
Web marketing
A means by which one Web site or computer can be accessed from another. It can be used by a Web site owner such as a company, to enable visitors to access product information on another site belonging to the company. The visitor needs no effort to do this, beyond clicking a button on the company's Web page, and transition is fast and accurate. A gateway can be used for more complex operations, such as sending information to a computer for collection.

Generation *Audio, Photography, Reprographics*
A term describing each succeeding stage in reproduction from an original copy. Thus, a print taken from an original negative is first generation. A photocopy taken from a first generation image is second generation; and so on. It is important to remember that with each succeeding generation some quality is lost. This does not happen with digital reproduction, because each 'copy' is actually an original. A similar deterioration problem also occurs in reproduction on audio and other magnetic tape applications.

Generic advertising *Marketing communications*
Collective or cooperative advertising by companies in the same product area. This is done by mutual agreement among the advertising parties, even though they may be in competition. Notable generic campaigns have been those for white fish, milk, butter, bacon and videos.

Generic product *Marketing*
An overall term indicating a particular type of product, rather than a particular brand. One of the oldest and best-known generics is aspirin. This is sold under many different brand names and labels, but the active ingredient in all of them is **aspirin**. Unbranded products are often cheaper than branded ones, and appeal to consumers seeking economies or bargains. The word cheap, of course, is not one to be associated with marketing.

Geo-demographic targeting *Marketing planning*
Marketing effort aimed at reaching specific target audiences using various demographic data and classification. These include the selection of targets by region, address, age, occupation, disposable income, lifestyle, credit card use, leisure activities and car ownership.
See ACORN, MOSAIC.

Geographical concentration *Marketing*
A geographical area used for the blitz marketing, advertising and selling of a product, or for the testing of marketing and promotional campaigns. Concentration makes good marketing sense where, for example, a product is under competitive attack in a particular region. Testing a product or market on a local or regional basis can offer strong clues on whether it will succeed when it goes fully national; a small expenditure to avoid a big mistake. Regional testing cannot, of course, totally eliminate marketing errors on a national scale. However, it is most effective when used as part of a comprehensive research programme.

GIF *Information technology*
Initials for **graphical interchange format**, a format for encoding high-resolution graphics. GIF files are widely used for pictures and icons on most Web documents. The most popular GIF versions restrict images to a total of 256 colours, but the technique also offers a worthwhile degree of compression, which allows fast transmission speeds.

Gift voucher *Marketing, Retailing*

A coupon offering worthwhile incentive to make another purchase. Vouchers may offer discounts, for example, and promotional incentives such as **buy one get one free**.

Give-away *Sales promotion*

A gift or premium, given free of charge to customers as an incentive to make further purchases. Usually a low-cost item, sometimes of practical value; often a sample of a product being promoted.

Global *Business, Marketing, Marketing research*

Commonly used to mean international. However, several other uses are popular. It can mean:

- across a product range;
- across an entire industry or profession;
- company-wide;
- throughout a document or report.

Gloss *Paper, Print*

The reflectivity of paper, or the printed image on it. Paper gloss is measured with a Gardner Glossmeter, which measures reflected light at an angle of 75°. The reflectivity is expressed in Gardner Gloss Units; the higher the number, the glossier the surface of the paper.

Glossies *Media, Publishing*

A generic term describing the range of up-market monthly magazines, such as *Country Life*, *Harpers* and *Vogue*. Although some glossies no longer print on glossy stock, the term persists.

Gondolas *Retailing*

In supermarkets, the banks of shelving units carrying products. The positioning of gondolas, and the aisle widths between them, are not a matter of random decision, or of the store manager's whim. They are determined by specialist store psychology. For example, high-priced items, such as wines and spirits, are given more space between gondolas, to encourage shoppers to spend more time and money there. Low-value items such as bread are sometimes given less aisle space; shoppers are made to feel less comfortable, and to hurry through, grabbing items as they go.

Graining *Plate-making, Print*

In lithography, subjecting the surface of a metal printing plate to the action of abrasives. The metal is non-porous, and cannot hold water or ink. Graining imparts greater water-retention and adhesion of coating to the surface of the plate.

Grammage *Paper terminology*
The system for expressing, in metric units, the weight of paper used for printing. The basic unit is grams per square metre. A particular weight of paper is said to be, for example, 80 grams per square metre, 80 gsm or 80 g/m². Its **grammage** is 80 g/m².

Grant projector *Art direction, Production, Studio equipment, Typography*
A large camera-like studio enlarger, used for reducing and enlarging illustrations. A more advanced version produces production-quality photoprints, termed **photo-mechanical transfers** (PMTs).

Graphics *Advertising, Art direction, Artwork, Design, Print, Television*
In print media, a term usually applied to the drawings used for illustrating text, including line drawings, graphs, histograms and charts, and everything else but type. Often also applied to pictures and halftones used in press and print. In television, it refers to anything on screen other than live action, including captions.

Graphics tablet *Artwork, Studio equipment*
Also known as a **digitizing tablet**. An electronic device for drawing or tracing images for input to a computer.

Gravure *Printing processes*
Five printing processes are today used in marketing communications. Each has its own production characteristics, advantages and disadvantages. One thing is common to all these processes: the transfer of images on to paper or other material.

- **Digital** prints electrostatically with toner fusion, or with liquid inks, without film or printing plates.
- **Flexography** uses thin, flexible, metal-backed neoprene plates with a raised printing surface (relief printing).
- **Gravure** uses engraved copper-plated cylinders (intaglio printing).
- **Litho** also termed **lithography** and **offset**. Prints from a flat printing surface using thin, flexible metal plates (planographic printing).
- **Screen** prints by forcing ink through a mesh (stencil printing).

Gravure, also termed **photogravure**, uses copper-plated cylinders engraved with myriad cells. During the print run, each cell, filled with a thinnish, volatile printing ink, prints a dot on the paper. Surplus ink is removed from the cylinder by a sprung metal blade, called a **doctor** (*qv*).

Unlike the other high-speed printing methods, litho, letterpress and flexography (*qv*), in gravure printing the entire image area is dot-screened. Type and line-work are screened, as well as halftones. In other words, the whole cylinder is a single, uninterrupted halftone.

Preparation of gravure cylinders
Several methods exist, including:

- Lasergravure – works direct from computer data. Uses a laser to engrave a special epoxy and plastic coating on the cylinder.
- Helio-Klischograph – artwork is scanned electronically; cylinders are engraved with diamond-tipped engraving heads, in a movement similar to that of a sewing machine needle.

Advantages of gravure

- High speeds. 2,000 ft a minute or more.
- Uses continuous webs.
- Can print up to 48 pages in one continuous operation.
- Can print eight colours in a single pass.
- Delivers high-quality colour, in a wide tonal range.
- Prints a wide variety of substrates, surfaces and materials.
- Cylinders are hard-wearing. They can be made more long-lasting by chromium plating.

Disadvantages of gravure

- Cylinders are very expensive.
- Machine proofing costs are exorbitant. Dry proofing or computer-aided proofing is cheaper.
- Once engraved, pages on a cylinder cannot be changed or modified; a new cylinder is required. Failing that, it may be possible to insert a specially prepared patch.

Optimum and economical uses of gravure

- long-run newspapers and magazines; mail-order catalogues;
- security printing, such as postage stamps and share certificates;
- packaging; wallpaper.

Greenwashing *Advertising, Public relations*
A current term describing marketing and corporate communication activity that exploits environmental issues.

Grey scale *Artwork, Photography, Print, Production, Reprographics*
A strip of standard grey tones ranging from white to black, placed beside original copy during photography, to measure tonal range and contrast.

Greyscale *Artwork, Information technology, Pre-press,*
Reprographics, Studio equipment
In computer graphics, each pixel on a greyscale monitor can display gradations
from white to black. This is important for the display of halftone black-and-white
images.

Grid *Art direction, Desktop publishing, Editorial design,*
Print, Typography
A guide used by designers, visualizers and typographers for layout work. The grid
consists of vertical and horizontal lines, usually printed faint blue, either on opaque
or translucent paper. The grid sets out the complete format of the page or spread.
This enables the designer to work accurately, and conform to the format of the
pages throughout the publication.

The grid includes the overall page size, the top, bottom and side margins; the
trim; the width of the columns; the spaces between the columns; and the areas
earmarked for illustrations.
See Gutter.

Grocery *Retail and wholesale business*
A term describing the grocery business, retail and wholesale. It also describes the
wide range of products sold in grocery outlets.

Gross circulation *Media marketing, Media planning, Press media*
The circulation of press media; that is, the sale of such publications, not their
readership. Gross circulation for a publication is calculated before duplication and
wastage are taken into account. Strictly speaking, you should not give a sales figure
for your publication and call it circulation, without first having it audited by an
independent third party such as ABC, the Audit Bureau of Circulations.
See Audit Bureau of Circulations.

Gross margin *Business*
The figure added to the cost of a product by its manufacturer, wholesaler, reseller
or retailer, in order to arrive at a selling price.

Gross opportunities to see *Broadcast media, Media planning, Press media*
A figure calculated to determine the total number of opportunities for viewers to
see a particular series of commercials, or readers to see a particular advertisement
or campaign.

Gross reach *Media planning, Press media*
A figure calculated to determine the total number of opportunities for readers to
see a particular advertisement. It can be calculated for a specific publication, or
across a whole schedule. The figure is arrived at by multiplying the number of
insertions by the readership of the publications on schedule.

Group discussions *Advertising research, Marketing research*

A popular research technique for evaluating marketing and advertising issues, and for testing advertising themes and copy. Groups are selected and assembled, and their discussions guided by a psychologist or trained professional briefed for the assignment. The proceedings are recorded, and analysed later by marketing teams and other specialists.

Group interviews *Advertising research*

A research technique for testing advertising copy and design, printed literature, radio and television commercials. Interviews are conducted by trained professionals, briefed to elicit opinions, suggestions, recall and other essentials about the material presented, or about the products they are promoting.

GSM *Paper, Print*

Grams per square metre. The unit of weight of paper stock. Also appears as **g/m²**. *See* Grammage.

Guarantee *Business, Retailing, Marketing*

An undertaking by a manufacturer, advertiser or promoter to indemnify the buyer against failure of the product. The guarantee must be specific: repair, replacement or refund, for example. Guarantees, and the responsibilities and liabilities of the guarantor, now have the support of legislation.

Gutter *Design, Print, Publishing*

The column of white space between two facing pages. This is the area that takes the stitching, stapling or other binding. *See* Grid.

Gutter crossing *Advertising, Art direction, Editorial, Press media, Publishing, Typesetting, Typography*

A headline extending across the centre gutters in magazine pages, bridging two facing pages. Although magazines are printed accurately enough, there may be inaccuracies in binding. This can result in two facing pages, together with two halves of a headline, becoming misaligned. This is because facing pages are printed on two separate sheets. Misalignment does not happen with a centre spread, which is printed on a single sheet. Care should be taken at the advertisement or editorial design stage to prevent this unwanted effect. In other words, the art director should be told that the insertion or feature will be on two facing pages; and his fee depends on his getting it right.

Hh

Hairline   *Artwork, Desktop publishing, Print, Production, Typesetting*
A very thin line laid down or drawn on artwork; equivalent to a very thin rule used
in typesetting. To quantify this: in desktop publishing, rules are designated line
styles; these range from ¼pt to 6pt, in quarter or half point steps. Hairlines are
much thinner than ¼pt; usually deemed the thinnest of lines and not included in
the range of line styles.

Halftone   *Artwork, Photography, Plate-making, Print, Production*
In technical terms, the representation of tonal gradation by an image composed of
dots of varying sizes, the centres of which are equidistant. Don't worry, it gets
much more interesting as you read on. To understand halftones, you must first
know something about photography.

Photographs, and their halftone counterparts, are produced in the following
sequence of techniques:

1. Light and image capture
    Most objects you see are made visible by reflected light. Light hits the object
    you are looking at and reflects the image to the eye. A camera captures the
    reflected image on film with a light-sensitive coating. When you release the
    shutter, an instant of light from the object is projected on to the film. This
    creates a latent image on the film, which needs 'development' with chemicals
    before it can be seen.
2. Negative image
    The film is processed chemically, producing a negative image of the object you
    have photographed. On negative film, the tones are reversed. Areas that will
    print white are black on the negative; black areas on the negative print white.
    The tonal areas between these extremes are called mid-tones.

    To make a photographic print, you must expose the negative on to another
    negative, usually of paper. You project the negative film image through an
    enlarger on to a sheet of photographic paper with a light-sensitive coating. In
    the marketing communications studio this is usually called a bromide (*qv*). The
    bromide is developed chemically; the image latent in the photographic coating
    then becomes visible.
3. Range of continuous tones
    The picture you have produced will have a wide range of tones, from black to
    white. The bromide shows all the tonal values of the object captured by the
    camera. In black-and-white photographs, the colours of the object will show

up as shades of grey. In colour photographs, the colours of the object will be more or less true to the original.

4. Contiguous tones

When correctly exposed and printed, the light areas (highlights), dark areas (shadows) and the mid-tones should give a balanced picture. This is called a continuous-tone print. The tones are contiguous – that is, they flow into each other, with no line showing where one tone ends and another begins. Obviously, it is impractical to print newspapers, magazines and brochures using continuous-tone prints. After a few copies had been run, the results would be muddy splodges on the paper, rather than clear, sharp images.

5. Halftone screens

The solution is to convert the continuous-tone image into dots. Each dot becomes a spot of ink on the printed page, and together they become a recognizable image of the original you started with. To create the dotted image, the bromide is re-photographed on to film, using a grid of fine, opaque lines. The grid – called a screen – breaks up the continuous tone into dots. Effectively, this gets rid of about half the continuous tones in the image, leaving the remaining half on the film. Hence the term halftone.

6. Optical illusion

The effect on your brain of a halftone screen is interesting. When your eyes scan the screened image on the page, your brain cannot separate them out. The dots are so small and so densely packed together that the eye and brain cannot resolve the dot pattern into its individual elements. The screen creates the optical illusion of a continuous-tone image, and the picture becomes recognizable. Dot screens vary widely in size, shape and density. There are other types of screen, such as line screens and random screens. But the result is the same: a recognizable image on the printed page.

7. Measuring halftone screens

Halftone screens are measured by the number of lines per centimetre. The more lines per centimetre, the finer the quality of the halftone printing. A 22-line screen has 484 dots per centimetre; an 80-line screen has 6,400. In the USA dot screens are given in lines per inch. If you are to achieve the best results the halftone screen must be matched to the paper stock, board, substrate or other surface to be printed. When printing on newsprint, or other coarse, absorbent paper, you should specify a coarse screen; for example 22 to 34 screen. Otherwise, the spaces between the dots will fill with a mixture of ink and tiny fragments of paper fibre, producing a muddy image.

With smoother paper surfaces you can employ finer screens, and get sharper images. Coated art paper is among the smoothest you can get, and the printed images can be spectacularly sharp and bright. Take a look at the latest Jaguar, Rover, Cadillac, BMW or Porsche brochures, and judge the quality for yourself.

Remember, the smoother the paper, the finer the screen you should use. As always, consult your photographer, art director, plate-maker, pre-press house and printer before spending your budget.

See Keyline, Paste-ups, Screen, Tint.

Hall research   *Marketing research*
A research technique for gathering public views on marketing issues such as advertising concepts and copy, new products and services, branding schemes, corporate images and political ideas. One popular technique works like this: members of the public are invited to an auditorium or hall, where they are entertained, shown a film or video. During the breaks, they are shown the marketing material being tested. Sometimes they are given product samples, to eat or take home. They are asked to fill in two questionnaires, one before being exposed to the issues in question, and one afterwards. The results are analysed by specialists, and appropriate advice offered to the clients paying for the research.

Handout   *Marketing, Sales promotion*
Sometimes termed a **flyer,** or flier. A promotional leaflet handed out in large numbers in public places, exhibitions, large stores and supermarkets. Such material is often cheaply produced, with quantity the name of the game. This is acceptable when promoting a bargain. However, part of the art of the successful handout is to make the product or service being promoted look reasonable in quality, appealing appropriately to the target audience.

Handshaking   *Electronic communication, Information technology*
The exchange of electronic signals between two computers or fax machines, before any data is transmitted. This ensures the establishment of recognition and compatibility at both ends of the communication.

Hard copy   *Desktop publishing, Internet communications,*
                                           Typesetting, Word-processing
The tangible version of a document or graphic created on computer. It is the permanent visual record of the computer's output. Hard copy output devices can produce paper copies, pen plots, transparencies, slides and prints. When produced on a printer, it is usually termed a **printout** (*qv*).

Hard copy   *Composition, Desktop publishing, Print, Production*
Advertising, editorial or other written material in typed form, sent to a typesetter for composition.

Hard news   *Editorial, Public relations, Publishing*
News that has been checked for accuracy and facts, and which can be substantiated by an independent third party. True hard news does not contain, and is not coloured by, the opinions and views of the reporter, editor and publisher. In public relations practice, the essential quality of hard news is not always recognized and honoured by the team producing the copy. It should be borne in mind that editors can smell from a great distance product promotions masquerading as news. Such material usually winds up on the spike or in the shredder.

Hard proof   *Desktop publishing, Print, Production, Word-processing*
A proof on paper, as distinct from a **soft proof**, the same image on a computer or word-processing screen.

Hard sell   *Advertising, Marketing, Sales promotion, Selling,*
Tele-sales
A sales technique relying on a mixture of aggression and manipulation. It is usually based on certain consumer benefits of the product being sold, sometimes backed up with strong hints of what might happen if the punter fails to take up the offer. When in print, hard sell needs to be backed by true product facts, benefits and features; otherwise the advertiser can fall foul of the Advertising Standards Authority (*qv*).

Hardware   *Computing, Information technology, Retailing,*
Wholesaling
The main electro-mechanical parts of a computing system; usually the computer itself and its peripherals. Monitor, printer, scanner, external disk drive, modem and so on, are the usual peripherals, but are nevertheless hardware. If you can drop it on your foot, it's definitely hardware.

Hardware   *Retailing, Wholesaling*
Products such as kitchen and cooking utensils, garden equipment, hand-tools, construction materials and cleaning products. These are retailed in hardware outlets, and the hardware departments of department and other large stores.
See Software.

Heading   *Media relations, News releases, Public relations*
The main title line at the head of a news release. The heading should tell the editor at a glance what the story is about. If it looks right for his publication and readers, he may read the whole story. If not, he will stop right there and bin or shred it. The heading should be informational and straightforward; do not be tempted to be clever or funny. Editors employ sub-editors to write headlines that entice readers into their stories. The sub-ed will probably do the same with your news release, so just stick to the central, most important fact of your story.

Headline   *Advertising, Promotional literature*
One of the principal attention-grabbing elements of an advertisement or brochure. Usually in large type, often in colour, it should convey the advertisement's most tempting benefit. Seen from the reader's point of view, it should express the most motivating sales-point. In an advertisement, it should be worded to encourage the reader to continue reading with rising interest. On the front page of a brochure, it should tempt the reader to turn the page and discover what other worthwhile benefits are waiting to be enjoyed. To learn how to write headlines, and the full implications of headline-writing technique, see *Creative Marketing Communications* (Kogan Page, 3rd edition, 2001).

Head-on site *Outdoor advertising*
A poster site positioned so that it faces approaching road traffic.

Heavies *Media, Publishing*
Another term for the quality press. In the UK, this includes the *Daily Telegraph*, *The Times*, the *Independent* and the *Observer*.

Heavy *Desktop publishing, Typesetting, Typography*
An alternative typographical term for **bold** (*qv*).

Heavy user *Marketing*
A consumer whose purchase of a product or service is considerably above the average for those in his market, eg when a quarter of a product's consumers buy more than three-quarters of what is on sale, they can be deemed heavy users.

Heavy viewing *Television*
The above-average viewing of television by individuals or groups. It is difficult to quantify this, but over 42 hours of viewing a week might be considered heavy. Radio listening is not in the same league; while television viewing demands a certain amount of concentration by viewers, radio is regarded as audible wallpaper. It is possible to do virtually anything else while listening to radio programmes: working, gardening, cooking, decorating or bathing the baby. Listening figures may be higher than those for viewing, but its use as a marketing tool is different.

Hickeys *Print*
Spots and imperfections in the printed output of offset litho presses. These are caused by dried ink skin, dirt on a plate, paper particles and other unwanted nasties. The term is of uncertain origin, but probably comes from the USA.

Hidden Persuaders, The *Advertising techniques, Marketing*
The title of a book of the mid-20th century by Vance Packard (Longman Green, London, 1957; updated edn, Penguin, London, 1991). One of its main hypotheses was that consumers could be persuaded by certain advertising techniques to do or buy almost anything. A technique used for this allegedly dishonest purpose was termed **subliminal advertising**. This comprised inserting a single frame conveying a promotional message into film used in cinema and television commercials. The individual message on the frame would not be discernible by the viewer's eye, but would nevertheless be conveyed to the brain. What's more, the viewer would be unaware that she had received a message. Thus, the subliminal message could be 'Buy Sudsy washing powder today', or 'Eat more white fish'. More subversively, subliminal techniques could be used for political messages; for example, 'Vote for H Dumpty', or 'Take an axe and kill your neighbour'. After years of debate and research, subliminal stimulation techniques were shown not to work. On the other hand, with today's technology, they just might. *Caveat*: before embarking on a project like this, consult the British Codes of Advertising and Sales Promotion, or your local regulatory codes and laws.

Hidden price increase *Marketing, Retailing*

Keeping the price of a product the same, while secretly lowering the quality or reducing the quantity. Many of the blue-ist of blue chip manufacturers and advertisers do this, without comment from consumers or legislators. For example, the weight of chocolate and other confectionery products in vending machines in public places has gone down over the last 20 years; the price has remained the same, or has increased.

Hierarchy of effects *Advertising, Marketing, Marketing planning*

A theory that a buyer's behaviour, following exposure to advertising, conforms to certain patterns. Various models of consumer behaviour were produced during the 20th century, and may well continue to be produced in the 21st. All are designed to guide advertisers and marketers towards the fulfilment of their commercial goals: consumer enquiry, trial, purchase, re-purchase, perpetual brand loyalty and profitability.

It might be prudent to point out that some of these models work in certain circumstances, and others do not. It is, as always, down to the business acumen and judgement of the marketing team planning the campaign. And, of course, that of the advertising account management and creative teams working at the sharp end.

Compare these models, all structured routes to advertiser and customer satisfaction, and decide which might work best for your next advertising campaign:

A	B	C	D	E	F
See	Attention	Attention	Exposure	Awareness	Unawareness
Read	Interest	Interest	Perception	Knowledge	Awareness
Believe	Desire	Desire	Integration	Liking	Comprehension
Remember	Action	Conviction	Action	Preference	Conviction
Act		Action		Conviction	Action
Sources:					
D Starch, 1923	E K Strong, 1925	Various	Sandage & Fryburger, 1935	Lavidge & Steiner, 1961	R H Colley, 1961 (DAGMAR)

Hierarchy of needs *Advertising, Marketing*

A technique used by marketers, which helps them to target the most profitable consumer groups. Basically, this comes down to what consumers need to possess, and to use, in order to survive and maintain their lifestyles. This is clearly not enough. For marketing viability, the hierarchy of needs must be closely coupled with the hierarchy of wants. These are different only in that they may also be luxuries. We are talking here about Western industrialized, well-developed communities, where money is the means of exchange, and people are entitled to make as much money as they can.

The concept of human needs structured into a hierarchy was developed by **A H Maslow**, in his theory of self-actualization. He divided human needs into five groups, arranged in a hierarchy of importance. Theoretical texts usually portray this as a pyramid, which shows the relationship between the groups of needs and their relative importance. From top to bottom, these are:

1. self-actualization;
2. esteem needs;
3. belonging needs;
4. safety needs;
5. physiological needs.

Crudely analysing this list, it seems that **self-actualization** is an inner desire to develop to the full one's human capability; it is therefore the only source of true human satisfaction. This seems also to suggest that the entire gamut of human needs works towards self-actualization.

Esteem needs include self-esteem and self-respect, success, achievement, prestige and status. **Belonging needs** embrace love, identification and affiliation. **Safety needs** include personal security, family stability and general order in the community. Finally, or rather at the bottom of the pyramid, **physiological needs**, including sex and the satisfaction of other instinctive urges; and the avoidance of hunger, thirst and other discomforts. These basic needs can be fulfilled through achievement, identification, stability and other elements in the hierarchy.

For decades, Maslow's model has served marketers well. It works for marketing planners who use the hierarchy at a number of levels at the same time. It gives advertisers strong clues about what messages to create, and which media to use for reaching their targets. A sweet, fizzy drink, for example, is not only capable of slaking your thirst, but also of making a statement about your lifestyle. A Ferrari parked outside your front door suggests that you not merely go down to the shops in it, but that you have substantial investments and know lots of rich and powerful people.

Hi-fi paper   *Paper-making, Print*
Machine-calendered newsprint; short for **high-finish paper**. This helps to impart a substantial smoothness to the paper, which is rough in its natural condition. Hi-fi newsprint can accept finer halftone screens than basic newsprint, and therefore produce sharper images and better reproduction.

High involvement products   *Marketing*
Products and services possessing qualities believed by their owners and users to confer status and high regard. These products are sometimes given a good deal of thought before purchase, or may be purchased on impulse. Switching to another brand of cigarette might give the potential buyer some trouble; for example, changing from Disque Bleu to B&H Gold, or vice versa. On the other hand, buying a Rolls-Royce, provided that you have the money, presents no problem and can be arranged in 10 minutes.

High key   *Photography, Reprographics*
A photographic technique, in which the contrast and brightness of a transparency or photoprint are adjusted so that the lightest tones predominate. A photoprint that contains mostly light tones is referred to as high key.

Highlight   *Artwork, Desktop publishing, Photography, Plate-making,*
Reprographics
The lightest tones of a photographic illustration or drawing. Extreme highlights can be achieved by eliminating tones altogether, letting the whiteness of the paper form the highlight.
See Halftone.

High pressure selling   *Sales technique*
A bullying or threatening attitude, usually accompanied by dogged persistence, often used by field sales and telephone sales staff, in order to urge customers to order products and services. This may sometimes be approved or sanctioned by sales management, especially when faced with the possibility of not achieving sales targets.

Hire purchase   *Sales*
A contract for the purchase of goods, where the purchaser pays in instalments, and does not own the goods until they have been paid for in full. In the UK, hire purchase offers and agreements are controlled by legislation.

Histogram   *Decision tools, Graphical representation, Graphics,*
Marketing planning, Marketing research, Spreadsheets
A graphical method of displaying research data. The figures are presented as horizontal or vertical bars, so that it is easy and quick to compare one set of data with another.
See Pie chart.

Hit   *Web site evaluation*
A record of each time a visit is made to a Web site, or to a page within a Web site. More accurately: a record of each time a file is requested from a server. This appears to be a basic unit of measurement, but many advertisers do take it seriously. This is because site owners, to boost the value of their sites, often quote hits on each page of a site; sometimes also each element or link on a page. Moreover, no standard time exists for the length of a visit to a site. Time-outs vary from 15 minutes to two hours.

Hoarding   *Outdoor advertising*
A large poster site, or group of posters, facing the road, usually parallel to the pavement. Also sometimes termed a **billboard**.

Hold *Commercials, Film, Video*

Another term for **freeze**: an instruction in a script to arrest movement on screen by successively printing from a single frame of a negative.

Hologram *Artwork, Creative, Display, Reprographics*

An illustration in the form of a flat image, giving an optical illusion of three dimensions. The effect is created with the use of lasers and special lighting. Some banknotes and credit cards carry small holograms to help avoid counterfeiting.

Home audits *Marketing research*

A technique employing panels of consumers keeping records of products purchased for home use. The records are usually in the form of diaries; the results are sent regularly by telephone to the research company. The findings can be related to retailing, and to advertising and other promotional effort.

In one type of home audit, householders are asked to keep the packaging of products bought. These are collected by the research organization, and the packs documented for brand, origin, retail outlet, price, frequency of purchase and other essential data. This technique is commonly termed **dustbin research** (*qv*).

Home page *Information technology, The Web*

The first or opening page of a Web site. This usually contains links to other pages on the site, and often some advertising material. When the site offers a range of products and services, menus of these items will be displayed on the home page. A browser, when entering a site, usually takes the user automatically to the site's home page. Most home pages are stored in a file named index.html.

Homogeneous products *Marketing*

Products competing in the same marketplace, which closely resemble each other in terms of design, quality, working life, reliability, warranty and after-sales service. In such cases, consumers may shop around for the best bargains; price may be the decisive factor in making a purchase.

Horizontal circulation *Media*

The circulation and readership of a publication aimed at subscribers across a range of businesses or industries. For example, the *Financial Times, Business Week* and *Forbes* are read by management executives and directors in a variety of industries. The other type of circulation is **vertical**. In this context, subscribers and readers work at all levels in specific businesses. For example, *Marketing Business*, read mostly by individuals in the marketing business; *The Accountant*, read predominantly by accountants.

Horizontal diversification *Marketing planning*

The planned expansion of a product portfolio, even though each product does not complement any of the others in the mix. Thus cameras, plus mobile telephones, plus picnic hampers, plus raincoats do not seem to be connected, but they are a way of hedging a manufacturer's bets for possible hard times. Certain Far Eastern manufacturers, for example, produce television sets and cars under the same brand name; motor bikes and electronic organs; photocopiers and video cameras. The main advantage is that an excellent brand image or track record in one product area or market carries over into the others.

Horizontal integration   *Marketing planning*
The opposite of horizontal diversification. In this case, products and services are grouped together at every level, both for pure sales and marketing purposes and for promoting the corporate brand. Integration can take place in a number of ways. In manufacturing, for example, standard components may be used in a variety of different items of equipment. It is used as a unifying badge both for similar and for different products under the same brand.

Horizontal marketing   *Business, Marketing*
Collaboration among companies working the same markets. In setting up a combined manufacturing, marketing and sales operation, they can bring more power to the market, offer better prices and better service than either of the individual companies working alone. The term may also apply to individual companies within the same organization, seeking savings, economies of scale, and other mutual benefits achieved from collaboration.

Host   *Information technology*
A computer system used for processing data, such as those on a database provided by an information supplier. Host computers are part of communications networks, over which they transmit messages.

Hot shop   *Advertising agencies and consultancies*
An advertising service business specializing in creative work. The service sometimes extends to pre-press and other production activity, though this may be sub-contracted to specialists.

House account   *Marketing, advertising and PR agencies*
A term applied to the largest or most important account whose business is serviced by an agency. A house account often provides the mainstay of an agency's business in terms of revenue earned from it. On the other hand, the term can apply to a smaller account of high prestige, such as a member of a Royal Family, foreign embassy or entertainment celebrity.

Household   *Marketing research*
For marketing purposes, a domestic establishment, usually residential, though not specific as to type of accommodation. It can be a house, bungalow, cottage, flat, apartment, penthouse, caravan, boat or any other type of living unit. The important feature of a household for marketing research purposes is its residents, taken as a single unit. This can be one person living alone, a whole family including grandparents, or configurations in between.

Household name *Marketing*

A well-known popular brand or product, with high profile, and with national or international reputation. Household names usually considered at the top of the list include Coca-Cola, the BBC, Marks & Spencer, Pizza Hut, Cadbury's Chocolate, Budweiser and Chanel.

House journal *Public relations*

A magazine or periodical published by a company, for circulation to its own mailing list. Where a company has a number of target publics, which is usually the case, different versions of the house journal may be produced. These are usually of two kinds, internal and external. Target internal publics include a company's workforce, management and shareholders. Externals include customers, suppliers, well-wishers, politicians and the government, and members of the public. Each target public, and therefore the journals aimed at it, usually requires different content and editorial treatment. Many organizations do not recognize the need for this diversity, and believe that one message is suitable for all their publics.

House mailing *Direct mail, Direct marketing, Public relations*

The posting of material to a company's own mailing list.

House style *Artwork, Creative, Desktop publishing, Print, Publishing, Typography, Word-processing*

A specific, distinctive, identifying style, used by a company in its advertisements, promotions, Web site, packaging, brochures, sales and technical literature and other publications. The style is inherent in such elements as logo, house colours, layout, typeface and typographical design. House style is usually incorporated in a company's stationery, livery, the design of its retail outlets, showrooms and exhibition stands, and staff uniforms.

House to house *Direct marketing, Distribution, Marketing research, Sales promotion*

Selling to, or distributing product samples to households by physically calling on them. Also, calling on households for the purposes of research interviews, and for collecting research data of various kinds. Samples and promotional material, of course, can be dropped through letterboxes. In the UK, the Post Office is often given this job. In this case, houses or householders are not addressed individually; postcodes (zip codes) are used as the mailing database.
See ACORN.

HTML *Communications, Information technology*

Initials for **Hypertext Mark-up Language**. This is the coding language employed in the creation of hypertext documents used on the Web. HTML defines the typeface and style to be used when displaying text, and allows hypertext links to other parts of a document, or to other documents. It is also used for the creation of documents for the Web, which is the graphical part of the Internet. It usually takes browser software to interpret HTML.

Hue *Design, Photography, Print, Reprographics*
The main attribute of a colour that makes it what it is, and distinguishes it from other colours.

Hype *Marketing, Public relations*
A vulgarism, denoting over-the-top publicity for an individual, product, activity or event. Public relations is usually blamed for this kind of exaggeration. In point of fact, it is a carefully planned, carefully controlled, professional activity, designed to bring an event to public attention. It is not unlike public relations effort, but much more highly focused and concentrated. Hype usually lasts only for a short period, while public relations is long term and sustained. The word probably comes from hyper-activity; or from hyperbole, a rhetorical term meaning an exaggerated statement not to be taken literally.

Hypermarket *Retailing*
A very large supermarket of 3,000 square metres or more. Because of its size, it is usually sited out of town or on town fringes. There is always a large car park, since access is usually only via a busy main road, motorway, turnpike or freeway.

Ii

Icon *Computing, Desktop publishing, Information technology,*
Word-processing
A thumbnail graphic image or symbol on a computer screen. Each symbol
represents an **application** (*qv*), a file or a document or a file already in the system.
The icon is used to access it.

IFC *Design, Desktop publishing, Layout, Print, Publishing*
Initials for **inside front cover**. *Caveat*: it is unwise to use initials when issuing
instructions to a printer, production house or publisher. They can easily be
mistaken for something you do not intend. IFC could easily stand for In Front of
Copy, which is not only misleading but unintelligible.

Illustration *Advertising, Artwork, Creative, Design,*
Desktop publishing, Print
Any drawing, painting, photograph, or other graphic used in artwork or print. It is
sometimes used to distinguish a drawn image from a photographic one.

Illustrator *Design, Desktop publishing, Information technology*
A popular, proprietary software package dedicated to the design and creation of
digital artwork.

Image *Advertising, Branding, Corporate identity, Marketing*
communications, Public relations
Image refers to the way brands, products, corporations and individuals are seen,
recognized, understood and appreciated. Although there is general agreement on
the concept of image in marketing communications, it tends to break down in
detailed explanation.

The concept of image is closely linked to identity. Image is concerned with how
a brand, product or company is perceived by its markets and target audiences.
Identity is concerned with the way a product or organization identifies and projects
itself. In building its image, an organization strives to create mental pictures of
itself, its brands or products, and place them in the minds of its targets. It can do
this in several ways. First, by persistent advertising and public relations effort,
using the same theme over a long period. Second, by developing a reputation for
whatever it does best; for example high quality, excellent design, outstanding
after-sales service, good value, friendly staff. Sooner or later, its image becomes a

shorthand by which a company, its products and other attributes are quickly and easily identified. This is a marketable commodity, and can be treated as part of a company's goodwill. Of course, given the wrong treatment, messages and promotion, image can also work in the opposite way, and damage a company and its products. When this happens, it may take years to restore, if ever.

Image editor   *Artwork, Desktop publishing, Information technology, Print*
A software program dedicated to editing, changing or over-painting parts of a digital image. It has the capability, for example, for removing blemishes from a scanned photographic image.

Imagesetter   *Desktop publishing, Print, Production*
Pre-press equipment that converts computer-generated data into physical output, such as halftone colour separation film. Most imagesetters are compatible with PostScript.
See PostScript.

Imitation art   *Paper, Print*
Paper loaded with china clay, and given a high finish so that it resembles true art paper. True art has a china clay coating applied to a conventional base.

Impact   *Advertising, Marketing communications, Public relations*
The effect a marketing communication has on its recipients. It is measured in different ways, and depends entirely on the brief to which the communication was created. It is reasonable to expect an advertising campaign to produce enquiries, sales leads and sales; and for a public relations campaign to change attitudes in target publics. In both cases the impact, its extent and value, can be determined by research.

Imposition   *Artwork, Desktop publishing, Print, Production*
The correct arrangement of multiple pages of artwork, film and printing plates. This must ensure that all pages will appear in the correct order when the printed sheets are folded and trimmed.

Impression   *Media planning and buying*
A single exposure to an advertisement or broadcast commercial. This is one of the factors determining the value of a campaign to the advertiser paying for it.

Impression cylinder   *Print*
The cylinder on a press against which the paper picks up the impressions of type and illustrations. On a litho press, the impression is transferred to the paper from a plate or offset blanket. On a direct print press, such as letterpress and flexography, from an inked plate.

Impulse products   *Marketing, Retailing*
Products bought on the spur of the moment or after a minimum of consideration. Such products are usually fairly low-value items, where price is the main consideration in the quick decision to buy. In many UK supermarkets, sweets were positioned next to check-outs, so that customers and their children could grab them while waiting to pay. This practice has now been abandoned.

Impulse purchase   *Consumer behaviour, Marketing, Retailing*
A purchase made on the spur of the moment. This kind of buying behaviour is normally unpredictable in individuals, but may be predicted when considered as part of mass consumer purchasing patterns. The income and social grade of a purchaser, as well as his mind-set, may influence his buying habits. Impulse purchasing is usually outside a consumer's usual purchasing behaviour pattern.

Incentive   *Advertising, Marketing, Marketing communications,*
Sales, Sales promotion
A gift or service offered by an advertiser, to encourage customers to carry out a particular task. An incentive is an inducement to buy more of the same product, or to try or buy another product in the range. Among the tools and techniques used in incentive marketing are competitions, free prize draws, coupons, trading stamps, premium offers and local tactical pricing. Another main application is in offering incentives for getting retailers, resellers and wholesalers to sell more products. In the best example I know, the salespeople had a choice of holidays, furs and jewellery. The sales director got a car. In this case, the product area was international financial investment.

Income   *Economics, Marketing planning*
Payments made to individuals and companies in exchange for work, goods and services. Payment, weekly, monthly, quarterly or some other period, can be made in cash or kind. For marketers, the important aspect of consumer income is usually termed disposable income. This is what is left when a consumer's regular and obligatory expenses have been paid: income tax, national insurance, mortgage, travel, local taxes, rates, community charge and so on. What remains is the arena for intense competition by every company with something to offer.

Incorporated Society of British Advertisers, The   *Representative*
organizations
Founded in 1900, the ISBA is the organization in the UK dedicated entirely to caring for the needs of advertisers. It represents its members on all aspects of advertising, and defends their interests vis-à-vis government, the media, advertising agencies, key opinion-formers and the general public. Any advertiser can belong to the ISBA, with the exception of advertising agencies and media owners. *See* BARB, IPA, ITC, ITVA.

Indent   *Copywriting, Desktop publishing, Typesetting, Typography,*
Word-processing

Starting a paragraph or line of text with a blank space of one or more characters. Experience suggests that three or four characters are enough blank space for an indent. Any less would not show up well; any more would look eccentric, and possibly render the copy more difficult to read.

The whole point of using indents is to guide the eye easily and smoothly from the end of one paragraph into the next. In advertising copy, which consumers generally don't really want to read, you have to seduce them into doing so.

Making copy easy to read and understand helps readers to get to the point where you encourage, urge and seduce them into taking action. Art directors and typographers should ponder this well. Advertising is not an art form – it is an essential tool of marketing. And marketing pays their salaries.

Independent local radio   *Broadcasting, Marketing*

The generic term for local commercial radio stations and networks in the UK. As with all radio stations in the country, they are licensed by the Radio Authority (*qv*). It is usually abbreviated to **ILR**.

Independent retailer   *Retailing*

A retail outlet, store or shop owned and run by a sole trader, an independent individual, a family or a company. Also termed **single outlet retailer**. A multiple retailer with fewer than 10 branches falls into the same category, and is termed **small multiple retailer**.

Independent Television Commission, The   *Broadcasting, Controls,*
Television

A government statutory body controlling the activities, standards and conduct of television broadcasting in the UK.
See BARB, IPA, ISBA, ITVA.

Index   *Research, Statistics*

A technique for referencing statistical data, so that it provides a basis for comparison with other data. The cost-of-living index provides a good example. If the reference year for the index was, say, 2000, it would be given a reference index of 100. Any rise in the cost of living in subsequent years would be a figure higher than 100; a fall would be a figure below it. This allows direct comparisons to be made between years.

Indirect cost   *Manufacturing, Marketing*

In manufacturing, any cost not actually incurred in the production of a product; quality control, for example. In marketing, this refers to any cost not incurred in getting a product to market; warranties, after-sales service, customer relationship management, for example.

Industrial advertising   *Advertising, Sales promotion*

Also termed **business-to-business advertising** (*qv*). Advertising aimed at industrial buyers and users, and not at consumers or the general public. Formerly called **trade-and-technical** advertising; in some places and cases, it still is.

Industrial marketing   *Marketing*

The marketing of industrial products and services to industrial buyers, users and manufacturers. As with consumer marketing, when planning an industrial marketing operation, your marketing team needs to take into account who is buying and using the products and services being offered. And also what you are *marketing* vis-à-vis what the customer is *buying*. They are not the same.

In promoting products and services to industrial companies, one of the marketer's principal skills lies in targeting the right executives and getting appropriate messages to them. Extensive knowledge of targeted companies is therefore vital.

Company buying processes involve a number of key executives, some of them at high level. A company purchasing decision-making stack can look like this:

- managing director;
- finance director;
- production director;
- human resources director;
- marketing director;
- sales director;
- company secretary;
- company legal adviser;
- administration director;
- purchasing manager;
- financial administration manager;
- IT manager;
- production manager;
- sales manager;
- distribution manager;
- personnel manager;
- training manager.

A managing director's corporate task is to run the company, smoothly and profitably, and deliver the highest possible dividend to shareholders. At the other end of the scale, a personnel manager's job is to recruit and retain the best employees, train them, so serving the interests of the company. Although these jobs are different, consultation may take place at all levels. It is prudent, therefore, to build into marketing communications appropriate arguments, messages and motivations for each of the directors, managers and executives involved in consultations for decision-making. This is the essence of successful communication in industrial marketing.

Industrial products *Manufacturing, Marketing*

Products manufactured, distributed and promoted to industrial buyers, users and manufacturers, and not to the general public. There are four main types of industrial product:

- capital equipment;
- consumable supplies;
- manufactured goods;
- raw materials.

Inertia selling *Direct marketing, Marketing*

A sales technique adopted by some suppliers in order to sell more products without promotional or sales effort. Goods are delivered to past or prospective customers, without their order, consent or prior knowledge. The supplier's intention, naturally, is for the recipient to pay for the goods. However, in the UK the recipient is not obliged to pay for or keep unsolicited goods, or to return them, since there is no contract with the supplier. If the recipient decides not to return the goods, they must be kept in good condition in case the supplier decides to collect them. If the recipient decided to dispose of or destroy the goods, due notice must be given to the supplier. Some recipients will think they are actually obliged to pay for the goods, and thereafter become the owners whether they want to or not. For this reason the whole idea of inertia selling is sneaky, and largely disapproved of by the marketing community.

Inferior goods *Economics, Marketing*

Products that sell well to a particular target consumer group, and which suffer a fall in demand when the income and lifestyle of that group improves. It might be thought that with a better lifestyle of the group, demand for the product would rise. Experience shows that this is not always the case. As the lives, circumstances and status of consumers get better, their expectations rise; they demand better products and services. This often means more expensive products, better product support, customer care and after-sales service. Demand for the inferior product goes down. A consumer may exchange a motorbike for a car; a family car for an executive car. Instead of a local annual holiday, she and her husband may opt for a foreign holiday or two.

Infinity *Photography, Reprographics*

The distance from a lens at which focal adjustment for sharp images becomes unnecessary. On some lenses, this is no more than 9 m, 30 ft. Beyond this point, with the lens set at its basic focal length, all parts of the view will be in focus.

Inflation *Economics, Marketing planning*

A situation in a national economy, which leads to a rise in prices and a fall in the purchasing value of money. An increase in workers' salaries and wages over time always causes prices to rise. Manufacturers and suppliers always seek to recover their profit margins from their customers. The inflationary effect is continuous and long term.

In-flight magazine   *Advertising, Marketing, Marketing communications,*
Publishing
A magazine published for airlines and distributed to passengers on board their aircraft. The current trend is for a substantial amount of full-colour advertising for high-priced products, supplemented by a small amount of richly embroidered editorial.

Influencer   *Campaign planning, Marketing planning,*
Marketing research
An individual or organization capable of, or actively engaged in, influencing decisions on the purchase of products and services. In domestic life, influencers include:

- children;
- parents;
- partners;
- spouses.

In business activity, influencers include:

- buyers;
- decision-makers;
- end users;
- gatekeepers;
- identifiers;
- senior managers;
- specifiers.

Gatekeepers are, of course, those formidable individuals employed to shield senior executives and managers from being bothered by salesmen. This is a pity, since one can often learn more about market conditions, and competitors, from other company's salespeople than from one's own staff.

.info   *E-commerce, Internet activity*
An Internet domain name, open to anyone including business, non-commercial users and government.

Informant   *Marketing research*
An individual selected by market researchers as an appropriate subject for research questioning. Having answered a questionnaire, an informant becomes a **respondent**.

Information *Business, Marketing, Marketing communications,*
Research
An item of knowledge or news. Increasingly abbreviated to **info**, it has spawned a wide range of blends and compounds mostly related to business and computer activity. Popular examples include:

- **Infomania.** A morbid obsession with information, and an uncontrolled desire to amass facts for their own sake.
- **Infomercial.** The broadcast equivalent of a press advertorial. A television or radio commercial in the form of a pseudo documentary, presenting information either instead of persuasion or in massive support of it.
- **Infopreneur.** An entrepreneur in the information technology business; sometimes, not always accurately, termed a **dot.com entrepreneur**.
- **Infotainment.** Television or cinema entertainment in the form of facts and figures, presented in a dynamic, entertaining and easily understood way.

Informational advertising *Advertising, Marketing communications*
Advertising that concentrates on giving or displaying facts about a product or service. The facts and features themselves are used as persuasion. The amount of contrived persuasion is kept to a minimum, or avoided altogether.

Information technology *Business, Marketing*
Often abbreviated to **infotech**. Information, usually generated, stored in, processed and manipulated by computers, related to knowledge about people and their activities. Such information is held in computer folders, files and documents. These are capable of being transferred or networked to other computers, telephones and a variety of other equipment. Marketing, especially that aspect of it using databases, makes wide-ranging and continuing use of infotech.

In-house activity *Advertising, Marketing, Public relations*
A company's marketing activity and communications planned and produced within the company, instead of using outside suppliers such as agencies and consultancies.

Ink fountain *Print*
The device that stores and dispenses ink to the inking rollers on a press. On litho presses there is also a water fountain.

Ink-jet printer *Computing, Desktop publishing, Word-processing*
A printer with a printing head that does not make contact with the substrate. Instead, it squirts tiny droplets of ink on to the substrate to form the image. The dot density of some inexpensive printers is 300 dpi (dots per inch). Better quality printers deliver a density of 600 dpi or higher, which increases the quality of the printed image.

Innovation *Business, Marketing*
Conception, creation and development of new products and services in competitive markets. It is widely agreed that no product is immortal, no market remains unchanged forever. Innovation has to be part of every organization's development, lest it fall behind or risk total failure. This is why products and services are relaunched from time to time. The need for innovation reaches into research, production, promotion, sales, distribution, retailing and wholesaling systems.

In-pack give-aways *Sales promotion*
A free item of low-cost merchandise, such as a toy or a household gadget, placed in a product pack. Such premiums are used as an inducement to consumers, in an effort to keep them buying the product. Sometimes give-aways are collectable in planned series, which offers the advertiser a degree of brand loyalty.

In pro *Artwork, Desktop publishing, Print, Production, Typography*
An abbreviated version of **in proportion**. When photoprints or line drawings are used as illustrations, enlargements and reductions are two-dimensional. In specifying the enlargement or reduction of one of a group of illustrations, to fit a layout for example, you may want the others in the same degree of enlargement or reduction. You therefore specify that the others be enlarged or reduced in proportion to it: and therefore **in pro**.

Inquiry *Advertising, Marketing communications, Public relations*
A request from a potential customer for information, product literature or a sales call. Inquiries can be generated by advertising – press, broadcast, outdoor, direct mail – or public relations activity. According to the profitability of a product or service, and the amount of attention that justifies it, the prospective customer is sent the most cost-effective follow-up item. This can vary from a leaflet or brochure, to a demonstration video or salesperson.

INR *Commercial broadcasting*
Initials for **independent national radio** in the UK. The first commercial operating licences were awarded by the Radio Authority in 1992, to Virgin Radio and Classic FM.

Insert *Film, Television commercials, Video*
A short, explanatory scene inserted into a piece of action. A pack shot, for example, a swift demonstration of a sales point, a passing car, or a clock.

Inserts *Advertising, Print, Production, Publishing*
Leaflets, catalogues or printed cards inserted into a publication, either loose, glued or bound. Insertion takes place after the publication itself has been printed and is on its way to be bound. Often when a catalogue insert is bound into a publication it is stapled in such a way as to make it easy to detach without interfering with the rest of the publication.

Institute of Practitioners in Advertising, The   *Representative organizations*
The organization representing the interests of UK advertising agencies. It helps its members through the minefield of legislation affecting agency business and activities. Since the volume of legislation emerging from the EU is growing at a frightening rate, the IPA's specialist advice is becoming more and more valuable.

Among the activities and services offered to its members, the IPA's specialist departments guide and advise members on problems relating to government action. It helps them negotiate with their clients and the media, and advises on marketing research and other specialized activities.

The IPA has close connections with similar organizations throughout the world, and is therefore able to help its members on international advertising matters.
See BARB, Chartered Institute of Marketing, ISBA, ITC, ITVA.

Institute of Sales Promotion, The   *Representative organizations*
The organization representing the interests of companies in the sales promotion business.

Institutional advertising   *Advertising*
Advertising undertaken by industrial groups or associations, such as the White Fish Authority or the Meat Trades Federation. It is usually designed to promote awareness of an organized group or industry, and often its generic products as well, rather than an individual company.

In-store demonstration   *Retailing*
A live demonstration of food, appliances, gadgets and so on, carried out in a store.
See In-store promotion.

In-store promotion   *Retailing*
A promotion carried out in a retail outlet. This can take several forms:

- a mini exhibition promoting a product on sale nearby or on the stand itself;
- a live demonstration of a product or a food;
- a static demonstration; for example a video programmed to loop endlessly until changed or switched off;
- an interactive video demonstration, programmed so that shoppers can input their individual requirements into the system and receive appropriate information in return.

In-store promotion is often part of a wider marketing promotional effort, including press and broadcast advertising, direct mail, local leaflet and money-off coupon distribution.

Intaglio   *Print, Printing processes*
Printing from a recessed image. The image is engraved into the printing surface. Gravure, which uses a cylinder to hold the image to be printed, is the only intaglio printing process in widespread commercial use today.
See Gravure, Photogravure.

Integrated marketing communications   *Marketing communications,*
                                                  Marketing practice, Marketing theory

The fundamental definition of integration in marketing communications is: 'A company's total marketing communications programme, complete with its planning, research, tools, techniques, media and messages, acting in concert'.

While it would be ignoble to denigrate the narrow implications of this accurate but simplistic approach, real-life marketing reveals many side-routes down which such a programme can drive. This is especially the case where an organization's communications have international reach and incorporate the World Wide Web as a marketing tool.

In 1993, *Marketing News* reprinted a working definition developed by members of the marketing communications faculty of the Medill School at Northwestern University. Under the title 'Marketing Communications: Maybe Definition Is in the Point of View', Don E Schultz offered the following:

> Integrated marketing communications (IMC) is the process of developing and implementing various forms of persuasive communications programs with customers and prospects over time. The goal of IMC is to influence or directly affect the behavior of the selected communications audience. IMC considers all sources of brand or company contacts which a customer or prospect has with the product or service as potential delivery channels for future messages. Further, IMC makes use of all forms of communication which are relevant to the customer and prospects, and to which they might be receptive. In sum, the IMC process starts with the customer or prospect and then works back to determine and define the forms and methods though which persuasive communication programs should be developed.

Even this definition may not go far enough. In its management form, integrated marketing communications is the practice of coordinating the various communications elements, media and messages, setting objectives, establishing budgets, designing specific communications programmes to achieve specific marketing objectives, evaluating and acting on the results; and taking remedial action when results do not meet stated goals.

Intensive distribution   *Retailing, Wholesaling*

A company's policy for selling a range of its products intensively through as many retailers and wholesalers as possible. This is how toys come to be sold in pharmacy outlets, for example, and computer software in bookshops.

Intensive selling   *Advertising, Sales activity, Sales promotion*

Coordinated sales and promotional effort aimed at getting new potential customers to try a product, existing customers to buy more, or users of competitive products to switch brands. Intensive selling is usually done over a limited period, or over a limited geographical area, or both at the same time.

Interface   *Business*

Executive collaboration between organizations or departments that have a potential or actual common interest.

Interface   *Computer hardware, Information technology*
In computing, a physical or software link between two different pieces of computer hardware or electronic channels of communication.

Interline spacing   *Desktop publishing, Typography, Word-processing*
A term, used in many word-processing packages, for the horizontal spacing between lines of text. In printing, it is called **leading** (*qv*), pronounced 'ledding'. In the days of hand composition and hot-metal typesetting, increasing the space between lines was achieved by inserting strips of lead between them.
See Galleys.

Inter-media comparison   *Advertising, Media planning and buying*
A technique for comparing media on the basis of cost, cost-effectiveness, audience demographics and characteristics, circulation, readership, audience and other data essential for efficient media buying. The term is usually applied to comparisons within different media or channels, for example press and broadcast. Comparisons within the same media area are usually termed **intra-media**. *Caveat*: used carelessly, the two terms can cause expensive confusion.

Internal communications   *Corporate communications, Internal marketing,*
Public relations
Messages aimed at, and prepared specifically for, a company's personnel. Techniques include house journals, memoranda, internal e-mails and bulletin-board messages. The term sometimes extends to communications aimed at shareholders. However, shareholders have different motives from company staff; usually to do with dividends and other benefits.

International Colour Consortium   *Information technology, Standards*
organizations
The body set up to define a standard of viewing colour from input devices, such as scanners. The standard applies to the complete process, from computer input to peripheral output, including colour printers and proofers.

International marketing   *Marketing*
Marketing operations carried out in more than one country or continent. The term usually applies when these operations function under direct control from head office. The method varies from one company to another. International marketing operations may be conducted by a company's own offices overseas, using its own staff supported by local expertise; or by autonomous local contractors.

Interview   *Marketing research*
A research technique for obtaining information from individuals or groups. Interviews are conducted under a variety of circumstances and formats. Respondents are interviewed in the street, at home, at the office; by telephone, post and e-mail. Group interviews, conducted and guided by a professional researcher, are

designed to give participants opportunities to express opinions and attitude freely, uninhibited by a rigidly structured questionnaire.

Introductory offer   *Marketing, Sales promotion*
To encourage consumer trial and take-up when a product or service is launched, the supplier may offer potential customers a special incentive for a limited period. This can take the form of extra product for the same price, a discount, or an associated product – such as free film with a new camera. A competition or contest may be offered in promoting the product, with worthwhile prizes.

Invisible exports   *Economics, Marketing*
International trade without the involvement of physical goods. Such products and services include financial services, insurance, tourism, haulage and shipping. Although invisible and intangible, these products are included in a government's balance of trade statements.

Invitation to treat   *Advertising, Law, Marketing, Retailing*
An advertisement is not an offer; it is an invitation to do business and create a contract. A contract comprises three elements: offer, acceptance and consideration – a price, either monetary or in kind. It can be verbal or written. There is an anecdote about a woman passing a department store, seeing in the window a full-length mink coat with a price tag of £50 ($70). She rushes in, tries on the coat and takes it to the checkout. 'That will be £5,000,' says the cashier. The customer protests, indicating the price tag. The cashier, who has a degree in commercial law, points out that the display in the window is merely an advertisement. It is an invitation to treat – that is, to do business, to come inside and make an offer for the coat. This applies even where there is an error on a price tag or show-card, as in this case. Should the store agree to the offer, and both parties agree on the price, a verbal contract is made, and the coat can change hands. The term applies to advertising in all its forms, including catalogue selling, and to transactions on the Internet.

IPA   *Representative organizations*
The Institute of Practitioners in Advertising (*qv*).

Iris diaphragm   *Photography, Reprographics*
In a camera, the adjustable aperture mechanism, similar to the iris of a human eye, controlling the amount of light reaching the film.

ISBA   *Representative organizations*
The Incorporated Society of British Advertisers (*qv*).

ISDN   *Electronic communication systems*
Integrated Systems Digital Network. A high-quality data transmission system, used for fast transmission of computer-generated and other electronic files via

telephone lines. Text, artwork and PostScript files, for example, prepared in a studio, can be sent to a printer via ISDN. Both parties need to have the appropriate equipment.

Another super-fast transmission technique is **ADSL**, Asymmetric Digital Subscriber Line. This is a system for high-speed access for businesses and home Internet users. It allows access at between 10 and 40 times normal speeds using a standard telephone line.

Island display *Retailing, Retail merchandising*
A display sales unit in a supermarket or self-service store. The unit usually stands in an open area or gangway, isolated from product bays. Its function is to attract passing customers and encourage them to take products from it. Often, an island display unit contains special offers.

Island position *Media planning and buying, Press advertising, Production*
A press advertisement surrounded by editorial copy, or by a combination of editorial and margins. Where an advertisement is the only one on a page, its position is termed **solus** (*qv*).

Island site *Exhibitions, Media buying*
An exhibition stand with gangways on all four sides.

ISO *Professional organizations*
The International Standards Organization.

ISO paper sizes *Design, Paper-making and buying, Print*
An international metric system for paper sizes used in printing. In its A series, the basic area is a square metre – definitely not to be confused with a metre square. The A series comprises paper sheet sizes in which the area from one size down to the next varies by a factor of ½. There are also B sizes, intermediate between A, RA and S stock sizes. In Europe the standard size for stationery and much printed literature is A4, 210 × 297 mm. The nearest US size is Letter, 8½ in × 11 in.

ISO rating *Photography*
A measure of the light-sensitivity of photographic film stock and paper; their 'speed' rating. The higher the ISO figure, the 'faster' the emulsion speed, and the greater its sensitivity to light. The speed of film stock and photographic paper determines camera lens aperture and exposure time. For example, in bright light, a fast film will need less exposure; a slow film will need more.

ISP *E-commerce, E-marketing, Internet activity*
Initials for **Internet Service Provider**. A local or national company that you connect to by telephone line or cable modem. The ISP connects you to the Internet. ISPs usually provide e-mail software, and an Internet browser for viewing Web sites.

Issue   *Advertising, Media buying, Press media*
A single edition of a publication. The period between one issue of a publication
and the next is termed its **issue life**.

Issue date   *Publishing*
Sometimes termed **cover date**. The publication date of a newspaper, magazine or
directory. This date usually appears on the cover, but in reality may not be the
actual date on which the publication hits the bookstalls, newsagents or news-
stands. With national and regional daily newspapers, the issue date is always the
actual date of publication.

Some full-colour consumer, business and technical magazines appear a month
or more ahead of the issue date. *Amateur Photographer*, *Ideal Home*, *Cosmopol-
itan* and *Vogue* are examples of this phenomenon. It is based on every publisher's
compulsive desire to get on to the news-stands first, well before the competition.
It was probably a good idea when it started. However, since many publishers are
doing the same thing, the advantage for all of them is completely lost. Why do they
continue to do it? As John Wayne used to say: 'It sure beats the hell out of me'.

Issue readership   *Media research, Press media*
The readership of a publication, calculated as an average. This must not be
confused with **circulation** (*qv*), which is the paid-up sale of a publication, certified
by independent audit.
See ABC, Verified Free Distribution.

Issues management   *Media relations, Public relations*
Identifying, investigating, analysing and dealing with issues affecting an organization or industry group. This is normally followed by the drawing up of plans to
manage the issues, and implementing them using appropriate measures and media.
See Crisis management.

Italics   *Composition, Copywriting, Desktop publishing, Typography,*
                                                      Word-processing
Type characters that slope to the right. Usually abbreviated to **itals**. Most often
used for the names of publications, such as the *Wall Street Journal*; foreign words
and phrases, and for emphasis in copy. *The Oxford English Dictionary* indicates
that it was introduced to Europe about 1500 by Aldus Manutius of Venice. Upright
characters are called '**roman**' (*qv*), spelled without a capital r.

ITC   *Media controls*
The **Independent Television Commission**. The UK government body responsible
for licensing and regulating commercially funded television services provided in
and from the UK. These include the commercial terrestrial channels, public teletext
and a range of cable, local delivery and satellite services. They do not include
services provided by the British Broadcasting Corporation. Under its powers
derived from the Broadcasting Act, 1990, the ITC:

- Licenses commercially funded television services in the UK, whether delivered terrestrially or by cable, local delivery or satellite. It licenses services provided from the UK to viewers in other countries.
- Regulates these services through its published licences, codes and guidelines, and has a range of penalties for failure to comply with them.
- Seeks to ensure that a wide range of television services is available throughout the UK and that, taken as a whole, the services are of a high quality and appeal to a variety of tastes and interests.
- Seeks to ensure fair and effective competition in the provision of these services.

One of the ITC's most important functions is to see that the programmes and advertisements on the services it regulates maintain proper standards. The ITC publishes programme, advertising and sponsorship codes applying to all channels, and a technical performance code applying to the terrestrial channels.

ITC staff monitor licensees' programme and advertising standards with the assistance of audience research and comments from viewers. Its range of advisers includes the ITC's 10 regional viewer consultative councils, the Advertising Advisory Committee and the Central Religious Advisory Committee.

Should a licensee fail to comply with the conditions set out in the Broadcasting Act and its licence, or the requirements of the ITC codes, the ITC can impose penalties. These range from warnings and broadcast apologies, to fines and the shortening or revocation of the licence.

The ITC replaced the Independent Broadcasting Authority and the Cable Authority in 1991. Its costs are met principally from licence fees payable by its licensees.

ITV *Broadcast media*
The general term for independent commercial television; so called to differentiate it from the BBC – the publicly funded British Broadcasting Corporation. ITV's income comes from advertising and other commercial activities; the BBC's from licence money, a form of taxation, forcibly extorted from British television audiences.

ITVA *Representative organizations, Trade associations*
The **Independent Television Association**. The organization representing the interests of UK commercial television companies and contractors.
See BARB, IPA, ISBA, ITC.

Jj

Java *E-commerce, Information technology, Internet, Web sites*
A programming language for creating applications enabling enhancements to be made to Web pages. With Java, it is possible to add multimedia effects to a Web page, which cannot be done with standard HTML commands. A JavaScript program is a series of commands included in a Web page HTML file, and carried out by the Web browser. Java was developed by Sun Microsystems from the C++ programming language.
See HTML.

Jaz *Information technology, Storage media, Studio equipment*
A proprietary, removable cartridge system for storing substantial amounts of digital information. It is capable of storing 1 gigabyte of data, which makes it ideal for artwork, graphics, halftones, animation and other large files.

JICCAR *Broadcast media, Media research*
In the UK, the Joint Industry Committee for Cable Audience Research.

JICNARS *Media research, Press media*
In the UK, the Joint Industry Committee for National Readership Surveys. The organization responsible for issuing and controlling the official industry contract for national readership surveys.

JICRAR *Broadcast media, Media research*
The Joint Industry Committee for Radio Audience Research. The UK organization responsible for issuing and controlling the official industry contract for radio audience research.
See BARB.

JICREG *Media research, Press media*
In the UK, the Joint Industry Committee for Regional Press Readership Research. Previously run by the Regional Newspaper Advertising Bureau.

Jingle *Advertising, Cinema, Commercial television and radio,*
Copywriting, Creative work
An advertising slogan set to music. The term can also apply to the music alone. Music for jingles can be composed specifically for the slogan or campaign, or can

be taken from a published work. Copyright law needs to be checked, and complied with, in every country in which the jingle is to be run.

JIT   *Distribution, Manufacturing, Retailing, Wholesaling*
Initials for **just-in-time purchasing**. Management policy and procedure, where virtually no stocks of components or product are held by the company, production unit or store. In manufacturing, components are delivered to the works on a daily or other short-term basis. In retailing, the same applies. In both cases only the absolute minimum is stored overnight.

While this procedure offers worthwhile operating benefits, including savings in storage space, personnel and capital tie-up, it does demand certain conditions to be set up and maintained on a permanent basis:

- accurate forecasts of demand for components or product;
- accurate stock control;
- confidence and capability of the company's marketing and sales departments;
- insurance against failure of supply;
- reliable suppliers and long-term contracts;
- staff with the ability to administer the system;
- suppliers with the ability, and the capacity, to handle changes in specification.

Joint demand   *Economics, Marketing theory*
In a marketplace, demand for products and services that stimulate demand for other products and services. This usually happens when such products are closely linked. For example, a rise in the sale of bread may stimulate butter sales; fish sales may result in a rise in the sale of chips (French fries); demand for shirts may positively affect the sale of ties.

Joint venture   *Business, Enterprise, Marketing*
A collaboration of companies or individuals, aimed at creating, developing or marketing a product, service or business activity. Costs and profits are shared, as are the risks.

Journey cycle   *Marketing planning, Sales management*
The frequency of calls made on a customer by a sales representative. The term usually refers to the time lapse between one call and the next. The planning and organization of a salesperson's customer calling schedule is termed **journey planning**. In many organizations this is done in the sales administration office, and is aimed at making the representative's work as time-effective as possible. Details usually include daily, weekly and monthly call schedules, customer priority, routes to be taken, and optimum time to be spent with each customer. This frees the sales representative from the tedium of working out who to call on next, how long the journey will take, and how long the interview should be. She can then devote all her skills and energies to making sales.

Journey mapping   *Media research, Outdoor advertising*
A slightly oblique term describing a research method for determining and measuring audiences for poster advertising. Respondents are asked to complete a weekly diary of their journeys within sight or proximity of a particular poster site.

Jumbo pack   *Merchandising, Packaging, Retailing*
Also termed **family pack**. An extra-large pack of a consumer product, offered for sale at an appropriately lower unit price than smaller ones.

Jump cut   *Cinema and television commercials, Film and video editing*
The removal of a portion of the length of a filmed shot, so that the action appears smooth and continuous. The technique helps to eliminate awkward momentary pauses. *Caveat*: in unskilled hands, a cut may be made ahead of its appropriate position in the shot, and the action may seem to 'jump'. The results can resemble a production of the silent film era, and be hilarious. However, when carried out deliberately, the technique can be highly effective.

Junior page   *Advertising, Media planning and buying, Publishing*
Advertising space in a newspaper or magazine, normally about three-quarters of a page. Its position is usually solus, with editorial on two sides and margins on the others. The format offers a chance to dominate the whole page without actually paying for the whole of it. This special position may cost more than the same space run-of-paper; but it's worth the extra money if you can also specify on which page it should appear. The term **mini page** is also used.
See Matter, Run-of-paper ad, Solus.

Junk mail   *Direct mail, E-mail marketing, Internet activity*
Unsolicited and unwanted mail, delivered either by post or by electronic means. This is a cruel way of describing such activity, since mailings often contain useful information, and many have interesting and attractive offers. Mail becomes junk when sent to the wrong target audiences. There is a strong lesson here for marketing planners.

Justification   *Composition, Copywriting, Desktop publishing, Typesetting,*
                                              Typography, Word-processing
Arranging copy so that it is set in columns with left, right or both edges perpendicular. The lines are spaced out automatically to the correct length. This option is available on all fully featured word-processing software.
See Full out, Justified, Measure, Ragged right, Range.

Justified   *Composition, Copywriting, Desktop publishing, Typesetting,*
                                              Typography, Word-processing
Type set in a block or a column, in which the edges are either evenly aligned – straight up and down – or ragged. Justified left, the copy has a straight, vertical left-hand edge. Justified right, the right-hand edge is straight and vertical. Fully justified, or **full out**, both edges are straight and vertical.

In word-processing and desktop publishing, to achieve fully justified copy, the software inserts small spaces between words to make each line of uniform length. *Caveat*: when a large chunk of copy in small type is set full out, it can look like a wall of words, and be extremely difficult to read.
See Full out, Measure, Ragged right, Range.

Just-in-time printing *Print*
A highly flexible system used in digital printing; also referred to as **on-demand printing**. It allows documents to be stored digitally, and printed at any specified time. It also allows the printer to produce the exact number of copies specified in the print order, with no **overs** – copies printed in excess of the specified number.

Kk

k *Marketing, Measurement*
A universal unit of measurement representing 1,000. For example: kilobyte, Kb, 1,000 bytes; kilogram, kg, 1,000 grams; kilohertz, kHz, 1,000 cycles per second. It is often used in marketing terminology as a short form representing 1,000 readers or viewers, 1,000 pounds sterling or 1,000 dollars. In this case, it is a suffix pronounced 'kay'; as in '$25k', 25,000 dollars. Its derivation is Greek *khilioi*, meaning 'a thousand'; in a composite word containing kilo, the stress should always be on the first syllable.

Kelvin *Film, Photography, Reprographics*
A unit of colour temperature. In a scale starting at absolute zero, – 273°C, it measures the colour value of light. The blue end of the spectrum gives the higher meter reading. Film stock and film processing are balanced for a certain colour temperature, and camera work must be within fine limits for correct exposure. Colour temperature is different from degree of illumination, and should not be confused with it.

Kerning *Desktop publishing, Typesetting, Typography, Word-processing*
The tightening up of letterspacing between characters in a typeset word, so that they are printed closer together. This gives the word a neater look and more satisfactory appearance. Most fully featured word-processing and desktop publishing programs offer manual kerning adjustment between pairs of characters. In the word AVAILABLE, for example, the first three characters appear to be further apart from each other than the next two. This illusion can be avoided by kerning. *Caveat*: don't overdo it.

Key *Advertising, Creative, Direct marketing, Print, Production, Research*
A code word, symbol or number within a coupon in a press advertisement. This should indicate the name and issue date of the publication in which it appears. Unless advertisements are keyed, your marketing team or researchers may have no idea where the replies have come from. Keying helps marketers evaluate the effectiveness of publications used in campaigns.

The only other way to identify an unkeyed coupon is to turn it over and see what's on the back. This cannot be regarded a professional research technique; it is tedious and time-consuming, especially when the volume of coupons from advertisements is heavy.

Key codes are equally essential on reply cards included in mailshots, especially where a series of shots is mailed in a planned direct marketing programme. Coding should always be computer-compatible. You can then access all the information you need for improving on your highest response so far. Unfortunately, not all advertisers do this – even some of the most marketing-aware.

Keyboarding   *Desktop publishing, Information technology, Typesetting,*
                                                    Typography, Word-processing
Inputting or entering data into a computer through its keyboard. The term is sometimes shortened to keying.

Keyline   *Artwork, Production*
A rectangle or outline drawing of an element of finished artwork, included on a paste-up (*qv*). This shows the exact position, shape and size of the element in the layout. Keylined external elements include halftones (*qv*), line drawings and transparencies.

Key plate   *Print*
In colour printing, the plate used as a guide for the registration of other colours. This plate usually contains the most image detail.

Key prospects   *Marketing*
Groups of potential customers who not only have the highest purchasing power, but who are most likely to use it. This applies to individuals with appropriate disposable income, and to organizations with viable purchasing budgets. Determining factors are demographics, company profiles, and likely targets indicated by marketing and media research. The whole point in identifying key prospects is to help marketers allocate promotional money and sales effort where they are most likely to achieve their targets.

Keyword   *Communications, Information technology*
A word typed into a search engine, with the objective of finding information on a Web site within a specific range. The obvious keywords for accessing information, for example on the Chartered Institute of Marketing, are 'chartered', 'institute' and 'marketing'. Keywords should make it easier for enquirers and potential customers to find what they are seeking more easily and quickly. Therefore additional keywords, determined by the Institute, may include training, education, membership, excellence, branches, professional, business, development, students, qualifications, examinations, research and library, all of which are appropriate.

Kicker   *Press advertising, Print*
A short line of copy above the headline of an advertisement or page of print. This position serves well for a comment, a product feature or sales point, or a consumer benefit, introducing the major point on which the headline is based.

Kill *Advertising, Editorial*

A verb used by advertisement managers who have decided to delete an advertisement from the pages of a publication. The term is synonymous with **dump** or **scratch**. This drastic measure is often taken when an advertiser shows signs of being unable or unwilling to pay for the insertion. Editors use the same terms for stories that need to be deleted. In editorial departments, the word **spike** is sometimes used; a relic from the days when thrusting a proof or a piece of copy on to a spike on the editor's desk meant the story had been killed. Spike is used in modern newsrooms even when the disposal method is a shredder.

Kiss impression *Print*

Also referred to simply as a **kiss**. A very light printing impression, just enough to produce an image on the substrate (*qv*).

Knock down *Retailing*

A product such as furniture supplied in component form, and which the customer needs to assemble in order to use it. Because the customer supplies the labour for assembly, the price of the product is usually lower than a similar one already assembled. Instructions for assembly usually come with the product; sometimes tools as well.

Knock down *Exhibitions, Expositions*

To dismantle an exhibition stand after the close of the show.

Knock-down price *Retailing, Salesmanship*

Another term for a low price that the customer can be persuaded represents a real bargain.

Knocking copy *Advertising, Controls, Copywriting, Creative, Marketing*

Advertising copy, where the advertiser disparages competitors' products or services and makes unfair or misleading comparisons. Little harm is done where the comparisons are true and fair, and product differences are marked. However, the Advertising Standards Authority (*qv*) takes a dim view of this practice.

On comparisons and denigration, The British Codes of Advertising and Sales Promotion state:

- Comparisons can be explicit or implied and can relate to advertisers' own products or to those of their competitors; they are permitted in the interests of vigorous competition and public information. (Clause 19.1)
- Comparisons should be clear and fair. The elements of any comparison should not be selected in a way that gives advertisers an artificial advantage. (Clause 19.2)
- Advertisers should not unfairly attack or discredit other businesses or their products. (Clause 20.1)

- The only acceptable use of another business's broken or defaced products in advertisements is in the illustration of comparative tests, and the source, nature and results of these should be clear. (Clause 20.2)

A British government directive on the control of misleading advertisements came into force in 2000. It defines comparative advertising as any advertising that 'explicitly or by implication. . . identifies a competitor or goods or services offered by a competitor'.

The directive makes clear that comparative advertising is permissible, in the interests of competition and public information. It requires that comparative advertising shall, as far the comparison is concerned, be permitted only when the following conditions are met:

- It is not misleading.
- It compares goods or services meeting the same needs or intended for the same purpose.
- It objectively compares one or more material, relevant, verifiable and representative features of those goods and services, which may include price.
- It does not create confusion in the marketplace between the advertiser and a competitor nor between the advertiser's trademarks, trade names, other distinguishing marks, goods or services and those of a competitor.
- It does not discredit or denigrate the trademarks, trade names, other distinguishing marks, goods, services, activities or circumstances of a competitor.
- For products with designation of origin, it relates in each case to products with the same designation.
- It does not take unfair advantage of the reputation of a trademark, trade name or other distinguishing marks of a competitor or of the designation of origin of competing products.
- It does not present goods or services as imitations or replicas of goods and services bearing a protected trademark or trade name.

The directive also states:

> . . . any comparison referring to a special offer, such an advertisement is not permitted unless it indicates in a clear and unequivocal way the date on which the offer ends or, where appropriate, that the special offer is subject to the availability of the goods and services, and, where the special offer has not yet begun, the date of the start of the period during which the special price or other specific conditions shall apply.

Known value items   *Marketing, Retailing*
A set of key brands within a retail environment in which their prices are well known by the average consumer. Consumers cannot be aware of every price, so the known value items are the brands that will make a store look inexpensive, average or expensive. Sometimes abbreviated to **KVI**.

Kodatrace   *Artwork, Production, Studio techniques*

Kodak's brand of translucent film, used for overlays in finished artwork. It is used for positioning additional material, and for carrying instructions to printers and plate-makers. With computerized artwork production now virtually universal in industrialized countries, flat artwork and overlay techniques are disappearing.

Kraft   *Packaging, Paper and board*

A German word meaning **strong**. The term used for certain grades of exceptionally tough paper and board used in packaging. The material contains unbleached wood pulp treated with a sulphate.

Ll

Lacquer *Print, Print design, Production*
A coating, usually clear and glossy, applied to printed covers or sheets for their protection, and to enhance their appearance. Lacquer is often used as a design feature, aimed at imparting a distinctive appearance or 'handle' to a piece.

Laggards *Marketing, Marketing planning*
Consumers who will usually not purchase a new product until after it has become well established, and proved its value, by being owned by a large number of other consumers.

Laid *Paper, Print*
Printing and writing paper with a ribbed surface imparted by a wire roll during manufacture. The other popular grade used for these purposes is **wove** (*qv*), which has a smooth, uniform, unlined surface.

Laid lines *Paper-making*
A continuous watermark consisting of close parallel lines. These are crossed with more widely spaced lines at right angles to them, termed **chain lines**.

Laminate *Print, Production*
An ultra-thin film applied to the cover surface of printed paper or board after printing. Although its main function is to protect print against damage, deterioration and greasy thumb-marks, lamination is regarded as a worthwhile extra process that also enhances the look and feel of printed material. Popularly used for covers of high-cost brochures and booklets, and good quality point-of-sale material. A wide variety of laminates exists, including plastic and metallic foil.

LAN *Communications, Computing, Information technology,*
Marketing communications
The acronym for **local area network**. A system for linking computers and other equipment into a single, operational network. This is done both with software and hardware, and a lot of extra wiring, including satellite equipment and telephone lines. A local area can be a single office, a building or a campus, or an office on the other side of the world. Advertisers, their agencies, suppliers and printers, for example, may be linked together in a LAN, which is a highly efficient method of exchanging images, graphics, text and data.

Landscape   *Art direction, Design, Desktop publishing, Photography,*
                        Reprographics, Word-processing, Press advertising

A horizontal page or advertisement design format. The orientation of an advertisement, printed page or photoprint, where the short sides are on the left and right. In other words, a shape wider than it is high. Some DTP software packages call this **wide format**. Some computer screens are so configured.

Brochures in this format work as well as in portrait; copy can be designed to be easy on the eye, and produce the required response. *Caveat*: print designed in one format does not adapt readily from the other. Sometimes advertisers adapt press advertisements to leaflets. Where both are in portrait format, there should be few problems. However, when portrait is being adapted to landscape it should be treated as a completely new page design. Liaise closely with your art director when considering a landscape format for your next advertisement or brochure.
See Portrait.

Laser   *Information technology, Optics, Reprographics*

The acronym for **light amplification by stimulated emission of radiation**. An intense beam of light with a very narrow bandwidth, capable of producing images by electronic impulse. It makes possible imaging by remote control from computers and fax equipment.

Laser plate-making   *Artwork, Pre-press, Print, Reprographics*

The use of laser equipment for the scanning of artwork, and the preparation of printing plates.

Laser printer   *Communications, Desktop publishing, Information*
                        technology, Marketing communications,
                        Word-processing

A printer using a laser beam, capable of producing print of a very high quality. The laser reproduces images and characters as minute dots on a revolving drum. These attract a fine toning powder, which is transferred to paper. The toner is melted by heat, forming a permanent image on the paper.

Laser printing   *Communications equipment, Desktop publishing,*
                        Information technology, Marketing communications,
                        Word-processing

A printing system using lasers emitting electronic impulses, a technique in widespread use with computers.

Lateral diversification   *Business, Marketing*

An extension of a business into areas remote from its current activity. An organization having done this is usually termed a **conglomerate**. As examples, a tobacco company extending its activity into cosmetics, or a distiller expanding into pharmaceuticals.

Launch *Marketing*

A marketing activity, injecting a new product or service into a marketplace. This nearly always involves marketing communications effort, including advertising, sales promotion and public relations.

Layout *Artwork, Creative, Design, Desktop publishing, Production, Word-processing*

An outline, sketch or drawing of a printed page, advertisement, brochure or other material to be printed. Also, a positioning guide for the various elements within an advertisement, set out on a grid, ready for production. When the graphic interpretation of editorial, advertising or print ideas is laid out on the drawing board or computer screen, this is termed a **visual**.

Lead *Marketing, Sales*

Pronounced *leed*. An enquiry, from an advertisement or piece of print, where the enquirer has indicated an interest in the product or service being promoted. This is an opportunity for the sales representative to turn the lead into a sale.

Leader *Creative, Desktop publishing, Publishing, Typography, Word-processing*

A line of full points, dots or dashes at the beginning of a sentence, or between two words or sentences. A leader is used to link two sentences, usually where the ideas expressed in them are similar. In publishing, the term is used for the leading article in a newspaper, magazine or house journal.

Leader *Audio, Film, Photography, Video*

A length of film or tape without pictures or sound, added to the beginning and end of a reel, roll or cassette, to permit threading up in equipment.

Leading *Composition, Desktop publishing, Print, Typography, Word-processing*

Pronounced *ledding*. Space between lines of type, usually measured in **points**; sometimes in **millimetres**. So-called because in former times, when hot metal typesetting was used, strips of lead alloy were inserted between lines of type in the galleys. This opened up the lines and increased the white space between them. In desktop publishing the term used is **line spacing** or **inter-line spacing**. Hot metal typesetting has now virtually disappeared in Europe, the USA and many industrialized countries.
See Galleys, Letterspacing.

Lead time *Advertising, Business, Marketing, Publishing*

Elapsing time between two planned activities. The time it takes for a planned activity to be carried out, before it moves into another planned activity or phase. For example, the time between the creation of a product and its launch; between the giving of an advertising brief and its implementation; the time between the copy date of a publication and its appearance on the bookstalls; between the receipt of an order and its fulfilment or delivery.

Leaflet   *Advertising, Marketing, Print*

An item of printed promotional or informational literature, printed on single or multiple sheets of paper. A single or double-sided page can be called a leaflet, with the number of pages rising to four or eight before becoming a **brochure** (*qv*). *Caveat*: these terms are not carved in stone; they may vary from company to company.

Legend   *Copywriting, Creative, Editorial*

An outmoded term for a caption to a photograph or other illustration. Also sometimes termed a **citation**. Legend is more usually applied to the explanation of symbols used on maps; and to some computer system activities, where the activity is represented on screen by symbols.

Letraset   *Artwork, Creative, Production, Reprographics, Typography*

The name of a company and its brand of dry-transfer lettering used in drawing board layouts and artwork. Letraset sheets are of translucent paper, on which are mounted type characters. The backs of the characters are sticky. To transfer a character on to a layout, it is positioned accurately over the chosen spot, then rubbed down with a special tool or the tip of a ballpoint pen. It can then be burnished with the blunt end of the tool or pen.

When compared to desktop computer typesetting this method is somewhat low-tech. However, it is brilliant for ad hoc headlining, particularly in the event of a power cut or a computer crash.

Letterset   *Printing processes, Reprographics*

Also known as *dry offset*. A printing process employing a **blanket** (*qv*) for transferring images from plate to paper. It uses a relief plate and, unlike litho, needs no dampening system.
See Litho.

Letterspacing   *Desktop publishing, Print, Typography, Word-processing*

The adjustment of the spacing between typed or typeset characters, by adding or reducing space between letters of a word. **Kerning** (*qv*) adjusts the spacing between particular pairs of letters depending on the font design; character pairs such as A and V can be nestled closer together to improve the visual effect. Some desktop publishing programs refer to it as **character spacing**.
See Kerning.

Library shot   *Artwork, Creative, Photography, Production*

A picture or illustration sourced from a photo-library specializing in this kind of service. Most large libraries provide photo images and line illustrations on CD ROM; others supply material downloaded online. High quality transparencies are also popular. Some libraries issue catalogues, classified into general or specialized photo subjects.

Most national newspapers and magazines, and many regionals, have photo-libraries. The main advantage in using libraries is that it may be more economical buying from them than taking your own shots. The best of these carry up-to-date material, and the quality is first class. Newspapers carry newsworthy photographs, adding to their collections on a daily basis.

Life cycle   *Consumer behaviour, Demographics, Marketing planning, Marketing research*

A slightly misleading term used to describe the chronological development or progression of people, products, behaviour and events. A cycle, by its nature, is a circular activity, in which the activity described comes full circle, and may recur. In life cycle theory the activity is linear; people and their relationship with products are the main considerations.

As target audiences for marketers, people are considered for their willingness, and ability, to spend money on products and services. As the table below shows, this can vary according to where people are in the various stages of their lives. Research helps to indicate the lifestyle and disposable income of consumers at different stages.

Life stage	*Situation*
1. Single, living with parents	1. Few financial commitments. Fashion-following and 'trendy'
2. Single, living in rented or shared accommodation	2. Basic household goods; car; fashion; concentration on leisure and entertainment; convenience and take-away foods. If in well-paid job, good supply of cash available
3. Married couple, or living together; no children	3. If both working, double income and high spending on fashion, personal products and services, household items. Cars, foreign holidays. Plenty of cash available
4. Full nest 1; first child under 6 years	4. Dynamic house-purchasing period; child takes up much cash and product purchase; not much spare cash available
5. Full nest 2; other children	5. Food and household products bought in bulk; many purchases made for children and their needs; school fees, music lessons and sports equipment; teenage fashions, usually expensive

6. Empty nest; children no longer at home, living independently or at higher education establishments	6. Replacement expenditure on house and household products, eg brown and white goods, bedrooms, bathrooms, kitchens. Better and longer holidays and breaks; larger sums invested. Desire for better lifestyle now this is possible with more money available
7. Retirement	7. Lower disposable income; often moving to smaller house or to apartment; less furniture. Higher spend on medical products and services
8. Solitary survivor	8. Simpler life altogether; more medical and physical attention needed

See Product life cycle.

Life cycle   *Marketing*
Every stage in the life of a product, from raw materials to disposal. It includes the production and supply of raw materials, processing and manufacture, storage, transportation, distribution and use; finally, disposal and recycling.
See Product life cycle.

Life cycle analysis   *Marketing, Product research*
The measurement of the total environmental effects in the preparation of materials for a product. This includes the generation of the energy needed for production and transportation, the manufacture of the product, its distribution, use, disposal and recycling.

Life cycle monitoring   *Marketing research, Product research*
Observing and analysing the progress of products in their markets, on the basis of their life cycles. In theory this is sound practice. On the other hand, it can be more like tunnel vision, and seen only in linear form. To explain: in product life cycle terms, a product may seem near to its death. In terms of business and marketing acumen and experience, it may need only a new ingredient, or a new label, to ensure its continued life and profitability.

Lifestyle   *Marketing, Marketing research*
More accurately, consumer styles of life, defined and analysed in relation to individuals, families, communities and nations. This refers to the way these groups either prefer to conduct their lives, or the way their lifestyle is determined by circumstances. For marketing purposes, the factual points of reference are those usually given in demographic analysis, including:

- age;
- disposable income;
- education;
- household composition;
- income;
- leisure pursuits and holidays;
- location;
- marital status;
- occupation;
- sex.

For lifestyle analysis, a number of other factors are taken into account, such as:

- allocation of personal time, energy and effort;
- aspirations and ambitions;
- personal and family possessions.

Ligature   *Composition, Desktop publishing, Typography, Word-processing*
Two or more characters joined together to make a single unit. For example æ, œ.

Light-fast   *Print, Reprographics*
The quality of an ink formulated so that it will not fade to any extent, even during prolonged exposure to light.

Light-pen   *Computer-aided design, Computing, Information technology,*
                                                Desktop publishing
An electronic hand-tool shaped like a pen, used rather like a mouse on a desk pad. Its function is to move a cursor around a computer screen, to draw and design, and to move data and images from place to place. With appropriate software a light-pen can not only draw, but also remove, insert and retrieve images and fragments of images. Like a mouse, it can also carry out some of the work done by a keyboard.

Some light-pens work on alpha-numeric pads, on which alphabetical characters, numbers and symbols are manipulated. This is slow and tedious; a keyboard is faster and less frustrating, and useful for working in foreign languages.

Light viewers   *Television audience research*
Viewers whose television viewing time is slight, or lower than the average determined by appropriate research.

Limbo   *Cinema and television commercials*
A term used in advertising agencies to indicate a nebulous background in the shooting of commercials. The term is deemed appropriate since it is elsewhere defined as 'a region on the borders of hell'.

Linage *Advertising, Editorial, Publishing*
The number of lines in an item of editorial or other printed matter. In classified advertisements, the number of lines and the method of paying for them. Pronounced line-age.

Line and tone *Artwork, Plate-making, Print, Production*
A film and plate-making technique for combining line art and halftone material in the same illustration. In the days of hot metal letterpress printing, line and tone negatives were combined mechanically, and printing plates made from this.

Line artwork *Artwork, Plate-making, Print, Production*
Artwork in black and white only, with no middle tones. This can be printed without halftone screening. Pen and ink drawings are an example of line art.

Line copy *Artwork, Plate-making, Print, Production*
Copy suitable for reproduction without the use of a halftone screen.
See Halftone.

Line drawing *Artwork, Plate-making, Print, Production*
An illustration in black and white only, with no grey tones.

Line extension *Marketing, Retailing*
A newly introduced product bearing the name of an existing brand. With retail lines, a new item in a line amounts to differences in size, colour or materials, or in more advanced models of the same brand. Food products may emphasize new flavours when introducing new product lines.

Linefeed *Computing, Desktop publishing, Information technology, Print and production, Teleprinter communication, Word-processing*
An alternative computer keyboard term for **enter** or **return**, for producing inter-line spacing or leading (*qv*). This originated with teleprinter keyboards, which served for many decades as the fastest, most efficient means of text communication.

Line manager *Administration, Advertising, Organization, Public relations*
Head of a team or department, holding executive responsibility for the physical implementation of a project. An account manager in an advertising or public relations agency is effectively a line manager.

Line spacing *Composition, Desktop publishing, Print, Typography, Word-processing*
See Leading.

Lip-synch *Film, Internet, Television, Video*
A short-form term for **lip synchronization**. The synchronization of an actor's lip movements on screen with the sound track. When they get out of synch, the results

can be hilarious; in a commercial, they can be damaging. Electronic editing makes inefficient lip-synch less common, and less frustrating, than in the days of cut and splice. Video material and animation over the Internet suffers from poor lip-synch. This is because of inadequate computer processing power and memory, and from inefficient line capacity.

List *Direct mail, Direct marketing, Marketing*
A common short-form term for a mailing list. Often also used to refer to a database. A list can exist within a database, but not vice versa.
See List broker, List cleaning.

List broker *Direct mail, Direct marketing*
An individual or company specializing in the marketing of mailing lists. A competent broker identifies, scrutinizes, analyses and evaluates a list offered by the company that owns it, and matches it to the needs of advertisers who want to use it. She prices each list, offering it for hire with the aim of making a profit. Brokers usually issue and mail out catalogues of their lists as part of their own marketing effort.
See List cleaning.

List cleaning *Direct mail, Direct marketing*
Correcting mailing lists and bringing them up to date. Under proper professional supervision, the cleanest lists are those in frequent use. People whose names are on mailing lists have the irritating habit of dying, moving house, changing jobs and dropping out of sight. Frequent use of a mailing list will reveal the gone-aways and not-knowns, so that the list operator can eliminate them. A clean list is usually more valuable than a dirty one, and may cost more to hire or buy.
See List broker.

List manager *Direct mail, Direct marketing*
An executive with responsibility for managing and updating a mailing list.

List price *Distribution, Marketing, Retailing, Wholesaling*
The price a manufacturer or distributor puts on a product, before applying discounts. In the UK in former times many wholesale and retail prices were fixed by the manufacturer, and could not be changed by distributors. This practice, known as **re-sale price maintenance**, was declared a restraint of trade in the UK, and abolished. Some products and services are still subject to RPM, though few admit that it exists.

Literal *Copywriting, Creative, Desktop publishing, Print, Production, Typesetting, Word-processing*
A literal error in a piece of copy. An uncorrected spelling or typing error in typeset copy or printed text. It is made by a compositor rather than copywriter or author. Literals include wrong fonts and defective type.

Litho *Printing processes*

A form of **planographic** printing. Printing from a flat printing surface using thin, flexible metal plates. Also called **litho** and **offset**. Points to note about litho:

■ This is by far the most widely used printing process, certainly in the UK, the EU and the USA. It accounts for over 70 per cent of all printed matter.

■ It is a printing process based on the use of greasy ink and water, and on the fact that these two do not mix.

■ The printing plate is prepared so that the printing areas attract ink, the non-printing areas attract water.

■ During printing, the plate is first dampened with water. When the oil-based ink is applied, the image areas attract it and the water-coated areas repel it.

■ Litho uses thin, flexible metal printing plates wrapped round plate cylinders on the press.

■ In offset litho printing, the plates do not print direct to the paper. The image is first transferred on to a cylinder covered with a rubber or neoprene **blanket**, which then prints the image on the paper. The blanket offsets the image; hence the term **offset litho**.

■ The offset blanket minimizes wear on the metal printing plate. This gives it a much extended working life, and the ability to print longer runs.

■ Offset litho presses have at least three printing cylinders:
 – a plate cylinder, which carries the metal printing plate;
 – a blanket cylinder;
 – an impression cylinder, which presents the paper to the blanket cylinder for receiving the printed image.

■ Litho presses use a system of inking and dampening rollers and reservoirs.

■ The printing plate comes into contact first with the dampening rollers, then the inking rollers.

There are two types of offset printing press, sheet-fed offset and web-fed offset:

Sheet-fed offset

■ Prints on single sheets.

■ Prints at speeds up to 11,000 impressions an hour.

■ Presses have single or multicolour units.

■ Multicolour presses print up to eight colours in a single pass.

■ Perfecting presses print both sides of the sheet in the same pass.

■ Sheets can be varnished on the run.

■ Sheets are delivered at the dry end in a stack, ready for finishing: cutting, folding, binding and guillotining.

Advantages of sheet-fed offset

■ Prints all international sheet sizes.

■ Prints a wide range of materials, from paper to board.

- Prints well on poor-quality materials.
- Delivers excellent colour reproduction.
- Printing plates are economical and easy to make.
- Make-ready is simple and economical.
- Economical for short or medium-long runs, from a few thousands to over 50,000.

Disadvantages

- There is manual paper-handling, for example:
  - manhandling it through the finishing stages;
  - manhandling paper to and from the press;
  - removing it at the dry end;
  - stacking paper at the wet (input) end.

Optimum and economical uses of sheet-fed offset

- leaflets, brochures and booklets;
- long- and medium-run newspapers, magazines and catalogues;
- short-run house magazines;
- stationery, letterheads, business cards.

Web-fed offset

- Prints on continuous reels of paper, usually termed webs.
- Prints both sides simultaneously.
- Prints at high speeds, 660 m (2,200 ft) per minute and more.
- Many web-fed presses have in-line finishing performed on the run. This includes folding, cutting, slitting, saddle stitching, inserting, gluing of inserts, perforating and numbering.

Advantages of web-fed offset

- Extremely high speeds.
- Long runs are possible, 1.5 million and more.
- It can compete with sheet-fed litho on medium–short runs, from about 12,000 copies.
- Prints up to eight colours in a single pass, depending on the capacity of the press.
- Excellent colour reproduction.
- Good depth of colour and gloss, aided by advanced drying and curing processes.
- Economical, easily made printing plates.
- Simple make-ready.

Optimum and economical uses of web-fed offset

- catalogues;
- long-run newspapers;
- magazines.

Lithography   *See* Litho, Offset.

Litho negatives and positives   *Film and plate-making, Pre-press, Print,*
Production
Screened film, ready for plate-making. Negatives and positives supplied to printers
by production houses are based on creative material and artwork produced by
advertisers and their agencies.

Livery   *Corporate and product branding, Marketing communications*
Originally, the provision of food and clothing for retainers in aristocratic households. Today, the term is applied to a company's branding and house style, and
the distinguishing aspects of a company's appearance. This includes product logos,
badges and packaging, delivery vehicle design, store fronts and showroom
designs, staff uniforms.

Local media   *Broadcast media, Cinema, Press media*
Press and radio with local circulation, readership and audience. For advertising
purposes, cinema may be regarded as a local medium, since cinemas carry local
as well as national advertising. In the UK, the local press often serves several
thousand streets in a locality. Local radio reaches a wider audience, but is still
regarded as local, even when its audience is a capital city such as London, Paris
or New York. Television, on the other hand, is usually regarded as a regional
medium; its coverage is carefully delineated, and may attract more national than
local advertising.

Location   *Cinema, Commercials, Film and television production,*
Photography
Any location used for filming or photography, except a studio. **On location** can
mean filming in a private house, in a field, at sea, down a mine or up a mountain.

Lock up   *Print*
In letterpress printing, to position and secure a forme in a chase. A forme is a frame
in which type and illustrations are positioned. A chase is a frame holding all this
material securely in the bed of a press. The type is locked up in the forme, and the
forme locked up in the chase.

Logistics   *Distribution, Marketing, Retailing*
Planning, organizing, moving and warehousing resources, supplies, equipment and
personnel. This is a principal function of project management. When applied to

marketing and marketing communications, it includes management, human resources, distribution, budgeting, and financial and stock control.

Logo　　　　*Artwork, Branding, Creative, Design, Marketing communications,*
Print, Typography

An abbreviation of **logotype**. The trademark of an organization or company, in the form of a distinguishing symbol, by which it is known by its target audiences and publics. In book publishing, this is known as a **colophon** or **imprint**.

In business and marketing, a company's logo is part of its branding and corporate identity scheme. Some products and services carry the company's logo, as well as the logo of the product itself. Among the best-known logos in the world are Coca-Cola, the BBC and Mickey Mouse. There can't be many people who have not seen them, and understand what they stand for. It goes even deeper than that. If you see the Rolls-Royce logo, for example, even out of context, you do not need to be reminded that it represents the best cars in the world.
See Brand, Branding, Brand loyalty, Positioning.

Log off　　　　*Communications, Computing, Desktop publishing,*
Information technology, Internet, Word-processing

Signing off when you have finished with the computer or terminal. This has to be done, as with all computing procedures, in a pre-determined, orderly manner.

Log on　　　　*Communications, Computing, Desktop publishing,*
Information technology, Internet, Word-processing

Entering personal identification details into a computer or terminal before starting work. Without these details, access can be denied. This is a security measure, designed to prevent confidential or trade-sensitive information getting into the wrong hands. When logging on to the Internet, a user name and a personal password are usually required.

Loose insert　　　　*Advertising, Marketing communications, Newspaper and*
magazine publishing

An advertisement sheet, page, leaflet or brochure, printed separately, inserted into a publication, and distributed with it. It is not bound in with the pages of the publication.

Loss leader　　　　*Retailing techniques*

A product used as a promotion in a store. It is usually seductively priced, at cost or less, in order to attract customers into the store and encourage them to buy copiously while they are there.

Lower case　　　　*Composition, Desktop publishing, Typesetting, Typography,*
Word-processing

The small letters in a typesetting alphabet. The capital letters are termed **upper case**, **capitals** or **caps** (*qv*). The origin of this, like many terms used in printing, is both historical and fascinating. Before the adoption of mechanical and computerized typesetting, type was assembled by hand by compositors, working in a composing room. The wooden or metal type, comprising capital letters, small letters, numerals and symbols, was stored in drawers, in cabinets known as **cases**. The upper cases contained capitals; the lower, small letters.

Low involvement products *Retailing*

Products bought on the spur of the moment or after minimum consideration. These are usually fairly low-value items, where price is the main consideration in the quick decision to buy. In supermarkets, such products are often displayed in racks or dump-bin dispensers, positioned in open areas or at the ends of gondolas. In dump-bins, the arrangement of products is higgledy-piggledy, seemingly random and unorganized. The aim of this lack of symmetry is to encourage customers to reach out and take an item while passing the dispenser. While many customers dislike disturbing orderly displays, here order is not disturbed since there is none. In many UK supermarkets sweets used to be positioned next to checkouts, so that customers and their children could grab them while waiting to pay. This practice has now largely been abandoned.

Low key *Photography, Reprographics*

A photograph containing a majority of dark tones.
See High key.

Low pressure selling *Advertising, Marketing communications,*
Sales technique

Popularly termed **soft selling**. A sales technique using seduction and user benefits, rather than aggression, to encourage a customer to buy. This applies as much to advertising as to field and shop-floor salesmanship. Often advertising concentrates on lifestyle themes; this can be seen in press and television advertising for cars. With this approach there is no mention of major features such as engine capacity, steering lock, aerodynamic bodywork, or resistance to rusting; or of miles per gallon. Play is made on status, beauty, and other intangible benefits.

Loyalty scheme *Marketing, Retailing*

A marketing technique designed to build relationships with consumers, usually by obtaining detailed information about their purchasing and usage habits. Under such a scheme loyal customers are rewarded for staying with a brand, or continuing to purchase from a particular outlet, which helps to prevent their switching to a competitor.

Ltd *Business, Legislation, Trade*

The abbreviated form of **Limited Liability Company**. In the UK, a private company engaged in trade or commerce comprises directors and shareholders. The company is considered a legal entity in its own right, the financial liability of each shareholder being limited by the value of personal shares held. The conduct of UK companies is regulated by a Companies Act, updated from time to time. Similar systems, and abbreviations, exist in other countries; the USA (Incorporated, Inc); Australia (Private, Pte); France (Société Anonyme, SA).

Mm

Machine proof *Print, Production*

A proof made on a printing machine, using inks to be used in a forthcoming print run. If this is done on a production press, the cost can be prohibitive. You will probably need no more than a dozen sets of proofs – for you, your agency, the printer, the files, and possibly one for the chairman's wife. Some printers maintain a special proofing press for short-run proofs, but the cost is still likely to be high. Other, more economical, proofing methods are available; for example, Cromalin, a branded, dry-proofing system. Proofs can also be made electronically, and uploaded to the computer terminals of all the above recipients. This can save time as well as cost.

See Cromalin, Proof.

Machine-readable characters *Information technology, Marketing research, Product coding, Retail auditing, Retail stock coding*

Special printed characters capable of being read, interpreted, processed and analysed by computer. These include characters and numerals printed in magnetic ink, and bar codes, representing numerals 0 to 9. Machine-readable systems can represent virtually anything written in the normal way: prices, weights, countries of origin, research responses, personal and confidential information, musical notation and so on.

Macro marketing *Business, Economics, Marketing*

A concept representing the broad picture of a national economy, expressed in marketing terms, and for marketing purposes. It encompasses all the factors needed for the study of the economy. These include its political, economic, sociological, cultural, ethnic, technological, legal and environmental climate; plus its strengths and weaknesses, and the opportunities and threats it faces.

Madison Avenue *Advertising*

The generic name for the upper end of the advertising industry in the USA. This New York street is where many of that country's largest advertising agencies had their head offices during the heyday of the business. The name has parallels in other fields. Tin Pan Alley symbolizes the popular music industry. In London, The City, or The Square Mile, is a synonym for the capital's financial centre; in New York, Wall Street. Whitehall symbolizes the UK's government; Westminster its parliament. Capitol Hill symbolizes that of the USA.

Magenta   *Artwork, Design, Print, Reprographics*
One of the subtractive primary colours used in four-colour process printing; a kind
of strong bluish-pink. It reflects blue and red light, and absorbs green. Used with
cyan, yellow and black, it enables you to print virtually any colour at reasonable
cost. The standard range of four-colour process inks is manufactured in huge
quantities worldwide, which helps to keep costs down.
See Process colours, Black, Cyan, Pantone, Yellow.

Magnetic ink   *Communications, Security printing*
A printing ink formulated with magnetic particles. Its main uses are security
printing for cheques and bonds, and for computer sorting. Characters and numerals
so printed are recognized and recorded by character-reading equipment and
appropriate software. Reply cards accompanying brochures sometimes have alpha-
numeric keys printed in magnetic ink, so that those recipients who reply can be
identified. More often, keys are represented in bar code form (*qv*).

Magnetic media   *Communications, Information technology*
A technique for storing computer-generated data, using magnetic tape and pre-
formatted disks. Video cassettes and some still cameras store images on magnetic
media. Magnetic media are, of course, at risk from distortion and erasure by
magnetic sources. Non-magnetic storage media exist, including CD ROM (compact
disk read-only memory), and solid-state devices.

Mailing list   *Advertising, Direct mail, Direct marketing, Direct response*
A list of names, addresses and other information essential for operating direct
marketing operations and campaigns. A computerized list should be capable of
being organized, classified and arranged in any order the list manager requires for
accurate targeting. Mailing lists can be bought, or they can be compiled and built
up using a company's own resources, from response to its advertising. It should
be borne in mind that compiling an in-house list is labour-intensive and time-
consuming, and demands a good deal of painstaking administration. However lists
are acquired, frequent updating and cleaning are essential.
See List broker, List manager.

Mailing piece   *Advertising, Direct mail, Direct marketing, Direct response*
A mailshot comprising an envelope and its contents.

Mail merge   *Databases, Direct mail, Direct response advertising*
Inserting a recipient's name, job title, company and address into a computerized
letter. This involves two separate pieces of software. One contains copy for the
letter; the other, name and address data. Each time a new letter is printed, a
different name, address and salutation is inserted in the appropriate position. The
recipient's name may also be inserted in the body of the letter; this is usually
termed **personalization**. *Caveat*: don't overdo it, otherwise it may look contrived
and insincere; once is usually enough.

Mail order *Advertising, Direct marketing, Direct response*
Buying through the post. The term applies to postal purchasing whatever the media used by the advertiser. The term also applies to buying from catalogues. The customer orders a product and sends payment with the order. The order goes direct to the advertiser; no intermediary is involved. The goods are delivered by post or courier. Often the order is physically fulfilled by a company specializing in storing, packing and dispatching products for mail order advertisers. Mail order should not be confused with **direct mail**, which is *selling* through the post (*qv*).

Mailshot *Advertising, Direct mail, Direct marketing, Direct response*
The mailing of a single piece to a target audience. A mailing operation comprising more than one shot could be considered a campaign.

Make-ready *Print*
Preparing a printing press so that the paper receives the highest possible quality of image. On letterpress machines, this is a painstaking and expensive activity – one reason why litho printing has become the widest-used process.
See Machine proof, Plate, Pull.

Make-up *Artwork, Desktop publishing, Print, Production,*
Typography, Reprographics
The arrangement of copy and illustrations into sections and pages, so that everything fits perfectly. **Making up** is also a technique for assembling the various elements of a page, prior to producing artwork, film and printing plates.
See Composition, Mark-up.

Making good *Advertisement management, Broadcast advertising,*
Press advertising
A measure adopted when an error or omission has occurred in the insertion of an advertisement, and the fault is the publisher's. The advertiser is entitled to ask the publisher to reimburse the cost, or to make good by running the insertion correctly, free of charge. The term applies to television and radio advertising, where an error or omission has occurred in the transmission of a commercial.

Management by objectives *Business, Marketing*
The application of management audits and techniques to secure increasingly efficient performance by a company's management staff. Every manager, at whatever level, is required to consider and submit personal and departmental objectives for a pre-defined period. Senior management and their professional advisers then put in hand techniques for improving company performance as a whole. Coordination is called for, together with close monitoring of personal and departmental management performance, measured against the agreed objectives. In some organizations, penalties are applied where performance falls below that specified by the objectives. The concept reached peak popularity in the 1980s and 1990s.

Marketing management is particularly sensitive to MBO techniques. This is because in economically difficult times marketing has to justify its existence more than other departments. In many organizations it is among the first to be considered for downsizing.

Manufacturers' agent   *Sales technique*

An independent sales organization or individual, with active contacts among buyers in various markets and businesses. The agent is hired by manufacturers to sell products and services to these contacts. Payment for this effort is usually commission on sales; sometimes a retainer is included, to maintain the agent's interest and loyalty.

Manuscript   *Advertising, Copywriting, Creative, Editorial*

A piece of handwritten copy. After it has been typed, it is termed a **typescript** (*qv*). *See* Copy, Hard copy.

Marcoms   *Marketing jargon*

A contrived word popularly used as a handy short form for **marketing communications**.

Margin   *Artwork, Copywriting, Creative, Desktop publishing, Print,*
                                            Production, Word-processing

On a printed page the blank, unprinted area on the edges of a sheet, outside the printed matter. Margins can be top, bottom, left or right of the copy, and all round it. The term includes the blank area of the **gutter**, the column of white space between two facing pages.

Margin   *Distribution, Retailing, Sales*

Margin is the difference between the price a distributor or retailer pays in purchasing a product and the price charged to customers. The selling price needs to take into account the distributor's overheads and other costs, and an element of profit.
See Grid.

Marked proof   *Artwork. Copywriting, Desktop publishing, Print,*
                                            Production, Typography

A proof supplied specifically for proof-reading. Corrections are marked on this proof by those qualified or assigned to handle it. This includes copywriter, proof-reader, approver and printer. To distinguish who has done each check, copywriters and proof-readers usually mark their corrections in red, authors in black or blue, typesetters and printers in green. *Caveat*: this is simply a convention, not a hard rule.

Another caveat: you may be asked to sign a marked proof you have checked, even though you have found no errors or omissions on it. This means that you have to be thorough in your proof-checking, and also stand by your decisions. Apart from any other considerations, accurate proof-checking saves time and money.

Market   *Business, Marketing, Marketing communications,*
                                        Trade and commerce

Originally, a market was a regular rendezvous where vendors would meet buyers for trading goods, tools, provisions and livestock, and for hiring staff. Today, the concept is much the same, but the increasing sophistication of technology has changed almost everything else:

- Advertising and the media have become the marketplace.
- Communications are faster.
- Customers can be accessed at high speed, and in their homes and offices.
- Customers can be targeted very accurately.
- Market sizes are vastly greater.
- They can be local, regional, national and international.
- The central physical venue is no longer essential.

The current concept of a market lies in the demand for a product or service by specific groups of customers and prospects, and the capacity of vendors to meet it.

Market acceptance   *Marketing, Marketing communications*

A situation in which a product or service is in sufficient demand for the producer to carry on producing it. This is a management decision, based on the estimated future of the product, its capacity for development, and the ability of the company to profit from it.

Market attrition   *Marketing*

A decline in customer loyalty for a brand. This may come about through competitive activity; apathy or indecision by the brand's management; its inability to recognize or respond to competitive attack; lack of funds for effective promotion. Or, just that the market no longer wants the brand. It happens.

Market awareness   *Marketing, Marketing communications*

A brand's position, and its continuing recognition, in its marketplace. This can be worn away by **market attrition** (*qv*).

Market coverage   *Distribution, Marketing, Marketing communications, Sales*

The amount of exposure a product or service receives while aimed at its target audiences. This can be both estimated and calculated, using data based on promotional effort and expenditure, response volume, and the conversion of leads and enquiries into sales. In the case of consumer products, additional factors such as physical coverage of sales forces and stocks taken up by distributors and sales outlets are taken into account.

Market coverage strategy   *Management, Marketing*

Marketing strategy designed to achieve maximum coverage, using a selection of measures in the **marketing mix** (*qv*). No product lasts forever, and no market is immortal. Everything changes with time, even for old-established brands. Each market therefore, and each marketing situation, demands constant re-examination of its individual strategy.

Market indicators   *Business, Management, Marketing, Research*
Changes in individual, national or international markets, revealed by research and analysed for management decision-making. In most cases, a standard set of indicator factors is examined and applied to the research, as well as maverick factors that arise with unusual circumstances. In modern, fast-moving market conditions constant monitoring is necessary, so that appropriate counter-measures can be taken by marketing management.

Marketing   *Marketing*
The UK's premier weekly newspaper for professional marketers and others involved in the marketing of goods and services. It provides news and features covering all areas of marketing, including marketing techniques, advertising and media; perceptive features on key marketing issues; and exclusive industry league table supplements. Target readership: marketing professionals in the UK's leading companies, and executives in advertising agencies and marketing services companies, including public relations, sales promotion, direct marketing and marketing research. Published in London; established 1964.

Marketing   *Marketing concepts*
There is more than one definition, and all leave something to be desired. This is not meant to denigrate either the definers or the definitions. It is simply that marketing is so all-encompassing that a single, handy definition cannot be entirely adequate. The Chartered Institute of Marketing defines it as follows: 'the management process responsible for identifying, anticipating and satisfying customer requirements profitably'.

Without much effort, you can see that marketing encompasses the total commercial activity of an enterprise – itself a viable definition. In considering marketing activity, it is important to understand a number of widely accepted factors:

- Marketing operates on the belief that a business, and its decisions, should be governed by its markets and customers, rather than by its own motives, technology and production capability.
- It is an orderly, systematic process of business planning, decision-making, implementation and control.
- It is a form of management by objectives, and places strong emphasis on innovation.
- It is considered a means of employing dynamic business strategy, and demands commercial acumen and organization of a high order.
- It employs advanced techniques and systems based on scientific principles. These are drawn from economics, research, statistics, finance and behavioural sciences.

- It employs a system of commercial intelligence, including information on activities in its own markets, and on its competitors'.
- It takes into account the political, economic, sociological, technological, legal and environmental climates in which it operates.
- It demands constant training at a high professional level.
- The common purpose of these activities is to serve customers, meeting their needs with products and services.

Marketing audit *Marketing planning*
A technique for gathering data on a company's marketing activities over a pre-defined period. Normally, an audit is carried out as part of marketing planning for a forthcoming campaign, or when planning activities for the next viable period. A marketing audit is essential when planning a company's business expansion or extension of its product range. It may also be required if a company is concerned about the lack of progress in its markets, or when things seem to be going wrong.

Marketing budget *Marketing planning*
The allocation of finance for a company's marketing activities for a pre-defined period; usually, a year. Budgeting needs to take into account all marketing activities, including marketing communications, sales and other promotion, trade promotion activities, exhibitions, marketing research; often also the cost of running the marketing department, and its commitments to suppliers, agents and consultants.

Marketing channels *Distribution, Marketing*
The means by which a company's products and services get to its customers. This includes wholesalers, retailers, direct marketing routes and the Internet. However, the Internet may also be considered a marketing communications medium as well as a channel of distribution.

Marketing communications *Marketing*
Techniques and media for reaching target audiences with promotional messages. These include:

- advertising;
- aerial advertising (eg airships, hot-air balloons)
- body media (eg T-shirts, tracksuits, with promotional messages);
- carrier bags, sports bags;
- catalogues;
- cinema;
- e-commerce;
- exhibitions;
- interactive video;
- Internet;
- livery design and display;
- mini media (eg book matches, ashtrays, beer mats);

- outdoor;
- packaging;
- point of sale material;
- promotional give-aways (eg diaries, calendars, keyrings);
- public relations;
- radio;
- sales literature;
- sales promotion;
- sponsorship;
- television.

The term is often, though vulgarly, abbreviated to **marcoms**, making it possible to avoid the tedious business of writing or speaking the whole phrase.

Marketing communications director   *Marketing personnel*
Another title, used in some organizations, for advertising or publicity director; a senior manager usually responsible for all a company's marcoms activities.

Marketing communications mix   *Marketing, Marketing communications*
The selection of marketing communications tools, techniques and media needed to carry out a specific marketing campaign. Products, markets, market conditions and target audiences change with time, predictably and sometimes unpredictably. The marcoms mix may therefore need to be considered afresh with each new marketing plan.

Marketing concept   *Marketing operations, Marketing philosophy,*
Marketing planning
A company's marketing mission statement; the basic motivation behind its marketing policy. When properly applied, a marketing concept involves a company's attitude towards every element and stage of its corporate and product marketing operations, from prototype to profit. Customer satisfaction is often a substantial element in marketing concept formulation, since it holds the promise of long-term prosperity. In certain circumstances, it may also involve considerations of moral and social responsibility.

Marketing effort   *Marketing management, Marketing operations*
A company's human, financial and physical resources invested in its marketing operations; or in an individual marketing operation. Not surprisingly, since all resources cost money, a company needs to include maximum sales, profits and development in its calculations for marketing effort.

Marketing intelligence system   *Marketing operations, planning,*
development and control
A system for identifying, gathering and processing marketing intelligence. Its aim is to provide marketing management with information on which to make decisions

on current and future marketing operations. Such a system needs to be capable of coping with and adapting to changing marketing situations and environments over a long period.

Marketing management *Marketing operations*

The team responsible for running a company's marketing operations, normally headed by a marketing director. The activity in which the team is involved is itself termed marketing management. It includes all a company's marketing functions and responsibilities, from concept and planning to implementation, evaluation and control.

Marketing mix *Marketing planning*

The mixture of tools, techniques and media commonly used in planning marketing operations. These are usually summarized in what has become known as **the four Ps**: product, price, place and promotion. Obviously, this simple formula can serve only as the basis of a wider concept for running marketing operations at worthwhile profit levels.

Seen in a more realistic and practical way, the marketing mix comprises a wide range of considerations and activities. Obviously not every campaign will include every element in the mix, but every viable campaign must incorporate some of them. They include:

- advertising and advertising research;
- after-sales service;
- branding and positioning;
- CRM, customer relationship management;
- developing a product range;
- distribution systems;
- exhibitions;
- Internet activities; e-commerce;
- market awareness and education activities;
- market segmentation;
- marketing research;
- media research;
- packaging;
- pricing;
- product concepts and conceptual planning;
- product naming;
- product or service innovation and invention;
- product research, development and modification;
- public relations;
- sales operations, field and call-centre;
- sales promotion;
- sponsorship;
- test marketing;
- Web site creation and operation.

Marketing modelling *Marketing management, Marketing planning*
The testing of marketing plans, procedures, campaigns and their likely outcomes. Usually this is computer simulation of marketing data, where every element in the model is variable. This enables marketing managers and planners to manipulate data in any way they wish; particularly, to aim for the most profitable solutions.

Marketing objectives *Marketing management, Marketing planning*
The setting of a company's marketing goals for a pre-determined period. In certain circumstances this could be synonymous with business objectives; where, for example, a company is entirely marketing oriented, as with direct response operations. Marketing objectives can be both short and long term. Long term can be anything from 5 to 10 years. Short term is usually 1 year to 5. A typical marketing objectives plan will include:

- overall objectives for the period;
- overall strategies, eg:
  - customer relationship management;
  - customer service;
  - marketing communications;
  - new customers;
  - new media, eg the Internet;
  - new products;
  - pricing policy and strategy;
  - selling strategy and tactics;
  - targets for:
    - □ annual growth rate;
    - □ profitability;
    - □ sales;
  - market share;
- action details, eg:
  - costs;
  - responsibilities;
  - timing;
- contingency plans, eg:
  - critical assumptions and their management;
  - financial implications and consequences;
- operational results:
  - financial ratios, including:
    - □ adjustments;
    - □ bank interest;
    - □ cost of administration;
    - □ gross margin;
    - □ marketing costs;
    - □ net revenues;

☐ overall operating result;
☐ return on investment;
☐ return on sales;
☐ sales to profit ratio.

Marketing plans   *Marketing management, Marketing planning*
Comprehensive plans covering all the thinking, activity and cost of achieving
marketing objectives over a specified period. Once completed, this is the planning
bible used by management and internal staff, and external suppliers such as
agencies, assigned to carry out the marketing plan.
See Marketing objectives.

Marketing research   *Marketing operations, Marketing planning*
The use of scientific and statistical techniques for gathering, processing and
analysing information for the marketing of products, services and corporations.
The term **marketing research** covers more than market research, which is limited
to research into markets and their characteristics. Marketing research extends, for
example, to information and studies on:

■ branding and positioning studies;
■ changes in consumer attitudes;
■ customer and end-user motivation;
■ effectiveness of communications tools such as media and advertisements;
■ packaging design and its effectiveness.

Marketing services   *Marketing practice*
Specialized professional services engaged in support of marketing operations,
either in-house or external. These include:

■ advertising creative and production activities;
■ direct mail;
■ educational and awareness activities;
■ exhibitions;
■ graphic design;
■ marketing research;
■ media selection and purchase;
■ merchandising;
■ packaging, design and production;
■ pre-print services;
■ print and production;
■ public relations;
■ sales promotion;
■ sponsorship;
■ test marketing.

Marketing services manager *Marketing administration*
A company executive responsible for commissioning and running marketing services (*qv*).

Marketing strategy *Marketing management, Marketing planning*
The setting of overall goals for a company's marketing operations, or these for an individual product or service. This is usually done by senior management, or at product management level subsequently approved by marketing management. The formal marketing strategy statement may also include, in broad terms, the methods by which the goals are to be achieved.

Market intelligence *Marketing, Marketing research*
Data on markets in which a company operates, techniques used for gathering it, and the data itself.

Market leader *Marketing*
A company, brand or product with the largest share of a particular market.

Market measurement *Marketing research*
The collection of data on a particular market, covering its value, volume and brand shares. Measuring a market over time enables a marketing management team to see its trends, and estimate the potential for the entry or development of their brand.

Market niche *Marketing planning and practice*
A small part of a market in which a company can devote effort, money and other resources towards making a worthwhile profit. This occurs where a company is unable to compete with its larger and richer competitors. In such a case, a company actively seeks viable market niches, or creates them by offering new products and services to meet their needs and wants. The company usually plans to achieve competitive advantage, eventually gaining domination or exclusivity.

Market penetration *Marketing practice, Marketing research*
The extent to which a product or service has succeeded in gaining its share of sales in a market. This applies also to its competitors. This information, and that from market measurement, helps marketing management teams to plan their next moves.

Market positioning *Marketing management, Marketing practice*
Entering or developing a market, or market segment, in which a company can gain recognition, ranking, competitive advantage, domination or monopoly.

Market potential *Marketing*
A company's estimate of the share it can achieve in a particular market over a predetermined period. The term also applies to a company's estimate of a market or niche which, with appropriate effort and resources, it might exploit profitably.

Market price *Business, Marketing*
A common price, price bracket or price range charged for a product or service. This is as much related to the price customers are willing to pay for a product as to that which the supplier decides is appropriate to ask for it.

Market profile *Marketing campaign planning, Marketing research*
Characteristics of a market, in the form of facts essential to the planning of marketing campaigns. Accurate profiling is vital to the evaluation both of market segments and niches, and global markets.

Market reach *Marketing activity, Marketing campaign planning*
The estimated number of customers or potentials a company believes it can reach with a marketing campaign. For this figure to be realistic, the budget and resources of the campaign may need to be taken into account. The term also applies to the number of enquiries, leads or sales actually achieved by a campaign once it has ended.

Market recognition *Marketing activity*
Recognition in a company's marketplace of the company, its products and services. Evidence for such recognition lies in enquiries, leads and sales, at wholesale, retail and direct response levels.

Market research *Marketing operations, Marketing planning*
A research activity related to marketing research, but usually limited to the gathering, processing and analysis of information on markets.
See Marketing research.

Marking down *Distribution, Retailing, Sales*
The practice of reducing prices to customers. This is usually done for a limited period, as an extra inducement to buy, and promoted as a sale of goods below normal prices.

Mark it! *Commercials, Film, Video*
The cry of a film director when a scene is ready for shooting. The clappers boy, a member of the crew, then darts in front of the camera, holds the **clapperboard** in front of it and whacks the clapper down on the board. The data on the board is recorded on the film or tape, and the sound recorded simultaneously. This is essential for editing, when each scene and take must be correctly identified, and the sound and picture brought together and combined in the editing suite.

Mark-up *Artwork, Print production, Typography*
Carefully calculated written instructions on how a piece of copy should be typeset. Computerized word-processing, artworking and typesetting has made this much easier; and in many cases eliminated conventional mark-ups altogether.
See Make-up.

Mark-up   *Direct marketing, Retailing, Sales*
A figure added by the seller to the cost of a product, so that the sale price gives
him a viable profit. The combined figure is the one offered to the customer.

Married print   *Film, television and video post-production*
Film or videotape on which picture and sound have been synchronized in the
editing suite. This is the final stage in film-making. The tracks are married with
great accuracy so that video and audio run in absolute synchronization. Also
termed a **combined print**.

Mask   *Artwork, Computer imaging, Production, Studio work*
A protective mask, cut, shaped and placed over a piece of artwork or photoprint.
This ensures that while the artwork or print is being worked on, the shielded parts
are not marred, damaged or distorted. In computer imaging, masks are used to
isolate areas of an image for manipulation. Masks are created by sampling colours
within an image to define the areas. Elements not selected are unaffected by editing
or manipulation. Masks can also be drawn on screen using a mouse or digital
tablet.

Masking   *Artwork, Production, Studio work*
When part of an illustration or photoprint is to be airbrushed or painted over, the
rest of the artwork is usually protected from unintentional spraying or splashes.
This protection is termed masking. It is usually done with special transparent or
translucent film and masking tape.

   Where part of an image itself needs to be painted out with opaque medium so
that it will not reproduce, this technique is termed **blocking out**, or sometimes
alternatively, **masking**.

Maslow, A H   *Human behaviour, Marketing theory, Motivational theory*
The well-known US psychologist. His hierarchy of pre-potent needs is used by
marketers to define human behaviour in relation to how it can be satisfied with
products and services. This makes some sense, when you consider how need is
defined by James Drever in *A Dictionary of Psychology* (Penguin, 1971): 'A
condition marked by a feeling of lack or want of something, or of requiring the
performance of some action'.

   Maslow published his theory of self-actualization and hierarchy of needs in
Motivation and Personality (New York, Harper & Row, 1954). In it he states that
human behaviour is characterized by a priority of needs, in five distinct groups:

1. self-actualization needs (inner need to develop one's full capabilities);
2. esteem needs (prestige, success, self-respect);
3. belonging needs (love, affection, affiliation, identification);
4. safety needs (security, order, stability);
5. physiological needs (hunger, thirst, sex, physical activity).

The hierarchy is usually shown as a pyramid, physiological needs at the foot, self-actualization at the top. While Maslow's theory is a useful marketing tool, it is wise to treat it with discretion. Needs, wants and desires can sometimes be interchangeable; for example, there may be a conflict between the need to eat and the desire to possess a television receiver. Both are legitimate, but not at the expense of each other. Marketing exploits human priorities; it uses the consumer's need to take action in order to relieve the tension generated by the need. In other words, 'When the going gets tough, the tough go shopping'.

Maslow's hierarchy of human needs   *Human behaviour, Motivational theory*
See Maslow, A H.

Mass advertising   *Advertising, Marketing, Media*
The use of mass media to reach and promote products and services to a mass market. Television, the press, radio and outdoor advertising are the four mass media popularly used in industrialized countries.

Mass communications   *Advertising, Marketing, Marketing communications, Public relations*
The use of creative techniques and media to deliver promotional messages at high speed to target audiences on a large scale.

Mass market   *Marketing*
A market for products and services, large enough to warrant the use of mass communications, and to justify the expense of doing this.

Mass media   *Advertising media*
Television, press, radio and outdoor, which convey advertising and public relations messages to mass audiences.
See Mass advertising.

Master proof   *Print, Production*
A definitive proof, containing all corrections and remarks, held by a printer for current and future reference. And to protect his rear.

Master sample   *Marketing research*
A major control sample from which further samples can be extracted. This is most valuable when the characteristics of the master sample do not change frequently, as with postcodes (zip codes) or parliamentary constituencies. Using a master sample can make field research cost-effective.

Masthead   *Editorial, Press, Publishing*
The title at the head of a newspaper or magazine, running across the top of its front page. Often also applied to the title heading on its contents and leader pages. The title of a newspaper or magazine along the top of its inside pages is termed a **running head**.

Matched samples *Marketing research*
Two or more samples with matching characteristics, to be brought together and compared with each other. This technique helps to arrive at more viable survey results, when used as an aid to decision-making. Characteristics compared can be those of age, occupation, location and so on. Weighting techniques can also yield results of similar accuracy.

Matching in *Advertising, Direct mail, Production*
Personalizing a sales letter when used as a mailshot. Adding the recipient's name, job title, company and address to the address section, and a salutation at the start of the text. With appropriate software, this can be done during the production run.

Matter *Creative, Desktop publishing, Editorial, Media campaign planning, Print, Production, Typography, Word-processing*
A term generally used to denote copy in any form – manuscript, typescript or printed text and illustrations. In media scheduling, the term **facing matter** is an instruction to place an advertisement directly facing editorial material on a spread. The instruction **next matter** indicates placing an advertisement right next to a piece of editorial on the same page. Advertisements facing or next to matter usually cost more than those that are run-of-paper; that is, anywhere the publisher fancies. *See* Mini-page, Run-of-paper ad, Solus.

Matt finish *Paper, Print*
A coated paper with a dull, smooth finish, without gloss or lustre.

Matt print *Photography, Reprographics*
A photoprint with a dull surface finish.

Maximum brand exposure *Advertising, Distribution, Marketing, Marketing communications*
Maximum marketing effort in the promotion of a concept, company, brand, product, service or political philosophy. All the appropriate tools of marketing communication are used, including:

- advertising;
- direct mail and direct response techniques;
- distribution techniques;
- exhibitions;
- field sales effort;
- in-store merchandising;
- public relations;
- seminars;
- sponsorship;
- trade promotions.

The over-riding objective usually is to raise brand awareness, and sales, to the highest possible level in the shortest possible time.

MEAL *Advertising media research*
The acronym for **Media Expenditure Analysis Ltd**, the UK research organization specializing in monitoring and reporting advertising expenditure.

Mean audit date *Retail auditing*
In retail auditing, the date on which a particular store's audit is carried out. With computerization and online reporting, the date can be fixed precisely. In the case of smaller stores with no computerization, which need to be visited by research personnel, the date is averaged to within specified limits.

Measure *Artwork, Composition, Creative, Desktop publishing, Typography, Word-processing*
The length of a line of type, and the width of the column it makes.
See Full out, Justified, Make-up, Margin, Mark-up, Ragged right, Range.

Mechanical *Artwork, Print, Production, Reprographics*
The complete version of layout, artwork and copy, ready for reproduction, with all instructions in place.
See Make-up, Mark-up.

Mechanical binding *Print, Production*
A binding method for printed pages, using metal or plastic wire or strip. The pages are first collated, and perforated or punched along one edge; the binding is then inserted. This binding method holds the pages together so that they lie flat when opened.

Mechanical data *Creative, Media campaign planning and buying, Production, Publishing*
Also termed **production specifications**. Production information supplied by newspaper, magazine and directory publishers, giving dimensions and other physical characteristics of their media. The information includes:

- artwork and film requirements;
- colours used;
- column widths;
- copy dates;
- delivery instructions;
- halftone screen;
- page size;
- printing process;
- type area.

The information is usually supplied in the form of a media advertising pack or kit. It is also given in digest form in publishers' listings in the UK media directory *British Rate and Data* (*qv*). Similar national media directories are published in Europe, the USA and elsewhere.
See BRAD.

Media   *Advertising, Marketing communications, Media planning and buying,*
Public relations
A term denoting the range of communication channels used for entertainment, news, advertising and public relations activities. Colleges and universities now offer courses in media studies.

Media, in a marketing communications connotation, are tools by which marketers are able to reach specific target audiences. Media owners offer a huge volume of research information on their subscribers, readers, viewers and listeners. They offer the opportunity, and the means, to reach virtually every target audience campaigns need – from accountants to zoologists. They are capable of doing this accurately, and with minimum waste.

Creatives working on advertising and public relations campaigns need to study media research, as much as does account management. The data can provide illumination on the targets that campaigns are required to influence; valuable insight into their lifestyles and buying behaviour; and how they are likely to react to advertising and public relations messages.

Media   *Desktop publishing, Information technology, Word-processing*
The means by which material generated by computer is stored. Magnetic media include hard, floppy and zip disks. CD ROM and re-writable compact disks also store computer material, but are not magnetic.

Media analyst   *Advertising agencies, Advertising research,*
Media independents
A research professional specializing in assembling and evaluating advertising media data. Most larger agencies offer this service to clients, as do the media independent specialist companies.

Media appropriation   *Advertising campaign planning, Advertising*
finance, Media planning
A budget for advertising activities. Advertising media scheduling is limited to the amount of money in the appropriation.

Media broker   *Advertising media services*
A company or individual specializing in buying advertising space or airtime for advertisers and agencies. Leading companies in the business may also offer media analysis, planning and administration services.
See Media independent.

Media buyer   *Advertising agency personnel, Marketing department personnel*
An agency or marketing department specialist executive responsible for purchasing media space and airtime. In many advertising agencies, press and broadcast media buying are separate functions.

Media commission   *Advertising agency practice, Agency remuneration*
Remuneration granted by media owners to advertising agencies on media bookings. Some agencies hand the commission to their clients, and are paid by fee instead.

Media data form   *Media auditing and research*
A document supplied by the Audit Bureau of Circulations, showing press media information in a set format. Used by media planners and buyers, advertisers and their agencies, for media analysis and comparison, evaluation, selection, scheduling and buying. Principal data include:

- advertising rates;
- editorial policy;
- geographical distribution;
- net paid circulation;
- readership;
- readership profile.

See ABC, Audit Bureau of Circulations.

Media evaluation   *Media planning and buying*
Comparison of media for planning selection, scheduling and buying. Media planners take everything into consideration, including:

- advertising rates;
- audiences;
- circulation;
- cost-effectiveness;
- coverage;
- publication and air dates;
- readership.

Media independent   *Advertising planning and buying*
A company specializing in the planning and purchasing of media for advertisers and agencies. They do not offer creative and production services; these are the domain of regular advertising service agencies and consultancies.

Media mix   *Advertising campaign planning*
The combination of appropriate media to be considered for advertising campaign planning and scheduling. The overall budget for a campaign usually influences

which media are selected and how much money is devoted to each. The final selection is determined by how effectively the mix fulfils a campaign's objectives.

Media owner   *Broadcast media, Media planning and buying, Publishing*
In press media, publishers are the owners; in television media, the contractors; in radio, the station owners; in outdoor, the site owners. The term is generally applied to the companies from which advertising insertions, airtime and outdoor media are reserved, bought and paid for. The term also includes cinema networks and Web site owners.

Media planner   *Media planning and scheduling*
A specialist in media analysis, evaluation and planning. The planner usually works to an objective, brief and budget. Her recommendations will be considered by, among others, the advertiser's marketing and advertising management; the advertising agency's account management and media buyers; often, also, their senior creative and production specialists.

Media relations   *Public relations*
A company's effort to set up and maintain relationships with press and broadcast media. This is usually done by personal contact over a long period. The objective is to enable the company's corporate and product messages to reach their ultimate publics via the media, without damage to their content or integrity en route. In the UK, it is regarded as ignoble actually to try to influence editorial integrity and content in this way. The quality of editorial material offered to the media by organizations and their consultancies should be sufficiently high, and newsworthy, to secure publication.

Media research   *Advertising and marketing campaign planning*
The gathering, analysis and evaluation of media used in campaigns, usually carried out on a continuous basis. The main elements carried forward to campaign planning are press media circulation, coverage, readership and cost; broadcast media and cinema audiences, and cost; outdoor traffic and cost. The media owners usually supply their own figures. In the UK the principal independent research organizations are:

- Internet: ABC//electronic;
- outdoor: POSTAR;
- press media: ABC, VFD and National Readership Survey;
- radio: RAJAR;
- television: BARB.

Media schedule   *Advertising media campaign planning and buying*
The comprehensive document compiled by media planners, showing the range of media to be booked for an advertising campaign. A schedule usually includes:

- channels;
- costs;
- discounts;
- insertion dates;
- insertion sizes;
- media titles;
- packages;
- spots;
- times.

In the UK, the European Union, the USA and most industrialized countries, media schedules are computerized, making them easy to process and manipulate. Some companies and advertising agencies prepare comprehensive schedules including all media; some prepare separate schedules for each medium. For press media, a schedule should include at least:

- advertiser's name;
- campaign executive's name and signature;
- campaign period;
- cost per insertion;
- job number;
- number of insertions;
- product name;
- publication titles;
- schedule issue date;
- schedule of insertion dates;
- space size;
- total cost for each publication;
- total cost of press campaign.

A schedule for broadcast media should include at least:

- advertiser's name;
- campaign executive's name and signature;
- campaign period;
- cost per spot;
- job number;
- number of spots;
- product name;
- running time for each spot;
- schedule issue date;
- schedule of spots: dates, times, programme names;
- station name;
- total cost for each station;
- total cost for the airtime campaign.

Media selection *Media campaign planning and buying*
Selecting advertising media for the cost-effective fulfilment of campaign objectives. In-depth coverage of this complex subject can be found in Martyn Davis's excellent book *The Effective Use of Advertising Media*, Century Business, London, 2000.

Media shop *Advertising media planning and buying*
Jargon for an independent company specializing in the planning and purchasing of media for advertisers and agencies.
See Media independent.

Media strategy *Advertising planning*
One of the two main tools of advertising strategy; the other being **creative strategy**. Media strategy is the plan and means by which a marketing team reaches its target audiences. Creative strategy is the conception and creation of messages for the eyes and ears of those audiences. Not only are they equally important; either they are interdependent or they are ineffective.

There is often conflict between the requirements of media and creativity. For example, media demands may dictate large-size insertions, high frequency or a long campaign. Creativity may demand full-colour insertions rather than spot colour or black and white. Since advertising budgets are usually fixed at the start of a company's financial year, and cannot normally be augmented, management conflict of this kind may arise. A prudent compromise may satisfy both parties.

Medium *Advertising, Marketing communications, Public relations*
In marketing terminology, a channel of communication for advertising campaigns. That is to say, press, television, radio, outdoor, cinema, and the Internet. The word is often also applied to exhibitions, sponsorship and public relations activity.

Merchandise *Distribution, Marketing, Retailing*
Products for sale, usually applied to products destined for, or actually offered in, retail outlets. Also termed **goods**.

Merchandising *Distribution, Marketing, Point-of-sale display, Retailing*
A wide range of marketing activities conducted at the point of sale. The objective is to sell as much product as possible in the shortest possible time, or encourage the fast take-up of a new product.

The point of sale is the marketer's final opportunity for influencing customers and prospects. You want them to make buying decisions in favour of your brand, and to take action immediately. It follows that, having spent money on other marketing communications, such as advertising and public relations, you would want to go the whole way. No so in many cases. Astute advertisers put money into merchandising. Others do not, and wonder why their brand leadership has disappeared.

Merchandising activities tools include special packaging, in-store displays, banners, showcards, posters and mobiles; live demonstrations and interactive videos. Pricing offers, discounts and deals are often trailed and promoted in advertising.

Merchandising pieces are usually designed, produced and offered to retailers by advertisers for the promotion of their branded products. For good examples, look around supermarkets and department stores. Dixons, the British electrical product retailers, produce their own displays, even though they sell many different brands. On the other hand, high street retailers such as Marks & Spencer and Ikea produce their own merchandising displays; their goods carry only one label.

Merge and purge   *Databases, Direct mail, Direct marketing,*
                                          Direct response advertising
Setting up a database by merging two different or related databases, and eliminating duplicate data. The result should be a good basic database, ready for testing. A test should reveal recipients who have gone away, changed occupation or status; the database should then be ready for use or hire.

Micro marketing   *Marketing techniques*
A form of marketing activity aimed at individual companies or groups of companies. Unlike **macro marketing** (*qv*), which is broad-scale in its function, micro marketing aims to satisfy the needs and aspirations of its target companies by finding out what they are. Therefore, if you are marketing electrical equipment to automobile or aircraft manufacturers, research into the needs of the target companies is as vital as knowing what their customers want.

Microperf   *Marketing communications, Paper, Print*
A perforated edge, very finely cut. This technique is often used to simulate the effect of a guillotine-cut edge. Sales literature sometimes uses this technique, where a page is designed to be detached by the recipient and faxed to the advertiser.

Middleman   *Business, Distribution, Marketing, Trade*
An intermediary. A company or individual who brings together the producer of a product or service and its customers or consumers. This is a useful function, despite the poor reputation middlemen may have earned in the past. Sometimes there is no other way of setting up or activating a trade relationship or transaction, especially where the parties involved want to keep the activity confidential.

Migration   *Media research*
A term describing what happens when television audiences switch channels to avoid viewing commercials. In audience samples used for research, migration can be monitored accurately. The term is also used in research into newspaper readership, though it cannot be quantified with such accuracy.

Mileage   *Advertising, Marketing communications, Public relations*
The value, impact or income obtained from an advertising medium, insertion, campaign, or budget; and from public relations effort and budget.

MIME *Communications, Information technology*
The abbreviation for **Multipurpose Internet Mail Extensions**. A method of
formatting non-ASCII e-mail so that it can be sent over the Internet. It enables the
sending and receiving of audio, video, formatted text and graphics, and a variety
of character sets.

Mini-page *Media planning and buying*
Also termed a **junior page**. An advertising space in a newspaper or magazine,
about three-quarters of a page; usually solus, with editorial on two or three sides.
This format offers an opportunity to dominate a page without actually paying for
the whole of it. Naturally, this special position costs more than the same space run-
of-paper; but it is worthwhile if you can also specify on which page it appears.
See Matter, Run-of-paper ad, Solus.

Minus leading *Desktop publishing, Typography, Word-processing*
Also termed **negative leading**. Type set with less space from base-line to base-
line than the height of the characters themselves. This can be done in computer
setting, but not in hot metal. For example, when 16pt type is set with 14pt leading,
the ascenders and descenders overlap. This technique is useful for achieving
special typographic effects, though it can look eccentric when used solely for the
sake of design. It can also easily render copy unreadable.

Mission statement *Business, Marketing planning*
A statement by a company, corporation or organization, setting out its *raison d'être*
and intentions. Although the statement may be brief, it is the central guide
governing the organization's conduct and operating policy for the foreseeable
future. A marketing plan may also begin with its mission statement.

Mix *Film post-production, Sound recording, Television, Video*
An optical dissolve (*qv*), in which one scene gradually fades while another takes
its place. The term is also used for the technique of combining several sound tracks
on to a single track, and adjusting each track to optimum level.

Mock-up *Artwork, Creative, Desktop publishing, Production, Typography,*
Word-processing
A rough design rendering of a leaflet, brochure, booklet, showcard, poster, pack,
and any other two- or three-dimensional promotional tool. In this form, the creative
team can present the design to its clientele at reasonable cost; or at least without
incurring the much higher expense of a more finished presentation.
See Origination, Visual.

Model *Marketing planning*
A marketing plan where every variable is represented by a mathematical calculation. This enables the marketing team to change any variable and see how the
change affects every other variable. Computer modelling is a fast, reliable method

of carrying out marketing modelling operations, and an important aid in decision-making.

Modem *Communications, Desktop publishing, Information technology*
A computer hardware device that accepts signals and converts them for transmission over an analogue channel such as a telephone line. It also receives and accepts analogue signals from remote modems, and converts them into a digital form, which a computer can recognize and process. A modem enables text, full-colour designs, pictures, illustrations and proofs to be sent at high speed by telephone, ISDN or ADSL (*qv*) to the media, printers and other suppliers, with no loss of quality.

Mods *Artwork, Copywriting, Creative, Marketing,*
Product development
Short for **modifications**. Changes, usually but not invariably improvements, to copy, designs and artwork. In manufacturing, product modifications are usually made for the same purpose; to improve performance, marketability or profitability, or all three at once.

Moiré pattern *Artwork, Creative, Photography, Plate-making,*
Print, Production
A bizarre and usually unwelcome pattern of dots, produced when two or more blocks of lines or screens clash. In print, the effect is produced when halftone screens are incorrectly angled during filming, plate-making or printing. It can be seen on television, when an actor or presenter is inappropriately dressed; say, wearing a chequered jacket or a tie with narrow horizontal stripes.

One of the finest examples of this effect on television is John McCririck, the UK's Channel 4 racing correspondent. A great showman, resplendent in sideburns, he is often seen wearing deer-stalker, check or chintz waistcoat, carnation button-hole, pince-nez, and other Victoriana. John is a truly original English eccentric, and his copy magnificent journalism. His waistcoats and ties, however, sometimes produce bizarre effects on television screens, including moiré patterns.

Television screen lines are horizontal; John's waistcoat stripes, checks, polka dots and wiggles can clash with them. The resulting myriad multicoloured sparks, flashes and whorls are a visual delight – though not to the programme's director. Similar effects can appear on the printed page, followed by the printer's nightmare. Unless there is a need to incorporate them into brand imaging, they are best avoided. If they are definitely not what the marketing team wants, reimbursement may be obtained from the supplier who fouled up.
See Halftone.

Monitor *Desktop publishing, Information technology, Word-processing*
A computer screen used as an output display. All screens now supplied with computers handle full-colour material, though the resolution varies from model to model.

Mono *Artwork, Photography, Print*
Print jargon shorthand for **monochrome**; ie print or reproduction in a single colour, but popularly taken to represent black and white.

Monopoly *Business, Economics, Marketing*
A situation in which a single producer, distributor or service provider dominates and controls a marketplace, and excludes all competition. In some countries, the government has a monopoly on many products and services. In this case, there being no rivals, monopoly usually makes for stability in the marketplace. On the other hand, the monopolist can change prices at will, make changes in product specification and distribution, create scarcities, and even withdraw products altogether.

Monopsony *Business, Economics, Marketing*
A situation in which there is only one purchaser of a product or service. In this case, the purchaser can also be the distributor, as with stores owned by a government.

Monoscanner *Artwork, Production*
A high-resolution device used for scanning line work and film.

Monotype *Artwork, Composition, Print, Production, Typesetting, Typography*
A US company, producers of typesetting software; formerly specializing in hot-metal typesetting machines setting type in single characters. The alternative system was **Linotype**, typesetting machinery that set hot-metal type in **slugs** – whole lines. Monotype now produces hardware and software for computer typesetting. It may still make hot-metal machines for use in developing countries; but not, presumably, for Europe, the USA, Australia, Japan and other industrialized economies where the computer dominates.
See Character, Nought, Null, Proof, Proof-reader, Proof-reader's marks, Quote, Zero.

Montage *Artwork, Marketing communications*
In artwork, design and studio practice, a collection of different images in a single illustration.

Montage *Commercials, Film, Film post-production, Television, Video*
A quick-cut assembly of shots or sounds. This is often used, for example, to convey aggression or the passage of time. In television commercials, the technique is often used for the sake of mere artistry, often resulting in bizarre, confusing and hostile effects. There is little place in marketing for such techniques, since clarity is the essence of marketing communications.

Mood advertising *Advertising techniques, Press, Print, Radio, Television*
Advertising that concentrates on creating an atmosphere rather than using hard sell. The technique aims to encourage the reader or viewer into a particular mental attitude. This allows the product being promoted to look desirable for the viewer's

own reasons. Mood advertising sets the stage for mental reflection on benefits to be gained from using the product, without mentioning the effort of acquiring or using it. Or, for that matter, the money needed to purchase it. Often, a change of lifestyle is the major benefit offered by this approach.

MOPS *Direct marketing, Mail order*

Initials for the UK's **Mail Order Protection Scheme**, operated by the **NPA**, Newspaper Publishers Association, and **PPA**, Periodical Publishers Association. This governs the conduct of display advertisements in UK newspapers and magazines. Mail order advertisements are checked and cleared before being released for publication. Advertisers are required to contribute to a financial pool; this may be used to compensate readers who lose money where a trader goes bankrupt or into liquidation.

MOSAIC *Marketing planning, Marketing research*

A proprietary neighbourhood classification system, developed by credit reference agency CCN, which defines 58 lifestyle categories. At its core is a geo-demographic database, with data held on customers, prospects, retail outlets and media in specified geographic areas of the UK. Its main usefulness in marketing is its ability to enable planners to identify an area's unique characteristics, and to analyse its suitability for the promotion and distribution of a product or service.

Motivation *Marketing communications, Promotional psychology, Public relations*

The promotion of a mental state encouraging target audiences to act in fulfilment of their personal objectives. In marcoms terms, this can vary from seduction to blackmail. Take, for example, a person who habitually drinks and then drives. He may be motivated into not doing both at the same time. In motivating such a person by seduction, he can be shown that not mixing drinking and driving can result in a long, healthy and happy life. In a blackmail approach, he can be shown how his own life is at risk. He may be deterred by showing how badly passengers or pedestrians can be injured in a vehicle accident for which he is responsible. In business-to-business communications, a higher motive can be invoked by indicating a person's responsibility to a company, or to a charitable cause.

Looking at Maslow's hierarchy of human needs (*qv*), it appears that self-actualization is the ultimate human objective and motivation. However, all human need can be rendered down to fear. The desire for physical security arises from a fear of physical injury. The desire for food is a fear of hunger. Love is a fear of rejection, as is the desire for recognition. One might even say that the desire for self-actualization is the fear of death, and of being forgotten throughout eternity; a truly frightening train of thought. One cannot condemn marketing communications that use blackmailing treatments, however effective they might be; they are the natural order in a brutally competitive world. On the other hand, such techniques are illegal in some countries. They are certainly declared unacceptable by organizations such as the UK's Advertising Standards Authority (*qv*).

Motivational research   *Behavioural research, Marketing research*
A branch of marketing research dedicated to establishing and understanding why people buy products and services. It gathers and evaluates responses to question-naires, and considers the attitudes and motivations of the respondents. Responses can be reasoned and logical, or emotional and irrational. For this reason, the skill and experience of psychologists in evaluating such responses has to be coupled with the acumen of the marketing team commissioning the research. There are no simple, straightforward answers, but the team still needs to decide whether to invest advertising money in *The Times* or the *Reader's Digest, Accountancy Age* or *Playboy*.

Moving average   *Marketing research, Statistics*
A statistical technique for demonstrating how a company's sales are progressing from period to period, allowing for seasonal variations. Average sales are calcu-lated using an agreed formula. For example, an annual average is arrived at by dividing the year's sales figure by 12. Using this average as a base, from then on the weekly or monthly average is increased or decreased according to an agreed seasonal weighting.

MPEG   *Communications, Digital audio and video reproduction, Internet,*
                                    Marketing communications
Initials for the **Moving Picture Expert Group** of the International Standards Organization. The Group's standards are designed to improve audio and video quality, and simultaneously to increase data compression. The data retains its quality during transmission and storage, yet takes up less space and is therefore more economical than the same data uncompressed. The current equivalent system for still images is JPEG (Joint Photographic Expert Group).

MPS   *Consumer protection, Direct marketing*
The **Mailing Preference Service**, one of the British Direct Marketing Assoc-iation's services to consumers. A consumer can have her name added to or deleted from an advertiser's database, by invoking the MPS and contacting its operator. If the advertiser fails to comply, he can be forced to do so by legal action.

Multi-brand strategy   *Marketing*
A brand strategy designed to protect a supplier's brands and increase market share by excluding competitors. The strategy is based on the infidelity of some con-sumers to a single brand. In any market, some consumers will always switch from brand to brand. Switching is often based on price, special offers, convenience or persuasive advertising. Sometimes they switch for irrational reasons; they may merely want a change from time to time.

Suppose you manufacture and supply household detergents to supermarkets and other retail outlets. To minimize the risk of having consumers switch from your brand to a competitor's, you create a second brand of detergent, seemingly in direct competition with the first. Since some consumers will inevitably switch brands, you increase the likelihood of a switch to one of your brands, rather than your competitor's. By creating third and fourth brands, apparently in competition with each other, your company increases its potential for gaining share of the market overall.

Multicast *Direct marketing, E-commerce, Internet, Marketing communications*
A technique for the transmission of a message to a number of recipients or groups of recipients. It can be used for the distribution of a news release to every daily, weekly and evening newspaper in the USA, for example, or an e-mailed offer to 10,000 carefully targeted customers. This technique is different from **broadcasting**, where a message is distributed on a large scale, and reception depends on who is in a position to receive it. This means that reception is sometimes largely a matter of chance, and is difficult to measure.

Multi-channel marketing *Marketing strategy*
A strategy using several channels of distribution for the same product at the same time. This includes distribution of a product direct to the public, as well as through wholesalers and retailers; publishers' distribution of books via the Internet, for example, as well as through the usual trade channels. The introduction of new or direct channels often creates friction between producers and their established conventional intermediaries and distributors.

Multi-level marketing *Marketing strategy*
Marketing to the public through several levels of distribution, such as importer, wholesaler and retailer. Each intermediary adds a mark-up to the cost incurred by buying from the previous one.

Multimedia *Information technology, Marketing communications*
Various combinations of text, images, sound, video and animation, within the same application or production.

Multinational *Business, International business, Marketing*
A company manufacturing, marketing or distributing products and services in several countries at the same time.

Multiple choice questionnaire *Marketing research, Research*
A questionnaire in which there are a number of possible answers to each question. The answers are prepared in advance and shown as alternatives in the question paper. The respondent is asked to consider each question, and to indicate by a tick or an x which answer she prefers. One disadvantage of this system is that the answers may not accurately reflect the respondent's preference. This will, of course, have been considered by the compiler, who works to a brief, and whose questionnaire has been agreed by the sponsor.

Multiple exposure *Photography, Plate-making, Production*
A visual display technique that involves printing an image several times to form a single image. Multiple exposure can also involve several different images at the same time. Images may be laid down on one another, obliquely superimposed, slightly offset, or laid alongside one another in columns or rows. In fact, any variation is possible, limited only by the brief and the creative imagination of the art director.

Multiple readership *Newspaper and magazine publishing*
A newspaper or magazine that enjoys more than one reader for each copy sold. This characteristic must not be confused with **circulation**, where each copy is purchased by its subscribers, and therefore has an audited readership of one. This is the figure that advertisers pay for. Daily newspapers – the *Los Angeles Times* and *The Times* of London, for example – have an established circulation of one per copy, and a theoretical readership of one per copy. In bachelor households, they have one reader per copy. However, in family households, they may have two or more readers per copy. The *Reader's Digest*, on the other hand, has an audited circulation of one per copy, but may have a readership of up to 12 per copy. This may run possibly to hundreds, when you take into account how often you find it in hospital, dentists' and doctors' waiting rooms. Business publications may have more than one reader per copy.
See ABC, Controlled circulation, Rate card, Readership, Verified Free Distribution.

Multiple retailing *Distribution, Retailing*
A number of retail outlets owned by a single company; chain stores, for example. The owners can centralize their personnel and administration operations, and their purchasing of merchandise, with consequent worthwhile economies.

Multiple unit pricing *Distribution, Retailing*
A retail marketing and pricing technique, in which several identical products are offered as a single packaged unit. This is designed to encourage customers to purchase more economically. The technique sometimes involves offering several different products in a pack; breakfast cereals, for example.

Multiplex *Cinema*
A cinema complex incorporating several screens, each showing a different film.

MVO *Film and video post-production, Radio commercials*
Abbreviation for **male voice-over**. A male actor's disembodied voice heard while a television commercial is being screened; the actor is not seen. In radio commercials, a man's voice doing a similar job.

Nn

Name   *Databases, Direct mail, Direct marketing*
An individual entry, usually the first two fields, in a consumer or business mailing list.

Name acquisition   *Databases, Direct mail, Direct marketing*
In the compilation of mailing lists, the gathering of names, addresses and other essential data. A number of sources are used, including the inclusion of reply coupons in press advertisements, reply cards in sales and other literature, data taken from a company's own sales records and credit card transactions, and Web site hits.

Nanny state   *Economics*
A nickname for the Welfare State. It has been given this name because, in some eyes, the government interferes and controls citizens' lives, as a nanny might do with the infants she looks after. The term **cradle to grave** is associated with this term. In the UK, the situation does actually exist to a certain degree, and governments would like to extend it. On the whole, although it does offer opportunities, marketers do not favour it.

Narrator   *Cinema, Film, Television commercials, Video*
A person who voices a commentary for a film or video. A voice-over (*qv*).

Narrowcast   *Television, Video*
All forms of television and video activity not actually put out on air by terrestrial or satellite transmitter, aimed at specific target audiences. The coverage achieved is deliberately smaller than that of broadcast transmissions.

Examples of narrowcast include cable television, videos and video games, multimedia and Internet activities. However, the Internet is now so huge that it might as well qualify as broadcast. Research suggests that more than 3 million businesspeople in the UK alone currently have access to the Internet in their places of work. By the year 2005, over a billion people worldwide may be connected to the Net.

National brand   *Marketing*
A brand or product advertised nationally, distributed and available to customers on a national scale. A national brand may be marketed in different countries under different names.

National magazines   *Advertising, Public relations, Publishing*
Weekly and monthly consumer magazines with national distribution, circulation
and readership. Business publications with national circulation are usually termed
the **business press**.

National marketing campaigns   *Advertising, Marketing*
Marketing campaigns conducted on a national scale, with national coverage
involving advertising, public relations, sales force effort, distribution, merchandising, sales promotion and sponsorship. It may also include direct marketing and
Internet activity.

National press   *Advertising, Public relations, Publishing*
Daily and Sunday newspapers published for national distribution, circulation and
readership.

National Readership Survey   *Media research*
A continuous programme of research into the readership of the UK's newspapers
and magazines. The survey is carried out on the basis of personal interviews with
a sample of respondents. The questionnaire includes respondents' demographic
data and readership habits. The research is commissioned and co-ordinated by
JICNARS, the Joint Industry Committee for National Readership Surveys.

Natural break   *Television*
A break in television programming, specifically for commercials.

Need   *Advertising, Human behaviour, Marketing planning*
A physical or emotional demand made by the human body, requiring satisfaction.
According to Maslow (*qv*), physiological needs are at the foot of a pyramid of a
hierarchical pyramid of needs, with self-actualization at its peak. Food, shelter,
clothing and sex are at the bottom. Once these have been satisfied, goes the theory,
other needs come into play. On the way up are the need for safety; the need to
belong to someone or something; the need for esteem and recognition. Bear in
mind that this is a theory which, although widely accepted, has its sceptics. When
formulating marketing plans, it may do no harm to take Maslow's ideas into
account, but not at the expense of sound marketing principles, business acumen
and experience, and common sense.

Negative   *Artwork, Creative, Photography, Plate-making, Production*
In photography, a negative is photographic film that, after being exposed in a
camera and developed, carries an inversion of the original tones. A positive can
be made of this by exposing light through it on to a second, photographically
sensitive stock such as film or paper. All the colours and tones of the original image
are reversed. In black-and-white photography, black is represented by clear film;
white represented by dense black. Intermediate tones are also present, but in

reversed form. Thus, light grey is shown as dark grey, and vice versa. The negative is an intermediate stage, between the object being photographed and the printed image it is eventually processed into. Since two negatives make a positive (in photography as in many other aspects of life), the final result is a positive image that looks like the original.

In colour photography, much the same principle applies. Colours are reversed, but each colour in the original is represented by its complementary in the negative. Red, for example, is represented by green. A yellowish greeny-blue in the negative represents flesh tones in the positive.

Some photographic films produce positive images without an intermediate negative. These are termed **reversal films**. They are used for the high-quality transparency photography in printing and screened presentations. The quality of reversal film is much better than prints taken with negative film, because there is no second stage printing, and consequently no loss of quality. For evidence, look at brochures produced for expensive cars, or look through glossy magazines such as *Vogue*.
See Photograph, Positive.

Negative advertising   *Marketing communications*
An advertising technique designed to expose the weaknesses of competitive products. An advertiser embarking on such a technique should take care not to make it look like knocking copy (*qv*), which could infringe local and national laws and voluntary codes of practice.

Negative leading   *Desktop publishing, Typography, Word-processing*
Also termed **minus leading**. Type set with less space from base-line to base-line than the height of the characters themselves. This can be done in computer setting, but not in hot metal. For example, when 16pt type is set with 14pt leading, the ascenders and descenders overlap. Useful for achieving special typographical effects. Be careful, however, to minimize eccentric effects of this kind; they can seriously damage the legibility of any promotional messages they carry.
See Minus leading.

Net paid circulation   *Advertising, Media statistics, Newspaper and magazine publishing*
The number of newspapers or magazines actually sold. This figure does not include complimentary copies of the publication, or unsold copies. Independent auditing by the Audit Bureau of Circulations is widely, possibly universally, accepted by publishers, advertisers and their agencies. Net paid circulation does not apply to readership.

Net price   *Business, Retailing*
The final price of a product or item of merchandise, after trade discounts, commissions, concessions, special offers and other deductions have been made.

Net reach *Advertising, Media statistics, Newspaper and magazine publishing*

A figure representing readers with one or more opportunities to see a press advertisement. This figure excludes duplication.

See Net readership.

Net readership *Advertising, Media statistics, Newspaper and magazine publishing*

The number of readers of a publication, excluding duplication. The figure does not include, for example, readers of a morning newspaper who also read other morning newspapers.

Net weight *Packaging*

The weight of a packaged product, not including the weight of packaging materials.

Network *Communications, Information processing*

A system comprising a series of points and their inter-connections. The term is usually used in relation to telecommunications networks and the Internet.

Networking *Broadcast media*

News or entertainment programming made available to a number of television and radio stations for broadcasting. The press equivalent term is **syndication**. Telephone companies and service suppliers sharing lines and facilities are also described as networks.

The term is also applied to face-to-face marketing and personal business contact. This is a much slower method of marketing, but it is useful in establishing new contacts that, although regarded as a long-term investment, can sometimes produce immediate results. Joining an organization such as the Chartered Institute of Marketing and attending its conferences, meetings, events and workshops is a popular form of networking.

Network marketing *Business, Distribution, Franchising, Retailing*

The marketing and distribution of products and services through a network of agents. Household goods, lingerie, cosmetics and slimming systems are popular products for networking.

New product development *Brand management, Business, Marketing, Product management*

Techniques for bringing new products and services to market. Having anticipated or identified a need or want in a marketplace, a product management team puts the concept through a number of stages through to launch. This includes product research and testing; consumer research – to be sure the need is actually there and that potential customers will buy it; product prototyping; product performance testing; packaging design and testing on consumers; pricing and testing on consumers; test marketing; trade promotion; distribution; consumer promotion campaign; regional or national product launch.

News agency *Media activity, News distribution, Public relations*
An organization specializing in the distribution of news to the media. PR Newswire Europe, in London, is an example of an experienced international news agency. The agency offers traditional newswire, fax, e-mail, Web site and online global databases, to ensure that journalists, analysts and the public receive information by the method most convenient to them. In the UK, the agency uses the Press Association wire to distribute clients' news. This service is replicated with news agencies overseas, via a global agency access network. The services include distribution of graphics, photographics, sound and vision.

Newspaper Publishers' Association *UK trade associations*
The organization representing and promoting the interests of UK national daily newspaper publishers, and that of the *London Evening Standard.*

Newspaper Society *UK trade associations*
The organization representing and promoting the interests of UK regional daily and weekly newspaper publishers.

Newsprint *Artwork, Creative, Paper, Print, Production*
A coarse, absorbent paper made mostly from wood pulp and small amounts of chemical pulp. Mostly used for printing newspapers; hence the name.
   Care should be taken when preparing artwork for reproduction on newsprint. Consult the advertisement or production department of the publication, your photographer, art studio and pre-press house. Printing on newsprint differs from printing on any other stock; you may find the results completely different from your expectations. The absorptive quality of the paper alone should give you pause for thought. Take care over the halftone screen you are specifying. Always consult the production specifications issued by the media you are using.
See Halftones.

News proof *Print, Production*
A proof taken on newsprint (*qv*). This should be capable of reproducing the image, ink density and colour quality expected from the actual print run. Always consult your printer before specifying news proofs; they can be expensive. There are special proofing presses for this job, but not every printer has them.
See Newsprint, Wet proof.

News release *Press and broadcast media, Public relations*
A piece of informational copy, written for publication in the press or for coverage in broadcast media. Ideally, a news release should be conceived and written specifically for the particular publication in which it might appear. Limitations in time, effort and expense prevent this. Nevertheless, a news release should be of

intense and immediate interest to its target readers, viewers or listeners. It should be immediately apparent to the editor that the news or information offered is of direct value for her readers or audience.

For the complete technique for planning and writing news releases, see *Creative Marketing Communications* (Kogan Page, 3rd edition, 2001).

Next matter   *Advertising, Editorial, Publishing*
A press advertisement insertion appearing, or scheduled to appear, right next to editorial. This is regarded as a special position, and subject to an additional charge.

Niche marketing   *Marketing planning and techniques*
The identification and selection of specified groups of customers and potentials, in order to market appropriate products and services to them. Such markets may be segments of larger markets or market groups. The essential requirement of this marketing technique is that the offerings meet the needs or wants of the targets. The situation often arises when a small supplier with a small marketing budget realizes that he cannot compete with larger, more powerful competitors. A small company may well be able to compete in a niche market; even eventually dominate it. The term niche is derived from Latin *nidus*, a nest; a niche being a shallow recess in a wall, capable of containing a vase or statue. Or, in this case, a product or service marketed successfully on a modest scale.

Nielsen Retail Index   *Marketing research, Retail auditing*
A retail auditing services offered by A C Nielsen Ltd, an international research organization. The index comprises information and analysis on retailers' purchases, stocks, prices and promotions. This subsequently indicates market size, market shares and other information important to manufacturers and suppliers subscribing to the service.
See MEAL.

Node   *Communications*
A device connected to a network cable. The term often refers to a computer workstation; sometimes to a repeater or passive network junction.

Noise   *Communications*
Interference with electrical signals. Devices such as computers, mobile telephones, household electrical appliances, electric motors and fluorescent lighting equipment can generate noise. Internet communications can be affected and corrupted by such noise. Special care should be taken to isolate computing equipment used for online transmission of data files to printers and the media; corrupting of data can be time-wasting and expensive.

Noise level   *Filming, Television, Video*
The level of unavoidable, unwanted sound generated on a sound track, or electrically within a recording playback or reproduction circuit.

Non-business marketing *Marketing*
Marketing techniques practised by non-profit organizations, such as charities, academic institutions, healthcare trusts and local government.

Non-durables *Marketing, Retailing*
Products purchased frequently and consumed within a short period after purchase. The term applies to fast-moving consumer goods, which may often be bought daily and consumed within the day; chocolate, cigarettes and perishables, for example.

Non-price competition *Marketing*
Competitive marketing and related activities based on any factor except price, and concentrating on product choice, for example, or outstanding service. However, all competition, particularly in consumer and business-to-business markets, is price-related in the end. In situations where price differences are small across a range of competitive products, marketers may choose to gain an edge by promoting other factors. These include:

- brand reputation;
- customer service;
- ease of product use;
- product performance;
- reliability;
- technical excellence;
- warranty and guarantee;
- worldwide availability;
- worldwide technical service.

Non-profit making organization *Organizations*
A non-commercial organization, such as a government or a charity, with a remit to serve the public, or work for the benefit of good causes.

Non-synch *Film, Television, Video*
Speech, sounds and sound-effects not required to be in synchronization with action in a picture. Sometimes a television commercial is aired with action and speech out of synch. The results can be hilarious or disturbing, depending on whether you are paying for the commercial or merely viewing. If it is the result of an error, it can be expensive.

Normal lens *Film, Television, Video*
A photographic lens giving a normal angle of view and natural perspective without distortion.

Noting *Advertising research, Editorial research, Readership research*
A test of awareness. A respondent is asked to name an advertisement, advertiser or news item seen in a particular edition of a newspaper or magazine. At this stage

of the research, the respondent is not required to describe the contents of the advertisement or editorial. The objective is to determine whether the reader has paid attention to it, or whether the item has slipped by unnoticed.
See Reading and noting

Noting score   *Advertising research, Editorial research, Readership research*
The number of readers claiming to have noted an advertisement or news item in an edition of a publication. The noting score is calculated as a percentage of the readership of the publication.

Nought   *Creative, Desktop publishing, Typography, Word-processing*
A word used by compositors, typesetters and proof-readers to differentiate between the characters 'o' and '0'. On screen, a nought is usually represented by a dot in the centre of the character, or an oblique stroke running through it. In proof-reading, if the distinction is not made, it can cause confusion and errors. Many typesetters refer to nought as null (*qv*) or zero (*qv*). Always say 'nought', 'null' or 'zero' when proof-reading and reading out copy, especially over the telephone.
See Character, Monotype, Null, Proof, Proof-reader, Proof-reader's marks, Quote, Zero.

Novelties   *Sales promotion*
Give-away items bearing an advertiser's name or logo. Most give-aways are not actually novel – keyrings, diaries and beer mats, for example. Some can be spectacularly novel, such as CD ROM business cards and disposable cameras.

NRS   *Media research*
The National Readership Survey (*qv*).

NTSC   *Broadcasting transmission standards, Television, Video*
National Television System Committee, the broadcasting transmission system used in the USA. Also known in Europe, rather cruelly, as 'Never The Same Colour'. This was coined after British and other European television engineers had rejected the US system on grounds of unpredictable colour results during test transmissions.
If a video recording has been made in NTSC, it cannot be used on a European PAL video-cassette player. Likewise, video material made in PAL should not be exported to a country using another television broadcasting standard. Videotapes can be converted, but there is a risk of quality loss in the conversion. Some video players have built-in converters.
See PAL, SECAM, Television transmission standards, VCR, VTR.

Null   *Desktop publishing, Proof-reading, Typography, Word-processing*
A word used to differentiate between the character 'o' and '0'.
See Character, Monotype, Nought, Proof, Proof-reader, Proof-reader's marks, Quote, Zero.

Numbers board   *Film and video production, Television commercials*
Also called **clapperboard**. A small, distinctive blackboard or whiteboard carrying identification details of a production during filming. Details include production title, scene number, take number, director's name, date and time. This information is vital during post-production, when the film is edited. The board usually has a hinged wooden or metal strip at the top; when brought down on the board it gives a crisp 'clap' sound, which is recorded. This enables the editor to synchronize sound and picture.

Oo

OBC *Advertising, Publishing*

Outside back cover. The outside back cover of a newspaper, magazine, directory, brochure or book. Publishers usually charge a premium rate for this position, on the grounds of higher readership or greater awareness. However, it is prudent to examine independent research before investing in special positions.

Objectives, budgeting by *Advertising appropriations, Finance,*
Marketing budgets

One of a number of methods used to determine advertising and marketing budgets. Essentially, there are only two task-based methods. One, to set objectives, then determine how much it will cost to achieve them. Two, to allocate a sum of money, then determine how much can be done with it.

A much more viable approach lies in considering all the factors contributing to the marketing, promotion and profitable future of the product or service in question. This composite technique includes:

- distributor system and network: familiarity, acceptability, efficiency;
- overall objective for the brand;
- overall trend in the market for the brand or product;
- past product trends and sales;
- PESTLE: market conditions – political, economic, sociological, technological, legal, environmental;
- product selling considerations: consumer awareness, price comparisons;
- production capacity and continuity;
- promotional media: cost, reach, impact; viability; past effectiveness;
- realistic anticipated sales;
- regional differences in terms of competition and own sales;
- sales force: strength, efficiency;
- seasonal differences and fluctuations in sales;
- SWOT analysis: strengths, weaknesses, opportunities, threats.

This is a dynamic mix both of calculable factors and influences, and the identification of factors to be addressed by business judgement. Using this objective-based technique makes it possible to build up a bank of experience for use in subsequent years.

Oblique *Creative, Desktop publishing, Typography, Word-processing*
Type slanted at an angle from the vertical. This resembles italic, but is more usually a leaning roman. Some software suites use the term **slanted** to describe this effect. Most software offering the oblique facility provides degrees of slant, as a percentage from the vertical, scaleable in size and infinitely variable in angle.

Obsolescence *Brand management, Product development*
A stage in the decline of a product in its market. Some products decline naturally; some are overtaken by competitive products, some by more sophisticated or advanced technology. In former times, products were designed and manufactured to last for human generations. Today, manufacturers build obsolescence into products so that they last, perhaps, for a single product generation. Computers are a case in point. Many computers and software suites are virtually obsolete on the day they are launched; there is always a new generation pressing forward into the marketplace. Passenger vehicles are another case; they are promoted as representing an increasingly sophisticated or moneyed lifestyle. The reality is somewhat different, since cars are bought on credit, which can be withdrawn if the buyer fails to honour the terms of his finance contract. Consumers, both in the domestic and business domains, have the power to end this unequal struggle, but consistently fail to do so.

Obsolete *Brand management, Product development*
The final stage in the death of a product, in which it may be available for purchase, but no longer produced.

OCR *Desktop publishing, Information technology, Word-processing*
Optical character recognition. A technique for converting copy into machine-readable form by scanning characters and matching them with their known standard characters. Typeset or word-processed characters read by an OCR scanner are converted to digital equivalents, then converted into normal word-processing file forms. They are then readable as human language on a computer screen. An optical character reader is the hardware for carrying out OCR.

Odd-even pricing *Marketing, Retailing*
A technique for encouraging consumers to purchase a product by making its price appear smaller. A product retailing at, say, £10 may appear more attractive when priced and displayed at £9.99. The price difference is minuscule, but the effect on sales may be worthwhile.

Off-card rates *Advertising planning, Advertisement pricing*
Special insertion rates not shown in advertisement rate cards. This may apply when an advertiser wishes to negotiate a rate for a campaign outside the limits of the rate card, such as special positions, frequency or volume discounts. However, card rates may sometimes be used as the starting point.

Offer *Advertising, Business, Contracts*
One element in the making of contracts for goods and services. The three elements that make a contract legally binding are:

- offer;
- acceptance;
- consideration (usually money).

A contract is legally binding even when made verbally; it is prudent to have witnesses to a verbal contract, otherwise lengthy proceedings could follow in the event of a dispute. Advertising and marketing contracts should always be in writing, if only because large sums of money are usually involved, and mistakes and misunderstandings can be expensive.

Offline *Communications, Information technology, Internet operations*
A computer software facility for compiling data before going online (*qv*), as with Internet activities, graphics and e-mail, for example. One can then switch to online, sending the data to a distant server. This is considerably cheaper than working online, as it takes up far less telephone time.

Off-peak *Broadcasting, Advertising planning and scheduling*
Television and radio airtime segments during which viewer and listener audiences are lower than at peak times. Although television audiences peak at lower levels at various times during the day and at weekends, the highest peaks are at breakfast-time and between 9 pm and 10.30 pm. It should be borne in mind, however, that many households have their televisions switched on during morning peaks even though nobody is viewing.

Offset *Print*
In litho printing (*qv*), a plate cylinder deposits the image direct on to the paper. In offset litho printing, a rubber or neoprene blanket cylinder picks up the image from the printing plate and deposits it on the paper. There is no contact between the printing plate and the paper; the blanket offsets it, and allows the printing plate a longer working life.
See Dry offset, Litho, Set-off.

Ogilvy, David *Advertising*
One of the world's greatest innovators of creativity in the advertising business. Born in England and educated at Oxford, he went to New York in 1949 and founded an advertising agency empire. He built Ogilvy & Mather into one of the largest international advertising agencies, with offices in over 40 countries. His two books, *Confessions of an Advertising Man* (Atheneum, New York, 1962) and *Ogilvy on Advertising* (Pan Books, London, 1983), are as witty, irreverent and unconventional as the man who wrote them. They also contain a great deal of wisdom on the practice of advertising.

Oligopoly   *Business, Economics, Marketing*
A market or an economic condition in a state of limited competition, dominated
by a small number of suppliers. From Greek *oligos*, small; *oligoi*, few.
See Monopoly.

Oligopsony   *Business, Economics, Marketing*
A market or economic condition in which there is a small number of buyers or
consumers. The automotive industry is a case in point: a small number of
customers with a large number of producers and suppliers chasing them.
See Monopsony, Oligopoly.

Omnibus survey   *Advertising research, Marketing research,*
Opinion research
An ongoing general field survey on topics of the moment, with a number of
questions on advertising or marketing topics added to it. The commercial questions
are sponsored by marketers or advertisers. Whereas the general parts of the
questionnaire may cover current political or economic issues, those on advertising
or marketing are specific to products, services or campaigns. For a sponsor, buying
into an omnibus is cheaper than setting up and carrying out an individual survey.
Participation in an omnibus makes it possible, for example, for an advertiser to
mid-test or post-test an advertising campaign at modest cost.

One-inch   *Television, Video*
A videotape standard used for originating and editing television commercials.

One-sided question   *Marketing research, Questionnaires*
A question that allows only one answer by the respondent. It does not allow
any alternative answer, or any leeway in developing an answer given by the
respondent. In a question such as, 'In your opinion, should cattle suspected of
having contracted BSE be put into the human food chain?', only 'yes' or 'no' is
possible. Having answered with one of the alternatives, the respondent cannot then
explain her reasons for her response, put the opposite view, or suggest another.
See Open-ended question.

One-stop shopping   *Marketing, Retailing*
A term sometimes used in connection with department stores or other large retail
establishments, where everything a customer needs is offered under one roof. It is
also used to describe what a consumer can expect from a shopping mall.

Online   *Communications, Information technology, Internet operations*
A general term for being connected to the Internet and the World Wide Web. When
a company or an individual is actually connected to the Net, taking up telephone
time, they are described as being 'online'. The term also means having an e-mail
address or a Web site, or both.
   Where a network of computers is connected under the control of a central server
computer, they are said to be online. They can be remote from one another,

connected by a telephone line. In this case, the operator pays the telephone company for the time it takes to stay online.

The opposite of this is **offline** (*qv*), which is a much cheaper method of working. You carry out a computing function or word-processing operation and compile all the data *before* you go online. When this is complete, you go online, sending the results down the telephone. This method is considerably cheaper than doing it online, because it takes up less telephone time. The Internet software package you work with should allow you to do this.

On-pack   *Packaging, Retailing, Sales promotion*
Information printed on a pack. This can relate to anything from a competition or prize draw, to a premium or a free gift.

On-pack goodie   *Advertising, Marketing, Sales promotion*
A jargon term for a give-away item attached to the outside of a retail product pack.

On-pack reduction   *Packaging, Retailing, Sales promotion*
A price reduction printed on a pack. This is a time-limited measure designed to increase the sales or uptake of the product being offered. Competitive attack often prompts the marketer or retailer to adopt on-pack reductions; slow sales in a particular region may do the same.

On-sale date   *Press media, Publishing*
The actual date on which a magazine is available in retail outlets and on bookstalls. This date may be different from the cover-date, the date printed on the cover of the magazine.

For many years publishers in Europe have been trying to outdo each other, by bringing their on-sale dates more and more forward. This can cause ludicrous anomalies, such as November issues appearing in October or even September. Naturally, publishers would not consider reverting to matching on-sale dates with cover dates. That would be far too sensible and logical; but it would make for sensible, logical and workable copy dates; and make life easier for advertising agencies' creative and production departments.

Open dating   *Packaging, Retailing*
Printing dates on a pack, indicating the latest by which it may be displayed, sold or used; or all three. The term 'open' refers to ordinary words and figures, easily readable by purchasers.

Open-ended question   *Marketing research, Questionnaires*
A question with no pre-selected answers prepared by the researchers. The respondent can provide the answer in any way he chooses, within the framework of the question. To the question, 'When did you stop beating your husband?', the respondent supplies an answer in her own words, which are recorded by the researcher.

Open systems *Information technology, Marketing communications*
Inter-connection and inter-working between data processing systems of different manufacturers, based on common standards of communication. In theory, this makes for simple inter-connection between PC-based systems used in many advertising and marketing departments, and the Mac systems used by most designers and printers.

Operating budget *Business, Marketing*
A sum of money allocated by a company for the fulfilment of a business or marketing objective. The money will be calculated and justified in the business or marketing plan for which it has been proposed.

Operational research *Business planning, Marketing planning*
A technique in aid of decision-making. The expression in mathematical terms of the facts in a business plan; almost always by computer. With this technique any variations in the plan, or the introduction of new variables or data, can be re-calculated immediately over the entire plan. The results, both specific and global, can be examined at once, and the results saved for future reference.

Opinion formers *Advertising, Marketing, Politics, Public relations*
Carefully researched, clearly defined groups of consumers, voters, shareholders, employees, etc, whose opinions or actions are capable of influencing others. Advertising or public relations messages may be formulated and aimed at these groups, achieving maximum impact. Using small, influential groups is always done for the fulfilment of objectives; sometimes also to save promotional money.

Opinion poll *Research*
Field, online and telephone research aimed at gathering opinions and views from representative samples of the general public.

Opinion research *Research techniques*
Techniques for gathering public opinion on specific issues and topics. Samples for this research are defined statistically, so that a small number of respondents represent the population or universe as a whole, accurately and economically.

Opportunities to see *Advertising planning, Media planning*
Usually abbreviated to OTS. The estimated or calculated number of times a reader or viewer is exposed to an advertisement or television commercial during a campaign. Taking into account the medium and target audience, the weight or impact of a campaign is often judged by its OTS. In considering OTS during planning, it should be borne in mind that OTS indications are different for different media. There may be no direct comparison between different media. The radio equivalent is **opportunities to hear**. The term also applies to outdoor and cinema campaigns.

Opportunity analysis *Marketing planning*
An element in SWOT analysis technique: opportunities. The whole technique comprises the strengths, weaknesses, opportunities and threats identified and analysed when planning a marketing campaign. SWOT analysis enables marketing teams to make the most of a product's strengths, minimize or eliminate its weaknesses, exploit opportunities for profitable marketing and employ counter-measures against threats.

Optical disk *Information technology, Studio equipment*
A compact disk for storing data generated by computer. The storage medium is non-magnetic, and therefore unaffected by unwanted magnetic fields. Optical disks are removable and portable, and do not rely on magnetic data transfer, as with hard drives. The data are written and read by laser.

Optical jukebox *Information technology, Studio equipment*
A device containing a number of optical storage disks, which can be requested to access individual disks, quickly and without human intervention.

Opticals *Film, Television, Video*
A wide range of effects added to film and video during post-production. These include an ever-growing variety of transition effects, such as fades, dissolves, wipes, explosions, implosions, fragmentations, superimpositions (supers) and page-turns; titles, captions and other typographical effects. In pre-computer times, these were achieved mechanically, using an optical printer, and sets of duplicate negatives and inter-negatives. They are now done by increasingly clever software. *See* Frame, Freeze-frame, Pan, Shot, Tilt.

Optimal impact *Advertising planning, Marketing planning, Media planning*
Having taken into account all elements planned into in an advertising or marketing campaign, the critical point at which the campaign reaches its greatest impact and cost-effectiveness.

Opt-in *Advertising, Marketing, Sales*
A statement by an individual, that he or she is willing to receive sales and marketing communications. In some countries there is a legal requirement for advertisers to make provision for consumers and enquirers to opt in or out. Advertisement coupons and print reply cards may have to carry declarations and tick-boxes indicating these options. The term is also used to denote an opportunity provided by a company to allow this.

Opt-out *Advertising, Marketing, Sales*
A statement by an individual, that he or she is unwilling to receive sales and marketing communications. In some countries there is a legal requirement for advertisers to make provision for consumers and enquirers to opt in or out. Advertisement coupons and print reply cards may have to carry declarations and

tick-boxes indicating these options. The term is also used to denote an opportunity provided by a company to allow this.

Order/call relationship   *Sales analysis*
More correctly, call/order relationship. The relationship between the number of calls made on customers and prospects by sales staff during a pre-defined period, and the number of orders obtained by them. This is often subdivided to indicate the most profitable relationship between calls and orders, to which more effort might be put.

Organic thinking   *Planning and development*
A system, of ancient Greek origin, for creating and building up individual and team thinking for the planning of projects and assignments. Today, using modern resources, it can be applied to almost any project, from building a greenhouse to creating an international marketing campaign. Its main function is to organize and structure individual and team thinking so that it grows organically, either logically or haphazardly. Either way, the individual or participants should eventually be able to:

- set objectives for a project;
- create and plan a project;
- develop ideas quickly;
- structure them;
- eliminate ineffective or inappropriate ideas;
- make appropriate management decisions;
- carry them out in logical sequence;
- create practical, logistical plans for implementing a project;
- create critical and linear paths for project activity;
- evaluate a plan against its objectives;
- predict consequences and avoid undesirable ones;
- implement plans for a project efficiently and cost-effectively;
- make a start on the practical work of a project;
- carry out or commission appropriate research;
- evaluate the results;
- apply the results to management decision-making;
- evaluate intermediate project work against objectives and plans;
- evaluate all a project's activities against its objectives and plans.

Organic thinking is often compared to **heuristics**, a system for proceeding by trial and error. Its basic purpose is discovery; for marketing, the discovery of facts and attitudes. It is essentially different from organic thinking, but may be employed as an element within it. Originally also of ancient Greek origin (*heurisko*, to find), the science of heuristic procedure is now rather loosely termed **lateral thinking**.

Organization and methods *Corporate management techniques*
A technique for maximizing the efficiency and impact of management effort. It comprises the investigation, analysis and implementation of findings relating to a company's management planning and procedures, their delegation, control, profitability and translation into profitable activity.

Orientation *Desktop publishing, Word-processing*
A page either in landscape (horizontal) or portrait (vertical) form.
See Landscape, Portrait.

Original *Artwork, Creative, Filming, Plate-making, Print*
Original material intended for reproduction. This includes text and illustrations.

Origination *Artwork, Copywriting, Creative, Design*
The preparatory stages of an advertising or print assignment. This includes concepts, visuals, graphics, mock-ups and presentation visuals (*qv* all these). What follows, after approval, is production, proofing and print.
See Estimate.

OTS *Advertising planning, Media planning*
Abbreviation for **opportunities to see** (*qv*).

Outdoor *Advertising media*
All forms of advertising appearing in the open air. Oddly, some indoor advertising is referred to as outdoor. Confused? Read on. Posters, billboards, adshels (*qv*), bus and taxi-cab exteriors, signs, store facias, and banners dragged by aircraft, are forms of outdoor advertising. However, bus and taxi interiors, car-cards on underground, metro, subway and mainline trains also come within the outdoor definition. They are more accurately termed transport advertising. Posters within underground and railway stations are also defined as outdoor; they too are transport advertising, but treated by media planners as outdoor.
See Adshel.

Outer *Distribution, Packaging*
Also termed an **outer pack**. A bulk container for several smaller units of a product. Its main function is to protect its contents during transportation, shipping and storage. It may also be designed to allow the easy unpacking of its contents at the destination. Outers usually feature the name and description of the product; often, also, the manufacturer's or supplier's logo and current advertising campaign slogan.

Outlet *Distribution, Retailing, Wholesaling*
Marketing terminology for a wholesaler or retailer; for example, **retail outlet**, meaning a shop, store, corner shop, supermarket, hypermarket, department store and chain store.

Output resolution *Graphics, Information technology, Marketing communications, Print, Studio work*

In a graphical production device, the number of separate points of image that the device is physically able to write. The output resolution of printers and image-setters is usually referred to in **dots per inch (dpi)**. This term can cause confusion; it makes no distinction between the fixed area dot **(spot)** of the output resolution, and the varying area dot used in halftones. Manufacturers of graphical production equipment refer to the smallest elements of their electronic halftone generators as **spots** or **addressable points**. A number of spots together build into a halftone dot. *Caveat*: some sources use the same terminology in reverse.

Outside broadcast *Radio, Television*

Broadcast material sourced or transmitted not from a studio but from a location, such as a street, field, factory, motorway incident, helicopter, rooftop or race track.

Out-take *Film, Television, Video*

A sequence shot during production, but taken out during editing. This usually ends up on the **cutting-room floor** – another piece of filmic jargon. During the filming of a television commercial, for example, when an actor inadvertently treads on the studio cat's tail, or trips over a power cable, this is usually taken out during editing; and often kept on file for the amusement of the crew.

Overheads *Business, Distribution, Manufacturing*

Costs involved in setting up and running a business, company, manufacturing or distribution facility and so on. Such costs are built into the end price of products and services produced by the business. However, overheads need to be paid whether a company sells its product or not: taxes, rent, electricity, heating, telephone, maintenance, wages and salaries, storage and so on.

Overlap coverage *Media planning, Radio, Television*

A situation where a designated geographical area or region is covered by more than one radio or television transmitter.

Overlay *Artwork, Studio techniques*

A transparent cover on copy or artwork, where instructions, keylines, corrections or colour-breaks are marked. A term also applied to transparent or translucent prints; when in position on each other, they form a composite picture.
See Keyline, Register marks, Registration.

Overmatter *Artwork, Copywriting, Creative, Desktop publishing, Print, Production, Typography, Word-processing*

Typeset or word-processed copy that does not fit a pre-determined area. If a specific space has been planned to be filled with copy, but more copy has been written than will fit into it, the overspill is termed overmatter; also termed **over-setting**.

Overprinted *Print, Production*

Type or illustrations printed on top of an already-printed area. For example, a distributor may have his name, address and telephone number printed on a leaflet provided by a manufacturer. The distributor's details may be printed in an unprinted, white area, and not actually on top of some other image; this is still termed overprinting.

Own label *Distribution, Retailing, Wholesaling*

A private brand, owned and used by supermarket and other national chains in competition with established brands sold in their outlets; often actually alongside them. Own labels are almost always sold at lower prices than established brands. David Ogilvy (*qv*) hated own-branded products. In *Confessions of an Advertising Man* (Atheneum, New York, 1962) he suggested that, when pathologists cut him open after his death, they would find 'Own label' engraved on his heart.

Pp

Package *Advertising, Marketing communications, Media planning, Radio advertising*
A schedule of radio spots. In the UK, advertising on radio is sold and purchased not as single spots; this is not considered worthwhile. Spots are purchased as packages, in which numerous spots are taken as a complete contract over a pre-determined period.

Packaging *Distribution, Marketing communications, Retailing*
Techniques for packing products in protective containers, which identify and promote their contents. A product pack on a shelf is the manufacturer's last chance to influence the purchaser. Identification with the promotional message delivered via press, television, radio, cinema and outdoor campaigns is vital. In a sense, this is the name of the game. In the European Union, packs also display information about products within: weight or volume, ingredients, nutritional data, information on possible allergic reactions and so on. Sometimes the materials from which the packs are made is displayed, plus information on how to dispose of them, and whether they are bio-degradable. The display of much of this information is mandatory, with penalties for default.

Packing *Make-ready, Printing presses*
Paper or other material used to underlay the plate or blanket on a litho press, or the image or impression cylinder on a letterpress machine. Its function is to get an accurate pressure or squeeze for printing the highest quality image possible.

PageMaker *Creative, Desktop publishing, Pre-press, Print*
A software package for the design and make-up of advertising and editorial pages, incorporating text and images. Simpler than QuarkXpress, but widely used nevertheless.

Page make-up *Artwork, Creative, Desktop publishing, Print, Production*
See Composition, Make-up, Mechanical.

Page make-up terminal *Artwork, Creative, Desktop publishing, Print, Production*
Sometimes abbreviated to **PMT**. A terminal at the sharp end of electronic publishing, used for laying out and making up pages of a publication, fitting type and

illustrations. The PMT is used for originating text and graphics, and retouching illustrations to an extremely high order of accuracy. *Caveat*: PMT is also a popular abbreviation for **photo-mechanical transfer**, a high quality studio photoprint (*qv*).

Page proofs   *Print, Production, Publishing*
Proof of a piece of print, arranged as pages assembled in the correct order. Before computerization, copy would be typeset in hot metal and proofed in galleys – single columns (*qv*). After checking and approval, the columns would be assembled into pages, and proofed again. These were page proofs; to be submitted for approval. A third stage of proofing could then be undertaken. These were machine proofs, with pages assembled in the correct order, produced on a specially designed proofing machine. When all had been approved, the job was put to bed, printed, finished and delivered. Page proofs can now be created, proofed, corrected, approved and delivered electronically, with no manhandling.

Page rate   *Advertising, Media planning*
The cost of a whole-page insertion in a newspaper, magazine or directory. This is shown in the publication's **rate card**.

Page scrolling   *Desktop publishing, Information technology,*
                                                          Word-processing
Displaying on a computer screen the pages of a document, a small section at a time or one complete screen page at a time. Pages can be scrolled backwards as well as forwards, and from side to side. Scrolling is done either with a mouse or via the computer's keyboard; some mice incorporate a scrolling ring. On laptop comp-uters, mouse-performed operations are done on a built-in finger-pad adjacent to the keyboard, or a roller-ball.
See Scrolling.

Page traffic   *Advertising research, Media research*
A calculation of the number of readers of a page in a newspaper, magazine or directory. This usually also gives it as a calculated percentage of the publication's total readership.

Pagination   *Print, Production, Publishing, Typesetting*
Organizing and arranging the pages of a newspaper, magazine, directory, brochure or other publication in correct page sequence. This term also applies to the number-ing of the pages. In computerized typesetting, make-up is handled by software.

PAL   *Television and video standards*
Abbreviation for **Phase Alternating Line**, the broadcasting system used in the UK and most countries in the European Union. *Caveat*: the PAL system is updated from time to time.
  Unfortunately, the three main technical systems used in the television broad-casting world are incompatible. You need to convert PAL videos to the SECAM

system used in, say, France and Russia, and the NTSC used in North America, before they can be viewed on their VCRs (*qv*). A PAL television, monitor or video-cassette recorder cannot be used in countries with incompatible systems unless they have built-in conversion capability.
See NTSC, SECAM, Television transmission standards, VCR.

Pamphlet   *Marketing communications, Political communications*
An inexpensive flyer or leaflet. In former times, the copy in a pamphlet was usually of a political or religious nature. Today the term is hardly used in marketing communications, except, perhaps, in political marketing.

Pan   *Film production, Television and video production*
A director's instruction to a camera operator. To slew a camera on its mounting in an arc to left or right, following the action during a shoot. The term derives from the word panorama.
See Shot, Tilt.

Panel   *Consumer research, Marketing research, Retail audits*
A group of individuals selected for the purpose of gathering information and opinion during a research programme. Members of such a group may represent themselves, their companies, political parties or other entity being researched. A version of this term is focus group. However, while a panel may be permanent or re-assembled again and again over a long period, a **focus group** is usually disbanded after a single session. Either way, each group is conducted, led, and its discussions monitored, by a professional researcher.

The discussions are usually recorded on videotape, and screened later for analysis by a research team. Television and radio audience research is panel-based. Panels' television and radio sets are fitted with equipment for recording viewing and listening habits. The information is automatically downloaded to the research company at regular intervals by telephone. Retail audits are conducted in panel format, with the agreement of retail managements.

Panel households   *Audience research, Consumer research,*
                    Marketing research
Consumer households that have undertaken to be involved in research panel activities.

Panel research   *Consumer research, Marketing research*
A technique for gathering information on consumer or business purchasing habits and product use. Consumer panels are asked to maintain records of their purchases, and diaries on how they use them. The records are sent by panel members to the research organization by mail, or submitted by telephone, fax or computer.

Pantone   *Artwork, Creative, Print, Production*
A palette of designer's colours, matched accurately to an established range of printing inks. The system enables you to produce designs in the range of colours

you have selected; then proof them and print them in exactly the same colours. In the designer's terms, what you see is what you get. It is also a practical control system, linking advertiser, designer and printer.

Pantry check *Consumer research, Marketing research*

A research technique designed to reveal the nature, quality and quantity of consumer purchases. It involves the regular inspection of the food and other domestic products bought and used by a panel of householders. Inspections are designed to reveal the quantity and quality of a household's purchases, and the amount of individual products consumed between inspections. The research covers such detail as retailers' names and addresses, product price, weight, capacity, brand names, flavours, colours, packaging, special offers, discounts, and the amounts of products wasted or discarded.

Paperboard *Packaging, Print materials*

Usually abbreviated to **board**. Stiff, laminated material used for packaging. Board is produced by bonding or compression-laminating thinner materials together to the required bulk, thickness and stiffness. The composition and quality of the finished board depends on its eventual use.

Paper-set *Advertising, Publishing*

Advertisements typeset by the publications in which they are to appear are termed paper-set. Usually, copy and layouts are supplied by advertisers or their agencies, and the publisher follows the accompanying instructions. Some publications offer layout and design services for advertisers without specialist design and pre-production help.

Paper sizes *Printing papers*

The paper sizes below are international. Metric size A0 has an area of 1 m^2 (one square metre; one square meter). Standard sizes then run in descending order, corresponding to the way the paper is folded or cut. The ratio of the sides A and B series papers is 1:$\sqrt{2}$, that is 1:1.414. A sizes are for most printing work. B sizes are mainly for posters and wall-charts. C sizes are envelopes or folders taking A series items.

A SERIES

Sheet size	Millimetres
2A	1,189 × 1,682
A0	841 × 1,189
A1	594 × 841
A2	420 × 594
A3	297 × 420
A4	210 × 297
A5	148 × 210

A6	105 × 148
A7	74 × 105
A8	52 × 74
A9	37 × 52

B SERIES

Sheet size	Millimetres
B0	1,000 × 1,414
B1	707 × 1,000
B2	500 × 707
B3	353 × 500
B4	250 × 353
B5	176 × 250

C SERIES
Envelopes and folders for A Series material

Size	Millimetres
C4	229 × 324
C5	162 × 229
C6	114 × 162
DL	110 × 220

PAPER STOCK SIZES FOR NORMAL TRIMMING

Sheet size	Millimetres
RA0	860 × 1,220
RA1	610 × 860
RA2	430 × 610

PAPER STOCK SIZES FOR BLEEDS AND EXTRA TRIMMING

Sheet size	Millimetres
SRA0	900 × 1,280
SRA1	640 × 900
SRA2	450 × 640

Parallel pricing   *Marketing, Retailing*
Pricing one's own products in line with the competition.

Pareto effect   *Marketing planning*
Also known as the **80/20 rule**. A market condition in which 80 per cent of purchases of a product or service are made by 20 per cent of the market. This is a common condition in consumer and business markets. It seems to suggest that

marketing planners should put 80 per cent of their budgets into motivating the potentially profitable 20 per cent of customers. The usual caveats apply; marketers might be better employed in an attempt to defy gravity.

Party promotions *Direct sales, Distribution, Marketing*
A network of individual agents, largely householders, who hold private coffee mornings and parties for friends and acquaintances. The purpose is to demonstrate and sell the products and services for which the party-givers hold agencies. Agents are paid commission on sales. Popular products for party promotions are cosmetics, underwear and kitchenware.

Pass-along readership *Media planning and buying, Media research,*
Publishing
A secondary readership, of newspapers and magazines, beyond that of primary readership. To define: primary readers are those who have paid for a copy of a publication and are the first readers of it. In a single household, members of the household are usually considered primary readers. Beyond that, any further readers are secondary readers. Business magazines, which get passed on by the subscriber to members of staff, are subject to pass-along readership. One of the best examples of pass-along readership in the consumer arena is the *Reader's Digest*, which may have 12 or more pass-along readers. *Caveat*: do not confuse readership with circulation (*qv*)
See: National Readership Survey.

Passed for press *Publishing*
Approval by a publisher or editor, indicating that the publication is complete and ready to go to press.

Passing off *Business, Criminal trading, Marketing*
Marketing a product using a spurious name, logo, trademark or pack, in order to mislead customers into thinking that the product on offer is another supplier's. For example, a company marketing a product using the logo Kelvin Clone might be seen as passing off the product as one of Calvin Klein's. Legal action will surely follow.

Password *E-commerce, Computer security, Information technology,*
Web marketing
A security measure to protect confidential computer files against unauthorized access. With a password engaged, you must enter it into your computer via the keyboard before you can access the material you want. Documents can be 'locked', so that they cannot be retrieved except by entering the password. You had better do it right first time, because computers are unforgiving of mistakes. Some systems lock you out permanently if you get it wrong three times. Password security of a high order is absolutely essential in commercial online activity such as Internet banking, shopping and data transfer.

There are several problems with this kind of security. For example, you may forget the password. Some software has no method of letting you retrieve your documents if you forget the password. The temptation to devise an unforgettable password is hard to resist. If you use your forename or family name, practically anybody can breech your security in about 25 seconds. If you write your password down, anyone may get hold of it, get into your files, steal or copy them and use them against you. You can try using numbers, but a lot of computer software is specifically designed to crack numeric passwords; there are also many alpha-numeric password-crackers on the market.

Paste-ups   *Artwork, Studio work*
The processing of a piece of finished artwork, where all the elements are mounted in place with precision. The elements include copy, display headlines, line drawings and other illustrations, and keylines (*qv*). Most paste-ups for press and print are now done electronically, via specialized computer software, without a drawing board in sight. The advantages lie in the savings in time and effort; in flexibility, great accuracy and the facility for saving the results to disk. Finished artwork can be sent to the printer digitally, and thus to press without loss of quality. *See* Halftone, Keylines.

Payback   *Business, Marketing, Product management*
The return on a company's investment in a product or service. A marketing or product management team when planning a product's future usually estimates how long payback should take. In former times, four to five years was a reasonable payback period. In today's brutally competitive business environment 18 months is all that many marketers give a product to repay their investment. This is one effect of the otherwise unacceptable risks some marketers take when getting a product to market. It is also why some new products – possibly most – are withdrawn before they reach the payback deadline.

Pay-TV   *Broadcast media*
Television channels that can be viewed only on payment of a subscription.

PDC   *Television, Video*
Program Delivery Control. A device built into video-cassette recorders, designed to switch machines on to record television programmes at pre-determined times. It also switches them off when the programmes are finished. The device is a US invention, used in the USA, where television programming and commercials are extensively networked. Programmes begin and end with accurate timing. However, in the UK and mainland Europe, where programme timing is imprecise, and programmes can begin and end late, the device is unsuitable. It can cause chunks of recorded programming to be missed. That is the situation as this edition goes to press. The manufacturer will almost certainly redesign the PDC for overseas markets. A similar, competitive product in the USA is VCR-PLUS; the UK equivalent is VideoPlus.

PDF *Information technology*
Portable Document Format. An electronic file format for pages, including text, fonts and graphics. It embeds all font and image information, and allows a document to be transferred from one computer to another

PDL *Information technology, Graphics,*
Marketing communications, Print
Page Description Language. A computer programming language, which allows the layout and content of a page to be sent to an output device such as a laser printer or image-setter. One of the most popular PDL software packages is PostScript. This enables many different output peripherals to reproduce the contents of a file, regardless of the manufacturer or model of the peripheral, or the technology used.

Peak time *Media planning and buying, Television advertising*
The most expensive segment of airtime for buying television advertising; the one with the greatest number of viewers. In the UK, this runs from about 9 pm to 10.30 pm. The radio equivalent of peak time is **drive time**, about 4.30 pm to 7 pm, when homeward-bound drivers, held captive in their vehicles, are sitting targets for advertisers.

Peer group *Marketing, Marketing research*
A group of consumers or businesspeople with similar characteristics of value to marketers. This generally comes down to their demographics, and their ability, and willingness, to purchase products and services, or accept new ideas and concepts.

Penetration *Advertising, Marketing research, Media planning and buying,*
Media research
In press media terms, penetration is calculated on the basis of the proportion of the total population represented by an active readership. One assumes that this core readership is exposed to, and looks at, the advertisements. In radio media terms, the equivalent is **weekly reach**. This is defined as the number in thousands, or as a percentage of the UK/area adult population, who listen to a station for at least five minutes in the course of an average week.
See Circulation, Controlled circulation, Opportunities to see, Rate card, Reader, Readership, Television rating points, Verified Free Distribution.

Penetration pricing *Distribution, Marketing, Retailing*
The pitching of the price of a product in order to encourage consumers to buy quickly, and in larger numbers. A measure often used during the launch or re-launch of a product or service, to gain as large a market share as possible in the shortest time. It is also used to prop up declining sales.

Per capita income *Business, Economics, Marketing*
A rough measure of average gross income in a national population. This is calculated by dividing the population figure by the total earned by it. This is not a

particularly reliable guide to the *disposable* income of the population, which is the figure marketers are most interested in.
See A,B,C1,C2,D,E, ACORN.

Percentage of sales   *Advertising, Budgeting, Marketing planning*
A technique for arriving at a budget for marketing activities. This is based on calculating a percentage of past sales, current sales and future anticipated sales. Using this method, a misjudgement can lead to over-spending and waste, or under-spending and failure to reach the full potential profitability of the product.

Perception of brand   *Advertising research, Consumer research,*
                                 Marketing psychology, Marketing research
A technique for arriving at consumers' views and understanding of a brand, compared with that of other brands. The results of this research may give clues to the way consumers select brands and products at the point of sale. It can also lead to the creation of successful creative strategies for advertising and sales promotion.

Perfect binding   *Print, Production, Publishing*
A technique for binding magazines, brochures and booklets. After folding, the pages are trimmed and glued at the spine. The cover is drawn on and held in place by the glue. No stapling is used. The effect is a flat, squared-up spine, rather than a rounded one. The main promotional advantage is that the spine is available for printing.
See Binding, Finishing.

Perfecting press   *Printing technology*
A printing press that prints both sides of a sheet in a single pass.

Performance audit   *Marketing, Product management*
Also termed performance analysis or appraisal. An audit of the performance of a product in the marketplace, measuring it against the marketing plan, its targets and performance estimates.

Perimeter advertising   *Advertising, Outdoor*
Advertising displayed on the perimeter of a race track, stadium or sports ground. The advertising becomes much more valuable, and more expensive, when events are covered on television.

Periodical   *Publishing*
A newspaper, magazine or journal published at regular intervals. The frequency can be weekly, monthly, bi-monthly, quarterly and so on. Annuals are not usually referred to as periodicals.

Periodical Publishers Association   *Media, Trade associations*
The trade association representing the interests of UK consumer, business, trade and technical and professional periodicals. It acts on behalf of periodical publishers

in industrial and legal negotiations, and offers members a range of professional services, events and activities.

Perishables *Retailing*

Products with a limited shelf life, on offer in supermarkets and other retail outlets. These include fruit, vegetables, milk, yoghurt, cheese and other groceries sold and consumed on a daily basis.

Permission marketing *Internet marketing activity, Marketing*

An interactive marketing technique which uses e-mail to advertise and sell to individuals, but only with their express permission. According to research figures available while preparing this edition of the *Dictionary of Marketing*, permission marketing has proved successful in Europe and the USA, alongside traditional methods.*

Personality promotion *Marketing, Sales promotion*

The use of celebrities to promote products and services. The most effective personality promotions are often those where the personality is appropriate to the product being promoted. Thus, a racing driver might be selected to promote cars; a fashion model for hair colourants. On the other hand, a well-known French footballer has been used for shampoo promotions on UK television and in women's magazines.

Personalization *Direct mail, Direct marketing, Print*

The incorporation of an individual's name, address and other personal details into a standard sales letter or piece of print. In a letter, personalization includes a personal salutation, the recipient's name in the body of the copy, and one or more personal facts and figures. A second-person-singular style of writing, using words such as 'you', and 'your company', are elements of personalization technique. Digital printing allows any amount of personalization; in a print run of, say, 1,000 brochures, each one can be personalized, with individual details included in the copy.

Personally identifiable information *Communications,*
Information technology

Information that can be traced back to an individual user, eg name, postal address or e-mail address. Personal preferences, tracked by a Web site via a cookie, when linked to other personally identifiable information provided by an individual user online, are also considered personally identifiable.

---

*According to figures available for this edition, e-mail marketing in the USA reached $98 million in 1999, and may increase by 417 per cent by 2003. A similar trend is expected in the UK and mainland Europe.

Persuasion *Marketing communications*

This is the objective of most, if not all, marketing communications. Persuasion is the conscious act of working towards and achieving a sale, or of changing a prospect's attitude about a product, service, concept or idea. It is in no way like merely presenting a calling-card to a prospective customer, as much advertising seems to do. Several proven techniques for persuasion are used by professional marketers. One of these is listed under AIDA (*qv*).

PESTLE *Marketing planning*

A popular acronym for six influences to which a market is subject:

Political
Economic
Social
Technological
Legal
Environmental

All products, services and markets are conditioned by these influences, as these examples show:

- *Political influences* – Many key influencers and opinion formers, especially at party political level, are antagonistic to marketing and the exercise of free trade. In recent years, alcohol and tobacco products have been banned from using television as a promotional medium in Europe. Throughout the world, particularly in industrialized countries, legislation is used as a tool to restrict marketing activity.
- *Economic influences* – Local, national and international economic movements influence marketing activity. Factors such as currency and interest rate fluctuations, local and national taxation, are strong contenders, and deterrents.
- *Social influences* – Population changes, and changes within population groups, influence marketing activity and growth. Rising and falling unemployment, baby booms, growth in the numbers of single parents and of pensioners, as well as local conflicts and national wars, for example.
- *Technological influences* – Technological advances are not a new phenomenon; they have been taking place since long before the invention of the wheel. In industrialized countries, the pace of change is accelerating, and having a chain-reaction effect on the rest of the of the world's economies. Products no sooner come on stream, and into the shops and the hands of end-users, than they are superseded by a more advanced generation. This offers marketers many opportunities for growth, but can also be a marketing planner's nightmare.
- *Legal influences* – In industrial economies, where legislation is closely linked to party politics, it is virtually unstoppable. In the UK, for example, over 250 acts of parliament, regulations and orders impinge on marketing activity; plus local legislation and by-laws. This is supplemented by European Union legislation, regulations, directives and decrees emanating from Brussels.

- *Environmental influences* – In industrialized economies, legislation is generated by governments under party political pressure, and stimulated and spurred on by unelected pressure groups. One of the best examples is Prohibition in the USA. It didn't work, and led to a great deal of wasted time, money, material and lives. Issues such as public transport, human warfare, animal welfare, agricultural and other issues have influenced corporations and governments on every continent. Their impact on marketing activity can be enormous, and marketing planning teams have constantly to take them into account.

Phased distribution   *Distribution, Marketing, Retailing*
In setting up national distribution, or a national distribution network for a product, phasing distribution into one region or area at a time. Phased distribution usually happens after the evaluation of test marketing.

Photocall   *Media relations, Propaganda, Publicity,*
                                                    Public relations
Also termed **photo opportunity**. An event organized specifically to bring together celebrities and camera crews. Celebrities include heroes, award-winners, sports persons, politicians, entertainers, and the like. The objective is to gain as much publicity as possible through media exposure.

Photo-composition   *Print, Production, Typesetting, Typography*
A method of typesetting using photographic techniques. This involves using a photographic negative matrix containing a font. The typesetting machine moves the matrix over photographic paper, one character at a time. It also keeps track of the matrix, and each individual character, as it proceeds. As the matrix moves over the paper, each character is exposed to the paper by a light source. In this way, the matrix is manipulated so that it sets lines of display and body copy.

In a way, this exposure method is rather like the way pictures are exposed in a camera. You wind the film on and release the shutter. Light coming through the lens exposes the film. You wind on again, and repeat the process to the end of the film.

In the UK, the European Union and the USA, photo-composition has largely given way to computer setting. This is because photo-typesetting is less flexible than the computer method, and involves chemical processing. For example, the photographic paper needs to be developed before you can see the image. You may find photo-composition in developing countries, or in places where the computer is not king. *Tip*: when entrusting artwork and typesetting to overseas suppliers, find out what production methods are in use.

Photograph   *Artwork, Creative, Plate-making, Print,*
                                                    Production
This term is so well known there is hardly any need to define it. But somebody will no doubt write complaining that I haven't covered it. A photograph is a

pictorial image, usually made in a camera, by the chemical action of light on light-sensitive film. The image produced is latent, until developed by chemical processing. The resulting image is either positive or negative. If negative, the image needs to be exposed again on to another negative, light-sensitive surface; then again developed chemically so that it becomes positive.

Where the final image is made on photographic paper, this is called a **print**, the abbreviated form of photoprint. This is still sometimes called a **bromide** (*qv*).

Photogravure *Print, Production*

Commonly called **gravure**. A printing process using printing cylinders rather than printing plates. This is intaglio (*qv*) printing, with myriad dots, or cells, etched or engraved into copper-plated steel cylinders. The sunken cells, representing the printing image, hold the thinnish, volatile ink. The cylinder rotates in a bath of ink, with the excess scraped away by a doctor blade (*qv*). In some gravure techniques, wrap-around plates are used.
See Flexography, Gravure, Litho, Screen.

Photo-litho *Print, Production*

Another term for litho (*qv*), where commercial litho plates are produced photographically. The image to be printed is photographically transferred to the printing plate, either direct or via film. In another technique, becoming more and more popular, direct imaging is done using a technique termed **CPT, computer-to-plate**. This is set to replace conventional film-to-plate methods.

Photo-mechanical transfer *Artwork, Graphic reproduction, Production, Studio work*

Usually abbreviated to **PMT**. A very superior form of photoprint, produced on a PMT camera. The sizing of the prints is very accurate, and the results very sharp and dense, to finished artwork standard. The PMT camera is precision engineered for the purpose, with very accurate controls. *Caveat*: PMT is also an abbreviation for **page make-up terminal** (*qv*).

Photo-montage *Artwork, Graphic reproduction, Photography*

Different photographic images brought together and mounted in position on artwork. This produces a combined image, which contains all the different photo elements. In former times, this was done by hand on the drawing board; today, it is done electronically, using appropriate computer software. This technique allows editing on screen, and no messing about with Cow Gum, spray mount or glue. Cow Gum mounting gel has been described as the greatest asset a studio could possess, with the possible exception of process white (*qv*). It used to be said that the more Cow Gum and process white a studio used, the more successful it was. Electronic montage techniques, and the use of scanning equipment are, however, faster and more flexible than drawing board methods. Vast libraries of digital images are available at reasonable cost, making photo-montage work potentially more profitable than conventional methods.

Photo-opportunity   *Media relations, Propaganda, Publicity, Public relations*
See Photocall.

Photoprint   *Artwork, Creative, Plate-making, Print, Production*
See Photograph, Print.

Photo-setting   *Artwork, Creative, Plate-making, Print, Production*
Display and body copy typeset photographically. Otherwise known as **film-set**.

PhotoShop   *Desktop publishing, Graphics, Illustration, Pre-print*
A popular, proprietary, image manipulation program. It is used for manipulating, retouching, cleaning up and generally enhancing computer graphics files.

Photostat   *Graphic reproduction*
A photocopy. An original document copied electrostatically by a machine dedicated to this technique, reproduced to paper or film. Sometimes called a Xerox, after one of the manufacturers that developed the process and popularized it. The quality of a photostat made by a copier is almost indistinguishable from the original. However, since the copy is a second generation, there is an inevitable loss of quality in the copying. One way of avoiding quality loss is in the use of a Docutech-type machine, which uses similar reproduction technology. In this case, the material to be copied is prepared on computer and saved to disk. The disk is presented to the machine, which reproduces the original without the loss of quality inherent in photocopying. There is no second generation; the output is actually an original.

Physical distribution   *Channels of distribution, Marketing*
The chain of distribution; the physical handling and shipping of products from manufacturer to distributor to retailer to consumer. This is one of the procedures and costs built into product marketing plans.

Pica   *Desktop publishing, Print, Typesetting, Typography,*
Word-processing
A unit in the measurement of type size. 6 picas = 72 points (pt) = 1 inch. This term has almost died out in the UK and the European Union, but is still popular in the USA. Type composed on computers is usually capable of enlargement or reduction on an infinite scale; or the size can be shown in millimetres. Some software packages offer a choice.

Manual typewriters usually have two type sizes: either pica, 10 characters to the inch; or elite, 12 characters to the inch. The typeface known as Courier is pica size. My first newspaper feature article was typed in Courier on a Remington Rand, which earned me my first fee. Why do I keep it? Not entirely for sentimental reasons. In the event of a power cut, which sometimes happens, I am the only person in the office who can actually do any work.
See Pitch.

PICT *Computer graphics, Studio work, Pre-press*
A Macintosh file format for bitmapped and object-oriented graphics.

Pictogram *Decision tools, Graphical representation, Graphics,*
Marketing planning, Marketing research, Spreadsheets
A graphic in the form of stylized symbols or icons, representing figures, mathematical and research data in an easy-to-understand form. The symbols relate to
the subject or activity being represented. Figures for, say, consumption of tea, are
represented by teacup symbols; petrol, by pump symbols; school attendance data
by children.
See Histogram, Pie chart.

Pictorial representation *Decision tools, Graphical representation,*
Graphics, Marketing planning,
Marketing research, Spreadsheets
A technique for displaying figures, models and other data in pictorial form. An
aid to decision-making. This can take the form of histograms, bar charts, pie charts,
graphs, curves, and so on, in colour or black and white. This makes it possible to
present complex arguments and figures in a form more easily understood and
digested than the bare text.

Picture caption *Film and video, Graphic reproduction*
See Caption.

Pie *Print, Proof-reading, Typesetting*
Type set indiscriminately in different faces, or jumbled in such as way as to distort
or destroy its meaning. Careless proof-reading resulting in the forwarding of
errors, if there is enough of it, is sometimes referred to as **printer's pie**.

Pie chart *Decision tools, Graphical representation, Graphics,*
Marketing planning, Marketing research, Spreadsheets
A graphic, in the form of a flat circle or a two-dimensional pie, representing
figures, mathematical and research data in an easy-to-understand form. The pie is
divided and subdivided just as the figures are, but shows more clearly how
quantities and differences relate to each other. Using a histogram (*qv*) or line chart
for the same figures, the data are represented by columns.
See Pictogram.

Piggy-back promotion *Retailing, Sales promotion*
A promotion where one product is promoted at the same time as another. For
example, a new coffee promoted with an established brand of tea; a film with a
camera; software with a computer. Promotions like these can also use coupons,
vouchers and other devices, either banded with a product or as stand-alone
distributions.

Pilot marketing *Marketing operations*
A basic feasibility test of a marketing project, manufacturing project, product launch, research operation and so on. Some companies prefer to carry out pilot surveys, to determine whether more costly, comprehensive tests should be made. Satisfactory outcomes of stages along the line may persuade the marketing team to continue to the next.

Pin register *Artwork, Pre-press, Production, Studio techniques*
Pins on a scanner frame, corresponding to holes in artwork mounting boards. The objective is accurate positioning and registration.
See Registration.

Pirating *Distribution, Marketing, Retailing*
The illegal use of another manufacturer's brand, logo, trademark, packaging design and intellectual property.

Pitch *Desktop publishing, Typography, Word-processing*
The number of typescript or typeset characters to the linear inch. With 10-pitch, there are 10 characters to the inch; this size is termed **pica**. 12-pitch is 12 characters to the inch; this is termed **elite**.
   This is not the same as **point size** (*qv*). 12pt typewriter type, usually termed Courier, has 10 characters to the inch; 10pt has 12. Confused? Don't worry; modern computerized typesetting and desktop software works it out for you.
See Point size, Typography.

Pitch *Agency new business activity, Sales technique*
Jargon for making a bid for a client's business. This has a formal presentation, or series of presentations, at its peak. When successful, a pitch is followed by a contract.

Pixel *Computer graphics, Information technology, Studio practice*
A portmanteau jargon word, a contraction of **Pi**cture **El**ement. The smallest addressable element on a display screen or in a raster computer graphic. In simpler terms, the smallest dot on a computer screen. For graphics displays, screens with more pixels provide higher resolution. More simply, the smaller the dot, and the more tightly they are packed together, the higher the definition, and the sharper the picture.
See Definition, Dot, Resolution.

Placement test *Marketing research, Product research*
A research technique for determining consumer attitudes to products. A product to be tested is placed by the researcher with a consumer or household. Later, the consumer is questioned about the product's performance, what she likes and dislikes about it; and about its attributes – size, quantity, packaging, price, value for money and so on.

Planned obsolescence   *Business, Manufacturing, Marketing*
Also termed **built-in obsolescence**. A marketing scenario in which the working
life of a product is limited by planning and design. This forces the purchaser to
decide, in the course of time, whether to continue to use the product until it actually
breaks down, or buy a new one. Obsolescence is usually driven by the introduction
of frequent changes in the design of a product, or by the introduction of completely
new ones at short intervals.

Consumers can be seduced by advertising and editorial coverage to believe
that the current product is inferior to its successor. This can be observed in the
marketing of computers, mobile telephones, televisions, videos and cars. With
computer software, new products are often incompatible with older computers.

Planographic   *Printing techniques*
A technique for printing from a flat surface. The current most popular method of
planographic printing is **litho** (*qv*).

Plans board   *Advertising planning, Marketing planning*
A team of executives and specialists, assembled for the purpose of discussing,
planning in outline, and evaluating a marketing or advertising campaign. This is
common practice in advertising agencies, particularly large ones. Members of a
plans board may or may not be members of the company's board of directors.
However, the main board director responsible for the conduct of the campaign,
and the client's account, may chair the plans board's meetings, and plans board
members may report to her.

Plastic comb binding   *Binding techniques*
A technique for binding a sheaf of individual sheets of perforated paper along one
of its edges, to form a booklet. The comb resembles a toiletry comb, but is larger
and curved into a tube. This is placed in a special machine that opens the tube to
receive the paper's perforations. The prongs of the comb go through the perforations. When all sheets are in place, the machine closes the tube, securing the
paper. The back edge of a plastic comb may be printed along its length, with the
title of the booklet, name of the author, company, recipient, or any other text; this,
of course, is done before binding. Another popular material for comb binding is
thin wire.

Plate   *Print*
A sheet of metal or other material carrying an image to be printed, mounted on
the plate cylinder of a printing press. When the press rolls, the image on the plate
is inked, then transferred to paper or whatever material is to be printed. Litho,
flexography and letterpress presses use plates of different kinds.
See Flexography, Litho, Pull.

Platform   *Advertising, Marketing communications, Public relations*
The central creative concept or theme on which an advertising or marketing communications campaign is based. Where campaign creation begins with copy and design concepts, this is usually termed **copy platform**.

Plinth   *Exhibitions, Presentations, Store window dressing*
A raised platform for displaying products, materials, posters and other exhibits, for convenience, emphasis or visual impact.

Plug   *Promotion*
Slightly cynical jargon for the free editorial mention of a product, service or company. The term is mostly associated with radio and television programming material such as news, reviews and entertainment.

PMT   *Artwork, Graphic reproduction, Production, Studio work*
See Photo-mechanical transfer, Page make-up terminal.

Pocket   *Direct mail*
An envelope in which the opening lies along one of the short edges. An envelope with its opening along one of its long edges is termed a **bank** envelope.

Point   *Desktop publishing, Proof-reading, Typesetting, Typography,*
                                                                Word-processing
More correctly, **full point**. Print term for a **full stop** or **period**.

Point of purchase   *Advertising, Direct marketing, Marketing, Retailing*
Virtually the same as point of sale, except that point of sale is usually confined to sales in retail outlets. Point of purchase can include direct marketing business, where purchases rather than sales are made; for example, via catalogues, the Internet and mail order.

Point of sale   *Advertising, Marketing, Merchandising, Retailing*
See POS.

Point size   *Desktop publishing, Typesetting, Typography, Word-processing*
The basic unit in the measurement of type. The size of a typeface is measured from the top of the ascender to the foot of the descender (*qv* both these).

The UK–US system is based on 72 points to the inch in the 12pt scale. Other type sizes are scaled appropriately in point units. This has served the printing industry well for more than a century. With the arrival of word-processing and desktop publishing, metric sizes have begun to take over. Don't worry: typefaces used in computerized setting are usually scaleable. This means that you can increase or reduce the size on a more-or-less infinite scale; the software works it out for you.
See Ascender, Descender.

Political correctness   *Advertising, Editorial, Internet, Marketing,*
                                                            Public relations

Popularly termed **PC**. A particularly nasty and damaging form of political censorship, practised by ambitious individuals and groups lusting after power. Single-agenda pressure groups intervene in, and interfere with, the democratic process. The bullying tactics of the proponents of PC, developed in the second half of the 20th century, are based on measures used by Stalinist and Fascist regimes in the first half. Initially a hobby of small, unelected, single-agenda pressure groups, political correctness has leached into the legislation of most industrialized countries, and is practised in many undeveloped countries.

The pursuit of political correctness inevitably leads to the infringement and destruction of the legitimate human rights of individuals and minorities. Reference to democracy is no excuse, since it works against individual freedoms. Stalin wrote: 'Democracy is the ruthless suppression of the minority by the majority'. Neither is there any moral basis for political correctness. As Lenin wrote of morality, it is: 'that which serves to destroy capitalism and unites working people around the proletariat'. History has answered both assertions.

Penalties for infringement of PC law now include fines and imprisonment. Any company, any citizen, can fall foul of politically correct legislation in areas such as race, sex, employment and disablement. Though not as draconian as penalties imposed by totalitarian regimes, they are just as pernicious in stifling genuine democratic debate and true free speech. This leaves many ordinary citizens in fear of innocent and unwitting infringement.

Political correctness inevitably develops into the more aptly termed, and perhaps more ugly, *political censorship*. It has a damaging influence on the common language, and on that of marketing communications. The history of the 20th century has clearly demonstrated that if the word 'freedom' is removed from a vocabulary, freedom itself ceases to exist. Editorial communication has also been infected, extending to press and broadcast media, the Internet and children's literature. It has reached a point where English usage and grammar have been driven into tasteless and illogical change.

Examples of political correctness producing poor communication in written English are found in advertising copy such as:

- Everyone wants to improve *their* memory.
- John Smith, the new *Chair* of the company, said today. . .
- Any person walking into a shop is usually referred to as a customer, whether *he/she* makes a purchase or not.
- The programme will provide a reliable, consistent method of guiding the *individual* from the start of *their* study to the successful completion of the exam, regardless of *their* exposure or career stage.
- We therefore strive to ensure that no *customer* is denied access to our services simply because of *their* disability. (Bank publicity leaflet.)
- Any words in the masculine include the feminine, and any words in the singular include the plural, and vice versa. (Bank, general terms and conditions.)

These real examples highlight the incongruous results of political pressure on organizations and creative writers. The italics are mine. The unhappy and ungrammatical mixture of the singular and plural is a result of political pressure. All efforts to de-sex and de-nature human endeavour, in the name of equality, make no sense in the ordinary world of free human communication. For those observing political correctness as a philosophy, this is political opportunism masquerading as conviction. It has no place in marketing communications. It could be argued that personal comments of this kind have small relevance in a dictionary of marketing. However, marketing communications managers and creatives, especially those starting their careers in the discipline, deserve to know what they are up against when putting their ideas into print.

Population *Marketing research, Research sampling and surveys*
Sometimes termed **universe**. In research terms, any pre-defined group of individuals or companies being investigated. The term population encompasses the whole group. The other common definition of population is that of people inhabiting a continent, country, town or village.

Port *Desktop publishing, Information technology, Studio practice*
A computer output line, designed to connect to a peripheral device, such as a printer, scanner, modem, communication line, or to another computer.

Portal *Information technology, Marketing communications*
A Web site offering an array of resources and services, bringing together multiple services and channels. The term is often used to refer to a company hosting a number of banner advertisements, with the main aim of generating worthwhile revenue.

Portfolio *Business, Financial marketing, Investment, Marketing*
The range of medium- to long-term investments held by an individual or an organization. A portfolio can include stocks and shares, government stocks, unit trusts, mutual funds, property and bank deposits.

In marketing terms, a portfolio is the range of a company's products and services. A company can have in its product portfolio an airline, insurance services, music production and retailing, construction companies, securities and soft drinks. Such a company, offering a diverse range of products and services, is termed a **conglomerate**.

Portrait *Artwork, Creative, Desktop publishing, Photography,*
Word-processing
The orientation of a printed page, or a photoprint, where the short edges are top and bottom of the page. The term derives from portrait photography, in which portrait photoprints have the short-top-and-bottom-edges format. A4 letterheads have portrait orientation, 210 mm wide × 297 mm high.
See Paper sizes.

POS   *Advertising, Marketing, Merchandising, Retailing*

Abbreviation for **point of sale**. Usually applied to advertising display material on show at the point of sale. It is designed to call attention to the product, and often reminds the customer of the message used in an associated advertising campaign. This is the last chance for the supplier and retailer to influence the customer into making a decision about trying or buying a product. Yet POS is often the Cinderella of marketing communications, and under-rated as an advertising medium.

Position   *Press advertising*

The location of an advertisement in a newspaper, magazine or directory. Advertisements booked in positions determined by the advertisement manager, termed **run-of-pape**r, are charged at basic rates. Special positions, specified by the advertiser, cost more.

Positioning   *Advertising, Brand management, Creative, Marketing planning,*
Product management

A marketing technique for placing in customers' minds the unique, most distinguishing ideas you want them to remember when considering a product or brand.

In creating a position for a brand, you must consider what customers are actually buying. Is it simply the product itself? Is it the product's reliability; its specification, performance, size, shape or colour? Is it after-sales service? Is it the reputation of the company that made or supplied it? It might be all of these.

In point of fact, these are not in themselves reasons for buying a product. A customer's true reasons are based on the *benefits* gained from possessing it or using it. The basis for successful positioning:

1. You must decide in advance exactly what you want your customer to think, feel and consider, both before taking the decision, and while actually making the purchase.
2. You must identify your product or service, and consider precisely where it stands in relation to its competitors. You must be prepared to differentiate it in the most compelling and motivating way. Sometimes this may conflict with the business culture of your organization.
3. In creative promotional terms, you must use concepts, ideas, images and motivations that differentiate your brand from all others. You must demonstrate its uniqueness.
4. You must give the customer the most compelling reasons for considering it as a purchase. These reasons must be based on the customer's needs, wants and self-interest. They can be rational or emotional, or both. They must be based on *benefits* to be gained from possessing and using the product.
5. You must motivate your customer, using these reasons to guide your promotional rationale.
6. The essence of positioning is: your customer's view of your product must be what you say it is.

When all this is decided, you need to attract your potential customer's attention in a commercial or advertisement. You must appeal to her needs, wants and self-interest. You must motivate, seduce, offer worthwhile benefits. You must strive to get a decision in favour of your brand, more compelling than the others competing for her custom. Only then can you ask her to take the action you want.

Positive   *Artwork, Creative, Photography, Plate-making, Production*
A photographic image on film, paper or metal, usually obtained from a negative (*qv*).
See Photograph.

Postal research   *Marketing research, Research techniques*
A research technique in which selected respondents are sent questionnaires through the mail. There is plenty of evidence suggesting that response to postal research is low, compared with the numbers sent out. This might be improved if an offer of discounts on purchases, a gift token, or a prize competition is included. Selection of recipients also affects response. Chairmen of corporations generally do not complete research questionnaires; unless, of course, they are personally involved or affected. On the other hand, lone farmers in isolated mountain areas may be more inclined to do so. Researchers also consider whether they need quantity or quality of response, and this too influences their selection of respondents.

Post-call review   *Sales staff training, Sales techniques*
Systematic review and analysis of sales representatives' activity. Reviews are based both on sales call reports and personal sessions with sales staff. Constant attention to sales activity enables management to make the most of sales staff time, improve sales techniques, and tailor sales training to current findings.

Post-campaign research   *Marketing research*
Research into the effectiveness of an advertising or sales promotion campaign after the campaign has run its course. This technique yields the most effective data when combined with pre-campaign and mid-campaign research.

Poster   *Media, Outdoor advertising*
An advertising sign displayed in a public place. The size of a poster is usually linked to the viewing distance. On a London Underground, Paris Metro or New York Subway platform, the size is modest, since the viewing distance is a few metres. Across the track, a poster may be up to 16 times larger.

Poster sites are usually found in, opposite or near to shopping centres and malls, where customers' money is exchanged for products and services. The promotional messages are designed to influence consumer decision-making at the point of sale.

Often, messages displayed on posters bear no relation to products on sale nearby. Some of the posters displayed near where I live seem to bear no relation to any product, person living or dead, or anything alive or inanimate. This is not the fault of the site owners; they merely supply sites for poster display. It is the

result of eccentric creativity, with little marketing thinking involved. The marketing message is obscured by the creativity. Read what David Ogilvy writes about posters, in his brilliant books *Confessions of an Advertising Man* and *Ogilvy on Advertising*. To say he doesn't like them is a gross understatement.
See Adshel.

Poster site classification   *Outdoor advertising campaigns*
Classification of poster sites, by location (proximity to shopping activity; type of street or highway), visibility (prominent positioning), estimated human traffic (pedestrians and vehicles). Poster class influences the cost of advertising.

Post-production   *Advertising, Film, Television, Television commercials,*
Video
All activities carried out after a production has been shot or filmed. This includes editing, sound dubbing, voice-overs, colour grading and computer animation.

Post-purchase anxiety   *Advertising, Customer behaviour, Marketing*
A period following a purchase, when a customer experiences fear that he has made a mistake. However, the anxiety may be resolved by the very means that causes it. Apart from the common fear that a natural mistake has been made, such as having bought the wrong size, capacity, shape or colour, fears can arise on the wisdom of having made the purchase at all. When contemplating the purchase of, say, a computer, a potential customer can experience fear arising from ignorance of the product field, or of personal inadequacy in selecting the right one. Anxiety can be heightened by seeing a plethora of competitive advertisements.

Such advertising can also assuage a customer's fear after the purchase; as can reading reviews in the press and discussion with colleagues. Needless to say, post-purchase anxiety can be prevented by adequate reading and discussion with experts *before* a purchase is made. This may be too rational for many consumers, a fact that advertising creative teams too often fail to take into account. Post-purchase anxiety can be experienced by consumers in fields other than the technical. It can be strong even in the case of the purchase of shoes.

Post-purchase promotion   *Advertising, Marketing*
Campaigns, or parts of campaigns, designed to promote brand loyalty. The aim is to ensure that recent purchasers realize that they have received a good deal, and are set up for the next purchase. As an example, a company known for high-quality photocopiers, seeking customers for its computers, fax machines, mobile telephones and cameras. This is a case for trading on the company's reputation, as well as its technological excellence and track record.

PostScript   *Information technology, Pre-press*
A page description language understood by RIPs and many printers. It defines how fonts and images appear on the page.
See Raster Image Processing (RIP).

PPI *Computer graphics, Studio work*

Pixels per inch. A measure of the resolution of computer image scanners.
See Pixels.

Pre-campaign research *Marketing research*

Research into the awareness, attitudes and reactions in a market and its environment before a campaign breaks. It is particularly useful in helping to modify a campaign ahead of media exposure; this can be applied to copy, design, response mechanisms and media schedule. It may reveal hitherto undisclosed information on competitive activity; it can tell the marketing team how much, or how little, the market knows about the advertiser.

Pre-coded questionnaire *Information technology, Marketing research,*
Research

A questionnaire in which questions, and the pre-determined answers required, are given computer codes. For example:

Q1 When did you stop beating your wife?
A1.1 Last month
A1.2 Last week
A1.3 Not yet

The main advantage of pre-coding is the speed with which completed questionnaires can be processed, and the results analysed.

Pre-empting *Advertising, Commercial television*

A system of purchasing television airtime based on supply and demand. Airtime rates are given in a contractor's rate card. However, at certain times spots may be bought at a basic rate, or at a discount. A television media buyer may book a spot at one of these rates, but can be pre-empted by another buyer prepared to pay a higher rate for the same spot. A contractor's rate may specify rates on a rising scale, shown as F1, F2 and so on. This indicates that the rates are pre-emptable.

Premium *Sales promotion*

A small item of merchandise offered with a purchase by an advertiser, to induce customers to try or buy more of a product. The items are usually free to the customer, or obtainable for a small sum of money; sometimes merely for the cost of the postage.

Some years ago you could have heard a bit of doggerel doing the rounds among vociferous consumer protection groups: 'Have you heard the latest premium racket? A mouldy old duster in a half-empty packet'. Today, most premiums are of reasonable value, and customers actually want them. Recently Kellogg came up with an offer, on Rice Crispies packs, of model vintage cars and public transport vehicles. Many customers, probably families, went for the whole collection, and of course consumed vast quantities of Rice Crispies. They came to no discernible harm, and now have a collection that will no doubt be valuable in years to come.

Premium price   *Marketing, Retailing*
A product or service with a high price, usually sold on style, quality, uniqueness
or rarity value. They are often labelled 'exclusive', and sold through selected
outlets.

Pre-paid reply cards   *Advertising*
Reply cards included with promotional leaflets, brochures, booklets and catalogues, inviting reply to an offer made in the literature. On one side of the card,
the recipient is asked to fill in name, address, telephone number, and other personal
information. On a business reply card, job title, company name, fax number, e-
mail address and Web site are usually asked for. Sometimes, the recipient is asked
to reveal other personal information, such as purchasing, consumption or reading
habits. The reverse side of the card carries the return address of the advertiser, or
that of an agent organization. There is also a pre-paid formula, showing that the
advertiser is paying for the return postage, and that the recipient is not required to
affix a stamp.

  The obvious caveat here is that many people dislike committing personal details
to an open card, which can be read by anyone. This can be a deterrent to using the
card, and can affect response figures.

Presence   *Media research, Television audience research*
The actual time a viewer spends viewing television, as against that indicated by
official research. Research commissioned by BARB (*qv*) shows whether viewers
are watching television or not, and this includes the entertainment programming.
What advertisers need to know is whether viewers are watching television during
commercial breaks.

Presentation visual   *Artwork, Creative*
A highly finished visual, suitable for presenting to a board of directors; or, if in an
advertising agency, to a client. It is designed to give the closest possible representation of the finished product. Also called a **finished rough**.

  In pre-computer times, presentation visuals were usually mounted on board and
covered with transparent acetate. An acetate served two purposes: to prevent
accidental damage from coffee and other contaminants; and to deter clients from
making alterations during a presentation. This was a wise precaution, since
presentation visuals were expensive to produce, and there was usually only one
of each. Today, visuals of every kind can be computer-generated, and a board can
have as many copies as it wants. They can also be displayed on screen during
presentations, and distributed electronically across the globe.

Press conference   *Editorial, Media relations, Public relations*
A media meeting called by a public relations department or agency. Editors,
journalists and reporters are invited to a presentation of news about a corporate or
other event, a product, service or statement. They are encouraged to ask questions,
and to take away a kit of relevant information. Proceedings are usually short and

to the point; refreshments are sometimes offered. What a journalist wants, above everything, is a good story of interest to her readers. Refreshments are usually welcome, but no journalist goes to a press conference merely for lunch. The shorter the lead time, the more urgent it is to get back to the newsroom to write up the story. Lead times for daily newspapers are often a matter of minutes rather than hours or days. Monthly magazines may work at a more leisurely pace, but time is always in short supply even for them.

Press cutting *Advertising, Editorial, Public relations*
Printed evidence of the appearance of an advertisement or editorial, cut from a newspaper or magazine. A number of companies specialize in monitoring advertising and public relations campaigns. Among the well-known ones: Romeike, News Index, Press Select, CIS Information Services and Tellex. Some press cutting services provide electronic distribution of cuttings. Also termed **press clipping**.

Press date *Editorial, Media, Print, Production, Publishing*
The date on which a newspaper or magazine goes to press, with all copy passed for publication. Do not confuse this with the **cover date**, which is the date on the cover of the publication; or **copy date**, the deadline for submission of advertising and editorial copy for publication. A public relations manager submitting a news release on press day will have the material held over to the next issue, or discarded altogether.

Some magazines, of the glossy and housekeeping kind for example, arrive on the bookstalls a month or more ahead of their cover dates. The objective seems to be to steal a march on competitors. However, since many publications competing with each other adopt the same strategy, it defeats itself, and serves only to confuse media buyers and consumers. Agency creatives and production managers also suffer from this bizarre timescale, since it is completely out of step with the realities of working life.

Press kit *Editorial, Media relations, Public relations*
Various items of information made up into a kit or pack, for distribution to journalists at press conferences and at exhibitions. Material can include news releases, photoprints, CD ROMs, video and audio-cassettes, product samples, and anything else a PR manager deems relevant. Also termed **press pack**.

Press proof *Advertising, Print, Production, Publishing*
The final proof of an advertisement submitted by the publisher before going to press. This proof needs to be signed off by the advertiser, who takes responsibility for it, this being the final approval and authorization.

In print practice, the term describes a proof made on a printing press before a production run. This is unacceptably expensive, because it means devoting an entire press to pulling off a few proofs; no printer dare do it and hope to survive in business. Therefore, specially scaled-down versions of production presses are used instead. The production values of proofs taken from such mini-presses can usually be relied on to resemble the real thing.

See Cromalin, Plate, Proof, Proof-reader, Proof-reader's marks, Pull, Quote, Zero.

Press reception   *Editorial, Media relations, Public relations*
See Press conference.

Press relations   *Media relations, Public relations*
More correctly termed **media relations**, since it applies also to broadcast media. An extremely important function of public relations activity. It means getting to know the media used in public relations work, and getting them to know and understand you. The ultimate prize of good media relations is when newspaper, magazine, television and radio journalists habitually approach you as a reliable source of good stories.

Press release   *Editorial, Media relations, Public relations*
More appropriately termed **news release**. For the complete technique for planning and writing successful news releases, see *Creative Marketing Communications* (Kogan Page, 3rd edition, 2001).
See News release.

Press run   *Print, Production, Publishing*
A print run; that is, the number of copies produced in a print run (*qv*).

Press visit   *Media relations, Public relations*
A company event, held especially for specified media of interest to the company. This may be a tour of a new factory or a local facility employing local people. A visit may be set up, for example, for the media to meet a new senior executive; promote a new product; celebrate a corporate success or anniversary. Sometimes, a private corporate event to which selected senior members of the press and broadcast media are invited.

Pre-test   *Advertising, Marketing*
A test on a small scale of an advertising or marketing campaign. For an advertising pre-test, one or more geographical areas or regions are selected, and local media used. Product distribution is confined to those areas. Pre-testing enables marketing teams to evaluate the strengths and weaknesses of a campaign before going fully national with it. They can compare technique and expenditure with the results obtained from them. Sometimes pre-test campaigns are conducted in two areas with similar population characteristics, in different parts of the country and with no overlapping media. This enables different advertising themes, product packaging and pricing to be compared.

Preview test   *Advertising*
Also termed hall test. The testing of television and cinema commercials in a hall, cinema or auditorium, before a campaign is launched. An audience is invited, and

exposed to a programme of entertainment material and commercials. A two-part questionnaire reveals their attitude to the material, before and after screening. This technique offers the campaign team an opportunity to evaluate the campaign material, and to modify it on lines suggested by the preview test.

Price *Marketing*

Generally regarded as the value of a product or service. Price, of course, can go up or down, depending on supply and demand, and many suppliers take advantage of this. However, price at the point of sale does not always truly relate to the cost of production and distribution. All prices are artificial. Every time a product changes hands among distributors, for example, its price rises. The more intermediaries, the greater the number of mark-up opportunities. Other anomalies exist. In the UK, ludicrously, where a whole lamb can be bought from a farmer for £1 (US$0.69), it may be offered to consumers by supermarkets for £3 per lb (US$2). Whatever the product, this cannot be called a just profit. But as long as consumers fail to complain, or show their preferences with their feet (so to speak), the situation continues to exist, and price continues to equal value.

Price cutting *Marketing, Retailing*

A marketing technique involving temporary reductions in the price of a product or service, aimed at increasing market share. Some organizations such as supermarkets reduce prices selectively for short periods, often on a geographical basis; some adopt it as long-term or permanent policy. One obvious danger lies in management inflexibility; competitors may cut prices tactically, and destroy any advantage gained for early price-cutters.

Price discrimination *Advertising, Marketing, Retailing*

The application of different prices for different customers for the same product or service. This can be implemented on a geographical basis, by differences in consumption volume, or by method of payment. A telephone subscriber may pay his bill with cash once every three months, pay less by quarterly direct debit, or even less when paying monthly. The price of petrol (gasoline) can vary according to district, or whether the retailer is sole supplier in an area. In pricing policy terms, price level is pitched at what customers will pay at the time, or what the market will actually bear. While not being particularly noble, price discrimination is nevertheless legal.

Price haven *Business, Marketing*

The position of a product enjoying such high customer loyalty, that its sales or market share are not affected by price changes; particularly after an increase in price.

Price leader *Business, Marketing*

A company or supplier, the first in its field to change its prices to higher or lower levels.

Price sensitivity   *Business, Marketing*
The degree to which demand for a product or service responds to changes in price.

Price tag   *Advertising, Marketing, Retailing*
Jargon for the price of a product or service shown in an advertisement, or given in
a verbal description of the product. The term is also used for the actual price label
affixed to a product at the point of sale.

Pricing strategies   *Business, Marketing*
A number of viable strategies exist, all based on profitability, and gaining and
keeping market share. Among the factors needed to be taken into account in
devising a pricing strategy for an established product:

- consumers' view of the product's value and importance;
- how an increase or decrease in price will affect sales and profits;
- how consumers will react to a price reduction or increase;
- how many might remain loyal after a price increase or decrease;
- how the competition will react to a price reduction or increase;
- how they have reacted to price changes in the past;
- if a price reduction will increase its market share;
- its position in its life cycle;
- opportunities and threats in its market;
- opportunities for a re-launch, if any;
- the current loyalty of customers;
- the product's strengths and weaknesses.

Pricing structure   *Business, Marketing*
The practice of pitching prices for a product or service, according to the type of
customer, and the volume or frequency with which it is bought. Wholesalers, for
example, will be offered a product at a lower price than retailers or consumers,
since wholesalers' volume of purchases will be higher.

Pricing tactics   *Business, Marketing*
The management of temporary price changes over short periods. Pricing tactics,
with flexibility and adaptability, are useful countermeasures against competitive
attacks, market downturns brought about by PESTLE influences, and so on.
Tactics may be able to encourage non-users to try a product, existing customers to
use more, and users of other brands to switch. As always, business judgement
should be exercised over blind faith in research findings.
See PESTLE.

Primary colours   *Artwork, Creative, Photography, Print, Production*
The primary colours of light, known as the additive colours, are red, blue and
green.The colours used in four-colour process printing are cyan, magenta, yellow
and black. Most other colours can be made up by combining these four. This is

usually termed subtractive colour mixing. Four-colour process printing has a number of limitations. Your eye is a brilliant visual instrument, capable of detecting millions of colours. But four-colour process printing can reproduce only a small percentage of them. Hues produced by four-colour process printing are made up of dots – a combination of cyan, magenta, yellow and black. It is difficult, however, to reproduce some shades of colour; for example deep blues, violets, greens and oranges.

In colour science, colour is measured by three basic criteria: hue, saturation and luminance. In ordinary language, these are the colour itself, its depth and brightness. The four primary colours used in four-colour process proofing are designated CMYK, a useful shorthand. K stands for black, to distinguish it from blue and brown.

Primary data *Marketing research, Research*
Data collected by proactive research methods, such as field research, surveys and polls. This is often combined with **secondary data** (*qv*), compiled from existing research carried out for a particular purpose at some other time.

Primary readership *Media research, Press media*
Readership data based on the total number of readers of a publication who actually purchase copies of it, and includes members of these reader's households. Readership beyond this restrictive profile is calculated as **secondary** and **tertiary readership**. These terms should not be confused with circulation, which is restricted solely to paid-for copies.

Prime time *Media, Radio, Television*
Periods during the day when the highest number of people are viewing or listening. On television, this is between 9 pm and 10.30 pm. Television advertising rates vary with the size of the audience. Prime time rates are the highest. Other times are called **off-peak**.

Radio has two distinct peak times, commonly called drive time. This refers to the captive audience sitting in their cars during the morning and evening travel peaks. The hours are 7–9 am and 4.30–6pm. However, with ever-increasing congestion on the roads at peak times, these periods are extending at both ends.

Print *Print, Production*
Professional jargon for **printing**. The executive who buys printing services is called a **print buyer**, not printing buyer.
See Copy.

Print *Artwork, Creative, Photography, Production, Studio work*
An abbreviation for **photoprint**. Professional jargon for a photograph (*qv*).
See Photo-mechanical transfer.

Print media *Advertising, Editorial, Marketing, Media*
Jargon for newspapers and magazines; it can also sometimes include directories.

Printout   *Computing, Desktop publishing, Word-processing*
The recording on paper of a computer, DTP or WP file. Also called hard copy (*qv*).

Print run   *Print, Production, Publishing*
The number of copies of a publication – newspaper, magazine, catalogue, brochure or leaflet – produced by a printer. This is specified in the print specification briefing and subsequent printer's quotation. The actual printing of the copies is also referred to as a print run.
See Cromalin, Press proof.

Privacy statement   *Communications, Information technology,*
Internet activity, Web marketing
A page on a Web site that lays out its privacy policies. This can include what personal information is collected by the site, how it will be used, with whom it will be shared, and whether you have the option to exercise control over how your information will be used.

Private brand   *Marketing, Retailing*
An alternative term for an own brand, one created and marketed by a retail organization in its own outlets.
See Ogilvy, David.

PRO   *Corporate communications, Marketing communications,*
Product communications
A popular acronym for **public relations officer** (*qv*). A manager or executive within an organization, responsible for the planning, creation and implementation of public relations campaigns and activities.

Probability   *Marketing research, Research*
A theory in sampling for research activity, used as an aid to decision-making. Theoretically, if an event occurs once, or more than once, there is a likelihood that it will occur again. In theory, it can be calculated, and become a probability.

Probe   *Research*
A technique used by researchers to ensure a questionnaire is answered satisfactorily by respondents during interviews. Detailed questions are put to respondents, often at some length, including minute detail of the subject being researched, to elicit the response needed.

Problem child   *Marketing planning, Product portfolio planning*
One of the elements in the Boston Matrix (*qv*), together with star, cash cow and dog. The Matrix is a graphical representation of a product portfolio, and the relative positions and values of products within it.
See Product portfolio.

Process colours *Print, Production*
The subtractive primary colours cyan, yellow, magenta and black. These are four-colour process printing colours, designated CYMK. K stands for black, to distinguish it from blue and brown. Combinations and blends of these four can produce most colours in the spectrum. This is cheaper than using special colours to achieve the same results.
See Primary colours.

Process white *Artwork, Studio work*
A very white, opaque, water-based paint used for whiting-out errors and removing unwanted spots on artwork. Also used for re-shaping photographic images and illustrations.

Product acceptance *Campaign research*
The degree of acceptance or product take-up at the end of a product launch campaign. To function as an element of campaign research, and aid decision-making, the level of acceptance must be capable of calculation – quantitative as well as qualitative.

Product benefits *Advertising, Creative, Marketing campaigns,*
Product management
The lure of benefits to be enjoyed, presented to potential consumers during marketing campaigns. This technique is designed to influence consumers' decisions to try or buy the product or service being promoted. Product benefits should not be confused with product facts and features. Seen from the consumer's point of view, product features are what a product can do; product benefits are what a product can do *for the consumer*. The art of presenting products benefits to a market lies in getting consumers to visualize themselves using and personally benefiting from the product.

Product development *Marketing, Product management*
A management process for developing a product or service, based on customers' current or anticipated needs. This is often an ongoing routine, linked to a product's life cycle (*qv*), or one stimulated by acute market conditions. Such factors as commercial trends, competitive attack, technological advances, political and environmental changes can drive product development. Improvements to a product's design, specification or performance are relevant in product develop-ment. On the other hand, it may amount merely to putting an old mechanism into a new box.
See Boston Matrix.

Product image *Advertising, Marketing, Public relations,*
Product management, Product promotion
A mental process determining how a product or service is perceived in its marketplace. The groundwork will have been laid down by careful marketing

planning, and delivered by advertising and other forms of promotion. Part of the process takes place in potential customers' minds when considering a product's technical specification. Part of it arises from a product's reputation or track record, or that of the company that produces it. Part of it, sometimes even all of it, is emotional, ignoring or in conflict with a product's technical features. One result is the impulse purchase, made without examination of competitive products.

Production　　　*Editorial, Press advertising, Print, Public relations, Publishing*
Also termed **pre-press** activities. Specialized activities carried out after conception and creation, in preparation for printing. These include typography, production layouts, photography, retouching, illustrations, finished artwork, photo-mechanical transfers, colour mark-ups, colour grading, production artwork, typesetting, proofing, colour separations, filming, plate-making.

Production　　　*Radio advertising*
Activities carried out after scriptwriting, ahead of submission of tapes to a radio station. These include casting, studio recording, editing, dubbing, voice-overs, music, sound-effects, transfer to tape.

Production　　　*Television advertising*
Activities carried out after scriptwriting and storyboards, ahead of editing. These include planning, set design, creation or selection of props, music and special effects, titles, casting, shooting film or videotape. Editing, sometimes regarded as a post-production activity, is carried out ahead of submission of prints or tapes to the broadcasting station. This includes rough cutting, tape and film editing, the marrying of music, sound and visual effects and voice-overs, lip synchronization, colour grading.

Product life cycle　　　*Marketing, Marketing planning, Product management*
A popular marketing theory that products and brands have a cyclical life in a marketplace, with conception, gestation, birth, growth, decline and death. While the analogy with animal and vegetable life, particularly human life, is understandable, it should not be taken too far. As a theory, product life cycle is not infallible, or totally valid, but does represent a useful guide to product progress. The following considerations should make the distinction clear:

- No market is immutable, or remains unchanged for long.
- No product has an unlimited life, untouched by changes in the marketplace.
- The continuous, indefinite growth of a product is unlikely.
- Product life is often determined by management activities and decisions.
- Product life cycle – birth, growth, decline – is the likely shape of things to come, unless management takes corrective action in good time.
- Marketing and product management can often increase a product's sales and market share by ignoring life cycle theory.

- The introduction of extensions to product use can stimulate additional stages of growth.
- Tactical re-launching can extend a product's life.
- Extending products in a range may extend product life.
- Profit levels are not constant, but change throughout the life of a brand in a more or less predictable way.
- Brands require different marketing programmes at each stage of their lives.

The length of a product's life depends on such factors as:

- the rate of technological change;
- the rate of market acceptance;
- apathy among consumers, and rejection by the market over time;
- the ease with which competitors can enter the market.

When referring to products and brands, the term life cycle is inaccurate. Instead, product life may be thought of as developing in stages or phases, some brands developing in a flatter or steeper life curve. What is more, some brands appear to have an indefinite life; Guinness, Coca-Cola and Colgate toothpaste, for example. However, these phenomena are usually the result of extremely clever product management, and vast investments in promotion and product development.

The widely accepted theoretical life cycle curve should be considered a generalization, an idealization. It is simply a pattern many brands can be expected to follow. There is nothing infallible about it, or about the length of its stages; it is not, as one might say, set in concrete. What is more, marketing management can pre-empt the decline and death of a product by re-launching it; possibly more than once. For theoretical purposes, the life cycle of a product can be considered as six stages:

Development stage

- marketing research undertaken;
- product designed;
- prototypes built;
- production plant set up and commissioned;
- substantial investment;
- high costs;
- income probably nil.

Launch stage

- possible slow growth in brand sales;
- growth curve may not rise steeply.

Growth stage

- the brand gains acceptance;
- sales rise;
- profits grow;
- return on investment begins;
- product unit costs decrease with greater volume of production.

Maturity stage

- competitors come on the scene;
- greater reliance on replacement sales;
- sales increase more slowly;
- profits come under pressure;
- signs of impending decline.

Market saturation stage

- sales peak and fall off;
- profits decline.

Decline stage

- sales go into indefinite decline;
- profit margins come under severe pressure;
- sales are increasingly costly to maintain at a profitable level.

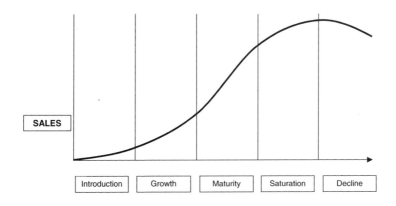

PRODUCT LIFE CYCLE
As product sales grow through repeat purchases, the rate increases.
Competitors often enter the market here, which further expands it. No market,
however, can expand forever, and no product is immortal. As competition
becomes fiercer, prices fall and some competitors drop out. Finally, the market
falls into decline.

Product manager   *Brand management, Marketing, Marketing management*
A term sometimes used for **brand manager**. A manager or executive responsible for the conduct of a product or brand in its markets. Duties include everything from the creation and implementation of the initial marketing brief for the brand, to the day-to-day running of the team handling brand affairs. This can include every product activity from package design to the pursuit of its profitability objectives and plans for future development. Close liaison with other managers and departments is usually essential, especially those in sales.

Product mix   *Brand management, Marketing, Product management*
The total product range of a company, managed in such as way as to appeal to a variety of markets and market segments. In a well-managed product range, products can be introduced to established markets at moderate cost. This can enable brand management to avoid or minimize the effects of product decline, and set up profitable new market segments. Some products in a company's product mix may deliberately compete with each other, even in the same market segment. In this case, consumers who habitually switch products have an opportunity to switch from one of the company's products to another, rather than to a competing brand. The bottom line, so to speak, is overall profitability of the company's entire product range over a long time-frame.

Product portfolio   *Business, Marketing, Product management*
A popular concept developed, if not actually created, by the Boston Consulting Group. Its main contention is that each product marketed by a company has a function in a company's overall profitability, and makes a contribution to it. Moreover, that some products in a portfolio perform better than others, and that some are a drag on it and need to be purged. It recognizes that a product will have an individual life cycle, comprising conception, gestation, growth, decline and death.

To simplify the concept, and make it easier to understand, the Boston Group produced a planning tool in the form of a diagram now known as the Boston Matrix. The terms used to describe products in a portfolio, and their performance, are problem child, star, cash cow and dog. An explanation of the terms used in the Matrix:

- *Problem child* – a product with high growth, low market share. Prospects are good, but possibly under-performing. May need high investment to reach its full profit potential; this could be a drain on the portfolio.
- *Star* – product with high growth, high market share. May need high levels of funding.
- *Cash cow* – product with low growth, high market share. Could be the main source of funds for the problem children and stars in the portfolio.
- Dog – a low growth, low market share product. Dubious performance. May qualify for removal from the portfolio.

See Boston Matrix.

Product recall   *Brand management, Marketing, Product management,*
                                                  Public relations
A situation arising from the discovery of defects or faults in a currently marketed product. The manufacturer asks for products to be withdrawn from sales outlets, and for customers to return them as soon as possible. This might be viewed as a public relations disaster for a company. However, many companies faced with product problems now minimize the impact by acting immediately, telling the truth, and using the situation as a media and public relations opportunity.

Product test   *Brand management, Marketing, Product management*
A research technique for evaluating a product in the marketplace before a launch.

Profiler   *Marketing research*
A computerized data analysis and query tool, designed to give marketers fast access to facts and figures on customers and prospects. It allows them to explore their own data, and provide information on key marketing issues, including:

- the crossover between products and services;
- the proportion of active customer profiles within a database;
- the profile of customers and enquirers;
- who should be targeted and selected for potentially profitable mailings.

The main advantages of a profiler are the accuracy and speed with which it delivers answers for decision-making.

Profiling   *Media research*
A technique for determining readership of newspapers and magazines. The difference between penetration and profile is this: a magazine read by half the women in the UK has 50 per cent penetration, but its profile is 100 per cent women. This calculation is theoretical, and also an over-simplification. In practice, the profile might be 85 per cent women and 15 per cent men, since women's maga-zines may also have male readership. Other profiles could be based on age bands, socio-economic groups, geographical areas or product usage. Bear in mind that however many sub-groups are included, profiles always add up to 100 per cent. *See* Circulation, Controlled circulation, Penetration, Rate card, Reader, Reader-ship, Television rating points, Verified Free Distribution , Viewer.

Profit centre   *Business, Marketing*
A business accounting practice, in which individual products and services are considered self-contained units for the generation of profit. Each unit is expected to make a profit contribution to the company that owns it. To this end, it usually sets up and maintains a corporate mini-hierarchy of its own; remembering, of course, that it is not a corporation but an element of one. Should the unit fail to make a profit, to the satisfaction of the corporation, it faces being purged without ceremony.

Pro forma *Business, Sales*
A Latin phrase used in business practice, translated as 'for form's sake'. A written advice, invoice or demand sent to a purchaser, for pre-payment before goods are supplied or delivered. It is designed to ensure the completion of business formalities before goods change hands. This is a useful measure to take in dealing with a new, untried customer, whose credit has not been established.

Progress *Advertising, Creative, Print, Production, Studio*
Also termed **traffic**. A department of an advertising agency, or section of a company advertising department, responsible for the orderly and timely progression of creative and production work. In many progress departments, it is also responsible for the forwarding of finished work to pre-production houses, typesetters, printers and publishers.

Progressive proofs *Artwork, Plate-making, Print, Production*
Also termed **progressives**; in the USA, **progs**. Proofs taken from individual plates or cylinders in colour process printing. They are produced to mimic the sequence of printing, and show the result after each succeeding colour has been laid down. This is a complicated way of saying that each colour is proofed separately, and also imposed upon one another, in this order:

Y   Yellow
M   Yellow + magenta
C   Yellow + magenta + cyan
K   Yellow + magenta + cyan + black

This technique enables advertiser, art director and printer to judge the hue, saturation and luminance of each colour, and evaluate the end result. They also see how the result compares with the original.
See CYMK, Press proof, Process colours, Proof.

Project Rain *Information technology, Pre-press, Print*
Also termed Megastream. An extremely fast form of file transfer, using fibre optic cables between a server and Digital Graphics Network subscribers. At 12Mb per minute, it enables the transfer of graphics files from pre-press to printer at high speeds.

Promotion *Marketing, Sales promotion*
Advertising and other forms of sales presentations, designed to encourage fast consumer or trade up-take of a product or service. The form of any promotion depends on the product, the marketing plan and its objectives, and on the imagination of the product management team. It can vary from a simple in-store demonstration of a range of cosmetics, or a sampling of Jaffa oranges, to a tie-in with a cinema blockbuster. A promotion for exotic vacations could be linked with a promotion for Martini. Travel insurance, for example, might be appropriate during a local screening of the film *Titanic*. A promotion for kitchen knives could

be mounted during a screening of *Fatal Attraction*. These are extreme examples, possibly in bad taste, but you see what I mean.

Promotional mix   *Advertising, Marketing, Public relations, Sponsorship*
Also termed **marketing communications mix**. A range of promotional tools, techniques and activities, mixed and matched to meet the needs of individual marketing campaigns. The mix can include:

- advertising;
- after-sales activity;
- body media;
- branding and positioning;
- catalogues;
- corporate communications;
- direct mail;
- direct marketing;
- e-commerce;
- exhibitions;
- interactive videos;
- Internet activity;
- livery design and display;
- market education;
- marketing research;
- merchandising;
- mini media;
- packaging;
- point-of-sale display;
- pricing strategy;
- print: consumer literature;
- print: trade literature;
- promotional give-aways;
- public relations;
- sales force support;
- sales literature;
- sales promotion;
- sponsorship;
- staff uniforms;
- stationery.

Prompt   *Advertising research, Marketing research*
A technique used by researchers to elicit answers from respondents. For example, a researcher shows a respondent an advertisement headline or a newspaper or magazine title, and asks a question about it. Questions can vary from 'What do you think this advertisement is selling? to 'How many times did you buy this newspaper during the last month?' The headline or title is the prompt.

Proof *Artwork, Creative, Plate-making, Print, Production*
An impression taken from an inked printing plate, cylinder or other printing surface, ahead of a production run. Proofing is done so that advertisements and pages can be checked for image, accuracy, colour and so on. When proofing is carried out on a printing press, using conventional printing inks, it is termed **wet proofing**.

Today, other techniques for evaluating printed material ahead of a run are available. This is done by computer; and by proofing techniques such as Cromalin (*qv*), in which case it is termed **dry proofing**.
See Progressive proofs, Proof-reader, Proof-reader's marks, Reader, Quote, Zero.

Proof of purchase *Advertising, Packaging, Sales promotion*
In conducting a competition related to a product or service, and publicized in the media, promoters may require proof that the product has been purchased in good faith. Proof can comprise a receipt, or a token cut from a pack. In the UK, promotions addressed to children must clearly indicate the number and type of any additional proofs of purchase needed for participation. They should not encourage excessive purchases in order to participate.
See Advertising Standards Authority.

Proof-reader *Copywriting, Creative, Print, Production*
A person whose job it is to read proofs, correct inaccuracies and revise copy. Copywriters and other creatives routinely read proofs of the work they create. Management often does the same.

Ideally, the way to read proofs is to have two people doing it. One reads aloud from the proof; the other, the copy-holder, holds the typescript or other original copy, and checks it against what is being read out. The reader calls out every word and all punctuation, and spells out names in full. Where numbers are part of the copy, the reader calls out each individual figure, including decimal points, commas, subscripts and superscripts.

If you have to read proofs alone, without the help of a copy-holder, life can be difficult, especially if you have written the copy yourself. One way of overcoming this problem is to turn the proof upside down and read it that way up. It's not ideal, or comfortable, but you soon get used to it.

There is a convention that copywriters and publishers' proof-readers mark their corrections in red ink for typesetter's errors; printers and typesetters use green for their comments and queries and authors use black or blue. This clearly shows who has made the corrections, and generally indicates who is to pay for them. If a printer has made an error, he is obliged to correct it free of charge. Where an advertiser, author or agent has made a mistake in original copy, and the printer sets it as it stands, the advertiser usually pays. The advertiser or author is then charged for **author's corrections**. Because it can cost £50 or more to change a comma on a proof, it always pays to take pains over the accuracy of original copy sent to printers.
See Proof, Proof-reader's marks, Quote, Zero.

Proof-reader's marks   *Artwork, Creative, Desktop publishing, Print,*
Production, Word-processing

A series of marks and symbols used by proof-readers for correcting and revising proofs. These are accepted and used by the printing industry in the UK and mainland Europe, and in other parts of the world. They are, of course, essential for correcting typescripts. Using them helps to reduce the risk of errors caused by ambiguous instructions, and avoid unnecessary expense and delay.

Because of the international trade in print, proof-correcting marks need to be international in character. This means that it is unwise to use words in the correction procedure. In the days before much of the English-speaking world went mad with decimalization, words and symbols were used together very effectively for proof correcting. I am glad to observe that the US printing industry has sensibly retained the combination of words, marks and symbols for correcting its proofs.

The British Standards Institution publishes a booklet that recommends to writers and printers the standardization of proof-reading marks and symbols. It can be obtained from Her Majesty's Stationery Office. Ask for BSI 5261 Part 2 1976. *Check*: there may now be a later version to be had.

See Proof, Quote, Zero.

Propaganda   *Communication techniques*

The use of media, print, entertainment and other tools and techniques, as a means of gaining support for ideas, opinions, beliefs, doctrines, causes, creeds and concepts. Its most dynamic use is in connection with politics and religion.

According to Dr Josef Goebbels, the highly successful Nazi propagandist of the 1930s and 1940s, propaganda is: 'The saturation of a group of people with propagandist ideas without their even noticing it. Of course, propaganda has a goal, but the goal must be so clever, and so brilliantly concealed, that the people who are to be influenced by it don't notice anything.'

There are clear differences between advertising, public relations and propaganda. The main one is that propaganda is designed to achieve changes in public thinking and attitude without being detected by its recipients. The means include covert persuasion, and the change has to take place naturally. The programme of change is created and conducted by professionals with a single, biased objective and agenda. The media are manipulated to achieve this; some media are controlled by the organizations issuing the propaganda. Other powerful tools are used, including education.

Propaganda is planned, systematic and ruthless; above all, it is covert. It exists and is used not only in dictatorial regimes but in democratic societies as well. Its ultimate aim is to encourage target audiences to conform and adapt to the attitudes and ideas being promoted.

On the other hand, marketing communications are, by their very nature, open and above-board, and can be seen for what they are. Propaganda is concealed and pretends to be something it is not.

313

Proportional scan *Artwork, Computer-aided design, Creative,*
Desktop publishing, Print, Production
Reduction or enlargement of an image or shape, where the height and width remain
in proportion to each other.

Proprietaries *Marketing, Pharmaceuticals, Retailing*
More correctly, **proprietary products**. Products manufactured to specifications
set or approved by a professional body or government department. In the case of
pharmaceuticals, some proprietaries need a licence before they can be distributed
to the public through retail outlets. In the UK, although doctors can prescribe them
proprietaries do not actually need a doctor's prescription, and can be sold over the
counter. Examples: certain painkillers, cough remedies and fungicidal creams.

Prospect *Marketing terminology*
Short for **prospective customer**. A term indicating a potential customer for a
product or service. It is common to confuse the terms customer, consumer and
prospect. The first assumes that the individual concerned has already bought the
product, or has bought from the same supplier in the past. Consumer is usually
applied to a member of the general public who routinely buys personal and
household products and services, including fast-moving consumer goods. Identifying and collating information on new potential customers is termed prospecting.
See Sales enquiry, Sales lead.

Prototype *Manufacturing, Marketing*
An early version of a product, built for testing and evaluation, and for decision-
making by product management and other management teams.

Provincial media *Press media*
Also termed **local** or **regional media**. In the UK, daily and weekly newspapers
and magazines circulating in areas outside London. The term includes the main
provincial conurbations. Local radio stations, whether BBC or commercial, are not
designated provincial; they are usually termed **local radio**. In the USA, virtually
all press media are local.

Psychographics *Consumer research, Marketing research*
A term combining psychology and demographics. It is applied to techniques for
researching, analysing and evaluating the lifestyles and behaviour of members and
groups of the general public. In marketing practice, target groups and market
segments are selected for psychographical analysis, evaluating their viability for
profitable marketing investment. Demographics includes details of:

- age;
- income;
- location;
- marital status;

- media reading, viewing and listening habits;
- occupation or profession;
- position in domestic life cycle;
- sex.

Psychographics in marketing research may add such factors as:

- attitudes to products;
- buyer psychology;
- buying and spending habits;
- decision-making processes for purchases;
- individual roles, such as purchaser, influencer and user;
- leisure interests and activities;
- lifestyle;
- purchasing motives;
- why, how and when products are used.

Psychological pricing *Marketing, Retailing*
Prices pitched at the right emotional level for a specific market. For example, a leading world brand of perfume may be worth £1 or $1.50, when ingredients, packaging, distribution and other costs are taken into account. However, if retailed at, say, £2 or $3, which would yield a just profit, the market might consider the product inferior, contaminated, not worthy of buying, using and giving. Raise the price to £50, or $75, and the product's psychological weight, and value, goes up. A further aspect of psychological pricing lies in pitching prices at levels acceptable to the general public. These prices may actually *seem* lower, and therefore better value. As an example: a jar of coffee at $2.95 seems better value than the same jar at $3. The psychological value is in the figures, not in the jar, yet the jar's contents acquire better value by association.

Psychometrics *Marketing research, Media research, Consumer research*
Techniques for evaluating a respondent's attitudes and behaviour to certain situations and circumstances. Standard psychometric tests can be used to quantify respondents' reactions and performance, and to classify, measure and compare them accurately for various purposes. These techniques are widely used in the selection of candidates for employment in commerce, management, the military and government. They are used for determining consumer behaviour; in marketing, their ability to understand, interpret and react to advertising, branding, public relations and editorial messages.

Public affairs *Media relations, Publicity, Public relations*
Also termed **corporate affairs**. Public relations activities conducted by a company, corporation or organization at corporate level. These are aimed at, or relate to, other corporations, local and national government, foreign governments, the military, the company's shareholders and supporters. Sometimes also at foreign

corporations, particularly customers and suppliers, at highest management levels. Some public affairs activity may be aimed at or relate to pressure groups, especially where such groups interfere with or disrupt a company's operations.

Publication date   *Publishing*
The date on which a publication is distributed or on sale. This applies to daily newspapers and most weeklies, but not monthlies. This is because many monthly magazines have cover dates that bear no relation to their publication dates. For example, computer magazines may have a cover date of, say, November, but are available on the book-stands at the beginning of October or earlier. Media buyers are usually aware of this anomaly. However, it can be confusing for advertisers, who may have time-related offers and pricing structures for their products and services.

Publicity   *Communications, Marketing communications*
A term sometimes confused with advertising, sales promotion and public relations. It could be regarded as a blanket term, incorporating all an organization's publicity activities acting together, or a single one. It is therefore wise to be precise when discussing publicity activities.

Publicity manager   *Communications, Marketing communications*
Another opportunity for confusion when referring to an organization's communications activity. This is a loose term for managers of advertising, public relations and sales promotion.
See Publicity.

Public relations   *Corporate communications, Marketing communications*
The UK's Institute of Public Relations offers this definition of public relations: 'The planned and sustained effort to establish and maintain goodwill and mutual understanding between an organization and its publics'.

A conference of public relations professionals in Mexico, after several days of deliberation, arrived at the following definition, popularly known as The Mexican Statement: 'Public relations practice is the art and social science of analysing trends, predicting their consequences, counselling organization leaders, and implementing planned programmes of action which will serve both the organization and the public interest'.

In essence, public relations aims to educate and inform, in order to create and increase knowledge and understanding about an organization and its operations. Although public relations is not in itself a marketing communications activity, it is an important tool used in marketing communications. Its basic aim towards its target publics is to achieve changes of attitude:

- apathy to interest;
- hostility to acceptance;
- ignorance to knowledge;
- prejudice to acceptance.

There are three basic 'publics' for public relations activities: primary, ultimate and internal.

Primary publics include:

- editors;
- feature writers;
- journalists;
- publishers;
- reporters;
- television and radio producers and editors;
- the media.

Ultimate publics include:

- academics;
- children;
- civil servants;
- competitors;
- customers and consumers;
- distributors;
- end users;
- financial institutions;
- general public;
- governments, national, local and foreign;
- health authorities;
- international influencers;
- investment analysts;
- investors;
- key opinion formers;
- legislators;
- local communities;
- medical profession;
- money market;
- opinion leaders;
- parliamentarians;
- politicians;
- potential employees;
- resellers;
- retailers;
- shareholders;
- stock market;
- students;
- suppliers;
- teachers;

- the professions;
- trade associations;
- trades unions;
- wholesalers.

Internal publics include:

- associate companies;
- employees;
- management;
- new employees;
- overseas associates;
- shareholders;
- trades unions.

The tools of public relations include:

- archival material;
- company newspapers;
- competitions, contests and prize draws;
- documentaries for television and radio;
- facility visits;
- feature articles;
- house journals, external and internal;
- media lunches;
- media receptions;
- news conferences;
- newsletters;
- news releases, printed and electronic;
- open days;
- PR functions and events;
- signed articles;
- the Internet.

Public relations consultant *Corporate communications, Marketing communications*

An independent specialist company or individual, whose services include the planning, creation and implementation of public relations activities and campaigns.

Public relations officer *Corporate communications, Product communications*

A manager or executive within an organization, responsible for the planning, creation and implementation of public relations campaigns and activities. He or she may be responsible for the PR activities of the whole organization, or that of a single product or service.

Public service advertising *Advertising*

Advertising by local or national government, or one of their agencies, containing information or advice of benefit to the general public. Topics include road safety, the dangers of smoking and use of alcohol and drugs, healthcare, education, taxation, employment opportunities and information technology.

Publisher's statement *Media planning, Media research, Publishing*

A statement of circulation issued by a publisher of a newspaper, magazine or directory. This is usually an estimate by the publisher, although some statements may be very accurate. Advertisers and their agencies usually look for completely independent audits of circulation, such as those provided by the Audit Bureau of Circulations (ABC), and Verified Free Distribution (VFD) (*qv* both).

Pull *Print*

A proof taken off a letterpress printing block or type forme. In hand-proofing, the block is inked with an inking roller, and the paper laid on it. Pressure is applied to the paper, then released. The paper, carefully pulled off the block, will have had the inked image transferred to it. In machine proofing, the same basic technique is applied, but on a production press. Specialized proofing presses simulate the action of production presses and their reproduction values.
See Plate.

Pull-out section *Print, Publishing*

A complete, self-contained set of pages in a newspaper or magazine. This is usually designed so that it can be detached and read separately. The editorial and advertising are usually closely related, but in the UK do not normally corrupt each other.

Pull-push activity *Distribution, Marketing, Marketing communications, Sales force effort*

A combined strategy aimed at getting the best possible distribution and sale of a product. It involves, on the one hand, substantial advertising effort; on the other, aggressive selling-in to wholesalers and retail outlets. Advertising, and other marketing communications activity, pulls the customers in; trade advertising and sales force effort ensure that products are available in sufficient quantity when the public comes in to buy. Point-of-sale advertising, plus inducement offers to resellers, help to pull the product through the distribution channel and push it to customers.

Qq

Q   *Business, Marketing planning*
Shorthand for **quarter**; that is, three months, or a specific three-month period of a
year. This is usually expressed as Q1, first quarter; Q2, second quarter, and so on.

Qualitative research   *Research techniques*
Research procedures dealing with data or material difficult or impossible to
quantify. However, it may yield important relationship data on which management
and marketing decisions can be based. The data is acquired by question and
discussion, and evaluated using the judgement and experience of the research
team. As an example: the question 'How many times a day do you clean your
teeth?' can be quantified, and a figure arrived at. This is quantitative research. The
question 'Why do you clean your teeth four times a day?', although yielding
important information, cannot be quantified.

Quality of life   *Marketing research, Social science*
A statement of individual or group lifestyle, easy to recognize but difficult to
quantify. The data and variables used to express it are principally financial,
familial, health, occupational and cultural. Thus, a rich, elderly individual, in poor
health, in a nursing home or living alone and in squalor, may be deemed not to
have a good quality of life. On the other hand, a young, impoverished artist, with
a university education and dynamic social and sex life, may be said to have a good
quality of life. To social science professionals, and others in the business of
manipulating populations, the first is no longer viable, the other highly so. The
estimated value of consumers in these circumstances, and at the extremes, is the
constant concern of marketing teams, in terms of purchasing ability and power.

Quantitative research   *Research techniques*
The collection, recording, processing, analysis and evaluation of research data,
which can be expressed in numbers.
See Qualitative research.

Quantity discounts   *Marketing, Media buying, Distribution, Purchasing*
Discounts given by a supplier, based on quantities of a product purchased. This
can be crudely summarized as 'The more you buy, the less it costs'. In point of
fact, such discounts apply to units of purchase, such as a case, crate, weight,
number, volume and so on. Media buyers expect discounts on volumes of
advertising space and airtime.
See Frequency discounts

QuarkXpress *Desktop publishing, Information technology, Print, Publishing*

A software package for the design and make-up of pages, incorporating images and text. It is currently the industry standard used throughout printing and publishing.

Quarterage *Budgeting, Marketing services*

A quarterly payment, as for example the payment of a marketing agency's fee, retainer or expenses.

Quarterly publication *Print, Publishing*

A magazine, house journal or catalogue published every three months.

Quarter-tone *Artwork, Production*

A dot-based method of reproducing continuous-tone images. Similar to the halftone (*qv*), but retouched in the studio so that some of the tones are eliminated. This produces a sharp, dramatic, high-contrast effect.

See Halftone.

Quartile *Marketing planning, Statistics*

In statistics, one of three values of a variable, dividing a population into four equal groups, relating to the value of that variable. Sometimes, perhaps in error, used to refer to one three-month period of a year.

Query *Information technology*

A question entered into a search engine to retrieve selected documents from a database.

Questionnaire *Marketing research, Research*

A highly structured document comprising a list of questions, used by researchers for gathering information. Space is provided for answers given by respondents. Questions and answers are numbered for the computer processing of the data.

Queue *Desktop publishing, Information technology*

A collection of computer documents or files waiting to be printed. The computer usually sends each file to the printer in the order in which it was created or processed. However, the operator can change the order of priority.

Quick cutting *Cinema, Television, Video*

A sequence of very short shots succeeding each other, without the intervention of optical devices or special effects.

Quota *International trade, Sales practice*

A government measure for restricting the importation of certain products, or of immigrants. It may also be applied to exports. In sales management, quotas are minimum targets set for sales staff.

Quota sampling *Marketing research, Research*
The specification of rules for a sample of a population required for a particular research project. For example, for 100 interviews, a quota of 30 red-headed people are required; for a survey of 100 stores, 20 must be food outlets.

Quotation *Creative, Marketing communications, Print, Production*
Also termed a **quote**. The costing of a job, prepared in advance, by a printer, production house, advertising agency or other supplier. Do not confuse quotes with estimates. In the UK, estimates are not legally binding; quotations are. The term can be applied to all goods and services.
See Estimate.

Quote *News, Propaganda, Public relations, Publishing*
A printed or verbal statement, reproduced exactly as it was written or spoken by the person who originated it.

In print, quoted speech is usually shown between dual turned commas at the beginning, and dual apostrophes at the end. Quotes from written statements are shown with a single turned comma at the beginning and an apostrophe at the end. With some publishers, the reverse applies.
See Proof, Proof-reader, Proof-reader's marks, Reader, Zero.

Qwerty *Desktop publishing, Information technology*
The arrangement of character keys, left to right, on the top line of an English language computer or typewriter keyboard. On French language keyboards, the top line begins AZERTY.

Rr

Radio Authority   *Media controls*
A UK body that licenses and regulates the independent radio industry in accordance with the statutory requirements of the Broadcasting Act 1990 (*qv*).

It plans frequencies, awards licences, regulates programming and radio advertising. It plays an active role in the discussion and formulation of policies affecting the independent radio industry and its listeners.

The Authority takes a firm and objective stance in support of the development and growth of a successful UK independent radio network that offers a wide listening choice.

The Broadcasting Act requires the Authority to draw up, periodically review and enforce a code that sets standards and practice in advertising. The Authority advises its licence-holders on interpretation of the code, and monitors compliance by investigating complaints.

By laying down clear, precise rules, the Authority encourages self-regulation. It believes that the ultimate responsibility for checking advertisements for compliance with its Code of Practice and the general law lies with the broadcaster.

It is a condition of a Radio Authority licence that radio stations comply with the Authority's Advertising Code, and that they employ trained staff to check all advertising carefully before accepting it for broadcasting.

In practice, local and regional advertisements are normally approved for broadcasting by station staff. National advertisements, and those that fall into certain categories, have the additional safety net of being checked by the Copy Clearance Secretariat of the ITV Association (*qv*), in an arrangement with the Broadcast Advertising Clearance Centre.

Ragazine   *Publishing*
In US media jargon, a cheaply produced magazine or news-sheet devoted to gossip and mild scandal.

Ragged right   *Creative, Desktop publishing, Typesetting, Typography,*
                                                                  Word-processing
A block or column of type with a vertically uneven right-hand edge. **Ragged left** indicates a ragged left-hand edge where the right-hand edge is justified.
See Full out, Justified, Measure, Range.

Rag paper *Print technology*

Paper made from stock containing a substantial amount of rag pulp. The rag is produced mainly from recovered cotton and linen.

RAJAR *Media, Radio audience research*

The acronym for UK Radio Joint Audience Research Ltd. A company jointly owned by the BBC and Association of Independent Radio Companies. AIRC is the trade association for commercial radio stations in the UK.

RAJAR was set up to implement and control a new, jointly agreed system of audience research for radio. It replaced two previous services, BBC Daily Survey and JICRAR audience research for commercial stations.

The purpose in establishing a joint system was to have one agreed audience currency. This would be accepted by the whole of the industry – including advertising agencies, advertisers and others with an interest in the medium. The remit of the organization is to:

■ operate the agreed research system;
■ oversee the quality of the service;
■ publish the results.

It is not a commercial organization in the normal sense of the word, and sets out to provide services as economically as possible to radio stations, rather than make a profit. It is managed by a small, full-time secretariat reporting to a board of directors, and supported by a technical management committee, which advises on technical and operational issues. It is structured as a 'deadlock' company – board decisions require the agreement of both parties.

The RAJAR research service encompasses national and local radio stations. Results are produced on a quarterly basis for national and large local services; twice a year for other participating stations.

The need to research stations covering a range of overlapping areas leads to a large and complex sampling arrangement. Around 150,000 respondents provide information during the course of a typical year. Information is obtained primarily through the completion of a seven-day diary, in which respondents record their listening, quarter-hour by quarter-hour. Published results and internal information are also made available to national broadcasters on a monthly basis.

Random sample *Research, Statistics*

A sampling technique that ensures that each informant within the population being researched has an equal chance of being selected.

Range *Creative, Production, Typesetting, Typography, Word-processing*

An instruction by a typographer to a typesetter, on how a piece of copy should be set in type. Range left asks for a straight, vertical left-hand edge. By implication,

the right-hand edge will not be so. Range right asks for the right-hand edge to be set straight and vertical. The left-hand edge will not be. In computer word-processing, the terms used are **align left** and **align right**.
See Full out, Justified, Measure, Ragged right.

Raster Image Processing   *Print technology*

Usually given as **RIP**. A device or computer program that interprets a page description language, abstracting from a pre-press file the instructions for printing. The RIP converts the instructions to dot patterns, enabling the printer to create a printed document.

Rate card   *Media, Media planning, Publishing*

A document, leaflet or brochure produced by a newspaper or magazine publisher, TV or radio station owner, giving its advertising rates. A rate card will also give production details and deadlines, and much other information. It is usually presented as part of a media advertising pack, with advertising rates accompanied by research information on circulation and readership; or viewing and listening audience. Among the information found in a typical UK local newspaper group rate card:

- a brief description of each paper;
- advertising agency commission;
- advertising rates for individual sections of the newspaper; for example entertainments, situations vacant, motors, property, sales and services, holidays, public notices and church notices;
- circulation and readership data; whether this is ABC or VFD;
- circulation area and map;
- cross-references to other publications in the group;
- frequency and volume discounts;
- mechanical data; precise information and dimensions on:
  - column length and width;
  - film required;
  - halftone screen;
  - image resolution;
  - no of columns;
  - page type area.
- representatives' names and addresses, e-mail addresses, telephone and fax numbers;
- run-of-paper advertising rates for each paper, expressed in £ per single-column centimetre;
- the newspapers in the group.

See ABC, Circulation, Controlled circulation, Penetration, Reader, Readership, Television rating points, Verified Free Distribution, Viewer.

Rate card cost   *Advertising, Media*

The cost of advertising space or airtime as shown in a current rate card. This is the basic cost on which discounts and other reductions are usually calculated and negotiated.

Ratings   *Advertising, Audience research, Broadcast media,*
                                                         Media planning

A short-form for **television audience ratings** popularly abbreviated to **TVRs**. A form of measurement used in television audience research. The calculation is based on 1 TVR = 1 per cent of the total estimated or potential audience for a particular item of programming. It therefore also applies to the commercials screened during the breaks. Not only is the popularity of a particular programme indicated by its TVR, it is a measure used by advertisers and their agencies in scheduling decisions. All television channels, commercial and public service, are in continuous competition over high TVRs. It might be argued that public service and other non-commercial channels, especially the BBC whose income is derived from taxation, have no reason to struggle for TVRs. But the battle for high ratings is as deadly and ruthless as in any commercial industry; in attempting to achieve them, programming quality often suffers.

Rational appeal   *Advertising, Creative platforms,*
                                                   Marketing communications

A form of argument and motivation used in the promotion of products and services. Rational factors, including facts and figures, advantages and benefits, are used in an appeal to consumers' intellects, rather than their emotions.

Rationalization   *Business, Marketing, Marketing communications*

The focusing of a company's resources only on products and services that produce maximum profit for a minimum of cost and effort. The term also applies to promotional effort. Simply explained: it might be worth putting additional money into a budget for persuading householders to clean their teeth three times a day. This objective may be achievable, and worthwhile in terms of extra toothpaste purchased and profits earned. An attempt to gain market share by persuading consumers to clean four or more times a day is almost certainly futile, whatever the estimated or calculated potential commercial rewards. It is not rational either to consider or implement it.

Raw materials   *Business, Manufacturing, Marketing planning*

Materials used in the manufacture of products. This term is slightly misleading, because most such materials have already been through a process of manufacture or conversion. Truly raw materials come out of the ground: water, coal, crude oil, mineral ores; perhaps also vegetables and wood. Plastics, on the other hand, are also considered raw material, even though they are usually the product of highly sophisticated industrial processes.

Reach *Audience research, Media research*
A term denoting the audience exposed to a television or radio commercial. It is sometimes expressed as a cumulative figure, and as a percentage of the total possible audience. In RAJAR studies, **weekly reach** is the number in thousands, or as a percentage of the UK/area adult population, who listen to a station for at least five minutes in the course of the average week.
See RAJAR.

Reader *Artwork, Creative, Desktop publishing, Print, Production, Publishing*
The person who reads and corrects hard copy produced by desktop publishing, and printer's proofs. Also termed a proof-reader (*qv*). Ideally, one half of a team of two; the other holds the original copy and checks the reader's reading-out of the proofed text.
See Proof, Proof-reader, Proof-reader's marks, Quote, Zero.

Reader *Media planning and buying, Media research, Press media*
A participating informant in a press media research sample. **Average issue readership** (AIR) is defined as the number of people claiming to have read or looked at one or more copies of a publication for at least two minutes during the issue period – the publication frequency.

In press terms, 'reading and looking' covers anything from reading a publication thoroughly, to a casual flip through it. The actual issue of the publication does not seem to matter; any issue will do for the purpose of this research.
See ABC, Circulation, Controlled circulation, Penetration, Rate card, Television rating points, Verified Free Distribution, Viewer.

Reader-friendly *Advertising, Copywriting, Creative, Print, Public relations*
Legal, insurance, computer and other gobbledegook, interpreted and written in clear, understandable language. Sometimes also applied to marketing terminology.

Reader involvement *Advertising, Creative, Sales promotion*
Advertising created for the purpose of gaining readers' confidence and participation. Product competitions are a case in point; readers are invited to take part, and offered reasonably worthwhile prizes as an incentive. This is a reliable technique for building and cleaning databases, as well as gaining new customers.

Reader reply service card *Advertising, Marketing communications, Publishing*
Popularly termed **bingo card**. A reply card, enclosed or bound into a publication, which readers use to send for information, or advertisers' product or service literature. Products and services advertised in a magazine are given key numbers; these are reproduced as a matrix on the reply card. The reader selects products she is interested in by ticking appropriate numbers on the card, then posts it back to the publisher. Return postage is usually, but not always, pre-paid by the publisher. Copies of cards are sent by the publisher to advertisers for fulfilment.

Editorial is often keyed in the same way, and for the same purpose. This tool is widely used in business, trade and technical publications, and by some consumer magazines. It is a popular technique for measuring response, both for advertiser and publisher. House journals also sometimes use reply cards.

Readership *Media planning and buying, Media research, Publishing*
The number of individuals reading an issue of a publication. Do not confuse with **circulation** (*qv*), since one who reads a newspaper or magazine is not necessarily the purchaser. Circulation is calculated on the basis of copies purchased.
See ABC, Circulation, Controlled circulation, Penetration, Rate card, Reader, Television rating points, Verified Free Distribution, Viewer.

Readership profile *Media planning and buying, Media research, Publishing*
Readership of a publication classified by demographics and other important characteristics. The information presented by the publisher may be quantitative or qualitative, or both. It may be augmented with information on readers' lifestyles, consumption patterns, and whatever the publisher deems appropriate for promoting the publication to advertisers.

Reading and noting *Advertising research, Media research, Readership research*
A research technique for gathering information on reading habits, aimed at measuring the effectiveness of press advertising. The results are presented as an average percentage of readers reading or looking at individual pages of a publication. Respondents are asked to describe various items in the publication being researched, as evidence that they did indeed read it on the day of issue. A range of questions follows, relating to specific pages of the publication. Some of the questions relate to advertisements on the pages in question.

Ream *Paper, Print buying*
Five hundred sheets of paper of the same size, grammage and quality.

Rears *Advertising, Outdoor*
Advertising panels at the rear of buses and coaches.

Re-branding *Marketing, Marketing communications*
Changing the name, image or logo of a brand currently on the market.

Recall *Advertising research, Audience/viewer research, Media research, Readership research*
A technique used in media research, aimed at determining the impact of press and broadcast advertising. Two variations are used. In **aided recall**, respondents are shown advertisements or commercials during an interview, then asked specific questions about what they have seen. Alternatively, **in spontaneous recall**, respondents are asked to discuss advertisements they have seen prior to an

interview, with prompting by the researcher. Both methods have disadvantages; for example in cases where a particular advertisement has been repeated with high frequency over a long period. This may distort the findings, especially where the research is limited to advertising appearing on the same day or the previous day.

Reciprocity *Optics, Photography, Physics*
The law of reciprocity states that exposure is equal to the intensity of light multiplied by its duration. In very brief or very long exposures, this law breaks down, and additional exposure is needed. Colour balance may also be affected.

Recognition *Advertising agency practice, Advertising media*
A status awarded by media owners and their trade associations to advertising agencies. Recognized status entitles agencies to receive commission from media owners. Two principal criteria are imposed, ensuring as far as possible that bad debts will not arise. First, an agency must be creditworthy; second, it must be professionally competent, to the satisfaction of those granting recognition. It should be noted that an advertising agency is not an agent in the generally accepted sense; it is in fact a principal, entering into contracts in its own right and with all the consequent responsibilities.

Recognition testing *Advertising research, Audience/viewer research,*
Media research, Readership research
A technique for studying consumer recall of brand messages.

Recruitment advertising *Advertising techniques, Media*
Also termed **personnel advertising**. Advertising dedicated to the recruitment of staff. This uses all techniques and media, especially the national, regional, local, professional, technical and trade press; display, semi-display (classified displayed) and classified (linage). In the UK, local commercial radio is also used, though not as widely as local press. Advertising agencies specializing in recruitment produce press and broadcast advertising and print; and, where appropriate, public relations campaigns and material.

Recto *Print, Production, Publishing*
A right-hand page of an open brochure, booklet or book, usually having an odd page number. **Verso** is the left-hand page (*qv*).

Recycled paper *Paper, Print*
Paper made wholly or partly from recycled pulp. Produced from waste paper or board, recycled pulp may or may not be de-inked. Fibres deteriorate with recycling, so that paper cannot be recycled ad infinitum.

Redemption *Advertising, Sales promotion*
The exchange of coupons and vouchers for products, services or benefits. For example, a coupon in a press advertisement for instant coffee may entitle the reader to a discount on a future purchase, or to a free sample. The coupon, when presented

at a retail outlet, is said to be redeemed. A collection of vouchers from cereal packets may be redeemed for a gift from the manufacturer.

Reel *Print*
Another term for a **web**, a large roll of paper used on high-speed printing presses. The paper is wound on a core, irrespective of diameter, width or weight. Large reels may therefore be wound into smaller reels, or slit into coils.

Reel-fed *Print*
A press fed by reels of paper or other material. Most high-speed offset litho and flexography presses used by national and regional newspaper and magazine publishers are reel-fed.

Reel-to-reel *Paper, Print*
A machine or press on which material is supplied in reels and comes off the machine also in reel form.

Reflectives *Artwork, Photography, Print*
Art, print or photographic originals prepared for scanning, from which light is reflected, rather than from transmitted light. Scanners offering a facility for scanning photographic transparencies can be set to **reflective mode**.

Regional press *Media*
In the UK, another term for the **provincial press**. This refers to virtually every-where outside Greater London; the demarcation is usually the M25 motorway.

Register *Artwork, Plate-making, Print, Production*
The precise fitting of two or more images on to a printing surface, in exact alignment with each other. In colour printing, the accurate positioning of colours with each another. The images and colours are referred to as being **in register**. In printing practice, it can also mean the correct alignment of pages, with accurately positioned margins.
See Colour bars, Register marks, Registration.

Registered trademark *Business, Marketing*
A design registered in the UK in accordance with current legislation. The design can be a picture, symbol, drawing or other graphic, a name or word in a particular typeface or style. Its use is to establish the clear visual identity of a product or corporation, and also represent the business of the trademark's owner. It can be used only by the registered owner. A properly registered trademark is a form of protection against passing off (*qv*) by competing organizations and by 'pirates'.

Register marks *Artwork, Plate-making, Pre-press, Print, Production*
Small cross-hair marks, lines or dots on artwork, negatives, film and colour separations. Hairline crosses or other symbols are drawn on or applied to original artwork before photography. These are important for:

- accurate lining up and positioning of colour separations;
- accurately positioning of overlays on artwork;
- cropping guides;
- indicating on proofs the trim areas of pages;
- keeping negatives and overlays precisely in correct positions;
- the accurate positioning of two or more colours in proofing and printing.

See Colour bars, Overlay, Registration.

Registration *Artwork, Pre-print, Press work, Print*
In artwork and pre-print practice, the precise alignment, or superimposition, of any artwork element with another. In press work, the precise positioning or alignment of colours with each other during a print run.
See Colour bars, Overlay, Register.

Reinforced paper *Packaging, Paper, Print*
Paper that has been strengthened mechanically, incorporating materials such as plastics, threads, cloth or metal strips.

Relational purchasing *Consumer behaviour, Marketing*
The way consumers habitually buy brands, products and services, based on their understanding of, and beliefs about, the brand, product, service or company. Such a purchase, and the decision process leading up to it, is usually emotional; possibly also with a trace of the rational, since this is never entirely absent. This is the basis of a customer's relationship with the brand or company.
See Transactional purchasing.

Relationship marketing *Marketing techniques*
Broadly speaking, a management process supporting a triangular relationship between marketing, quality and customer service, with the three arms serving each other. Relationship marketing has evolved from traditional, transactional marketing. It focuses on:

- a combination of high quality product and customer service, rather than product quality alone;
- customer identification, acquisition and retention, rather than one-off sales;
- frequent customer contact, rather than limited contact or no contact at all;
- highest commitment to customer service, rather than limited or reluctant commitment;
- long time-frames, rather than short ones;
- outstandingly high quality customer service, rather than mediocre service;
- personalization of marketing communications, rather than anonymous, impersonal ones;
- product benefits, much more than product features;
- the development of efficient customer databases for long-term relationships, rather than passing trade or random contact.

Re-launch *Marketing*

Re-presenting a product or service to its markets. Since no product is immortal – with very few exceptions, such as Coca-Cola – re-launch is often necessary. It helps to revitalize sales where they are declining, coming under competitive attack, or losing market share for one reason or another.

Relief printing *Print, Printing processes, Production*

A printing technique in which the image is transferred to the substrate from a raised surface. The system most popularly used for relief printing is the flexographic press.

See Blind embossing, Die stamping, Embossing, Flexography, Thermography.

Reminder advertising *Advertising techniques*

Advertising devoted to maintaining sales and customer loyalty, rather than creating new ones. Individual research determines which of these jobs it is doing best. It is sometimes used as a corporate or product message bridge between campaigns. Posters are a popular medium for this purpose.

Repeat purchase *Buyer behaviour, Marketing, Retailing*

A pattern of purchase by consumers or business and industrial equipment buyers. The temptation to avoid trial and adoption of a new brand is strong, and usually leads to buyer inertia. It is easier to buy from the same source than take time and make an effort to change. In business-to-business purchasing, it is easier to stay with a reliable supplier, especially if the relationship is a good one. This makes life difficult for suppliers seeking to break into established relationships, even if they are offering better products and service.

Reply card *Advertising, Direct mail, Editorial, Marketing communications, Publishing, Sales promotion*

A card inserted or bound into a publication, with which a reader can send for information or sales literature. Cards are used to solicit and encourage response both to advertising and editorial material. The reader fills in personal details, then returns the card to the publisher. The card is usually post-paid. Reply cards are used extensively in direct mail campaigns, providing a degree of quantifiable evidence of success or failure. *Caveat*: the success of a campaign is better calculated in actual profits and return on investment; enquiries and sales should be treated as guidelines only. Such benchmarks are most useful when built into the written objectives for a campaign.

Repositioning *Marketing communications, Marketing techniques*

Positioning is a marketing technique for placing in customers' minds the unique, most distinguishing ideas to be remembered when considering a purchase. In creating a position for a brand, consideration must be given to what customers are actually buying. Is it the product itself; its reliability, specification, performance, size, shape or colour? Is it the guarantee, after-sales service, manufacturer's reputation; or all of these? In point of fact, these may not be the only reasons for buying a product. A customer's true reasons may be based on the *benefits* gained from possessing it or using it.

Repositioning is a strategy for adding to or changing customers' ideas about a company, brand or product. It is, of course, done for a purpose. Its life cycle may be approaching its peak. Its position in the Boston Matrix (*qv*) may have changed. Constant repetition over many years may have created a blind spot in customers' minds to the dynamic merits of a brand. The brand may have recently come under fierce competitive attack; sales may be falling; new, more advanced products may have entered its market.

A repositioning may be based, for example, on a new or existing feature of a product, and on the benefits to be derived from it. It can also be linked to its use. Ice cream: repositioned from a cooling summer treat to an all-year-round food. A fizzy, sugar-laden drink: repositioned from a refreshing summer gulp to an energy-giving food for sports activities. Cornflakes: repositioned from breakfast cereal to all-day instant snack. Four-wheel-drive car: repositioned from rural workhorse to status-laden fashion statement.

Reprint   *Advertising, Direct mail, Marketing communications, Publishing*
An advertisement in a newspaper or magazine, reprinted as a leaflet for promotional purposes. Reprints are popularly used in mailshots linked to and supporting press and television advertising campaigns.

Repro   *Pre-press activity, Print, Production*
Production jargon for pre-press camera work, scanning and film make-up.

Reprography   *Print technology*
Another term for copying and duplicating.

Repro pulls   *Pre-press activity, Print, Production*
High quality proofs of typesetting.
See Plate, Pull.

Reputation monopoly   *Branding, Corporate identity, Marketing, Marketing communications*
A positioning strategy used by a manufacturer to convince his market that his product is the best in the field, and that there is no viable alternative. A brand of chocolate for years used the slogan 'The genuine Cadbury taste'. This strongly implied that not only did the product in question represent the standard by which all others were judged, it also suggested that the manufacturer had the ultimate reputation for quality. Therefore, the product was the best possible purchase, highest in quality and finest in taste; and no other brand came anywhere near it.
See Branding, Positioning.

Research brief *Marketing research, Research*
A set of instructions given to a research organization by a client, in the form of a project. This will be complete with objectives for the research, specific individual requirements for the current project, and the use to which the findings will be put. Since virtually all marketing projects are time-related, a deadline for completion of the research is essential; this is specified in the brief.

Resolution *Information technology, Photography, Print*
The density and size of dots or grain, and the ability of various systems to discriminate, register, resolve and reproduce them. This term also applies to the human eye.

Resolution *Desktop publishing, Information technology, Reprographics*
On a computer screen, the capability of a screen to reproduce images. A lot depends on the size of the pixels (*qv*). A high-resolution screen produces finer and sharper images than one with low resolution. The higher the resolution, the higher the quality of the image, the sharper the picture.

Resolution *Photography*
The fineness of detail that a lens, prism system or photographic film can discriminate.

Resolution *Print*
The number of dots per inch or per centimetre of a halftone screen. The greater the number of dots, the higher the reproduction quality, and the sharper the results. *See* Definition, Dot, Pixel.

Respondent *Marketing research, Research*
An individual selected by market researchers as an appropriate subject for research questioning. Strictly speaking, only after the informant has answered questions does she become a respondent; before that, she is an informant. In the UK, standards for research activity are set by organizations such as the Market Research Society and the Industrial Market Research Association. In the European Union, and various industrialized countries, standards are controlled or mediated by directives and local legislation. *See* Informant.

Response bias *Research*
A research error arising during the questioning of respondents. For example, for idiosyncratic reasons, a respondent may supply 'don't know' as an answer throughout a questionnaire. *See* Informant, Respondent.

Response-driven mechanism *Marketing communications*
A coupon, reply-paid card or other device used by consumers for acquiring information about a product or service, or placing an order for it.

Response function   *Marketing communications, Marketing research, Research*
A process of weighting in calculations for advertisement scheduling. Weighting is applied to a sequence of press advertisement insertions, in relation to their potential combined effectiveness. In theory, the more times an advertisement appears, the more effective the campaign becomes as a whole. However, each advertisement in the series has its own theoretical effectiveness, which can be calculated by a process of weighting. This measure may be necessary because each advertisement is both stand-alone and also relies on those appearing before it.

Response rate   *Advertising, Direct mail, Marketing communications*
The calculation of the effectiveness of a campaign, advertisement insertion or mailshot. In press advertising, this is based on the number of replies, enquiries, orders or sales per insertion. With direct mail, it is shown as a percentage response; sometimes, as replies per thousand shots. In both cases, it should be possible to calculate the cost of each reply, enquiry, order or sale, and therefore the viability and profitability of the campaign.

Response rate   *Marketing research, Research*
The ratio of respondents, those responding to research questioning, to the total number of informants planned for.

Retail audit   *Marketing research, Retail research*
An audit of retail outlets, for evaluating a retailer's marketing and retail strategies and tactics. It is designed to produce statistics on sales volume, stock levels and turnaround, company and branch turnover, and information on individual brands. This can be related to changes in store layout, and to promotional activity both of store chains and individual brands. It may also reveal information on the purchasing habits of individual customers, based on their use of store and credit cards.

Retail cooperative   *Retailing*
A group of independent retailers pooling their resources for buying products, and retailing under a common banner or brand. A cooperative may also be linked to, or owned by, a wholesale or distributive organization. In Europe, the original cooperative groups, such as Spar and Wavy Line, were set up to compete with supermarket chains, which could buy and sell more cheaply than independent outlets. Spar still survives in Europe, but supermarkets are slowly but surely driving independents out of business.

Retailer   *Retailing*
A company, organization or establishment, usually in a fixed location, selling products to the general public. The essence of retailing practice is the sale of goods in small or household quantities. The term is sometimes applied to companies selling domestic or personal products by direct mail or mail order.
See Direct mail, Mail order.

Retailing mix   *Marketing communications, Marketing planning, Retailing*
The development of a comprehensive plan outlining the optimum, cost-effective
way to attract customers. This includes store location, design and layout, services
offered, advertising and promotional budget.

Retail outlet   *Marketing, Retailing*
A shop, store, market, supermarket, showroom, warehouse or any permanent place
where goods are retailed to the public. Permanence, or fixed location over a
reasonable period, is important for continuity and consistency in research into
retail activity.

Retainer   *Consultancy practice, Professional services*
A retaining fee, negotiated by an individual or consultancy, for services to a client
over a fixed period. Terms are usually, and prudently, laid down in a written
contract. This often gives the client a degree of priority over the consultant's time
and professional skills.

Retouch   *Art studio practice*
Changing the appearance of a photoprint, positive or negative film, using studio
techniques and materials. Retouching is usually applied in order to remove
unwanted images or features, sharpen image edges, and otherwise improve image
quality.

Return on investment   *Business, Marketing planning*
Usually referred to as ROI. A management method of measuring the success of a
business or individual marketing project. A number of criteria are used, including
gross and net profit, assets and effort used, with gain set against expenditure.

Returns   *Retailing, Wholesaling*
Goods returned to a supplier, because they are damaged, of unsatisfactory quality,
or incapable of being sold.

Reversal film   *Photography*
Photographic film that produces a positive image, rather than a negative one. The
image is viewed by transmitted light. The term is usually applied to film used for
colour transparencies or slides.

Reversed   *Desktop publishing, Photography, Print*
Copy, including graphics and images, appearing white or unprinted on a printed
solid black or colour background.

Reverse side printing   *Print*
Printing on the underside of a sheet of paper.

RGB *Information technology, Print*

Short for **red, green, blue**, the primary colours of light, and of additive colour reproduction systems. Computers use RGB values to display images on monitors and scanners. When colours are to be printed, RGB values must be converted to **CYMK** – cyan, yellow, magenta, black (*qv*).

Right-angle fold *Binding, Print*

In binding, two or more folds to a printed sheet, at 90° to each other.

Ring flash *Photography*

A circular flash gun mounted at the front of a lens. This is designed to produce shadowless images in close-up photography.

Rolling launch *Marketing*

The introduction of a product to its markets in phases, rather than all at once. This gives the marketing team opportunities to examine the process at each stage, learn from this and improve the technique as it progresses. On the other hand, competitors are on constant alert for new products and campaigns, and may respond at high speed to a rolling launch.

Roll-out *Marketing, Marketing communications*

A technique for expanding a marketing campaign or product distribution, from local or regional test to full national scale.

Roman *Desktop publishing, Typography, Word-processing*

Type that stands perpendicular, as distinct from slanted, oblique or italic. The term is correctly spelled with a lower case r, and abbreviated as **rom**.
See Italics, Oblique.

ROP *Media, Media planning and buying*

Abbreviation for **run-of-paper ad** (*qv*).

Rosette *Halftone screens, Print*

A dot pattern produced by the overlay of conventional halftone screens in process colour printing. When correctly positioned, and when registration is good, the dots form into rosette groups.
See Register, Registration.

Rough *Advertising, Creative, Design, Editorial,*
Marketing communications, Print

A layout representing the design of an editorial page, advertisement or item of print. This is usually developed from a **flimsy** or **scamp**, with readable headlining and recognizable illustrations. Roughs are usually used for internal discussion by creative and account management teams.
See Visual.

Royalty *Branding, Intellectual property, Publishing*
A payment by a user due to the owner of copyright material when that material is used; to a patentee for the agreed use of a patent; to an author for each book sold; to a dramatist for each performance of a play. In book publishing, a royalty is usually a percentage of sales. Royalties can be levied on the agreed use of brand devices or trademarks.

Rule *Desktop publishing, Typesetting, Typography, Word-processing*
Print terminology for a printed line. Styles include single, double, solid, broken, dashed and dotted. From Latin *regula*, a straight stick.

Run *Print, Print buying, Print planning, Publishing*
The quantity – number of individual pieces – of a piece of print, packaging or publication, produced on a press. Usually also referred to as a **print run**. The term is also used to express the total quantity of a complete print order.

Runaround *Desktop publishing, Typesetting, Typography, Word-processing*
Type set to follow the contour of an illustration. The type literally runs round the shape.

Running head *Publishing*
A heading or title repeated at the head of each page of a publication.

Run-of-paper ad *Media, Media planning and buying*
An advertisement insertion in a newspaper or magazine, placed wherever the advertisement director decides, and charged at the standard rate. The alternative is termed **special position**. This gives the advertiser more control over where the advertisement appears, and is charged at a higher rate. Special positions may be specified; the advertiser can opt for a particular page, solus, facing matter, next matter, or other special position offered by the publisher. The term **ad** is the usual professional abbreviation for advertisement. Using **advert** is the mark of the amateur.
See Matter, Mini-page, Solus.

Run on *Print, Print buying, Print planning, Publishing*
Extra copies of a publication or item of print, produced while a press is still set up for the original order. Since there are no extra charges, eg setting up a press for the extra quantity, the run-on cost is comparatively low. Print quotations often include a separate slot for run on, usually as 'run on per hundred' or 'run on per thousand'.

Ss

Saddle stitching *Binding, Finishing, Print*
A technique for binding a multi-page publication – booklet, brochure, catalogue etc – by fastening it through the middle fold of the sheets. The sheets are collated and mounted on a metal 'saddle', in the form of an inverted V, then stapled together.

Sale of Goods Act 1979 *Consumer protection, Legislation*
In the UK, one of the principal laws governing contracts for goods and services.

Sales agent *Marketing, Sales organization*
An organization or individual selling or negotiating, by agreement or contract, goods and services on behalf of another. The sales contract is entered into and signed by the principals involved, not the agent, whose responsibility is to sell and not to act as principal.

Sales aid *Marketing, Sales management*
Any promotional item that helps field sales personnel to make sales presentations to customers. For example, a portfolio, folder, brochure, flip-chart, sample pack or video. The content, whether trade, technical or consumer, is specifically created and designed for sales-aid purposes.
See Sales literature.

Sales analysis *Marketing, Sales management*
A management tool, involving the analysis of collected data on sales performance for a company, sales team, product or service.

Sales approach *Marketing, Sales management, Sales techniques*
The basic theme or platform adopted by a sales team for the effective selling of a product or service. The approach is determined by sales management, often in collaboration with its marketing management. Acting with marketing management is prudent, especially when a marketing campaign is about to start or is in progress. Not doing this can result in conflicting messages.

Sales audit *Marketing management, Sales management*
Periodic review and assessment of a company's sales strategy, designed to indicate whether sales management, and its staff, are meeting their targets. The main

purpose is to improve the success and effectiveness of the sales force. It also helps to weed out ineffective sales personnel. In many organizations a sales audit is a component of their marketing audit procedure.

Sales broker   *Sales organization*
An independent sales agent whose responsibility is to negotiate the sale of products and services, and bring the principals together; not, however, to handle goods or be party to contracts.

Sales budget   *Sales management, Sales organization*
A sum of money dedicated to the running of a sales department, covering all its activities. This is usually allocated for a fixed period; a year, for example. It may be allocated from an overall marketing budget.

Sales call activity   *Sales management, Sales organization*
The organization of field sales teams and the activities of individual members. This may comprise:

- setting the sales call cycle, both for the sales team and its individual members;
- setting the frequency of sales calls;
- scheduling of individual visits to prospects and customers;
- determining the most time-effective sequence and route of all visits;
- determining the cost-effectiveness of each call;
- the duration and content of each call;
- the enforcement of sales report activity;
- regular analysis of individual and team sales activity.

Sales campaign   *Marketing planning, Sales force activity,*
                                                        Sales management
A sales effort, properly planned, coordinated and controlled. It has specific objectives, with targets for orders, sales volume, turnover, cost-effectiveness and profitability.
See Sales call activity.

Sales conference   *Sales management, Sales training*
In US English: sales convention. A structured meeting of sales personnel, organized and controlled by sales management. It is usually designed to:

- introduce new concepts and techniques;
- introduce new management, team and area structures;
- present awards for outstanding success;
- present new sales aids and support material, including advertising and sales literature;
- review sales activity for current or past periods;
- set targets for future activity.

Sales contest   *Sales management*
A competitive activity, designed and monitored by management, to encourage sales personnel to achieve and exceed individual sales targets. Prizes are usually worthwhile and often very valuable; eg holidays, cars, jewellery. Recognition is usually displayed at sales conferences and in house journals.

Sales decline   *Marketing, Sales activity, Sales management*
A stage in the life cycle of a product or service, in which sales fall, and can be predicted to continue falling. Countermeasures are called for; and indeed should have been taken well in advance of this stage.
See Product life cycle.

Sales drive   *Marketing, Sales activity, Sales management*
Also sometimes termed a **sales blitz** and **commando sales**. A dynamic, highly concentrated selling effort over a pre-planned period. Sales drives are organized to combat competitive activity or attack, and to maintain or increase sales during slack periods.

Sales engineer   *Sales activity, Technical sales*
A sales representative with special technical skills and qualifications, operating in a technical market. To operate successfully, she must be able to understand clients' markets, customers' technology, and talk clients' language.

Sales enquiry   *Marketing, Marketing communications, Sales activity*
An enquiry from advertising, mailshot, catalogue or other marketing communications activity. Reliable follow-up is required to convert enquiries into orders. Sometimes termed **sales lead** (*qv*), though in practice these terms are not synonymous.

Sales feature   *Sales management, Sales technique*
A specific feature of a product or service, highlighted during a sales interview or advertisement campaign. In planning sales presentations and advertisement campaigns, management usually sets priorities for sales features. These are based on a variety of motives, from profitability and user acceptability, to countermeasures against competitive attack. In any event, a sales feature should always be closely coupled to the benefits associated with it.

Sales forecast   *Sales management*
A management forecast of sales for a specific period, based on planning and predictions. This is often done by territory, because each may have individual geographical and commercial characteristics, call patterns and demands. Trade and business-to-business sales forecasts can be acceptably reliable; consumer markets are more volatile and susceptible to rapid and unpredictable change. Often, sales forecasts contain elements of current and past performance. While the gathering

of all available data on current markets and sales territories is reliable, since they are fact-based, predictions are not. Naturally, the shorter the time-scale for a forecast, the more reliable it may be.

Salesforce incentive   *Sales management*
An incentive offered to sales representatives as encouragement to achieve and exceed their individual sales targets. This can be financial, in the form of bonuses, commission, cash for achievement and so on; or in some other form, such as certificates of merit, holidays and luxury goods.

Sales incentive   *Marketing*
Gifts offered to traders, re-sellers and distributors, and customers, company, trade, technical and industrial buyers, to encourage increased sales activity.

Sales interview   *Sales presentations*
A planned meeting between a sales representative and a customer or prospect. A representative's objective is not only to present the product or service, but usually to close the sale and obtain an order. In industrial sales, and where the product is technical or the cost is high, several interviews may be necessary. The long-term view is necessary; product demonstrations may be called for.

Sales lead   *Marketing, Marketing communications, Sales activity*
An enquiry generated by press or broadcast advertising, direct mail or cataloguing. A sales lead is usually deemed more serious than a **sales enquiry** (*qv*), since it may be easier to convert into an order. Many of the most promising sales leads may come from referrals by existing customers.

Sales literature   *Marketing communications, Print, Sales techniques*
The huge variety of printed material produced by marketing teams. The objective is to provide information and motivation for customers and prospects at every level: consumer, retail, trade, industrial, technical and commercial. It includes:

- advertising bags and carriers;
- booklets;
- book matches;
- brochures;
- calendars;
- catalogues;
- competition entry forms;
- diaries;
- flyers;
- folders;
- guarantee cards;
- leaflets;

- newsletters;
- point of sale material;
- postcards;
- price lists and order forms;
- stickers;
- swing labels;
- timetables.

Increasingly, sales literature includes non-printed material such as:

- badges;
- body media (T-shirts, baseball caps and so on);
- CD ROMS;
- CDS;
- video material.

Sales management   *Marketing management, Sales organization*
In many larger companies, this is often a function of marketing management. It is dedicated to all organizational, planning and operational activities for efficient, cost-effective and profitable sales effort. It usually involves personnel recruitment, deployment and training; production and distribution of sales literature through a sales force; reporting to senior management and acting on board decisions.

Sales manager   *Management, Marketing management*
An executive responsible for the conduct and operations of a sales department, a single product or group of products. Responsibilities include reporting to the company's board of directors, reporting to its sales and marketing directors, the submission of written sales reports; and, often, the hiring and firing of sales and administrative staff.

Salesmanship   *Sales technique*
Persuasive sales techniques, pursued or employed as a professional craft, for individual or corporate profit. This is, of course, the simplistic and pragmatic view of salesmanship. There is far more to it. Foremost, the ability to persuade in speech, writing and body language. It involves an exhaustive knowledge of the product or service being sold; an instinctive or learnt understanding of customers, their strengths and weaknesses, and the motives that guide their behaviour; a dogged and persistent nature, and the determination to win orders; often, a killer instinct. This is sometimes defined as natural flair, but good training, knowledge and luck also play an important part.

Sales meetings   *Sales management*
Periodic meetings between sales management and staff, designed to review, discuss and improve sales team performance. Often part of, or associated with, sales training.

Sales objectives   *Sales management*

Sales targets, to be achieved by specific activities planned by sales management, by territory and individual sales representative. Time-scale is an important feature of sales objectives.

Sales office   *Sales organization*

A company in-house department organized for the support of field sales representatives. It deals with the fulfilment and delivery of orders brought in by field and call-centre sales staff. This includes invoicing, queries and complaints, sales follow-ups and further customer contact. It may also organize the day-to-day call programmes of field sales staff.

Sales penetration   *Sales management*

A calculation indicating how much of a particular market for a product or service has been gained through active sales. It is usually presented as a percentage of the total market.

Sales pitch   *Sales management, Sales presentations*

The basic theme or platform set by sales management for representatives' sales presentations to customers and prospects. This usually includes detailed arguments, cases, highlights, product features and benefits, their due priority within sales presentations, and relevant sales literature.

Sales platform   *Advertising, Sales management, Sales techniques*

A set of sales features and benefits, set by management, for a sales campaign. This is part of the brief given to sales representatives setting out on a programme of field calls. A sales platform often conforms to the theme and copy platform determined for an advertising campaign running alongside sales effort. Indeed, co-ordinating the two is sensible, if only to avoid conflicting messages being aimed at the same markets.

Sales policy   *Sales management*

The policy governing the conduct of a company's sales effort, and that of representatives in the field. This may include the company's objectives for a campaign, in the wider sense; and also many small but important details, such as discounts and warranties.

Sales portfolio   *Sales presentations*

Also termed a **sales organizer**. A sales aid folder carried by a representative, comprising the conduct of the interview and details, features and benefits of the product or service being sold. It is often lavishly illustrated. A **sales kit** is a portfolio prepared for trade sales calls. More complicated than a portfolio, it may contain samples of the product being sold, to be left by the representative with the customer.

Sales promotion   *Marketing*

Several definitions exist; for example:

- below-the-line activities aimed at increasing product take-up among non-users, and increased use among existing consumers;
- promotional marketing techniques, generally involving a range of direct or indirect additional benefits, usually on a temporary basis, designed to make goods or services more attractive to purchasers;
- special promotional schemes, usually of limited duration, at the point of sale;
- specialized marketing activities designed to sell a product or service, with or without the use of advertising;
- tactical marketing.

Whichever definition suits your current planning, certain features are common to most sales promotion schemes. Many involve giving away items of value, from free flights to coloured pens. The promotional value of a give-away is in its financial value, its design, its emotional value, or all three. Here are some of the most popular sales promotion techniques in current use:

- banded packs;
- cash dividends;
- cash premium vouchers or coupons;
- charity promotions;
- competitions and free prize draws;
- cross-couponing offers;
- flash packs;
- free gifts with products;
- free samples;
- gift coupons;
- high street redemption schemes;
- in-store demonstrations;
- jumbo and multiple packs;
- mail-in free offers;
- matching banknote or coupon halves;
- money-off deals;
- on-pack direct marketing;
- promotional games;
- self-liquidating premiums.

Sales report   *Sales management*

A report submitted by a sales representative, detailing sales calls and their outcomes during the current or previous week.

Sales representative   *Sales management, Sales organization*

An individual salesperson specializing in selling a company's products or services. The essence of representation is face-to-face contact with customers and prospects in the field, with the objective of obtaining orders.

Sales revenue   *Business, Marketing, Sales*
That part of a company's income derived from sales activity. Often synonymous
with **turnover**.

Sales targets   *Sales management*
Objectives, set by sales management, for representatives to fulfil in terms of orders.
Sales performance targets are often set in financial units; or as physical units such
as barrels, cases, tons, or square metres to be sold; per sales call, per day, week or
month. Usually, sales targets are set in accordance with management sales
forecasts.

Sales territory   *Sales management*
Usually defined as the geographical area allocated to a sales representative, for
the purpose of generating and developing new customers and servicing existing
ones. It is sometimes also applied to groups of customers, specific market segments, and groups of products, allocated to representatives for the same purpose.

Sales volume   *Sales management, Sales planning*
Sales targets, or sales turnover already achieved, expressed in quantities rather than
money. Units used may be crates, bottles, cases, gallons, litres, tons, wagonloads,
hundreds of components, and so on.

Same size   *Pre-press, Print, Production*
A production department's instruction to a printer, to reproduce an image in exactly
the same size as the original.

Sample   *Marketing, Retailing, Sales techniques*
A small, trial quantity of a product, usually packaged appropriately, given away free
to consumers or retailers, to create awareness, to stimulate uptake or increased use.

Sample   *Research*
For survey purposes, a small number of people selected to represent an entire
population. By matching those selected with the characteristics of the whole
population, the number selected is calculated to achieve accurate survey results.
Often, this is based on past experience with populations and samples. However,
where surveys and survey techniques differ, if only minutely, sampling techniques
are best tailored to each individual research project.

Sampling   *Research*
The selection of small, representative groups for research into wider groups and
populations.

Sampling error   *Research*
An error occurring in sampling procedures. Because no research technique is
perfect, bias usually occurs. This can usually be calculated and the research results
modified to reach a pre-planned degree of accuracy.

Sandwich boards *Advertising*
Portable advertising posters, mounted on boards, carried in pairs by a person hired
for the purpose. The boards are joined by straps worn over the shoulders of the
carrier; one board facing forwards, the other rearwards. In the UK, sandwich board
men are sometimes seen in town and city centres.

Sans serif *Desktop publishing, Typography, Word-processing*
Typefaces without serifs. Such faces are usually excellent for headlines, but may
be difficult to read in small sizes.
See Serif.

Satellite broadcasting *Radio, Television*
Television and radio transmissions via satellites orbiting the Earth. Consumers may
access transmissions direct from the satellite, or via cable.

Saturation *Marketing*
The point at which marketing effort no longer brings in a sufficient number of new
customers. Campaigns then need to be tailored to encourage existing customers
to use more of a product, or replace a product more frequently.

Saturation advertising *Advertising techniques, Media planning*
The selection of mass and main media for an advertising campaign, designed to
dominate in a particular product or geographical area for the duration of the
campaign.

SC *Printing papers*
The common abbreviation for **supercalendered**, a paper surface finish, indicating
its smoothness. Paper can be used exactly as it comes off the paper-making
machine, uncalendered, or it can be smoothed mechanically at the paper mill. It
can be machine calendered, using steel rollers – calenders. For greater smoothness,
it can be supercalendered, which involves the use of high-speed, very hot, steel
calenders.

Scaling *Artwork, Pre-press, Production*
Calculating the proportions of an artwork element, so that it can be enlarged or
reduced to fit a given area on a page.

Scaling *Marketing research*
A technique for evaluating a respondent's attitude to a product or proposition. The
results are ranked in order of strength, on a pre-determined scale.

Scanner *Art direction, Information technology, Studio work*
A photo-electric device for capturing typographical or graphic images and
converting them into data for computer processing. A scanner is connected to and
controlled by a computer, which displays the image on screen. A scanner dedicated
to converting text and other typed data is termed an **optical character reader**.

Most of today's scanners can do both jobs. In retail outlets, particularly super-markets, bar codes printed on products are read by a dedicated scanner at the checkout.

SCC *Advertising, Media planning, Publishing*

The common abbreviation for **single column centimetre**. A unit of advertising space one centimetre high and a single column wide. This is one of the basic media buying and billing units for display advertising space; in the USA, the basic unit is the single column inch.

Scenario *Marketing planning*

The description of a course of events, issues or factors, past and present. This is usually used as a planning tool for anticipating how they might affect the course of future events.

Schedule *Advertising, Media planning*

A popular contraction for advertising media schedule; a plan of proposed press advertising insertions and airtime for a campaign. Some companies and advertising agencies prepare comprehensive schedules including all media; some prepare separate schedules for each medium. For press media, a schedule should include at least:

- advertiser's name;
- campaign executive's name and signature;
- campaign period;
- cost per insertion;
- job number;
- number of insertions;
- product name;
- publication titles;
- schedule issue date;
- schedule of insertion dates;
- space size;
- total cost for each publication;
- total cost of press campaign.

A schedule for broadcast media should include at least:

- advertiser's name;
- campaign executive's name and signature;
- campaign period;
- cost per spot;
- job number;
- number of spots;
- product name;

- running time for each spot;
- schedule issue date;
- schedule of spots and segments: dates, times, programme names;
- station name;
- total cost for each station;
- total cost for the airtime campaign.

SCI   *Advertising, Media planning, Publishing*
The common abbreviation for single column inch. A unit of advertising space one inch high and a single column wide. In the USA this is one of the basic media buying and billing units for display advertising space; in the European Union and other countries using metric measurement the basic buying and billing unit is the single column centimetre.

Screamer   *Copywriting, Journalism, Print, Proof-reading, Typesetting*
Editorial, copywriting and PR jargon for an exclamation mark.

Screen   *Pre-press, Print, Production*
A short-form for halftone screen, the arrangement of dots used in printing full-tone images.

Screen advertising   *Advertising*
Another term for cinema advertising.

Screen angle   *Pre-press, Print, Production*
The angle of rotation of a halftone screen. When making colour separations, the screens need to be laid down at specific angles to avoid image distortion, disturbing patterns and other unwanted effects on the negatives.
See Colour separations, Halftone.

Screening   *Television*
The process of getting advertising or entertainment programming to the television screen. A commercial, for example, is 'screened' on a specified day and at a specified hour, or within specified programming.

Screening   *Marketing planning, Recruitment*
The structured evaluation of concepts and ideas brought to marketing management, and the rejection of those that do not meet the brief, or are otherwise inappropriate. In recruitment practice, the evaluation of candidates for employment or promotion, and their acceptance or rejection.

Screen printing   *Printing processes*
This process uses a porous, fine-mesh screen of tough material, such as nylon or stainless steel. Printing is done on paper or other substrate under the screen, by applying a paint-like ink to the screen and forcing it through the mesh with a

squeegee. Production rates, formerly limited by the drying time of the ink, is now fast through the use of ultra violet inks and efficient dryers. Automation is now common in screen printing shops; production is made faster still, and more economical, with rotary screen presses that allow continuous operation. Screen printing can usually be identified by the thick layer of ink, and sometimes by the texture of the screen on the printed surface.

Facts about screen printing

- A stencil printing process method, which uses a mesh screen, mounted and stretched in a frame.
- Screens are of man-made materials such as nylon; often of stainless steel.
- The stencil is produced photographically on to a light-sensitive emulsion on the screen mesh.
- Exposing the emulsion to ultra-violet light hardens the non-image areas.
- The non-printing areas are protected by solid material remaining on the screen after processing.
- The printing areas are open, the emulsion having been washed away during processing. They therefore let the ink through to the substrate beneath.
- The ink is forced through the screen mesh by a squeegee.

Advantages of screen printing

- Highly versatile. Can print virtually any surface, including paper, board, wood, cork, glass, metal, plastics and fabrics.
- Uses strong, opaque inks, giving rich depth of colour.
- Because inks are opaque, white can be printed on black, for example.
- Can print curved surfaces, such as bottles.
- Prints individual sheets or rolls of material.
- Commercial screen presses are highly mechanized.
- These can print up to 5,000 impressions an hour.
- The toughness of screen materials allows long runs and worthwhile economies.
- Most useful and practical also for short runs. Before commissioning screen printing for short runs, compare with other methods.
- Manual proofing is possible; simple but not always economical.

Disadvantages of screen printing

- Ink takes longer to dry than other processes.
- Printed sheets must be separated and racked individually, or put through a drying tunnel.
- Ultra-violet curing is also used, but this also takes time.
- Accurate registration may limit the printing speed.
- Because of the comparatively relatively coarse nature of the screen mesh, fine detail is difficult to achieve.

Optimum and economical uses for screen printing

- posters;
- point-of-sale and other material;
- packaging, bottles, book covers.

Screen ruling   *Pre-print, Print, Production*
The number of halftone dots per linear centimetre or linear inch.

Script   *Advertising, Creative, Radio, Television*
The copy written for a television or radio commercial. Sometimes also used to describe a typescript of editorial or advertising copy, though this is incorrect.

Scrolling   *Computer terminology, Desktop publishing, Word-processing*
Moving up and down a computer screen; or, rather, making the image on the screen move up, down and sideways. When there is more to a document than can be displayed on the screen, you are obliged to use the screen as a window. You therefore have to treat the material on screen like a scroll, moving the visible text up and down the window, or scrolling from side to side. You can then see only the bits of the document that fit into the window.
See Page scrolling.

Search engine   *Information technology, Internet, Intranet, Web activity*
A software program designed to carry out a search of a database for information, or the World Wide Web for particular Web sites. It has three basic components:

- A software agent. Termed the crawler or spider, it scours information sources, including the Internet. Where appropriate, it searches a company's Intranet and other internal information sources. The crawler visits a Web page, scans it, and follows any links to other pages on the site. It may revisit the site regularly to discover whether any information has changed since the last visit.
- An index. Pages found by the crawler are copied to it. The index is interrogated during each search.
- Scanning software. This scans information in the index for documents containing the search terms, using a formula to prioritize them. Ranking strategies are the main features that differentiate search engines. Many search engines use 'push' technology, which enables users to specify individual information requirements; relevant items are forwarded to them via e-mail.

A search engine uses **meta tags**, a range of key words, to find subject matter, and lists its findings with the most likely match first. It is possible to generate more than a million findings from a search; it therefore needs to be done in a way that produces only a shortlist of findings.

Seasonal discounts *Broadcast and press media*
Discounts on advertising rates offered to advertisers by media owners, as encouragement during quiet or off-peak periods when little advertising is anticipated.

Seasonal discounts *Direct marketing, Retailing, Wholesaling*
Discounts offered as encouragement to consumers during seasonal off-periods. These occur several times a year, for example at mid-summer and just after Christmas. This measure is popular during periods when retailers need to sell off stocks from the previous year or season; for example, spring and autumn.

SECAM *Television broadcasting standards, Video*
The initials for Système en Couleurs à Mémoire. The television transmission system used in France, Russia and countries of the former Soviet bloc. *Note*: incompatible transmission standards are equally incompatible for reception. Video recordings made in one standard must be converted for playback in any of the others.
See NTSC, PAL, Television transmission standards.

Secondary data *Research*
Data gathered from existing sources, such as company records, directories, official statistics and government publications.
See Primary data.

Secondary readership *Media research, Publishing*
Every reader of a publication beyond the person purchasing or subscribing to it. In the USA this is termed **pass-along readership**.

Security paper *Paper, Print*
Paper with identification features, such as metallic strips and watermarks. This helps to deter and detect fraud, and prevent counterfeiting.

Seeding *Direct mail*
The inclusion on a database or mailing list of individuals assigned to monitor mailings carried out with it. This is an essential check on the conduct of mailings, particularly for timing, frequency, punctuality and accuracy.

Segment *Advertising, Media planning, Radio, Television*
A time-band within which advertising spots are charged at the same rates. Segments on weekdays and weekends may differ in time and duration. For details, consult contractors' advertising rate cards.

Segment *Marketing. Marketing planning*
For the purpose of marketing, promotion and distribution, a carefully defined smaller group within a larger one.
See Segmentation.

354

Segmentation *Advertising, Marketing, Marketing planning*
In marketing planning, the identification and isolation of groups of individuals into cohesive groups, for the purpose of delivering appropriate, and cost-effective, products, services and promotional messages.

In plain language, this is the splitting, metaphorically speaking, of large markets into smaller ones. This is usually done for the purpose of developing different marketing tactics and approaches for each one, within an overall marketing plan. Most industrialized societies are made up of different social groups, each having its own lifestyle, attitudes and beliefs. Each reacts in its own characteristic way to internal pressure and external stimuli. Within each group, social activity and pressure result in conformity of behaviour. The art of segmentation lies in understanding how to identify these groups, and formulate promotional and product strategies expressly for them.

Segmentation may be based on demographics, lifestyle, psychographics, the ability or willingness to buy. Thus, *all women* is a large market; *married women* a segment of it; *young married women with small children*, a segment of that; *young marrieds with red-haired twins* a segment of that. Each segment may have different potential of interest to marketers; each may be approachable with different products, services and copy platforms of direct appeal to them.

A further example: the family is another huge market segment. To appeal to the entire segment with a single message and range of products would almost certainly be wasteful. Efficient segmentation reduces the risk of total or partial failure of a marketing campaign. The marketing planner needs to recognize the existence of segments within 'the family', and that they change over time. Each segment will have different disposable incomes, and therefore different purchasing abilities. For marketing segmentation purposes, the family comprises:

- **bachelor**: young, single people not living with parents;
- **newly married couples**: young, no children;
- **full nest 1**: young marrieds with the youngest child under six years old;
- **full nest 2**: young marrieds with the youngest child six or older;
- **full nest 3**: older marrieds with dependent children;
- **empty nest 1**: older married couples, the head of the household working, and no children living with them;
- **empty nest 2**: older married couples, the head of the household retired, and no children living with them;
- **solitary survivor 1**: the survivor working and earning;
- **solitary survivor 2**: the survivor retired.

Self-liquidating premium *Product marketing, Retailing, Sales promotion*
An article offered to consumers with a product, such as cereals or toothpaste, for a small sum of money. The price to the consumer is just large enough to cover the cost of the item, its promotion and distribution. Sometimes this brand-loyalty tactic is adopted as encouragement to consumers to continue collecting the premiums, and therefore to purchase the product. Sometimes the item is a one-off. Either way, it is usually of reasonable value and quality; the best ones are collectable.

Self-mailer   *Direct mail*
A direct mail shot in a self-contained format. The whole thing is in one piece, so that no envelope is needed. Generally, the idea is not to save money, but to make the mailer more interesting than others to the recipient. Sometimes the reply element will also be self-mailing, often carrying the recipient's name and address; and also the advertiser's return address.

Self-service store   *Retailing*
Another term for a **supermarket**; though self-service outlets are often smaller than supermarkets. Another type of self-service store is the **cash-and-carry** warehouse. Products are offered in bulk quantities and sealed cartons. The store is open both to consumers and traders – provided that they purchase appropriately. Some cash-and-carry stores are operated as clubs, with a small annual membership fee.

Sell-by date   *Product marketing, Retailing*
In the UK, the date marked on a product pack, indicating the date by which it should be sold. There is room for confusion here. Many packs are marked with 'BBE' followed by a date. For example, 'BBE 07/05'. This translates as 'Best before the end of July 2005'. It is not clear whether this means 'To be displayed by the end of. . .', 'To be sold by the end of. . .', or 'To be consumed by the end of. . .', which all imply different instructions. European Union directives compel manufacturers to mark even cans of food with sell-by dates. It is worth noting that a few years ago a number of cans of beans and bully beef issued to troops during the First World War were opened in London, and found perfectly edible.
See Best before.

Sellers' market   *Marketing*
A market condition in which demand for a product or service is greater than the supply. This gives suppliers opportunities to raise prices and offer poorer service to customers. However, no market condition is immortal and conditions usually change. This often results in a **buyers' market**, in which supplies of a product exceed the demand. In the meantime, competitors may come into the market. This is when consumers have their revenge; although consumer memory is usually short, and forgiveness is readily offered.

Selling proposition   *Advertising, Marketing, Sales promotion*
A major benefit or appeal used in consumer promotion, employed to persuade consumers to accept the idea of trying or buying a product. Often the advertiser creates and uses the strongest, powerfully identifying proposition, unique to his product, and different from those the competition is using. Some advertisers and agencies term this the **unique selling proposition**; this was originally coined and developed in the 1940s by Rosser Reeves, head of the Ted Bates agency. Others call it the **key proposition**, the **single-minded proposition**, and so on. Whatever it is called, it is the single, most powerful, most persuasive promotional benefit capable of moving the consumer towards the product, and getting a decision in favour of the brand.

Semantic differential   *Research techniques*

A structured measurement of respondents' attitudes to a question or proposition, based on a fixed scale between two extremes. For example, a question about the temperature of bath water may be answered on a scale varying from cold to hot. 'Do you find the water in this bath:

1. Very cold?
2. Cold?
3. Moderately cold?
4. Moderately warm?
5. Warm?
6. Hot?
7. Very hot?'

Similarly, a question about an advertising campaign could be put as follows: 'Do you find this advertisement:

1. Very persuasive?
2. Quite persuasive?
3. Moderately persuasive?
4. So-so?
5. Moderately unpersuasive?
6. Quite unpersuasive?
7. Very unpersuasive?'

Obviously this second example is slightly fatuous (moderately fatuous, seriously fatuous), in that it cannot be measured physically or arithmetically, as can the temperature of bath water. What is more, an advertisement cannot be described as 'so-so'. Either it persuades, or it does not. It is a matter of personal opinion, which is the essence of semantic differential techniques.

Semi-display   *Media planning, Press advertising, Publishing*

Classified advertising incorporating copy, logos, simple illustrations, bold and italic type; and sometimes set inside thin rule borders. The size is calculated in column centimetres (column inches in the USA). The sizes, costs and production conditions are laid down in the publisher's rate card. In the USA, **semi-display advertising** is termed **classified display**.

Semi-solus   *Media planning, Press advertising*

A term describing an advertisement position, on a page that it shares with only one other advertisement. They are usually not positioned next to each other. For a special position such as this, a rate higher than run-of-paper is usually charged. Where an advertisement has a page to itself, its position is termed **solus**.

Separations *Pre-press, Print*
See Colour separations, Screen angle.

Sequence *Copywriting, Positioning*
The pre-planned order in which facts, features and benefits are given in an advertisement. If the campaign comprises several advertisements, the sequence may be given in a different order, depending on the major emphasis of each advertisement.

Serial advertising *Advertising*
A campaign that tells a story over several advertisements. The classic serial in the UK during the 1990s was that on television for Nescafé Gold Blend. The story unfolded over many months, beginning with a chance encounter between two people sharing a taste for the product. It was claimed that every time the commercial was shown, with repetitions, product sales rose by 27 per cent.

Series discount *Media planning, Press advertising, Publishing*
A rate card discount offered to advertisers for booking a series of insertions on a single order. A time limit, or pre-determined number of issues, usually applies for the advertiser to qualify for the discount.

Serif *Desktop publishing, Typography, Word-processing*
A small terminal cross-stroke at the end of a main stroke of a character. Serifs come in various shapes, sizes and angles. Typefaces without serifs are termed **sans serif**.

Server *Information technology*
A computer on a network, providing a resource for workstations connected to the network. Resources include printers, disk drives, electronic mail, pages of information including Web pages, and connections to other networks. One server can serve several 'clients'.

Service department *Advertising agencies, Company organization*
A department within an organization, dedicated to providing specialized services to other company departments. A creative department, for example, provides specialized creative work for a company's marketing, advertising and sales promotion departments. Similarly, a production department provides commissioning and supervision of press and print production within an advertising agency.

Service fees *Advertising, Marketing and PR agencies*
Fees charged by an agency for services provided to clients. This sum, agreed in advance, can be charged in addition to any income derived by the agency from media commission and from mark-up on production, print, research and other professional services. In some cases, when a fee is charged, any commission earned by the agency is handed to the client.

Service industry *Business*

A commercial enterprise, business or industry offering products and services to customers, without physical, industrial or manufacturing activity. This includes catering, distribution, retailing, insurance, travel, education, entertainment, health care, financial and professional services.

Set *Film and video production*

A construction of scenery, usually in a studio, but sometimes also outdoors, with decor and properties in place, ready for shooting.

Set-off *Print*

An effect that occurs when the ink of one printed sheet marks the next sheet being delivered off the press. This used to be a printer's nightmare in the days before wet on wet printing. To some extent, it still is. Before the perfection of modern inks and drying techniques, one colour had to dry on the page before another could be printed on it.

With many modern printing presses, drying is not wholly a 'drying' process. This is now achieved as curing, by ultra-violet light. Most of the credit goes to the printing industry, which recognizes both the ecological soundness of this technique and the economies to be gained from using less volatile inks. It is possible to recover the volatile substances from the inks during printing, and to recycle them. But this is expensive, and probably not cost-effective except in the very long run. *See* Show-through.

Set solid *Typesetting, Typography*

An instruction to a compositor to set type in tight lines without leading or line-spacing. Also, type that has been set in this way; it will have been **set solid**. *See* Leading.

Set-up *Film, Television, video and cinema commercials*

The position of camera, microphone, lights, artists and so on, at any given moment. This is generally applied to the positions at the start of a **shot** (*qv*).

Shared values *Marketing planning*

A method of placing products of similar perceived quality within the same promotional setting, or within a company's product portfolio. This helps to justify the premium price of some relatively unknown brands.

Sheet *Outdoor advertising, Posters*

The basic unit size of poster formats, for design, display and billing purposes; 30 in × 40 in, usually referred to as **double crown**. There is some confusion here, since the minimum acceptable size for poster display is usually 60 in × 40 in.

Sheet-fed *Print technology*

A term describing a press that prints and delivers individual sheets of paper. *See* Web.

Shelf life   *Distribution, Retailing*
The time a product can acceptably be displayed on a retailer's shelf. The manufacturer usually limits this time according to the nature of the product. Therefore,
canned and glass-packed products may have a longer shelf life than those
packaged in waxed cartons. Fruit and vegetables usually have a shelf life of a
single day.

Shoot   *Advertising, Film and video production, Public relations*
To photograph a scene, performers or object with a cine- or video camera. In
advertising and public relations practice, photographing with a still camera is
usually termed a **photo-shoot**.

Shooting script   *Film and video pre-production*
The complete written content of a film or video, in precise detail. This is usually
separated into serially numbered scenes, complete with pictures and sounds, in
columns side by side. Simultaneous shots, actions and sounds are positioned
opposite each other in the script.

Shopper study   *Marketing research, Retail research*
A research programme held at retail outlets, designed to solicit opinions and
information from members of the public. Respondents may be asked about their
purchasing habits and behaviour; or about the outlet itself, products and services
on offer, its environment and customer service.

Shopping products   *Consumer behaviour, Retailing*
Also termed **shopping goods**. Consumer products, especially consumer durables,
purchased on consideration of quality more than just on price. Such products are
usually fairly expensive, such as furniture and electrical appliances, which justify
comparison at some length and in some detail with competitive products. The term
'shopping products' arises from this act of lengthy shopping around for information, and for demonstrations of best performance, quality or value.

Shot   *Advertising commercials, Film, Photography, Television, Video*
A set-up (*qv*), the content of a single photographed scene, complete with action,
sound, camera movement and so on. It is made as a single item in shooting.
See Frame, Freeze-frame, Opticals, Pan, Still, Tilt, Voice-over.

Showcard   *Marketing, Retailing*
An advertising mini-poster, printed on board, for display in retail outlets. Usually
these are displayed on counter-tops, and promote products on offer at the counter
or available elsewhere in the store. In many stores, especially where there is little
counter space available, larger showcards are displayed on walls or stand-alone
positions.

Showcard *Marketing research*

A card used by interviewers, displaying a number of alternative issues, answers, attitudes or opinions. This is shown by the researcher to respondents, who are asked to make a choice.

Showcase *Exhibitions*

Another term for an exhibition designed to show a range of products and services to an invited audience, or to members of a particular trade or profession.

Showcase *Retail display*

A display cabinet with glass panels, designed to promote its contents, and to protect them from handling and theft.

Show-through *Print*

An effect that occurs when the printed side of a sheet shows through the paper to its reverse side, and interferes with the copy. This is usually the result either of a bad choice of ink or of over-inking; or a bad choice of stock, which is too thin or not opaque enough.

See Set-off, Stock.

Shrink-wrap *Packaging*

A packaging technique, using thin plastic foil shrunk by heat over its contents. The plastic moulds itself around the product underneath, and takes on its form. This is a useful method both for displaying, labelling and protecting a product, and can avoid having to use a second layer of packaging.

Shutter-speed *Photography*

The speed of the shutter of a camera. It is usually calculated in whole seconds and fractions of a second.

See Film speed.

SIC *Research, Statistics*

See Standard Industrial Classification.

Side-head *Copywriting, Editorial, Publishing, Typography*

A heading or subhead positioned at the side of a piece of copy.

Side perf *Print*

Perforated lines running down the sides of a continuous business form; usually 12–13 mm (0.5 in) from each edge.

Silk screen *Printing processes*

A long-used form of printing using a length of fine silk stretched on a frame. In commercial printing, the use of silk has died out, modern materials having replaced it.

See Screen printing.

Simulation *Information technology, Marketing*
A computer program designed to imitate a real-life situation, the function of a piece of equipment or another type of computer. The term includes the creation of models for evaluating the theoretical behaviour of markets in different conditions. This is often used as a prelude to actual test marketing; and to decisions on avoiding test marketing where conditions seem unfavourable.

Single column centimetre *Advertising, Media, Publishing*
A basic billing unit of display or semi-display advertising space, one centimetre high and one column wide. Usually abbreviated to **SCC**. In the USA, the equivalent unit is the single column inch, **SCI**.

Single-sourcing *Purchasing*
Buying an organization's materials, equipment or services from a single source, usually accompanied by favourable discounts and priorities. A major disadvantage arises when a single source becomes inadequate, uncompetitive or goes out of business.

Sixteen sheet *Outdoor advertising*
A poster site size, comprising eight double crown sheets.

Skimming *Marketing, Retailing*
A marketing strategy for maximizing profits on higher-priced products. This is based on a retailing attitude, that consumers willing to consider buying expensive products will pay whatever is asked for them. The price is therefore pitched at a premium – 'cream' – level, which can be skimmed effectively without loss of customer interest.

Slant *Advertising, Editorial, Public relations*
An advertising copy platform with a particular bias, designed to influence the reader into seeing an issue or product in one way only. In editorial writing, a theme or idea selected by the writer as a basis or thread for the whole piece. Also termed an **angle**.

Slate *Advertising commercials, Film- and video-making*
A small black or white board carrying essential details of a production. This includes the production's name and number, the scene number, take number, name of director and cameraman and so on. The slate is photographed before the action with each shot, and clear of it, so that it can be identified later in the cutting room or editing suite. A slate is sometimes termed a **number board**.

Slitting *Paper, Print*
Dividing a web lengthwise into two or more narrower webs or strips.

Slogan *Advertising, Marketing, Propaganda, Public relations*
A phrase designed to represent a corporation, brand, product or service, used in promotional and educational material. It can become a brand property, designed around a product's unique qualities or a major selling point; or to reinforce a brand's positioning. Recent examples include:

BMW: The Ultimate Driving Machine
Compaq: Inspiration Technology
De Beers: Diamonds are Forever
Kenco: The Real Coffee Experts
Les Vins du Val de Loire: Noble Vineyards of France
Nokia: Connecting People
Rémy Martin: The world's favourite VSOP
Roc (moisturizer): We keep our promises
Sky: A digital vision for everyone

Slow motion *Advertising commercials, Film- and video-making*
A technique for shooting with the camera running above normal speed. During projection, the action will appear slowed down.

Small caps *Desktop publishing, Typography, Word-processing*
Small capital letters with the x-height of a particular font, as distinct from full-size capitals. A copywriter's or reader's instruction in the margin of a typescript or proof, for setting words in this form.
See x-height.

Smoothness *Paper, Print*
The surface smoothness of paper is measured by the Bendtsen test. This measures the amount of air escaping between an annular ring and the surface of the material. Results are measured in ml/min (millilitres per minute). Papers having a value higher than 50 are usually referred to as **matt**; below 50, as **silk**, sometimes termed **satin** or **velvet**.

Social group *Behavioural science, Marketing, Marketing research*
A group or community of individuals in distinct relationships with each other. Theoretically, their behaviour, and the way they interact with each other, can be evaluated, sometimes predicted and quantified. In marketing terms, a distinct social group can be expected to conform to a known variety of social customs, conventions and practices, make predictable purchases and use products in predictable ways. Distinct social communities include work, professional, tribal, religious, cultural and family groups.
See Segmentation.

Socio-economic grades *Marketing planning, Marketing research*
The theoretical classification of populations into groups and grades, under fixed social and economic criteria. It is a pragmatic system used by marketing planners,

for differentiating target groups. To understand these grades, it should be borne in mind that they are not political or class references, but based on individual and group lifestyle. They are not based solely on income. Two totally different individuals earning the same income may not qualify for the same grade listing. One may be an insurance underwriter, the other a coal miner. The underwriter may spend her disposable income on golf, foreign holidays and yachting; the miner on racing pigeons, the national lottery and football. The key, therefore, is partly *how* they spend their money, and how they are evaluated as target audiences for specific products and services.

Grade		Members	Approx % of UK population
A	Upper middle class	Top businessmen; other leaders; key opinion-formers	2.7%
B	Middle class	Senior executives; managers	15.2%
C1	Lower middle class	White-collar, white-blouse office workers	24.1%
C2	Skilled working class	Blue-collar factory workers	27.1%
D	Working class manual workers	Semi-skilled and unskilled	17.8%
E	Lowest level of subsistence	Poor pensioners; disabled; casual workers; unemployed	13.1%

See Segmentation.

Soft copy   *Information technology*
Computer output presented on a computer screen. Hard copy is printed output.

Soft goods   *Marketing, Retailing*
Marketing jargon for products that are literally soft, such as clothing, fabrics, curtains and bed-linen. Hard goods, on the other hand, are consumer durables, such as refrigerators, washing machines and cookers.

Soft proofing   *Information technology, Pre-press*
A technique for previewing pages on a computer screen. Difficulties may arise between the two technologies – electronic and printing – in achieving accurate representations of colour. Leading edge professional monitors are usually provided with calibration tools to ensure colour-matching.

Soft sell *Advertising, Marketing, Sales techniques*

Techniques of persuasion in advertising and selling, which may loosely be described as 'laid back'. Soft sell concentrates more on advising the customer of the benefits to be gained from possessing and using the product being sold than on bargains, discounts, savings and competitive razzmatazz.

Software *Computing, Information technology*

Programs and applications for a computer, or other interchangeable material for performing computing operations. Software contains instructions for the performance of hardware, including its operating systems. The counter-term is **hardware**. *See* Hardware.

Sole agency *Business, Sales activity*

A sales organization holding an exclusive agency, representing a client, product or service. The agency can be national, regional or local.

Sole trader *Business*

A business owned and operated by a single individual. Many freelance writers, art directors, film editors, photographers and marketing consultants are sole traders; they work for themselves and are not directors of a limited company or corporation.

Solid fibreboard *Packaging*

A board suitable for the manufacture of fibreboard packing cases and drums. It often incorporates a lining of kraft or other heavy-duty material.

Solus *Media planning and buying*

A newspaper or magazine advertisement space, positioned on a page with no other advertising matter on it. The advertiser usually specifies which page. The cost is therefore higher than the same space inserted run-of-paper ad.
See Matter, Mini-page, Run-of-paper ad.

Sound track *Film, Video*

Photographic or magnetic modulations, made in a narrow band to the left side of the picture area on 35 mm stock, on the right on 16 mm. This is sometimes simply termed the track; and nearly always, if mistakenly, used to represent the sounds themselves.

Space buyer *Advertising, Media buying*

Another term for **media buyer** specializing in or concentrating on press media. In broadcast media, the term used is **airtime buyer**.

Spam *Internet marketing*

Unsolicited e-mails, particularly those with marketing messages, sent to individual recipients without their permission. During the preparation of this edition, legislation is being proposed in Europe and the USA designed to prevent spamming. *See* Fax Preference Service, Permission marketing, Telephone Preference Service.

Special feature   *Advertising, Editorial, Publishing*
A section or supplement in a newspaper or magazine dedicated to one particular topic. There is a wide range of general topics, from property, finance, food and furnishings, to information technology. Special features are also produced to coincide with an event or an exhibition; the Ideal Home, air shows at Farnborough and Paris, a royal wedding or the opening of an important store.

Special offer   *Advertising, Marketing, Retailing, Sales promotion*
An inducement to try or buy a product or service; for example: a discount, usually time-limited, or an extra amount of product at the regular price.

Special position   *Advertising, Media buying, Publishing*
An advertisement occupying a specified position in a newspaper or magazine. Publishers always make an extra charge for such positions, on top of card rates. Examples of special positions: front page solus; inside back cover; page three left-hand bottom corner; next matter; opposite specified editorial.

Speed rating   *Film, Photography*
See Film speed.

Spend   *Advertising, Marketing*
Used as a noun, this term is synonymous with budget, appropriation or expenditure. For example: 'Next year our advertising spend will be a million dollars'.

Spike   *Editorial, Newsroom practice, Public relations, Publishing*
Used as a verb, this means to kill a story with no possibility of reinstatement. The term comes from pre-computer times, when editors used a piece of desk-furniture, a spike, to collect non-viable stories for disposal. It comprised a heavy circular base, about the diameter of a saucer, with a tall, vertical metal spike embedded in it. The editor would jam rejected stories and news releases on the spike; a messenger would collect the papers at intervals and put them out for the garbage collectors. If you were a public relations officer and your story or picture were spiked by an editor, you could be certain that it would never be published. The effect is as final as death. Today, editors use the 'delete' key or, worse, a shredder.

Spine   *Print*
The edge of a brochure, booklet or other publication that supports the binding. The back of a bound book connecting the covers.

Spinner   *Point-of-sale display, Retailing*
Jargon for a circular or rectangular display stand, holding products or literature, on a revolving base.

Spiral binding *Binding, Finishing, Print*
A publication bound with wire, in spiral form, inserted through holes along the binding edge.

Splash *Editorial, Newsroom practice, Publishing*
A main story featured on the front or back page of a newspaper. A **splash headline** usually occupies several columns horizontally, with the story running beneath.

Split run *Advertising, Print, Publishing*
In press advertising, a test and control technique. An advertisement appears in different editions of a publication on the same day and in the same position. The response from each is measured, compared and evaluated. With many campaigns, the same basic advertisement appears in two editions simultaneously, with differences in headline, offer, price and so on; the results are evaluated. Different advertisements are often tested against each other in a split run. In direct mail campaigns, much the same technique is employed. A mailshot is tested on half the target audience, and a modified or different shot tested on the other half. The results are measured, compared and evaluated. In all cases, the objective is to achieve the most profitable result at the least possible expense.

Sponsor *Cinema productions*
An organization or individual who finances production of a film usually for other than theatrical exhibition. This is done almost always for public relations purposes, and to keep a brand or corporate identity before a pre-defined public such as shareholders, governments and key opinion-formers.

Sponsored broadcasting *Advertising, Public relations, Sales promotion*
In the USA, companies advertise products and services by buying television and radio programmes at specified times. The sponsor commissions and provides entire shows for broadcasting, complete with its own advertising. This is not permitted in the UK, where different regulations apply.

Sponsorship *Advertising, Corporate publicity, Promotion, Public relations*
Several types of sponsorship exist. A company may sponsor an entire television or radio programme, such as entertainment or news. It may sponsor a sport or game, a public award or prize, a cultural event, an educational activity, an expedition on earth or in space. Sponsorship of charities and causes are popular, as are local events such as fairs and rallies. Companies sponsor publications of all kinds; the best-known are the *Michelin Guides*, Automobile Association country books and the *Guinness Book of Records*. Other forms of publication sponsorship include advertisements in local media, handbooks, yearbooks and charity function souvenirs.

In the case of sponsorship of broadcast entertainment, outright sponsorship is restricted under the rules of the Independent Television Commission. In defining programme sponsorship, the ITC states:

> A programme is deemed to be sponsored if any part of its costs of production or transmission is met by an organization or person other than a broadcaster or television producer, with a view to promoting its own or another's name, trademark, image, activities, products or other direct or indirect commercial interests.

The Radio Authority's sponsorship definition:

> A programme is sponsored if it is broadcast in return for payment or other valuable consideration (which includes the programme itself) to a licensee.

In this case, the rules are different from television sponsorship. The Radio Authority allows all programmes to be sponsored, with the exception of news bulletins. However, ultimate editorial control of sponsored programmes must remain with the licensee – the owner of the broadcasting licence. Endorsement of a sponsor's product or service within editorial is not permitted. As to programme contribution, sponsors may contribute to the editorial content of all sponsored programmes, except:

- addressing matters of political or industrial controversy or relating to current public policy;
- business/financial news or comment;
- current affairs;
- news features;
- news magazines;
- programme/documentary items.

Whatever the nature of the sponsorship, the objectives are similar: the widest possible exposure to the public. Often, sponsorship is used in support of advertising and public relations effort. Although products and services such as computers, insurance and soft drinks are featured in sponsorship activities, immediate product sales are not the principal objective. The main reason for sponsorship is usually to keep an organization, product or service in the public eye within an environment of concentration, enthusiasm and excitement. It is usually part of long-term planning. However, sponsors also usually expect a return on their investments. Those forms of sponsorship that achieve the widest media exposure are in constant demand: football, baseball, cricket, snooker, tennis, television game shows, entertainment awards.

Spontaneous recall   *Advertising research*

Advertising research often makes provision for recall by respondents. This involves the ability of a respondent to recall an advertisement, or elements of a particular advertisement, such as headline, body copy, offer, main benefit, illustration and logo. Recall-prompting visual aids can be used, such as prompt-cards. This is termed **aided recall**. Spontaneous recall is the term used when no devices are employed in the recall process.

Spot *Advertising, Media planning and buying, Television*

The airtime duration of a television or radio commercial; also its date and transmission time. There are usually fixed units of time: 7, 10, 15, 20, 30, 45, and 60 seconds. However, an advertiser may book longer spots, 1½ minutes or more. One of the longest television commercials in recent years was that of the Hanson Corporation, promoting its transatlantic business; duration, 2½ minutes.

Spot colour *Print*

In a black-and-white advertisement or item of print, one or more small areas of a single, usually solid, colour.

Spot rate *Advertising, Broadcast media, Media buying*

The rate card cost of a single spot. This is the most expensive way of buying advertising airtime; buying it in packages is the cheapest.

Spread *Advertising, Editorial, Print*

Two contiguous, facing pages. Do not confuse this with **double-page spread** (*qv*) or **centre spread**, which comprises two facing pages in the centre of a publication, printed on a single sheet. In the USA, this is termed a **centerfold**.

Spreadsheet *Information technology, Marketing planning*

A computer application into which alpha-numerical data are entered in the form of a grid of rows and columns. The information is processed, and can be changed, at the operator's will, with an infinite number of variables. This enables planners to compute different scenarios, for comparison and evaluation. For example, when a marketing budget is increased by, say, 5 per cent, and entered into the spreadsheet, the change may affect all the cells in the grid. This helps to calculate and evaluate a wide range of 'what if. . .?' situations.

Sprocket holes *Paper, Print*

A line of holes at each side of a continuous form, for feeding it through printers.

Standard Industrial Classification *Research, Statistics*

A UK governmental system for classifying commercial, industrial and economic activity. It lists manufacturing and service activities by codes. It was introduced into the UK after the Second World War, for use in classifying businesses and other statistical units by the type of economic activity in which they were engaged.

The classification provides a framework for the collection, tabulation, presentation and analysis of data about economic activities. Its use promotes uniformity of data collected by various government departments and agencies. It can also be used for administrative purposes and by many non-government bodies, as a convenient way of classifying industrial activities into a common structure.

A European Union regulation has general application, and is directly applicable in all member states. It does not have to be confirmed by national governments in order to have binding effect.

The SIC is divided into 17 sections, each denoted by a letter from A to Q. Some sections are divided into subsections, each with a single letter. The main sections are:

A Agriculture, hunting and forestry
B Fishing
C Mining and quarrying
D Manufacturing
E Electricity, gas and water supply
F Construction
G Wholesale and retail trade; repair of motor vehicles, motorcycles and personal household goods
H Hotels and restaurants
I Transport, storage and communication
J Financial intermediation
K Real estate, renting and business activities
L Public administration and defence, compulsory social security
M Education
N Health and social work
O Other community, social and personal service activities
P Private households with employed persons
Q Extra-terrestrial organizations and bodies

Curiously, marketing appears not to qualify as an economic activity, trade, occupation, profession or industry, since it has no classification of its own. However, certain marketing-related activities are mentioned, here shown with their SIC section letters and numbers:

Section DE, manufacture of pulp, paper and paper products; publishing and printing
22.22 Printing of advertising material
Section K, real estate, renting and business activities
74.4   Advertising
74.13 Market research
74.14 Public relations activities
74.40 Aerial advertising
74.81 Advertising photography
74.83 Direct mailing activities
Section O, other community, social and personal service activities
92   Production of commercial messages for radio, television and film

Similar systems are used in the European Union and the USA.

Standard letter   *Business, Direct mail*
A letter with an identical text, sent to a large number of recipients – staff, business contacts, charitable donors, customers, suppliers and so on. Usually the individual

names, addresses and salutations are matched in. Sometimes, small details within the body of the letter are changed to suit individual recipients.

Stapel scale   *Marketing research, Research*
A research evaluation technique in which respondents are asked to describe an object using words, numbers or both. It is often used where a qualitative opinion is required, one which cannot be actually measured, such as a taste. When asking respondents to describe a sausage, for example, a Stapel scale may be compiled to include very spicy, fairly spicy, moderately spicy, not very spicy, and tasteless. Each attribute is given a number, No 1 for very spicy, No 5 for tasteless. The **semantic differential** technique has similar characteristics.

Staple   *Distribution, Marketing*
A product bought and consumed on a daily or weekly basis, such as bread, cheese, potatoes, milk and rice. The main considerations among consumers are usually availability, convenience and price; consequently there is often little brand loyalty involved.

Star   *Marketing planning, Product portfolio planning*
A product with high growth, high market share.
See Boston Matrix.

Star   *Advertising, Cinema, Commercials, Television*
A loose term for a well-known actor or actress. Originally, this term was applied to an artist with so much public following that a management employing one would know in advance the likely box office earnings of a film, regardless of its quality. Today, the term has become badly degraded; even actors with minimal or mediocre talent may be dubbed stars. Their usefulness in television and cinema advertising, however, is well exploited. For advertising purposes, actors endorse a huge variety of products and services, much of the time regardless or not of whether they are mutually suitable.

Static market   *Business, Marketing*
A market situation, over a long period, in which rises and falls in demand are very small. The market for washing powders, for example, depends in part on the demand for washing machines. Both markets are far from dynamic, fluctuations are small. For planning purposes, in normal times, they can usually be described as static. During a property boom, demand for new washing machines tends to rise, but the washing powder market remains static nevertheless.

Status symbol   *Business, Consumer behaviour, Marketing*
A product acquired for the purpose of making an impression, rather than practical use alone. Porsche, Ferrari and Lotus cars, Rolex watches and country club memberships fall into this category.

Still *Film, Television, Video*
Also termed a **freeze -frame** (*qv*). A non-moving picture or illustration on screen. *See* Commercial, Frame, Freeze-frame, Shot, Titling, Voice-over.

Still *Photography, Publicity*
A photograph taken during film or video production, sometimes on the set, and usually used for publicity and public relations activity.

Stochastic screening *Pre-press, Print*
A halftone screening technique in which dots are scattered apparently at random on the printing surface. This produces an image in much smaller, irregularly shaped dots than conventional halftones. There are no rosettes. Stochastic screening is capable of producing high quality images at relatively low resolutions. The word stochastic derives from the Greek 'to guess'.

Stock *Photography*
Film used in still and cine photography. **Standard stock** is the term used for 35 mm film.

Stock *Print*
Paper or other material used in printing.

Stockist *Distribution, Retailing*
A distributor, seller, re-seller of a product, or range of products, usually with a reasonable knowledge of its technology and use. The term can be applied both to consumer and business products; domestic appliances and office equipment, for example.

Stockless purchasing *Manufacturing, Retailing*
The purchase by a retailer, and subsequent delivery of products on demand, from a supplier. Purchase and delivery of components for manufacturing. The supplier carries out this service usually, but not always, under contract, and takes responsibility for warehousing stocks of the product or component. For both sides to be satisfied, a fair amount of planning is involved. However, when the purchaser's demands are greater or smaller than planned for, problems are usually experienced by the supplier.

Stocktaking *Distribution, Retailing, Warehousing, Wholesaling*
The regular counting and valuation of items in stock at specific times. This practice is carried out periodically by wholesalers, retailers and factory management. It may include various company assets as well as trading stock. In the USA this is termed **inventory**.

Stock turn rate　　　　　*Distribution, Retailing, Warehousing, Wholesaling*
Also, **stock turnover**. A term describing the rate at which a manufacturer's or distributor's stock is sold and subsequently replaced, over a specific period. Stock turn audits can be carried out daily, weekly, monthly, quarterly and so on.

Stop motion　　　　　　*Cinema, Filming, Television, Video*
A technique for conveying the impression of movement in inanimate objects. The objects are manipulated between successively photographed frames. The film *Chicken Run* and the made-for-television *Wallace and Grommit* series are excellent examples of this technique.

Store audit　　　　　　　*Research, Retailing*
Another term for **retail audit** (*qv*).

Store brand　　　　　　　*Retailing*
Also, an **own brand**. A brand owned by a retailer. The product carries the store's own label, logo and pack design. Most own-brands are cheaper, and inevitably in competition with, the national and international brands carried by the store. Nevertheless, both seem to do well.

Store demonstration　　　　　*Retailing*
More properly, **in-store demonstration**. A live demonstration of food, appliances, gadgets and so on, carried out in a retail outlet; often by a professional demonstrator.
See In-store promotion.

Store traffic　　　　　*Research, Retail auditing, Retailing*
Measurement of the number of shoppers entering a store over a specific period, whether or not they make a purchase. In measuring the volume of customers, and comparing this with those actually purchasing, the retailer can obtain an indication of the success of the store's trading policy.

Storyboard　　　　*Cinema, Commercials, Creative, Film, Pre-production,*
　　　　　　　　　　　　　　　　　　　　　Television, Video
An illustrated script; a sequential series of illustrations showing the action highlights of a script. The illustrations are usually drawings created to summarize the action demanded by the concept and copy. Usually, extracts of the copy are shown beneath each frame. Sometimes a storyboard is created as a PowerPoint presentation, accompanied by a basic voice-over (*qv*). A storyboard is the basic document advertising agencies and production companies present to their clients for initial discussion and approval. Costs at this stage are modest, compared with the cost of the production. Film-makers plan their production work using storyboards, sometimes modifying them during a shoot.
See Animatic.

Strategic business unit *Business, Marketing*
Sometimes also termed a **strategic business centre**. A stand-alone department or unit in an organization, with its own management, objectives, strategies, market and product range. Although the unit is autonomous within the organization, it is expected to produce profits, and also make a financial contribution to the organization.

Strategic marketing planning *Marketing planning*
The high-level decision-making process that examines and recommends the best strategies for a company to market new and existing products. This involves the setting of an organization's long-term marketing objectives, together with its planned activities, products and services, markets, target audiences, marketing finance, human resources, production and supply sourcing, distribution channels and promotional effort. It particularly involves management planning and development, in terms of recruitment, decision-making, delegation and control.

Strategic pricing policy *Business, Marketing*
A skeleton plan to determine, as far as possible, the long-term pricing activity for a product or service. Such a plan may not be capable of forecasting daily fluctuations within a national economy, a competitive marketplace or a source of raw materials. However, with a strategic policy in place, management may be in a better position to maintain or increase its market share over a long period, and cope well in difficult times.

Strawboard *Paper-making techniques*
A general term for a range of boards, yellowish or grey, used for backing envelopes, writing pads, book covers, ring binders and so on. The original strawboard was board made from straw pulp; some strawboards are still made from this inexpensive material.

Straw pulp *Paper-making techniques*
Paper-making pulp obtained from various varieties of cereal straw.

Streaming *Broadcasting, Internet, Radio*
A technique used by radio stations, making their programmes available over the Internet.

Stringer *Journalism*
A journalist working for a local newspaper or magazine, who contributes local news to national media as local correspondent.

Stripping *Pre-press, Print*
Traditional colour printing involves manual work for final film assembly from a number of sets of separations, prior to plate-making. This is termed RIPping and stripping. Digital methods are more cost- and time-effective. The ideal is the

preparation of final, imposed film from a digital file, with no manual intervention. *See* Raster Image Processing.

Stroboscopic effect   *Film, television and video production*
An unwanted effect created by the relationship of the interval between camera exposures and the speed of a moving object being filmed. The most commonly observed effect is the wheels of a moving car appearing to revolve backwards.

Stuffer   *Correspondence, Sales promotion*
Promotional material inserted – stuffed – into a package or envelope, accompanying the main material, which may be a product, invoice or sample.

Sturgeon's theorem   *Advertising, Business, Consumer behaviour, Marketing*
This states: 'Ninety per cent of everything is cr*p'. Science fiction writer Theodore Sturgeon once wrote: 'Ninety per cent of science fiction is crud. That's because ninety per cent of everything is crud.' This was intended to convey the author's belief that the majority of the public is totally undiscriminating, has no interest in facts or how to evaluate them, and is interested only in immediate physical gratification.

Critics of marketing and advertising apply Sturgeon's theorem in numerous ways to marketing and advertising practice. Advertising, for example, they consider immoral, with sinister and destructive social and economic effects. They contend that marketing is secretive; that advertising is unnecessary, that it raises prices, fuels inflation, stresses unimportant differences between products, and makes the media dependent on a few rich companies.

In fact, the opposite is true. Advertising helps to add value to products and services. It provides consumer satisfaction, increases product variety, stimulates competition and technical progress. It subsidizes the media, helps them to survive and stay free.

Similarly, in the face of denigration on social grounds, advertising by its very nature is totally above board; everything can be seen, on paper and on screen. It helps to meet consumer demand and raise living standards. It stimulates freedom of choice, supports branded products and encourages product reliability. Above all, it encourages advertisers to be responsible. Finally, in answer to accusations of licence in marketing and advertising: both are heavily controlled, by legislation and voluntary codes of practice.

When Sturgeon's theorem is cited, the final word is usually changed to **cr*p**.

Style   *Internet communication*
A formatting tool for adding special emphasis or structure to e-mail message text. This usually comprises address styles, headings, numbered lists, bulleted lists, directory lists, menu lists and so on. HTML (Hypertext Mark-up Language) is the standard for formatting text for the Internet. Using HTML formatting also enables users to add graphics, and links to Web sites. Only e-mail programs that support MIME (Multipurpose Internet Mail Extensions) can read HTML formatting.

Sub-editing *Journalism, Publishing*

Also termed **subbing**. An editorial process, in which a journalist arranges and edits copy for publication. This skilled and painstaking work comprises purging copy of unnecessary material, rewriting and rearranging it if necessary; checking and correcting spelling and punctuation. Creating headlines and subheads is an important function of subbing. Unfortunately, most of these subbing activities need to be carried out on news releases submitted by public relations departments and consultants. In newsrooms, a sub-editor is usually referred to as a **sub**.

Subhead *Copywriting, Creative, Desktop publishing, Typography,*
Word-processing

A heading below a headline and above a paragraph. The main heading of a piece of advertising copy is the **headline**; in news release copy it is a **heading**. Subsidiary headings are subheads. Where a subhead sits centrally on a line above a paragraph, it is termed a **cross-head**.

The function of a subhead indicates a main division in copy. In advertising copywriting, it should be written as a benefit. In news releases, particularly long ones, subheads should be as bland as possible, conveying only the information essential to divide the copy. This is because editors and sub-editors usually prefer to create their own.

Subliminal advertising *Cinema, Controls, Promotional techniques,*
Television

A technique in visual presentation that delivers promotional messages below the threshold of conscious perception. In simpler terms, putting an advertising message in front of a television or cinema audience, so short that it does not register in the viewer's conscious mind. It does, however, register below the conscious level, and provides stimulus for action. In films shown in cinemas, it is possible to insert one single frame in 24. The message in the frame could be, for example, 'BUY ICE CREAM NOW'. Repeating the message a hundred times at intervals might, in theory, encourage the audience to buy ice cream while in the cinema. Opponents claim that any kind of subliminal message can be carried in this way, including propaganda and messages that encourage violence and criminal activity. In point of fact, nobody is quite sure whether or not the technique actually works.

In the UK, the technique is forbidden under Independent Television Commission regulations. The ITC Code of Advertising Standards and Practice states:

> No advertisement may include any technical device that, by using images of very brief duration or by any other means, exploits the possibility of conveying a message to, or otherwise influencing the minds of, members of an audience without their being aware, or fully aware, of what has been done. (General Principles, clause 6.)

In the UK, the Advertising Standards Authority is the independent body responsible for ensuring that advertising works in the public interest. Its Codes of

Advertising and Sales Promotion apply to non-broadcast advertising, including cinema and video commercials. Under the terms of the Codes, subliminal advertising is not allowed. The Codes state:

> Advertisers, publishers and owners of other media should ensure that advertisements are designed and presented in such a way that it is clear that they are advertisements. (Section 23.1.)

Subscription publishing *Publishing*
The publishing of a newspaper, magazine or directory, where each copy is intended for purchase, and is paid for. Purchasing can be at newsagents or street vendors, delivery by mail or by hand. Some publications distribute a number of copies free of charge, but this is not reckoned as part of their subscribed circulation. The other type of such publishing is controlled circulation (*qv*) where copies are distributed free to qualifying individuals.
See ABC, Audit Bureau of Circulations, Verified Free Distribution.

Substance *Paper*
A term defining and describing the weight of paper or board. Substance is defined in grams per square metre of a single sheet. This expressed as g/m². For example, the substance of a letterhead of moderate quality and weight may be given as 80 g/m².

Substrate *Print*
The surface of any material to be printed.

Sub-title *Film, Television and video post-production*
Wording appearing on screen at the same time as action or between scenes. For example, in a commercial for Haze room freshener, the passage of time is indicated by a sub-title on a black screen, '4 weeks later'. In the UK and mainland Europe, subtitles of programme scripts and news may be accessed on television by pressing the Teletext button and keying 888.

Super *Film, Television, Video*
The abbreviated form of **superimposition**: titling superimposed on to frames of a motion picture.

Supercalendered *Paper, Print*
A surface finish on paper, which may vary from relatively dull but smooth to highly glazed. It is produced by passing damp paper through a supercalender stack. This is broadly similar to a machine calender stack, except that is separate from the paper-making machine, and some of the rolls are of compressed fibre.

In paper-making, a calender is a metal roller, rather like a rolling pin but several metres wide. A calendered paper is one subjected to smoothing and polishing between stacks of highly polished, steam-heated calenders. This usually takes place at the dry end of a paper-making machine, though there are other forms of calendering carried out away from the machine, such as supercalendering.

Super-site   *Outdoor advertising*

A particularly large poster or billboard display, usually built by specialists because of its size or format. Some of the most spectacular super-sites are three-dimensional, in colour and, frequently, illuminated.

Superstore   *Retailing*

A supermarket or other self-service outlet, with a floor area greater than 25,000 sq ft (2,325 sq m).

Supplement   *Advertising, Publishing*

A section or supplement in a newspaper or magazine, dedicated to one particular topic, almost always with appropriate advertising.
See Special feature.

Supplier   *Business transactions, E-commerce, Information technology,*
                                                         Marketing communications

An individual or organization supplying products and services to a customer. In recent years, in the information technology business, a great jumble of suppliers has arisen. These include:

- **ASP** *Application service supplier*
  An application is a computing task. An application program is a specific set of instructions dedicated to operating the computer in carrying out the application; for example, invoicing (billing). An ASP is a company delivering applications, via the Internet, to a number of clients from a centralized data centre. The application, which may be a large and complex one, is hired by the client on an ad hoc or contract basis. For the client, this avoids the expense of owning the application, and all the training, updating and breakdowns this may incur. Thus, a client may need a suite of applications for promoting a product, soliciting orders, processing them, supplying the product, keeping track of stock, invoicing, receiving the money and banking it. All these functions can be provided by the ASP.
- **BDPAS** *Business document processing application supplier*
  An ASP specializing in the storage and management of business documents, via the Internet. Documents can be accessed direct from a client's computer.
- **CSP** *Content service provider*
  A service designed to transform client-generated information into Web-ready content. This includes creating online bookstores, document archives and e-catalogues, which can be made available on demand to a client via the Internet.
- **EBPP** *Electronic billing, presentation and payment service*
  A supplier service enabling clients to engage customers on a monthly basis, while increasing brand awareness. Designed to turn invoices into revenue-generating instruments.

■ **FSP** *Fulfilment service provider*
An invoicing service meeting the e-commerce requirements of clients' business transactions.

Swatch   *Design, Fashion, Print*
A range of samples, often in booklet form, of printing inks, design colours, fabrics, leathers and so on, available from a supplier.

SWOT   *Marketing planning*
The marketing planner's acronym for:

Strengths
Weaknesses
Opportunities
Threats

This is a popular technique used in strategic marketing planning, analysis, evaluation and decision-making. **Strengths** and **weaknesses** refer to the current position of an organization vis-à-vis its assets, resources, target markets, market share, products, services, distribution, competition and so on. **Opportunities** looks to future prospects and development, the anticipation of problems and possibly turning them into profitable opportunities. **Threats** include current and anticipated political, economic, sociological, technological, legal, environmental conditions, and competitive activity.

Symbol retailer   *Retailing*
An independent retailer with membership of a cooperative group. Membership of one of these groups, usually termed voluntary chains, endows individual retailers with the bulk buying power of the whole group. This helps them to compete on better terms with supermarket chains. The retailer features the group's logo on store-fronts, window displays, wrapping materials, stationery and elsewhere. Some voluntary chains have their own brands. In the UK and the European Union, SPAR and Wavy Line are popular voluntary chains; Londis is a chain run by a wholesaler. Some voluntary chains have their own marketing departments for handling local marketing and publicity operations.

Synch   *Film, Television and video post-production*
Short for **synchronization**. This refers to picture and sound that are coincident when properly married and reproduced together. The most commonly observed effect of faulty synchronization is lip-synchronization, or **lip-synch**. When this is faulty, the results can be hilarious. An actor on screen appears to be saying certain words, while entirely different words are heard by the audience. Funnier still, the actor's audible words are a fraction behind the lip movements. Sometimes the price of a cinema ticket is worth an opportunity of experiencing this effect. Faulty lip-synch may occur in live television reporting, when a transmission is bounced off several satellites and incurs a chain of delays.

Synopsis   *Business, Copywriting, Creative, Film, Marketing planning,*
Television commercials

A brief outline of a document, plan, report or proposal. In creative concept work, copywriting, or script-writing for commercials, this may be no more than a list of ideas to be considered. In film and commercial work, this is a very brief form of treatment, giving a bare outline of a concept, plot or other content of a film. Producers usually have to be satisfied by a synopsis before they will spend time reading anything longer.

Tt

Tab *Copywriting, Desktop publishing, Word-processing*
Short for **tabulation**. A jump in spacing to a position decided in advance. Horizontal tabs are sideways pre-set jumps across a page; vertical tabs are pre-set jumps up and down a page.

Tabloid *Print, Publishing*
A page size used in newspaper and magazine printing. The trimmed page size is approximately 425 mm high × 300 mm wide, varying with the size adopted by the publisher. Tabloid is about half the trimmed size of broadsheet. In the UK, the *Daily Express*, the *Mirror* and the *Sun* are tabloids. House journals are often published in tabloid format.
See Broadsheet.

Tabulation *Desktop publishing, Planning techniques, Spreadsheeting,*
Word-processing
The compilation, insertion or grouping of numerical data into tabular form.

Tack *Print*
The cohesion between particles of printing ink; also, the pulling power or separation force of ink. A tacky ink has high separation forces, which can cause surface picking or splitting of weak printing papers. The tack of an ink is governed by viscosity and adhesion.

Tactical pricing *Marketing, Retailing, Wholesaling*
Varying the price of products and services, to take into account peaks and troughs in sales, or seasonal demand patterns. During peak times, for example, prices may be adjusted upwards. When sales are flagging, or under competitive attack, prices may be reduced until the crisis is over.

Take *Filming, Video*
A complete photographing of a shot. The director may demand a number of takes, until satisfied that one of them is perfect or acceptable.

Target audience *Advertising, Marketing, Marketing communications,*
Marketing planning
An identifiable group of consumers, or other individuals, at which a campaign is aimed. This term applies particularly to advertising activity, since many campaigns

are aimed at population segments from which a particular response is expected. In most circumstances, a target audience can be considered the primary market for a product or service. More to the point, a target should be considered as the *individual* at whom an effective advertising message can be addressed, and from whom the campaign's desired response can be obtained.

Target consumers *Advertising, Marketing planning, Sales promotion*
A database of customers with common interests, forming the focus of a marketing promotion. The list can be one of individual names or, in the case of mass marketing, common characteristics such as age, sex and income. The information is used to create appropriately persuasive campaigns aimed specifically at such targets.

Target Group Index *Advertising research, Marketing research*
Popularly known as **TGI**. A subscription research service that provides links between consumer viewing, listening and reading habits and the consumption of a large number of brands. The research is based on information provided online by a panel of 24,000 adults, covering 400 product fields, their demographic characteristics and media exposure.

Task budgeting *Advertising planning, Marketing planning*
There are two basic techniques for arriving at viable marketing and advertising campaign budgets:

Task budgeting. Setting campaign objectives, then assessing the size of the task and calculating what it will cost to carry it out.
Budget tasking. Proposing a budget, then calculating how far it will go in fulfilling the campaign's objectives.

Of the two methods, task budgeting is the more sensible and prudent. However, some marketing and advertising managements are easily scared by its implications. It means setting a budget that will really do the job, without wasting money, and without under-spending and therefore under-achieving.

TC *Advertising, Media buying*
An abbreviation for **Till Countermanded**. An instruction by an advertiser to a publisher, to repeat the publication of an advertisement until specifically instructed to cease doing so. *Caveat*: When issuing media orders, it is always more secure to spell out instructions in full. Relying on initials as instructions is unsafe, since they can be misunderstood or misinterpreted. In the USA, the equivalent of this instruction is **Till Forbid**.

Tearsheet *Advertising, Production, Publishing*
An advertisement clipped from a publication, sent to the advertiser as proof of insertion. This is done nearly always by magazine publishers, less often by

newspapers. Small advertisers may receive tearsheets with invoices. A tearsheet is also termed a **voucher**. Tearsheets are often stored by advertisers and agencies, in outsize portfolios known as **guard books**. A complete copy of a publication, sent to an advertiser for the same purpose, is termed a **voucher copy**.

Teaser campaign   *Advertising*

An advertising campaign designed specifically to arouse public interest and curiosity. Teaser campaigns are usually followed by persuasive advertising, complete with product facts and features, strong consumer benefits, and information.

Technical media   *Advertising, Publishing*

Publications for a targeted technical and industrial readership, not for consumers. Also termed **trade and technical** publications. Many have a reader reply service, through which readers can send for literature on products and services advertised or featured in editorial.

Technological forecasting   *Marketing planning*

Part of the PESTLE technique for the evaluation of product portfolios and their future. With many technologies, such as mechanical engineering, the pace of technological change is relatively slow. Much of the technology used in the modern automobile, for example, is inherited from that of the 19th century. Its development, compared with electronics, is at a snail's pace. With computers and telecommunications, a complete technological generation can be turned round in as little as 18 months. Forecasting difficulty and risk is therefore relative to the speed of individual technological change. PESTLE is a popular acronym for six influences to which a market is subject: **P**olitical, **E**conomic, **S**ocial, **T**echnological, **L**egal, **E**nvironmental.
See PESTLE.

Telecast   *Broadcasting, Television*

A live television broadcast, often applied to news or outside broadcasting.

Telecine   *Film, Television, Video*

A machine that transfers film to videotape, or transmits picture and sound from film over a television channel.

Telecoms   *Information technology*

Popular shorthand for **telecommunications**; the transmission and reception of data by digital or analogue signals, using broadcast or transmission lines.

Telemarketing   *Marketing, Marketing research, Sales*

Selling carried out by telephone. Also termed **telesales** and **telephone selling**. Telemarketing is carried out either in support of an advertising campaign running alongside it, or as a stand-alone sales effort. It is popular among companies selling, for example, insurance, kitchen equipment, double-glazing and passenger vehicles. It is also a major medium for professional and technical sales, as well as an important tool in marketing research.

Telephone Preference Service (TPS)   *Controls, Direct marketing,*
Marketing

In the UK, the central register of individuals who have indicated they do not wish to receive unsolicited sales and marketing calls. It is now a legal obligation for anyone making unsolicited sales and marketing calls to ensure they do not call individuals who have registered their wish not to be called.

The TPS enables individuals to register their objection to receiving direct marketing calls with a central service. Telemarketing companies receive the list of numbers that have been registered by subscribing to the TPS.

The Telephone Preference Service, set up by the Direct Marketing Association (UK) Limited (DMA), was formed in 1995 as a voluntary, self-regulatory mechanism. It enabled consumers to opt out of receiving unsolicited sales and marketing calls.

Following the adoption of the Telecommunications Data Protection Directive by the European Parliament in 1997, the Department of Trade and Industry (DTI) and the Office of Telecommunications (OFTEL), entered into a public consultation period. This resulted in the Telecommunications (Data Protection and Privacy) Regulations 1999, which affected all telemarketers in the UK and came into force on 1 May 1999. The Directive and Regulations are wide-ranging in their scope.

In February 1999 OFTEL issued an Invitation To Tender for the management of the Telephone and Fax Opt-out Schemes. The Direct Marketing Association was awarded the contract to run both the Telephone Preference Service (TPS) and the Fax Preference Service (FPS).

Telephoto   *Photography*
A photographic lens for photographing distant subjects. Its focal length is greater than the diagonal of the negative it covers.

Tele-prompt   *Broadcasting, Television*
Equipment that displays a script or dialogue, positioned in front of a presenter or news-reader. The text scrolls up the tele-prompt screen at an appropriate reading pace. Also termed **autocue** (*qv*).

Teletext   *Advertising, Information technology, Television*
A data transmission system, conveying news and other information to consumers via television channels. The data runs alongside normal programming, and can be accessed by using special keys, usually on a hand-held remote control device. In the UK, commercial channels display advertising material; BBC channels do not. Although virtually all current analogue television sets have Teletext, the standard of reproduction is crude. It is adequate for text only. With digital television, the standard can be much higher, and interactive at consumer level.

Telethon *Broadcasting, Charity public relations*
A lengthy television entertainment programme featuring artists and their music, usually in support of a charity. The pioneer, *Live Aid*, was transmitted internationally, and millions of pounds and dollars were raised. Money is pledged by viewers over the telephone or online, and paid in by credit card. The word is contrived from two others, *television* and *marathon*.

Television rating points *Advertising planning, Media planning and buying,*
Media research
Popularly termed **TVRs**. The value of television to advertisers is calculated in TVRs. Each TVR represents 1 per cent of the potential TV audience. This is expressed in terms of individuals or homes with television sets. A viewer is defined as a person in a room with a television set switched on for at least 15 consecutive seconds. Within this definition, 'in the room' means anything from watching attentively, to a casual glance at the screen while doing something else. This may seem a rickety basis for buying airtime, but a commonly agreed one until another basis is found.
See ABC, Circulation, Controlled circulation, Penetration, Rate card, Reader, Readership, Verified Free Distribution, Viewer.

Television transmission standards *Television, Video*
There are three broadcasting standards:

PAL   Phase alternating line
NTSC   National Television System Committee
SECAM   Système en Couleurs à Mémoire

Unfortunately, these standards are incompatible. Worse, there are variations of PAL and SECAM. The following list is up to date at the time of writing, given the speed of change now taking place in broadcasting. As digital television standards are introduced, there will be further changes:

Country	Standard
Afghanistan	PAL-B
Albania	PAL-BG
Algeria	PAL-B
Angola	PAL-I
Antigua	NTSC
Antilles	NTSC
Argentina	PAL-N
Australia	PAL-BG
Austria	PAL-BG
Bahamas	NTSC
Bahrain	PAL-B
Bangladesh	PAL-B

Barbados	NTSC
Belgium	PAL-BG
Benin	SECAM-K
Bermuda	NTSC
Bolivia	NTSC
Botswana	PAL-I
Brazil	PAL-M
Brunei	PAL-B
Bulgaria	SECAM-D
Burkina Faso	SECAM-K
Burma	NTSC
Burundi	SECAM-K
Cameroon	PAL-BG
Canada	NTSC
Cayman Islands	NTSC
Central African Republic	SECAM-K
Chad	SECAM-K
Chile	NTSC
China	PAL-D
Colombia	NTSC
Congo	SECAM-K
Costa Rica	NTSC
Cuba	NTSC
Cyprus	SECAM-BG
Czech Republic	SECAM-DK
Denmark	PAL-BG
Djibouti	SECAM-K
Dominican Republic	NTSC
Ecuador	NTSC
Egypt	SECAM-B
El Salvador	NTSC
Ethopia	PAL-B
Finland	PAL-BG
France	SECAM-L
Gabon	SECAM-K
Germany (Former Dem)	SECAM-BG
Germany (Former Fed)	PAL-BG
Ghana	PAL-B
Gibraltar	PAL-B
Greece	SECAM-B
Guam	NTSC
Guatemala	NTSC
Guinea	SECAM-K
Haiti	NTSC
Hawaii	NTSC
Honduras	NTSC

Hong Kong	PAL-I
Hungary	SECAM-DK
Iceland	PAL-B
India	PAL-B
Indonesia	PAL-B
Iran	SECAM-B
Iraq	SECAM-B
Israel	PAL
Italy	PAL-BG
Ivory Coast	SECAM-K
Jordan	PAL-B
Kenya	PAL-B
Kuwait	PAL-B
Lebanon	SECAM-B
Lesotho	PAL-I
Liberia	PAL-B
Libya	SECAM-B
Luxembourg	PAL-BG +, SECAM-BG/L
Madagascar	SECAM-K
Malaysia	PAL-B
Maldives	PAL-B
Mali	SECAM-K
Malta	PAL-B
Mauritania	SECAM-K
Mauritius	SECAM-B
Mexico	NTSC
Morocco	SECAM-B
Mozambique	PAL-I
Nepal	PAL-BG
Netherlands	PAL-BG
New Zealand	PAL-B
Nicaragua	NTSC
Niger	SECAM-K
Nigeria	PAL-B
Norway	PAL-BG
Oman	PAL-BG
Pakistan	PAL-B
Panama	NTSC
Paraguay	PAL-N
Peru	NTSC
Philippines	NTSC
Poland	SECAM-DK
Portugal	PAL-BG
Puerto Rico	NTSC
Qatar	PAL-B
Romania	PAL-DK

Rwanda	SECAM-K
Saudi Arabia	SECAM-BG
Senegal	SECAM-K
Sierra Leone	PAL-B
Singapore	PAL-B
South Africa	PAL-I
Spain	PAL-BG
Sri Lanka	PAL-B
Sudan	PAL-B
Surinam	NTSC
Swaziland	PAL-BG
Sweden	PAL-BG
Switzerland	PAL-BG
Syria	SECAM-B
Tahiti	SECAM-DK
Taiwan	NTSC
Tanzania	PAL-I
Thailand	PAL-B
Togo	SECAM-K
Trinidad & Tobago	NTSC
Tunisia	SECAM-B
Turkey	PAL-B
UAE	PAL-BG
Uganda	PAL-B
UK	PAL-I
Uruguay	PAL-N
USA	NTSC
Russia*	SECAM-DK
Venezuela	NTSC
Virgin Is, Br	NTSC
Virgin Is, US	NTSC
Yemen	PAL-B
Yugoslavia**	PAL-B
Zaire	SECAM-K
Zambia	PAL-B
Zanzibar	PAL-I
Zimbabwe	PAL-B 90

Notes:
* Former USSR
** Now separate states

Tensile strength   *Paper, Print*
The maximum force a test-piece of paper will endure before it breaks. The
conditions are defined by an industry standard testing method.

Territorial franchise   *Business, Sales and marketing*

The right, granted by a supplier to an individual or company, to sell the supplier's products and services in a specified geographical area. It gives the franchisee the right to develop the sales potential in the area. The terms and conditions of the franchise are usually, and prudently, detailed in a contract.

Territory   *Sales and marketing*

The geographical area worked by a sales team or individual salesperson, allocated to them by their sales management.

Testimonial   *Advertising*

Also termed an **endorsement**. A statement by a celebrity, well-known individual, award-winner, professional expert, and so on, in an advertisement. The celebrity may praise the product or service, or merely be seen in its vicinity. The implication that by appearing in conjunction with the product the celebrity actually uses it should be taken lightly. However, the reading, listening and viewing public are very discriminating, and can often tell the wheat from the chaff. On the other hand, if the chosen celebrity is appropriate to the product, and his or her patronage is genuine, it can be very effective and often do some good. As, for example, in the case of campaigns to discourage the use of tobacco products and narcotics, and the installation of security devices in houses and cars.

Test marketing   *Advertising, Distribution, Marketing, Retailing*

The marketing of a product or service on a limited scale, within a limited territory, and within a limited time-frame. This is usually a pilot campaign, and a prelude to marketing on a national scale. The sample territory or market selected for the test usually represents the characteristics of the national market, and is a miniature of it. Compared with full-scale marketing costs, the cost of testing markets in this way is modest. Above all, it helps to minimize the risk involved in full-scale marketing operations. Often, a number of matching territories are selected for testing at the same time.

Test marketing helps the marketing team to evaluate important criteria, including the viability of:

- advertising: concept, message, media and performance;
- branding and positioning;
- competitive activity;
- decision to launch;
- distribution technique;
- distributor and public acceptance;
- packaging;
- price and discounts;
- product;
- regional variations;
- timing;
- type of outlet.

A test launch or campaign will, of course, alert competitors to the marketing team's plans; any element of surprise will be lost.

Text type *Desktop publishing, Typography, Word-processing*
Another term for **body type** (*qv*).

TGI *Advertising research, Marketing research*
See Target Group Index.

Thermography *Print*
A method of producing a relief effect similar to embossing and die-stamping, but without the high set-up costs involved. The inked image is coated with a powdered resin compound, and passed under a heated grill. The heat causes the resin and the ink to fuse, to swell and rise up in relief. There is usually a wide range of colours to choose from. Its principal use is in the production of stationery, such as letterheads and business cards. It is also used in brochure work.
See Blind embossing, Die-stamping, Embossing.

Throw-away item *Print, Sales promotion*
An inexpensive item of print, or a small, inexpensive gift, distributed or offered to the public as a reminder or encouragement to take action, or to purchase a product.

Thumbnails *Advertising, Art direction, Creative, Design*
Tiny versions of larger visuals or layouts, usually for discussion by an internal design, advertising or marketing team. The standard is usually very basic and sketchy, with only the main features shown. The main advantage of thumbnails is that they can be drawn and developed quickly, and in large numbers, to illustrate what subsequent versions could look like.

Tied house *Business, Distribution, Retailing*
In the UK, a pub, bar or other outlet selling alcoholic drinks and other products, owned and supplied by a single organization. The retailer is 'tied' to the products and policy of the organization. The opposite situation is enjoyed by the owner or manager of a **free house**, who can buy products, services and equipment from any supplier.

TIFF *Desktop publishing, Information technology, Print,*
Production, Reprographics
Initials for **Tagged Image Format File**. One of the most-used image interchange formats used by DTP software. It is a file format popularly used for storing graphic images, and for supplying copy to repro houses. Although the technique is proprietary, originally developed jointly by Aldus and Microsoft, in recent years it has become an industry standard.

Till Countermanded   *Advertising, Media buying*

An instruction, also known as TC, by an advertiser to a publisher, to repeat the publication of an advertisement until specifically instructed to cease doing so. *Caveat*: When issuing media orders, it is always more secure to spell out instructions in full. Relying on initials as instructions is unsafe, since they can be misunderstood or misinterpreted. In the USA, the equivalent of this instruction is **Till Forbid**.
See TC.

Tilt   *Film, Television, Video*

To swing a camera in the vertical plane. In other words, to move a camera on its mounting up or down in a vertical arc, following the action during a shoot.
See Pan.

Time segments   *Advertising, Media buying, Television*

Specified periods during the broadcasting day during which an advertiser may buy time for screening commercials. Each segment has a different audience popularity, and is therefore charged at a different rate on that basis.

Tint   *Artwork, Desktop publishing, Print, Word-processing*

A tone area of a solid colour, usually achieved with dots or lines. The end result is an apparent shade or pastel of the solid colour. There are endless variations of tint and dot patterns, from regular to random. In the computerized creation of art, computer software can generate a wide variety of dot shapes.
See Dot gain, Halftone, Screen.

Titling   *Film, Television, Video*

Words shown on a television or cinema screen, including credits and sub-titles.

Toner   *Reprographics*

A chemical used to form the image in photocopying and laser printing.

Tooth   *Paper, Print*

A surface characteristic of paper, implying a slightly rough finish that enables it to take ink readily.

Track   *Film, Television, Video*

A short-form term for sound track.

Trade and technical media   *Advertising, Publishing*

Publications for a targeted technical and industrial readership, not for consumers. Also termed **technical media**. Many have a reader reply service, through which readers can send for literature on products and services advertised or featured in editorial.

Trade Descriptions Act 1968 *Legislation*

A British law dealing with descriptions of goods offered for sale. Its aim is to prevent and deal with misleading statements in promotional material about products and services.

Trade discounts *Retailing, Wholesaling*

Discounts applied by wholesalers to list and catalogue prices, on products supplied to retailers and re-sellers, who sell on to consumers and end-users. Reduced trade discounts are sometimes offered to consumers by main suppliers and wholesalers, especially when the goods are bought in greater than normal consumer quantities.

Trade fair *Advertising, Exhibitions, Marketing, Sales promotion*

An exhibition held to promote products and services to professional, trade and technical buyers. Exhibitors usually invite existing and potential customers to these events. Usually, the trade press is used by event organizers, to advertise them to wider audiences.

Trade-in *Business, Retailing*

A discount offered by a supplier to a customer as part of a deal involving a previous purchase. The customer trades in the used product in exchange for a discount on the new. Since the used product may have a re-sale value for the supplier, both parties benefit. Cars and capital equipment are popularly traded in this way.

Trademark *Branding, Business*

A design incorporating a word or words, a name, a drawing, symbol or other graphic device, a picture, a colour or colours and, strictly speaking, is legally registered. Registration of the mark under an appropriate parliamentary act entitles the owner exclusive use of it. An organization's appointed agent may use its trademark, with the permission of the owner. A trademark can also be established by long use.

From the marketing point of view, the creation of a registered trademark has practical use. Ideally, it becomes a branding tool, identifying the owner and the product. It establishes a direct link with the product or service it represents; differentiates it from the competition; warns the competition off. It deters unauthorized use and passing off, because the penalties for doing so are usually severe.

A trademark can sometimes actually become a product in itself, as in the case of the BBC, which is known worldwide by its trademark. With BBC broadcasting, there is no tangible product. It exists only when the viewer or listener switches on the television or radio and tunes to a BBC station.

Trade name *Business*

The trading name of an organization, as distinct from its **trademark** (*qv*). A trade name may also be the name of a product in an organization's portfolio.

Trade press   *Media, Publishing*
Newspapers, magazines and journals published for, and devoted to the interests of, particular trades, industries, businesses and professions. Most of them carry advertising appropriate to the readership. Many of these publications have a reader reply service, through which readers can send for literature on products and services advertised or featured in editorial.

Trade prices   *Distribution, Retailing, Wholesaling*
Prices on goods offered by manufacturers and wholesalers to distributors, re-sellers and retailers. These are structured discounts, usually pitched at a level that enables the traders to sell on to consumers at a profit.

Trade promotion   *Distribution, Retailing, Wholesaling*
A promotional campaign mounted by a manufacturer or wholesaler, aimed at the retail trade. This usually incorporates advertising, public relations, direct mail, sales literature, field selling and, often, small regional exhibitions.

Trading stamps   *Retail promotion*
A retail marketing technique involving the distribution of discount stamps to purchasers of goods and services. Customers are encouraged to buy from outlets offering the stamps, to collect, and eventually redeem the stamps for products or cash.

Traffic   *Advertising and PR campaigns*
The department of an advertising or public relations agency responsible for organizing and progressing the flow of production activity. Its job is to ensure that work is commissioned and completed on time and, together with the appropriate documentation, everything ends up in the right place. The ultimate aim is that the agency should be able to bill its clients accurately, avoiding problems, post-mortems and delays in payment.

Traffic   *Marketing research*
The volume of people or cars passing a poster or specific point in a street; entering a store, or passing through a department in a store. Monitoring and recording this movement is termed a **traffic count**.

Trailer   *Broadcasting, Cinema, Radio, Television*
A short promotional item, containing advance notice of a broadcasting or cinema event.

Transactional purchasing   *E-marketing, Marketing planning*
The way customers habitually buy products or services based on the understanding of facts about the brand, its availability and price. Such a purchasing technique, rightly or wrongly, assumes that the customer has no particular preference either for supplier or brand. The decision to purchase is assumed to be non-emotional,

although emotional motives are never entirely absent. The popularity of Internet buying has increased transactional purchasing; marketers may therefore need to consider a different, more appropriate approach to Internet marketing campaigns. *See* Relational purchasing.

Transparency   *Advertising, Photography, Studio work*
A positive image designed to be viewed by transmitted light. Light must pass through it for it to be seen or reproduced. In popular studio and marketing communications terminology, it is referred to as a **trannie**; sometimes as a **slide**.

Transport advertising   *Outdoor advertising*
Advertising material displayed on public transport vehicles: buses, taxis, underground, metro and subway trains. The term is also used for advertising displayed at bus stops, stations – both underground and over-ground, airports and maritime ports. Oddly, 'outdoor' is used also in connection with advertising displayed inside transport vehicles and stations.

Transpose   *Proof-correction, Typesetting, Typography*
An instruction in copy editing, typesetting and proof-correction, to move letters, digits, words and lines from one position to another. To exchange the position of a letter, word or line of copy with another letter, word or line. The instruction '**tr**' is written in the margin, and a line or ring put round the matter to be transposed. Obviously, the new position is indicated also.

Trapping   *Print*
The ability to print a wet ink over a previously printed ink. **Dry trapping** is printing wet ink over dry ink. **Wet trapping** is printing wet on wet.

Treatment   *Advertising, Cinema, Commercials, Television*
The main content of a commercial, promotional film or cinema production, written in non-technical form. It is designed not only to describe the broad action and sequences, but often also to convey the atmosphere and environment of the production.

Trend analysis   *Business, Marketing management*
A technique for identifying and evaluating the drift or movement in the increase or decline of a business or marketing activity. This includes enquiries, sales, profits and Web site hits. Ideally, the trend should be capable of quantification – measurement – so that the numbers can be processed, charted and manipulated.

Trial order   *Purchasing, Sales*
A small quantity of a product, ordered and paid for by a buyer, generally for the purpose of test and evaluation. If the product proves satisfactory, and cost-effective, the buyer may be encouraged to order a larger quantity.

Trickle down *Retailing*
A trend by sections of the consuming public to move towards cheaper products.

Trim marks *Artwork, Print*
Marks placed on copy to indicate the edge of the page.

T-space *Advertising*
An press advertisement space in the shape of a T; and a T-shaped poster on the side of a bus. Neither need be symmetrical. The T-shaped press advertisement format is not often used, though very powerful on a newspaper or magazine page; it is usually priced by negotiation.

Tube card *Outdoor advertising, Transportation advertising*
The common term for an advertisement displayed inside carriages on London's Underground network.

Turkey *Advertising, Cinema, Television, Video*
A cruel, colloquial expression sometimes used in trade magazines, signifying an unsuccessful commercial, television programme or cinema film.

Turnover *Advertising, Business, Marketing*
A company's sales revenue, in financial figures, over a specified period. Advertising agencies that give their turnover on media sales usually term them **billings**. This should not be confused with an agency's total turnover, which may include sales of print, research and other services.

Turn-round rate *Sales*
Sales of a product over a specified period, expressed as the amount of stock held during the period and subsequently sold.

TVR *Advertising, Media, Media planning and buying, Television*
Shorthand for **Television Rating**. A technique for measuring television viewing audiences. One TVR is equal to 1 per cent of a specified television audience, segment or potential audience. A rating may be enumerated in terms of individual viewers, homes, families, children, and so on.
See Television rating points.

Twin wire *Paper, Print*
A two-ply paper or board, made on a paper-making machine with duplicated wire components. Two sheets of the same composition are formed and combined, wire-side to wire-side, so that the finished sheet has two identical printing surfaces.

Type area *Advertising, Press, Print*
The physical area of a newspaper or magazine page containing type matter and illustrations; it excludes the margins. Also, the area occupied by advertising matter

on a page of a publication. The same term and principle applies to printed literature. The dimensions used are centimetres or inches, depending on whether the publication is within the metric or US sphere of influence.

Typeface *Desktop publishing, Typesetting, Typography, Word-processing*
The design of a particular type style, with its own name. Arial, Baskerville, Bodoni, Garamond, Times Roman and Univers, for example, are typefaces. The term face is often applied in distinguishing styles of typeface. For example, serif, sans serif, slab serif, old face, transitional, modern and script are variations on face. Within this definition, Arial and Univers are sans serif; Bodoni, modern; Rockwell, slab; Baskerville, old face. Every marketing professional needs a good knowledge of typography; besides, it is a fascinating study in its own right.

Type high *Print, Typesetting*
In letterpress printing, the standard height of the printing surface of a character above the base of the forme: 0.918 in.

Typescript *Creative, Editorial, Publishing*
Typewritten copy. Do not confuse this with **manuscript** (*qv*), which is hand-written. Oddly, publishers usually refer to typescripts as manuscripts.

Typographer *Advertising, Creative and studio personnel, Editorial,*
Packaging, Print, Publishing
A studio artist specializing in the specification, use and manipulation of type. After a rough layout has been produced by a studio, a typographer may be assigned to specify the typefaces most appropriate for the readership, product, publication and so on. Typographers also design original typefaces for editorial pages and advertisements, and for products and their packaging.
See Copy, Hard copy.

Uu

UCR *Print, Reprographics*
Initials for **Under Colour Removal**. A technique used in four-colour process printing, replacing elements of cyan, magenta and yellow with black. This helps to avoid undesirable build-up of ink in dark areas on a printed sheet.

Ultraviolet *Optics, Photography, Pressroom, Print, Reprographics*
Part of the non-visible spectrum, with a wavelength shorter than blue light. Its presence causes blue colour distortion, which may need laboratory correction, and makes distant scenes appear hazy.

In pressroom practice, ink is now usually dried (actually, cured) by exposure to ultraviolet radiation. The more volatile inks are dried by jets of warmed or heated air.

U-Matic *Television, Video*
A video-cassette tape format, using ¾-inch tape. This is high-band, near-broadcast quality, and therefore a very practical format for commercial material. It is excellent for creative presentations, being able to deliver higher quality than VHS (*qv*).

Uncoated *Paper, Print*
Printing paper with no coating on the surface or surfaces to be printed. Coating is a material applied to the printing surface of paper; usually a mixture of china clay, latex and other loadings, to fill up surface pits and improve the surface as a whole. A number of techniques are used, including roll coating, blade coating, air-knife coating and brush coating, and combinations of these. Cast coating is one of the highest quality techniques.

Union paper *Packaging, Print*
Paper produced by combining two webs or sheets with bitumen, or similar moisture- or vapour-resistant material.

Unique selling proposition *Advertising, Marketing*
A concept created and developed by US advertising agency creative director, Rosser Reeves. The essence of the USP (as it became popularly known) was that with every product there is one unique and outstanding feature or consumer benefit that will seize the consumer's imagination and sell the product. Reeves maintained that, however the message is dressed up, a product's USP should be used relentlessly and continuously. Reeves set out this philosophy in *Reality in Advertising*,

a booklet he wrote for the staff of the Ted Bates Agency, which he co-founded. Needless to say, it became a best seller throughout the advertising business worldwide.

Unit *Pressroom, Print*
A complete printing unit in a pressroom or print shop. In multicolour presses, the combination of inking, plate and impression operations in printing each colour. Thus, a six-colour press has six complete units, each with its own inking, plate and impression functions.

Unit pack *Packaging, Retailing*
A pack containing a single product. Packs containing several products, such as cereals aimed at children, are termed **multiple packs**. Where two or more units of the same product are combined and sold as one unit, this is termed **banded pack**; they are usually held together with self-adhesive tape.

Unit pricing *Retailing*
The pricing of an item of merchandise by weight or volume. This usually means the indicating of the price of a specified weight or volume of product, together with the selling price displayed on the shelf. For example: a certain weight of pre-packed ice cream is marked at a particular price; alongside this is given the cost of 100 gm of the ice cream. This enables consumers to compare the cost of one brand of ice cream with others in the cabinet.

Universal product code *Packaging, Retailing*
A series of digits identifying a product, particularly groceries and other fast-moving consumer goods. The numbers are printed above a machine-readable bar code. In Europe, 13 digits are used, identifying the product and its origin. Thus, 3017760000109, with its bar code equivalent, represents Danone's 'Lu, Véritable Petit Beurre' biscuits, manufactured and distributed in France.

Universe *Marketing research*
The total number of a population from which samples may be selected.

Unload *Distribution*
To dump a quantity of goods on a company, or a country, at low prices, with a view to getting rid of them quickly. The European Union has quite tough regulations aimed at preventing the unloading of such goods from countries outside the Union.

Unsolicited goods *Controls, Marketing*
Goods sent to an individual or company without an order or prior consent. Book and CD distributors often do this, in order to encourage recipients to join and buy future selections. In the UK, the recipient is not legally required to accept or return the goods, but must take good care of them until the sender eventually collects

them. Should the sender not collect within six months, the goods become the property of the recipients.

Unstructured interview *Consumer research, Marketing research*
A technique for interviewing a respondent without the aid of a questionnaire. From the respondent's point of view, the interview seems informal, possibly even random. However, the interview is actually highly structured, the interviewer having a checklist of topics to be covered. The interviewer guides the discussion towards the topics to be covered, and the respondent is allowed to talk freely, and in depth. This produces the kind and quality of information almost impossible to elicit with a structured format. This technique is often used for interviewing groups of consumers, specialists and professionals, and focus groups.

-up *Print, Production*
To take full advantage of the capability of a press, the imposition of material on large-size sheets. For example, where eight complete pages of a publication are printed on a single sheet, this is referred to as '**eight-up**'.

UPC *Packaging, Retailing*
See Universal product code.

Up-market *Consumer behaviour, Marketing*
A slightly sardonic, but perfectly realistic, term for consumer purchasing behaviour and product use. It implies that the consumers in question have nothing to do with bargain, cut-price, discounted or low quality products, but always go for the best. This usually also means the higher-priced end of the spectrum. Retailers respond to up-market consumer buying habits by maintaining higher prices. Often, retailers in certain city areas may all follow the up-market trend; as in Bond Street, London and Fifth Avenue, New York.

Upper case *Desktop publishing, Typesetting, Typography, Word-processing*
The capital letters in a typesetting alphabet, also known as capitals or caps (qv). The small letters are termed lower case (*qv*).

The origin of this, like many terms used in printing, is both historical and fascinating. Before the adoption of computerized and mechanical typesetting, type was assembled by hand by compositors in a composing room. Wooden or metal type, comprising capital letters, small letters, numerals and symbols was stored in drawers, in cabinets known as cases. The upper cases contained capitals; the lower, small letters.
See Font, Lower case, Roman.

Up-rating *Photography, Reprographics*
Using a film or emulsion at a higher shutter-speed than that for which it was designed. This effectively under-exposes the film, which is compensated for by extra development time.

Up-weighted discount *Advertising, Media planning and buying, Television*
A negotiated discount on purchased airtime. This may be agreed to by the television contractor's sales department when an advertiser undertakes to spend more than can be accommodated by a regular discount. By a short stretch of the imagination, it may be compared to an upgrade given to a passenger on an airline.

URL *Information technology, Internet practice*
Initials for **Universal Resource Locator**; also referred to as **Uniform Resource Locator**. The obscure, confusing, but currently standard term for an address, page or any resource, on the World Wide Web. For example, the full URL of the Chartered Institute of Marketing is http://www.cim.co.uk; the British Broadcasting Corporation is http://www.bbc.co.uk.

Use by *Packaging, Product management, Retailing*
A phrase printed on a product pack, followed by a date. In current practice, this form of date coding indicates the time limit by which the contents should be used by the consumer. In theory, date coding is a measure designed to ensure that the customer receives the product in reasonably fresh condition; or at least in good condition. In practice, it covers the producer and retailer against accusations of negligence.

However, date-coding on packaging is a cause for confusion. 'Best before' is a popular date formula used in retail packaging in the UK. This is probably the most confusing of all, since it seems to imply that the consumer should open the pack by the date; or else use the product before the date. Either that, or that it should be displayed on a retailer's shelf until that date, and then discarded. This misleading terminology may be phased out in due course. In reality, products sold in packs, especially cans, can often safely be used months, years, or even decades after the 'best before' date.

Sometimes, packs bear the phrase 'Display until', followed by a date. This indicates more clearly what is meant – that the retailer should display the product on his shelves until the date shown, after which it should be removed. Moreover, some packs bear both 'Best before' and 'Display until'. There seems to be no national or international standard for date coding.

The French have a realistic and clear approach, using 'A consommer de préferénce avant fin', followed by the date by which the product should be *consumed.*

User-friendly *Consumer and technical products, Information technology*
An adjective implying that a particular product, service, piece of equipment or instruction manual is easy to use.

USP *Advertising, Marketing*
Unique selling proposition (*qv*).

Vv

Vacuum frame   *Photography, Print, Production*
A device for holding copy and reproduction material in intimate contact during
photographic exposure. In plate-making, the emulsion sides of film and plate must
be in absolute contact, with no air bubbles between them.

Varnish   *Print, Production*
A thin, protective coating applied to a printed sheet. A varnish can also be
incorporated into the ink vehicle.
See Vehicle.

VCR   *Television, Video*
Video-Cassette Recorder. Do not confuse with VTR, **Videotape Recording.** The
problem with using initials is that they will always confuse *somebody*. In issuing
orders, contracts, media instructions and legally binding documents, it is prudent
to be specific, and to spell out all terminology in full.

Vegetable parchment   *Paper, Print*
A specialized paper modified by the application of sulphuric acid. This gives it a
smooth, continuous texture, increased surface hardness, and high resistance to
penetration by oil, fat and grease. It also makes it resistant to disintegration, even
at the boiling point of water.

Vehicle   *Media*
A term sometimes used to denote a publication used, or to be used, for carrying
an advertisement or advertising campaign. Also used in the same context in public
relations practice.

Vehicle   *Print technology*
In printing inks, the fluid component that acts as a carrier for the ink pigment.

Vellum   *Paper, Print*
A paper made to simulate the fine, smooth surface of parchment. Often used for
certificates, diplomas, indentures, title deeds and so on.

Velox   *Photography*
Jargon for a photographic paper print made from a screen negative. This term is
used mainly in the USA.

Verified Free Distribution *Media*
Usually abbreviated to **VFD**. A circulation-auditing service for free newspapers and magazines; a subsidiary of the Audit Bureau of Circulations (*qv*). Like **ABC**, it offers publishers and advertisers independently researched, accurate data on the number of copies actually distributed.
See Audit Bureau of Circulations, Circulation, Controlled circulation, Penetration, Rate card, Reader, Readership, Television rating points, Viewer.

Verso *Print, Publishing*
A left-hand page, usually bearing an even number; the reverse side of **recto** (*qv*), a right-hand page.

Vertical circulation *Advertising, Marketing, Media*
The circulation and readership of a publication aimed at subscribers across a particular business or industry. For example, *Marketing Business*, read mostly by individuals in the marketing business; *The Accountant*, read predominantly by accountants. The other type of circulation is **horizontal**, where a publication is read by individuals across a range of industries. For example, the *Financial Times*, *Business Week* and *Forbes*.

Vertical integration *Business, Marketing, Retailing*
The merger of two companies, or the acquisition of one by another, within a market. Since they are within different parts of the same channel, eg a manufacturer merging with a retail organization, they complement each other.

Vertical publication *Advertising, Marketing, Media*
A publication aimed at subscribers and readers of a single type, profession or trade; or of one set of demographic characteristics.
See Vertical circulation.

VHS *Television, Video*
Video Home System. A video-cassette tape format, using half-inch tape. The quality is satisfactory for domestic use, but can be sub-standard for top-notch creative presentations. It is nowhere near good enough for use in broadcasting. VHS was conceived and developed by the Japanese company JVC. For some years, several systems competed for the commercial market, including Beta-max and Philips 2000; these have long since gone to the graveyard.

The quality of videotape reproduction depends on four factors: tape speed, head rotation speed, width of tape and the quality of the coating material. **U-Matic** uses tape wider than VHS, and has higher head and tape speeds; consequently, the quality of reproduction is higher.

VHS is intrinsically a good system, but is sometimes let down by camcorders (*qv*) and playback machines used with the cassettes. Digital recording and playback systems are overtaking and improving everything now in use, delivering very high-quality standards, especially at the broadcast end of the spectrum.
See U-Matic.

Video   *Film, Script-writing, Television and video pre-production*
In a script, usually divided into two columns, one column is devoted to describing the action. This is usually termed the video column, and headed, simply, **video**. The other column, termed **audio**, is devoted to the words. Audio and video run side by side in the script. Alternative terms for audio and video are **sound** and **picture**. Sometimes, **action** is used at the head of the video column.

Video News Release   *Broadcast communications, Editorial,*
                                                          Public relations
A corporate or product news item, prepared and edited before submission to television stations. Popularly referred to as **VNR**. Current wisdom on VNRs is that, on a busy news day a VNR can get an item on air mainly because it is already in the can; that is, complete and ready for transmission. However, mere submission of a VNR will not guarantee airtime.

At the time of writing this edition, pre-edited news packages are gradually being replaced by shorter news-bites and sound-bites. This applies particularly to company news, launches and mergers. Producers are realizing that it is more useful for viewers if there is someone available in front of a camera to answer presenters' questions. This is particularly the case when there has been a national, political, economic or corporate strategic shift, or when an important event has already occurred.

The keys to the success of VNRs are clarity, brevity, news-worthiness, editorial integrity and independence. A VNR must also be capable of being re-edited to suit an individual programme's style. *Caveat*: unless VNRs are properly researched, produced and tailored, they can resemble corporate advertising. Producers do not like them or accept them.

Viewer   *Advertising, Broadcast media, Media research*
A viewer is defined as a person in a room with a TV set switched on for at least 15 consecutive seconds. In television terms, in the room means anything from watching attentively, to a casual glance at the screen while doing something else. *See* Television rating points.

Viewer   *Film post-production*
A machine for viewing film, part of an **editing suite**.

Vignette   *Artwork, Photography, Reprographics, Typography*
The shading of a tonal area so that it gradually fades away. In artwork, this originally applied to an ornament around a capital letter, particularly one without a definite border. In current artwork and photographic practice, an illustration shaded off at the edges. With halftone illustrations, this is achieved by gradually tapering off the size of dots at the edges of an illustration. In information technology and desktop publishing, the technique is termed **degrade**, **graduation**, **graduated fill** and **fountain fill**. Two opposing vignettes in the same area are termed a **blend**.

Viscosity *Print, Printing inks*

The property of a fluid to resist physical change, such as internal relative motion and friction. With printing inks, a general term denoting the properties of **tack** and **flow**.

Vision mixer *Television studio personnel*

An assistant director, working in the control room, or **gallery**, responsible for switching from camera to camera during a production.

Visual *Artwork, Creative, Print, Production*

A drawing board layout representing the design of an editorial page, advertisement or piece of print. There are several qualities of visual, from the cheapest, basic scribble to the highly polished version used for boardroom presentations.

A **flimsy** or **scamp** is a pencil or marker rendering of first ideas. Flimsy is so called because the paper usually used for flimsies is itself flimsy; sometimes also termed **detail paper**. I'll buy a drink for the first reader of this dictionary who can provide me with the true origin, in this context, of the word **scamp**.

A rough is a step up from flimsy, indicating that it has developed from the original basic visual. Usually done to a better standard, with readable headlining and recognizable illustrations. Roughs are usually used for internal discussion, and are not for the eyes of clients or directors.

A **finished rough** is a good-looking visual of fair quality. Sometimes, clients are presented with visuals of this standard. Many design groups and agencies, however, are unwilling to go forward to client presentation stage with finished roughs, even though they are economical and show a prudent regard for clients' money.

Presentation visuals are first-class visuals, with typeset headlines and subheads. Where layouts are created on computer, which is the norm in industrialized countries, body copy is often shown as readable text.

Visual aids *Presentations, Training*

Physical materials used in lectures, presentations, education and training. These include audio and video recordings, slides, overhead projection acetates, whiteboards, flip-charts, and software-generated aids such as Microsoft PowerPoint. The general idea is to make the intellectual material being presented easier to absorb and understand.

Visualizer *Advertising creative personnel, Artwork, Professional titles,*
Studio practice

An artist who understands marketing, advertising and public relations briefs, interprets them and turns them into creative visual ideas. During the late 19th century, and the first half of the 20th, these clever creatives were generally termed commercial artists. In the 1950s and 1960s, the salaries and fees they were able to command increased, and they began to be called visualizers. After about 1970 the financial rewards again rose, steeply. They are now known as **art directors**.

Visuals   *Film and video technique*
Shots illustrating informative or explanatory speech, usually voice-overs, accompanying filmed or video action.

VNR   *Broadcast communications, Editorial, Public relations*
Initials, **Video News Release** (*qv*).

VO   *Film, Radio, Television, Video*
Voice-over (*qv*). The instruction in a script for a voice-over to begin.

Voice-over   *Film, Radio, Television, Video*
In television and film scripts, this indicates where spoken words are to be heard while action is taking place on screen. Blind voice-overs are usually not in **lip-synch** (in synchronization with an actor's lips), but linked to the action.
   In entertainment, voice-overs are the equivalent of speech bubbles in a printed cartoon. *Caveat*: when voice-over and titling are different, it can be very confusing to the viewer; and sometimes absolutely hilarious.
   In television commercials, voice-overs are used for delivering sales points, comments or thoughts. Widely used while a **caption**, a still picture, is on screen, often accompanying **titling** (*qv*).
   In scripting, a range of initials denotes who should be speaking a voice-over. **MVO** denotes a male voice-over; **FVO**, a female voice-over.
See Commercial, Still, Titling.

Volatile memory   *Computers, Information technology*
Computer memory requiring uninterrupted power supply to retain the data it stores. Once the power has been switched off, even momentarily, the data are lost.

Volume   *Audio, Film, Television, Video*
Intensity or loudness of sound. In the studio, this is controlled by a calibrated fader. An end-user can do this by operating a control on the equipment, or by the use of a hand-held remote control device.

Volume discount   *Media, Trade*
A discount applied by a vendor to the price of a commodity when purchased in higher-than-average quantity. In press media sales, a discount offered when a substantial amount of advertising space is bought by an advertiser in a single order; or when several orders are aggregated. The discount is applied to the total amount bought. Such discounts are sometimes given in publishers' rate cards; often, they are arrived at by negotiation. The other type of media discount is **frequency discount** (*qv*).

Voluntary chain   *Retailing*
A group of independent retailers functioning collectively, pooling some of their resources, sharing overheads and expenses, and acting as a single buying unit. In

this way they are able to take advantage of suppliers' discounts, negotiate from a position of strength, drive prices down, and compete with major players such as supermarket chains. In the UK and the European Union, SPAR is one of the popular voluntary chains. Also termed a **voluntary group**.

Voucher *Advertising, Media*

Proof of publication of a press advertisement. Where the advertisement has appeared in a newspaper, only a **tearsheet**, a cutting, is generally offered as proof. With magazine advertising, sometimes a complete copy of the magazine may be supplied. This is usually subject to the generosity of the publisher; but it may also be specified in the media order or contract.

VTR *Video production*

Initials for **Videotape Recording**. See my comments under **VCR**.

Ww

Walk-off *Print*
Deterioration of part of an image area on a plate during litho printing.

WAP *Communications, Information technology, Marketing, Telephony*
Initials for **Wireless Application Protocol**. A technology that allows a user to access information on an Internet server, using a hand-held radio communication device such as a mobile telephone. Currently, it can run on virtually any operating system or hardware. WAP devices provide basic browsers displaying basic graphics and text-based information on a small screen. Marketers have not been slow to exploit WAP technology. Advertising, and information on products and services, are becoming commonplace on WAP networks. This calls for owners' permission, and is regulated both by voluntary and legal controls.

Warehouse *Information technology, Marketing*
Also termed **data warehouse**. An electronic store for very large amounts of information collected via credit card or electronic transactions, or input from paper sources. Consumer data warehouses hold information essential to marketing and **customer relationship management**. Data can include customer demographics, lifestyle information, product purchase, frequency, preference and usage habits. Once the data required is specified, warehousing software can isolate it for processing and incorporation into a marketing programme.

Warm colour *Photography, Print*
In multicolour printing, a colour with a reddish or yellowish cast. In photography, a reddish cast, usually unintentional and unwanted, either through a fault in the film stock, or miscalculation in light values and the application of an incorrect optical filter.

Warranty *After-sales service, Marketing, Retailing, Sales*
An undertaking by a vendor, re-seller or retailer, to supply a product capable of performing as described, and to repair, replace or refund if it does not. Consumers' rights under the UK's Supply of Goods and Services Act 1982 are not affected, whatever the terms of a warranty.

Washing up *Press room practice, Print*
Also referred to as washing down. Cleaning the rollers, plates, formes or ink fountains of a press.

Wastage *Advertising, Media*

A term applying to press media circulation, and to broadcast channel audiences. However well targeted an advertising campaign, there will always be an element of waste in media selection. The advertiser pays for this, despite the wastage. For example, in targeting car owners for a television advertising campaign, there is always a proportion of poor, non-car-owning pensioners among the viewers. The advertiser cannot get rid of the wasted part of the audience, and has to pay for it along with the targeted part. The same applies to mass-circulation newspapers; some of the readership will neither own cars, nor ever be likely to.

Watermark *Paper, Print*

A design, trademark or logo, impressed into paper by a raised pattern in the dandy roll during manufacture. This feature is often used as a corporate or product branding feature, both by paper manufacturers and end users. Watermarks can be specially designed and commissioned.

Weak product *Marketing*

A product in decline, or one vulnerable to competitive attack due to its poor quality or to ineffectual marketing. Such a product could be at the end of its life cycle, with no realistic prospect of a re-launch.

Web *Print*

A reel or roll of paper used on rotary presses. The webs used to print national newspapers and magazines can be 14–19 km (9–12 miles) long. Smaller web-fed presses use webs smaller in length and diameter. There are also sheet-fed (*qv*) presses, which use individual sheets of paper.

Web *Communications, Computing, Information technology, Internet*

The current popular contraction for the **World Wide Web**; sometimes termed the **Internet**. This is the collection of millions of Web sites and pages that together form that part of the Internet most seen by users. The generic Internet also includes electronic mail, Usenet and newsgroups. The term Web is sometimes used to mean the graphical aspects of the Internet, since Web site pages usually comprise text, graphics, and links to other Web sites.

Web offset *Print*

A technique for printing from a curved printing surface using thin, flexible metal plates. In this case, presses print on continuous reels of paper, usually termed **webs**. The main characteristics of web offset are:

- Both sides are printed simultaneously.
- Prints at high speeds, 660 m (2,200 ft) per minute and more.
- Many web-fed presses have in-line finishing performed on the run. This includes cutting, slitting, collating, folding, saddle stitching, inserting, gluing of inserts, perforating and numbering.

See Flexography, Gravure, Litho.

Web tension   *Paper, Pressroom practice, Print*
The amount of tension or pull applied in the direction of travel of a web, by the action of a press. To avoid misprinting and stoppages, this needs careful monitoring and control, usually carried out by computer.

Weight   *Desktop publishing, Typesetting, Typography,*
                                                            Word-processing
The visual heaviness of a typeface, mainly the amount of ink it puts on the page when printed. Bold type is heavier than light type. The term also applies to the relative thickness of the individual strokes of a type character.
See Bold.

Weighting   *Planning, Research, Statistics*
Increasing or decreasing the relative importance of a statistical factor, figure or finding, by multiplying it by a pre-determined figure. This technique is designed to add to the weight of an argument and, eventually a management decision; or to subtract from it. For example: a small number of red-bearded individuals have spending power much greater than their number would suggest. To adjust their statistical influence relative to other spenders, it might be prudent to apply an appropriate weighting. On this basis, a decision could then be taken to adjust a marketing or promotional budget accordingly.

Wet end   *Paper-making*
The first stages of a paper-making machine, before the drying process begins. Once the basic pulp stock is on the machine, it is subjected to draining, pressing, drying and calendering. The far end of the machine is termed the **dry end**.

Wet on wet   *Print, Production*
In state-of-the-art multicolour printing, one colour printed on top of another before the first is dry.
See Cromalin, Trapping.

Wet proof   *Print, Production*
Using a printing press for proofing, ahead of a print run. This is slow, wasteful and expensive. There are better and more economical ways of doing it; using a special proofing press, or dry proofing.
See Cromalin, Dry proofing, Progressive proofs, Proof, Trapping.

White goods   *Marketing, Retailing*
Marketing jargon for certain consumer durables, usually those purchased infrequently, with high unit cost. This includes dishwashers, refrigerators, washing machines and food-mixers. When the term was coined, probably in the USA, in the 1930s and 1940s, such products were available only in white enamel. The term is used to distinguish them from **brown goods**, which include domestic furniture, storage units and carpets.

Widow *Composition, Copywriting, Desktop publishing, Typesetting, Typography*

A short line, or a single word on a line by itself, at the end of a paragraph. This sometimes happens naturally during type composition. When it does, copywriters are usually urged, or commanded, to rewrite the text so that the widow disappears. However, widows have their uses. A short line of two or three words at the end of a paragraph can encourage or seduce the reader's eye to jump quickly and easily to the next. Since advertisers need every possible potential customer to read all their copy, and take action at the end, widows make a positive contribution to this cause. No copywriter should be coerced into rewriting text for the sake of typographical symmetry. Why damage a promotional argument, or a perfectly competent piece of persuasive copy, for mere pedantry?

Wildcat *Marketing planning, Product portfolio planning*

Another term for **problem child** or **question mark**, one of the four conditions of a product within a portfolio, outlined in the Boston Matrix (*qv*). A product may have high growth, low market share, with good prospects, but possibly be under-performing. It may need high investment to reach its full profit potential; this could be a drain on the portfolio. The other three conditions indicated by the Matrix are:

Star

Product with high growth, high market share. May need high levels of funding.

Cash cow

Product with low growth, high market share. Could be the main source of funds for the problem children and stars in the portfolio.

Dog

A low growth, low market share product. Dubious performance. May qualify for removal from the portfolio.

See Boston Matrix

Window dressing *Retailing*

The art of designing and displaying products and promotional material in store windows. The idea is to put passing potential customers into a buying mood, and attract them into the store, as well as merely to show what is on offer. In mid-20th century London, Paris and New York the art of window dressing reached a peak of attraction and perfection. Some of it may still be seen in these cities today.

Window shopping *Consumer behaviour, Retailing*

A consumer habit of visiting and strolling round stores without actually making a purchase. All retailers know that this goes on, especially in wet and cold weather. However, they also know that consumers do shop around, looking for best buys. Whether or not retailers make the most of this perfectly reasonable aspect of human nature remains part of the management decision process.

Wipe *Film, Television, Video*
A technique for quitting one **shot** (*qv*) and bringing on the next, without cutting, dissolving or fading. This is usually done by reducing the existing shot in a movement from one side of the screen, with the next shot following it without a break. Sometimes this is done from top to bottom.

Popular wipes include the implosion, explosion, fragmentation and flying rectangle. Iris, circular and square wipes were favourite techniques during the silent film era. You can sometimes see them in today's commercials, though rarely in entertainment productions.

Wire binding *Binding, Finishing, Print, Production*
Also termed **wire-o binding**. A continuous double series of wire loops, run through punched slots along the binding edge of a booklet.

Wizard *Communications, Information technology*
A software utility that helps to create an application simply and easily, by offering a number of pre-designed alternatives. Microsoft Access, for example, offers a wizard for creating databases. The wizard prompts the user with questions, and creates a database based on the answers. Some publishing progams offer wizards for the creation of stationery, leaflets and brochures.

Wood-free *Paper, Print*
A paper that contains no mechanical wood pulp. In normal commercial practice, a small percentage of mechanical fibre is usually acceptable. It does not denote a paper or pulp made from materials other than wood. In newsprint, with papers used for newspapers, the furnish is mainly pulp, with some chemical pulp.

Wordspacing *Copywriting, Desktop publishing, Typography, Word-processing*
The space between individual words in typescript or typesetting.
See Letterspacing.

Work and tumble *Printing techniques*
Printing one side of a sheet, then turning it over from the gripper to the back, and printing the other side. The same guide and plate are used for the second side.

Work and turn *Printing techniques*
Printing one side of a sheet, then turning it over from left to right, retaining the same front edge but moving the side-lay edge of the sheet to the other side of the press. The same plate is used for printing both sides of the sheet.

Workgroup *Communications, Information technology*
A collection of computers connected by a network. The term is usually applied to a group of personal computers doing similar things within an organization. In an advertising or marketing agency, for example, a workgroup might comprise a sales department, an entire production department, or a number of individual researchers or copywriters.

Wove *Paper, Print*

Printing and stationery grade papers, made with a soft, smooth finish and uniform, unlined surface. In the 18th century, such paper was manufactured by forming it on a mould with a cover made of woven wire cloth. Stationery grades are usually **wove**, as described here, or **laid**, with a ribbed surface imparted by a wire roll during manufacture.

See Laid.

Wrap *Advertising*

Also termed **advertisement wrap**. Advertisements placed on the windows of vehicles – taxis, buses, trains – buildings, roadside shelters and so on. The image appears on the outer side of the vehicle, while remaining see-through from the inside.

Wraparound plate *Print*

In flexographic and rotary letterpress printing, a thin, one-piece plate wrapped round an impression cylinder, as on litho presses.

Wrinkles *Paper, Print*

Unwanted creases in paper caused by uneven moisture absorption. This sometimes happens when paper is transported or stored in unsatisfactory conditions, or stored over a considerable length of time. Apart from uneven printing, wrinkles can cause press stoppages. Both are among the wide range of printers' nightmares; a silent press is an unproductive one, and earns no revenue for the printer. This effect can sometimes occur with inks during drying.

Write-protected *Communications, Information technology*

A device on a magnetic storage disk, cassette or cartridge, protecting its contents from being overwritten. With computer disks, this is usually a slider, opening and closing a small aperture in one corner of the disk. When the aperture is open, the disk can be written to; when closed, it cannot. On VHS cassettes, the write-protect device is a tab at the back. If the tab is snapped off, the disk is safe from being over-written. On some types of disk, the reverse applies. When sending marketing data, production or promotional material on disk or cassette, extreme care should be taken to ensure that no over-writing is possible.

Wrong font *Proof correction, Typesetting*

In proof-reading, a mark in the margin indicating a character or numeral of the wrong face or size. International proof-correction marks use a symbol in the margin to indicate this; otherwise, the initials WF are used.

WYSIWYG *Computing, Desktop publishing, Information technology,*
Word-processing

Initials for **What You See Is What You Get**. A popular vulgarism, meaning that what you see on your computer screen resembles what will be printed after you hit the print button. Most word-processing packages have a 'view' mode, where you can see before you hit the button how the copy will be printed.

Xx

X   *Marketing communications*
This alphabetical character is commonly used in mathematics to represent an unknown quantity. In advertising and marketing, especially of domestic washing products, **Brand X** is any competitive brand, or a brand other than the one being shown in an advertisement. The term is used to imply that unknown brands, being anonymous, are inferior.

Xerography   *Graphic reproduction systems, Reprographics*
A proprietary electrostatic photocopying system, which uses a selenium-coated drum, and toner adhering to electrostatically charged paper, to produce the image. The term has, like Hoover, entered into English mainstream vocabulary, and can represent copying made on any similar system or machinery.

x-height   *Desktop publishing, Type, Typography*
The height of a lower case x. The x is regarded as typical of the lower case characters in a font without ascenders or descenders (*qv*). The higher this is, the more legible the copy. Some typefaces have quite low x-heights, making them unsuitable for body text; sometimes also even for display text.

XHTML   *Information technology, Internet practice*
Shorthand for Extensible Hypertext Mark-up Language. A Web page mark-up language combining HTML and XML. It provides a simpler method of creating Web pages capable of being displayed over a wide range of browsers.

XML   *Information technology, Internet practice*
Short for Extensible Mark-up Language. A Web mark-up language that allows designers to create their own tailor-made mark-up tags.

X-synch   *Photography, Reprographics*
On a camera, a shutter speed that synchronizes with electronic flash.

XXX   *Branding, Marketing communications*
Initials originally used to represent ale of triple strength. Today, four Xs are the brand-mark of an Australian canned alcohol product. The strength of the drink cannot be immediately assumed from the number of Xs used. However, the brand has become established in world markets without the aid of a comparative scale

of alcoholic strength. This illustrates the wisdom of using simple, timeless branding devices, acceptable in most cultures, and capable of being typeset without difficulty. Plus copious budgets for advertising.

Xylography   *Direct mail, Print*
A printing technique using wood blocks. The technique is sometimes used to achieve special effects for mailshots, often in combination with hand-made paper or specially made materials.

Yy

Y2K *Business, Information technology*
A popular abbreviation referring to The Year 2000. In 1998 and 1999 it was predicted that millions of computers throughout the world would be affected by a 'problem' appearing on 1 January 2000. It was assumed that many older personal computers and other devices would fail to recognize the date. This was because they were not designed to recognize the full four digits of the year, namely 2000, but only the final two digits. It was estimated that computers and devices with this fault would revert to 1980, or even 1900. Major fears arose: that guarantees of all kinds would be invalidated; that financial instruments such as investments and insurance policies would become useless; that aircraft would crash as their computers, and those of air traffic control, would fail. In the event, most organizations modified their systems in good time, and few suffered as predicted. Designers of computer operating systems may have learnt the lesson. . . but who knows?

Yahoo! *Information technology, Internet activity*
An Internet search engine that enables users to seek and find Web sites.

Yankee dryer *Paper manufacture*
A large drying cylinder that replaces the banks of smaller cylinders in paper-making machines. Diameters can be up to 5.5 m. It is widely used in the production of tissue paper.

Yearbook *Publishing*
An annual publication, most popularly that of a trade organization or association, in the form of a directory. Some yearbooks also carry editorial, dealing with issues of the current or previous year, obituaries, new developments, expectations, and so on.

Yellow *Print*
One of the subtractive primary colours used in four-colour process printing. It reflects red and green light and absorbs blue.
See Black, CYMK, Cyan, Magenta, Process colours.

Yield *Business*
Income or profit from a company's shares.

Yuppie   *Behavioural types, Media*
An amusing, if slightly sardonic, acronym, used by the media, for Young Upwardly mobile Professional, or Young Urban Professional. It is applied to members of a high-ranking socio-economic group of professionals working in cities. The term was coined in the mid-1980s.

Zz

Zahn cup *Print technology*
A device for the measurement of the viscosity of printing ink. This is achieved by measuring the time taken for ink to empty through a small hole in the base of the cup. Several standard holes are used, depending on the viscosity, density and composition of particular inks.

Zakazukha *Advertising, Editorial, Public relations, Publishing*
A Russian term indicating paid advertising masquerading as news. In 2001 a Russian public relations agency exposed the practice by offering a number of Moscow newspapers cash in exchange for editorial coverage of a store opening. Sixteen publications entered into negotiations, with 13 running the story. The agency later revealed that no store actually existed. The International Public Relations Association condemned the practice, stating that the issue was international, rather than simply a Russian one. It pointed out that as long as the practice of illicit paid-for editorial continued, the public could never have confidence in what they were reading in the press. The story, covered in UK public relations magazine *PR Week* in March 2001, reported that the IPRA was setting up an anti-zakazukha committee. Russian law requires differentiation between advertising and editorial copy.

In the UK, there is strong differentiation between editorial and advertising, and amazingly little zakazukha occurs. Editors hate it and will not be influenced either by money or advertising offered for editorial. Similarly, publishers dislike it; when exposed it can damage the reputation for honesty, trustworthiness and even-handedness of their media. This is particularly the case with business media.

Zapper *Television, Video*
A slang term for a hand-held, remote-control device, which enables television viewers to change channels without getting up from their chairs. Virtually all zappers now also operate teletext channels. Some zappers also operate video-cassette recorders; this enables viewers to speed through commercial breaks in video-recorded television entertainment or news, without watching them.

Zapping *Television*
Also termed **channel hopping**. Sometimes called the television advertiser's worst nightmare, it involves changing channels at high speed during commercial breaks.

Zero *Copywriting, Desktop publishing, Typesetting, Typography,*
Word-processing
A word used to differentiate between the characters 'o' or 'O', and the numeral
'0'. On screen, a zero is sometimes differentiated by a dot in the centre of the
character, or a slash running through it. In proof-reading, the difference is not
easily made, and can cause confusion and errors. Many typesetters refer to zero
as **nought, null** or **nuller**.
See Character, Monotype, Nought, Null, Proof, Proof-reader, Proof-reader's
marks, Quote.

Zero rating *Business, Taxation*
One of the ratings of European value added tax. Zero-rated products and services
are not liable for tax at the point of sale. The supplier, however, can recover from
the government the value added input tax paid on purchasing the products,
materials or services.

Zine *Advertising, Information technology, Internet marketing, Marketing*
Pronounced 'zeen' as in magazine. An Internet publication, usually free, usually
carrying and financed by advertising.

Zip code *Databases, Direct marketing*
In the US, a nine-digit numerical code used in the sorting and delivering of mail.
For example, Redmond, WA 98052-6393. The initials indicate Washington State.
The first three digits before the hyphen indicate the town; the last two, the local
area. The final four digits are an accurate location of the address of the office,
house or block. In some situations, a five-digit code is sufficient. For example,
Columbia, SC 29208. In the UK the term used is **postcode**; this uses an alpha-
numerical code, such as the BBC's at London: W1A 1AA. A similar system is used
in other countries including Canada.

Zip drive *Computing*
A computer peripheral storage device; a removable drive for disks, which can store
up to 100 megabytes of information. Capacity of 1 gigabyte is also available.

Zip pan *Film photography, Television and cinema commercials*
Also termed flash pan. A very quick camera panning move, giving a sudden
transition effect. This is a director's device designed to move the action to another
activity taking place at the same time; or to convey a feeling of bewilderment.

Zippertone *Artwork, Studio practice*
A proprietary system for applying a range of halftone screens to artwork on the
drawing board. It comprises backing sheets coated with self-adhesive halftone
material mounted on one side. Its main use is to add shades of grey toning to line
or wash illustrations. Screens in the range are either regular, irregular or random.
The halftone material is cut to shape and rubbed, adhesive side down, on to the

required part of the artwork. Alternatively, the material is roughly shaped, rubbed down, then cut accurately to the required shape.
See Letraset.

Zipping   *Audience behaviour, Video*
When viewing television programmes on video equipment, fast-forwarding through commercials. Some state-of-the-art video-cassette recorders can be programmed to zip automatically.

Zoom   *Cinema, Commercials, Photography, Television*
An optical effect used in filming, in which an object seems to draw closer to the camera, or the camera to the object (zoom in); or draw away (zoom out). This is achieved with the use of special, variable-focus zoom lenses, whose focal length can be varied during shooting, changing the magnification of the image. The change is made in a smooth, continuous action. A similar effect can be achieved using an optical printer during post-production.

Zoom   *Computer graphics, Information technology*
To enlarge a screen area containing graphics or text, so that it becomes easier to see and work on.

Zoom lens   *Photography, Reprographics*
A lens with movable elements, allowing the focal length to be varied. In still photography and reprographic equipment, zoom lenses allow any focal length in a range between two fixed points. The most popular photo zoom lenses are moderate wide-angle to standard, 28–50 mm; and short to medium telephoto, 80–200 mm. Zoom lenses offering ratios greater than 1:3 are sometimes of inferior quality, or give inferior results.

Appendix 1
US English, Queen's English

English is used throughout the world; it is the language of science, of the airlines and the Internet. For this reason, it is worth taking care over how you use it. This is particularly important when preparing campaigns for the USA and areas under US influence.

There are over 200 differences between Queen's English and the US version. There are differences in spelling, as well as in meaning. There are also differences in pronunciation. In England, buoy is pronounced 'boy'; in New England, it is pronounced 'boo-ee'; in New York, Houston is pronounced 'howston', not 'hewston'.

There is a pragmatic reason for this phenomenon. The British see more US films and television shows than Americans do UK ones. The British are therefore fairly familiar with how US English sounds. Some Americans, on the other hand, regard Queen's English as something of a medieval curiosity; perhaps even slightly alien. I have been misunderstood in upper-crust New Jersey, when I thought I was speaking Queen's impeccable English.

Some of the major differences between the two languages, in meaning and in spelling, are listed below. Proper nouns are capitalized.

QUEEN'S ENGLISH	US ENGLISH
admitted to hospital	hospitalized
aerial	antenna
aluminium	aluminum
analyse	analyze
angry	mad
anywhere	anyplace
autumn	fall
banknote	bill
barrister, solicitor	attorney
bill (restaurant, bar)	check, tab
biscuit	cookie
bonnet (car)	hood
book in (hotel)	check in
bowler (hat)	derby (pronounced derby, not darby)
boot (car)	trunk

braces	suspenders
brought up (in childhood)	raised
bumper (vehicle)	fender
buoy (pronounced boy in England)	buoy (pronounced boo-ee in New England)
called (a man called James)	named (a man named James)
car	automobile
caravan	trailer, camper
caretaker	janitor
centre	center
check it, check it over	check it out
chemist	drugstore
cheque (bank cheque)	check
chips	French fries
cider	applejack
cinema	the movies
colour	color
condom	rubber
constable (police)	patrolman, officer
cooker	stove
corn	maize
cot	crib
cotton (sewing)	thread
crash (vehicle)	wreck
crisps	potato chips
crossroads	intersection
cupboard	closet
curtains	drapes
defence	defense
deliver	ship
different from	different than
dinner jacket, dinner suit	tuxedo, tux
diversion	detour
draughts (board game)	checkers
drawing pin	thumbtack
drop in	drop by
dual carriageway	divided highway
dummy (baby's)	pacifier
dustbin, rubbish bin	trashcan, garbage can
dustman	garbage collector
dynamo (car)	generator
engine	motor
engine driver	engineer
estate agent	realtor
fag (slang, cigarette)	fag (homosexual, offensive)

Father Christmas	Kris Kringle
fewer (people, things)	less (colloquial)
film	movie
finished	through
first violin	concertmaster
flat	apartment
flyover	overpass
fortnight	two weeks
gaol, jail	jail
garden	yard
gear-lever	shift, gear shift
got	gotten
graduate	alumnus
grill	broiler
ground floor	first floor
guard (train)	conductor
handbag	purse, pocketbook
hoarding	billboard
holiday	vacation
honour	honor
Houston (pronounced hewston)	Houston (pronounced 'howston' in New York)
ill	sick
in a moment	momentarily
interval (theatre)	intermission
I suppose	I guess
jewellery	jewelry
jug	pitcher
ladder (tights)	run
leader (orchestra)	concertmaster
lift	elevator
lose	lose out
lorry, van	truck
luggage	baggage
macintosh, raincoat	raincoat
mad	crazy
main road	highway
maize	corn
marmot	woodchuck
maths	math
mean (not generous)	stingy
meet	meet with
mobile home	trailer home
motorway	freeway, expressway, parkway
nappy	diaper

nasty, vicious	mean
nowhere	noplace
nursing home	private hospital
oblique stroke	slash
offence	offense
offender (criminal)	perpetrator
off-licence	liquor store
optician, oculist	optometrist
out of bounds	off limits
pack of cards	deck of cards
paraffin	kerosene
pavement	sidewalk
peep	peek
petrol	gas, gasolene
plain	prairie
plough	plow
post	mail
postbox, pillar box	mailbox
postcode	zip code
poster	billboard
postman	mailman, mail carrier
potato crisps	potato chips
practise (verb)	practice
pram, perambulator	baby-carriage
pretence	pretense
programme (other than computer)	program
pub	bar
public toilet	rest room
pudding	dessert
pullover, jersey	sweater
pumpkin	squash
puncture (flat tyre)	flat, blow-out
purse	coin-purse
pushchair	stroller
pyjamas	pajamas
queue	stand in line
railway	railroad
railway carriage	railcar
railway station	train station
reel of cotton	spool of thread
return (ticket, journey)	round-trip
reversed charge	collect call
rise (salary)	raise
road surface	pavement
roundabout	traffic circle

route (pronounced root)	route (pronounced rowt)
routed (pronounced rooted)	routed (pronounced rowted)
rubber	eraser
rubbish	trash, garbage
saloon (car)	sedan
Santa Claus	Kris Kringle
sceptic	skeptic
schedule (pronounced shedule)	schedule (pronounced skedule)
school, college	school
secondary school	high school
Sellotape	Scotch tape
shop	store
shopping	marketing
silencer	muffler
single (ticket, journey)	one-way
singlet	undershirt
somewhere	someplace
spanner	wrench
speciality	specialty
staff (academic; college, university)	faculty
stroke (oblique)	slash
sump	oil-pan
sweet	dessert
sweets	candy
tailor-made	custom, custom-made
tap (water, indoors)	faucet
tap (water, outdoors)	spigot
taxi	cab
tea-towel	dish-towel
tennis shoes, gym shoes	sneakers
term (university, school)	semester
tights	panty-hose
timetable	schedule
tin (packaging)	can
titbit	tidbit
toll road, toll motorway	turnpike
torch	flashlight
tram, tramcar	streetcar
tramp	hobo
trilby	fedora
trousers	pants
turn-ups (trousers)	cuffs
tyre (car)	tire
underground, tube, metro (transport)	subway

underpants	shorts
up to you	down to you
verge, hard shoulder (highway)	shoulder
vest	undershirt
waistcoat	vest
wallet	billfold
walking stick	cane
wash hands	wash up
wash up	wash dishes
wellingtons (boots)	rubbers
windscreen	windshield
wing (car)	fender
zip	zipper

Appendix 2
Marketing-related business
and other terms

Many business terms are essential for efficient day-to-day marketing practice; these are given in the main body of the Dictionary. Other terms, closer to the fringe of marketing, are also used by marketers, usually at management level, when preparing marketing plans and pitching for business. Some of these are explained in this appendix.

Ad valorem *Business*
A Latin phrase, 'according to the value'. When applied to taxation or duty on goods, it denotes a calculation in proportion to the estimated monetary value of those goods.

Advice note *Business administration*
When a business activity has been carried out, a supplier may issue a document called an advice note to a client confirming that this has taken place. This is not an invoice, or a delivery note, but indicates that the supplier has carried out the instructions of the client. It is usually a prelude to the supplier's issuing an invoice for the work.

Anti-competitive practice *Business*
In March 2000 a new law came into force in the UK. The **Competition Act** is designed to protect businesses from anti-competitive behaviour. Under the new act, businesses that do not follow the new rules could face substantial fines. The government's Office of Fair Trading, long-time watchdog of business practices, is now taking even firmer control of business conduct. The previous law, 1980, affected business activities ranging from the production of products to their distribution, and also applied to services.
See Web site: www.oft.gov.uk.

Anti-dumping *Business*
Government action to prevent the dumping of goods on to its home market from another country. This embargo was applied by the European Union some years ago to products manufactured in Turkey, particularly textiles. While one can

understand that a government needs to take care of its home market, maintaining reasonable quality and price levels, anti-dumping measures tend to breed bad blood between countries and sour their trade relations. It can make export marketing difficult, particularly in the short term.

Back-hander   *Business*
A bribe. A covert payment, usually in cash (brown envelope effect) but sometimes in kind, made as an inducement to a customer or prospect in facilitating a business transaction.

Back-to-back credit   *Business*
Where a seller does not wish to make his identity known to an overseas buyer, a finance house may provide credit for a transaction between them. The finance house also does the contact work. This technique is also adopted in overt transactions. The terms of the credit reflect those of the sale.

Balance of payments   *Business, Economics*
A country's balance of credit and debit in its transactions with others. Where its credit is higher than its debit, this is called a balance of payments surplus. A government's policy towards the marketing community is often motivated by party political considerations and political ideology. In terms of an industrialized country's real marketing needs, either such a government's grasp is poor, or those needs are ignored. Under such circumstances, a country's balance of payments position can be affected by internal political strife. This is why a country's position in international trade is often in conflict with its actual needs, and the value of its currency distorted.

Barter   *Business*
A system for transacting business without using money. Products and services are exchanged on a value-for-value basis. In former times, barter was done between individuals, as is occasionally done today. It now increasingly occurs on corporate and international trading levels.

Bill of lading   *Exporting and importing, International trade*
A ship-master's consignment note, a receipt for goods he is transporting aboard his vessel. It shows, among other things, the parties to the contract, the contractual terms and the goods being shipped. Several copies are issued; for the vendor, the ship's master and the purchaser.

Capital gain   *Business, Economics*
The profit made from the sale of property or investments.

Capital intensive *Business, Economics*
Where the proportion of capital, used in an enterprise or industrial or commercial
process, is high in relation to labour used, this activity is termed capital intensive.

CIF *Exporting, Importing*
Initials for cost, insurance and freight. A condition of an exporting contract,
showing that the price to the customer includes these elements.

Closing prices *Stock market*
The price of a company's shares or stock at the close of a day's trading.

Conglomerate *Business*
A holding company with a group of subsidiaries controlled from the centre. The
essence of the term conglomerate lies in the nature of the companies in the group.
These are usually different from one another, both in structure and in their business
activities.

Cost/benefit analysis *Business planning*
A form of cost analysis applied to public projects. In this case, the social costs and
benefits, not always in financial terms, are also taken into account.

Credit *Business*
The supply of goods and services before payment is made. This kind of credit is,
in effect, an interest-free loan granted by the supplier to the customer. In the case
of bank credit, this does mean money loans, either by overdraft or sums lent
conventionally by the bank to customers.

Creditor *Business*
A person or company giving credit for money, goods or services, and to whom a
debt is owed by another.

Credit rating *Banking, Business*
A complex scoring system in which customers, individuals as well as companies,
are given points for credit-worthiness. The rating is based on the ability of a
customer to pay or repay, and his track record in this regard. Ratings can include
data based on personal income, household income, personal liabilities, age, marital
status, postcode and criminal record; and such intangibles as a customer's history
of success in business, personal reliability and probity.

JIT *Business, Manufacturing*
Acronym for **just in time**, a manufacturing technique designed to reduce stock
levels by planning to receive components or raw materials exactly when needed.
A more advanced development of JIT is **JIT 2**, where there is a closer relationship
between a manufacturer and its suppliers. Often a supplier will have its own

personnel working at the manufacturer's plant, to ensure close co-operation and continuity, and resolve daily issues promptly and efficiently.

Job lot *Merchandising, Retailing*

A quantity of merchandise, usually the unsold end of a product line, offered for disposal as a single purchase. A large retailer or distributor may dispose of a job lot to a smaller one, at an appropriately low price.

Kitemark *Controls, Standards*

The British Standards Institution's official symbol for the standard of quality in a product it has tested.

Leasing *Business, Finance*

A perfectly legal method of possessing and using business equipment without owning it. It is also tax-efficient. The lessee contracts to pay rent for the equipment in regular instalments for a specified period. When the period is up, she is given the option of returning the equipment to the lessor, or making a final payment ('balloon' payment) and becoming its owner.

Liquid assets *Business*

The cash kept aside by a company to enable it to pay its bills. It is calculated by comparing a company's assets with its liabilities, termed its **current liquidity ratio**. A further method is a comparison of a company's assets, with the value of its current stock deducted, against its current liabilities; termed its **liquid ratio**. This is important when a company's directors are considering its sale or soliciting further investment.

Liquidation *Business*

The winding up of a company, usually followed by the disposal of its assets.

Management audit *Business*

A professional, methodical study, assessment and evaluation of the management of a business or organization. This covers management personnel and their departments, together with their job descriptions and how effectively they are fulfilling them. Performance is a key characteristic of management audit; each personal and departmental function is studied and analysed in detail. A report of the audit and its findings is given to senior management, so that it can consider and implement the auditor's recommendations for improvement.

Merger *Business*

A situation in which two or more companies, corporations or organizations join together to form a single entity. Theoretically, such companies are of more or less the same size, and the merger is regarded as a 'marriage'. In reality, it is more often a takeover, with the more dominant company incorporating the weaker. Economies usually follow, with asset-stripping and with staff being laid off.

Naked   *Finance, Investment, Stock market*
An unhedged option or position, not covered, secured or backed by underlying stock, and therefore at high risk. This is because the writer of a naked option does not actually own the stock.

Net profit   *Accounting, Business*
The trading profit made by a company after all appropriate deductions have been made. Deductions include expenses such as overheads, direct costs, indirect costs, manufacturing and distribution costs, commissions to agents and others. In most cases this is the figure on which income and corporation tax liability is based. Profit before appropriate deductions is termed **gross profit**.

OEM   *Manufacturing*
Initials for **original equipment manufacturer**. These companies buy other manufacturers' products in order to make their own. Some motor vehicle manufacturers do not make their own car seats, windscreens (windshields), electric or braking systems; these are purchased from OEMs. There is a great deal of this activity among manufacturers of personal computers.

Organogram   *Corporate organization and planning*
A company's organization chart, usually including its departments and department heads, directors, management and personnel.

Price/earnings ratio (P/E ratio)   *Business*
The ratio of the price of a company's shares to its earnings, indicating how much the whole company is worth on the stock market. P/e ratio indicates the number of times needed to multiply the net earnings (post-tax profits). Thus, net assets x p/e = worth.

Price index   *Business, Economics*
A system for comparing prices at a particular time with those at another time. This enables analysts to make direct price comparisons over time. For example, if last year's price for beans was rated at zero, and this year's is 1 per cent higher, the current price is indexed at 1, relative to last year's. By next year the price may have risen a further percentage; in which case the price will be indexed at 2, compared with the first year's. Most price indices start at 100 at a specified point in time, this being the base for all future comparisons and calculations.

Reserve price *Business*

The minimum price at which a product may be offered or sold. Popularly used when auctioning an article or lot of goods. If the bidding does not reach the reserve price the lot is usually withdrawn from the auction. It may be returned to the owner or re-entered in a subsequent auction.

Tender *Business*

An application for a contract. An organization, usually a government or an institution, advertises that a substantial project is being planned, and needs a contractor to carry it out. In many cases the project is for the construction of a building complex, such as a hospital, oil refinery or housing estate. In others it can be for maintenance work or large-scale, continuing supplies of equipment and servicing to the organization and its branches. Specialist companies are invited to submit a detailed application – the tender – and to compete for the contract. The tender needs to be submitted by a specified closing date, complete with all documentation, work schedule, estimated costs and completion date. When all tenders are in, the organization selects the most viable and offers the work to the successful candidate.

Appendix 3
Marketing-related technology terms

Many terms used in information technology are either in daily use by marketers themselves, by their technology suppliers, or by marketers' own IT departments. Many of the most popular ones are given in the main body of the Dictionary. Some of the more fringe, but still useful, terms are explained here.

Algorithm   *Information technology*
A set of rules that a computer uses to solve problems, translated into a sequence of instructions.

Alpha-numeric   *Language*
A mix of letters and numbers.

Analogue   *Information technology*
'Analog' in US English. Varying continuously along a scale, rather than in fixed steps or increments. It is best described as the use of physical quantities to represent numbers. Voltage, weight and length, for example; the position of a pointer against a scale; the reaction of photographic film to light. A clock with hands and figures, in which time is represented as a continuous circle, is considered analogue. The mechanical speedometer of a car is analogue. Its ability to define fractions of kilometres-per-hour is determined by the physical size and movement of the pointer in relation to the scale. By way of contrast, a car's cyclometer or odometer is digital; it displays fractions of a kilometre only by the printed numbers on its revolving wheels.
See Digital.

AppleTalk   *Communications technology, Information technology*
A media-independent communications protocol, which enables file exchange over common network types, such as Ethernet and Apple's own proprietary, LocalTalk.

Archiving   *Business practice, E-commerce, Information technology*
The offline, long-term storage of data, which can be recalled, at full quality, on demand. Data can include artwork, video clips and invoices. Archive storage often

uses media such as tape streaming, usually considered too slow for day-to-day operations.

Auxiliary storage   *Information technology*
External magnetic or optical storage outside a computer's own internal memory.

Binary   *Computing, Information technology, Mathematics*
A counting system using base 2. In this system, only 0 and 1 are used. Thus:

Decimal	**Binary**
1	1
2	10
3	11
10	1010
20	10100
30	11110
100	1100100
200	11001000
300	100101100
1000	1111101000
2000	11111010000
3000	101110111000
Etc	

In computer technology, 1 represents positive, 0 represents negative; electrical current on and off respectively. When this system is incorporated into computer design it makes for fast calculations and data processing.

Chat   *Internet communications practice*
An Internet facility that allows a group of people to communicate simultaneously by typing messages to one another online. Everyone participating in the chat sees your message as soon as you send it. Designated chat areas are often referred to as **chat rooms**. Any individual or group you respond to in the room can contact you by e-mail.

Cookie   *Internet communications practice*
A block of text or a file, placed in a file on your computer's hard drive by a Web site you are visiting. The cookie identifies you the next time you visit the site, and is normally stored in the same directory as your Internet browser program. Cookies cannot identify an individual user specifically unless the cookie data is attached to personally identifiable information collected some other way, such as an online registration form. Cookies are normally innocuous, and usually held by remote sites for such activities as shopping. However, if a user wishes not to accept

cookies, she can prevent them being stored on her hard disk by using the options within her browser program.

CPS *Computer printers*

Initials for **characters per second**. A measure of speed, indicated by the number of characters a computer printer can print in one second.

Daisywheel *Computer printers*

A detachable printwheel containing a complete type font, with characters, numbers and symbols. This type of printer uses physical impact for getting characters on to the paper. The reproduction quality is high, usually described as **letter quality**.

DAT *Information technology*

Initials for digital audiotape, magnetic medium housed in a cartridge or cassette, capable of storing huge amounts of data. Usually used for backing-up computer data, its access speed is comparatively slow.

JPEG *Information technology, Studio techniques*

A standard for storing graphical images, in a file on disk and in compressed format. Using JPEG techniques, images take up a fraction of the disk space occupied by the same images when uncompressed. This means that they can be more economical to store and to transmit electronically, especially over a telephone line. The initials stand for **Joint Photographic Experts Group**.

Machine code *Information technology*

A language with which computers are programmed, and in which computer software is written and compiled.

Mass storage *Information technology*

Auxiliary or bulk memory, as distinct from computer memory. Disk drives and tape streamers are mass storage devices currently in universal use.

Megabyte *Information technology*

A measure of computer memory capacity, colloquially meant to represent a million bytes, but actually 1,024 kilobytes. The term also applies to the size of application software. Usually abbreviated to Mb. Kilobytes are Kb. The term is derived from the Greek, *megas*, great.

Memory *Information technology*

A hardware device into which data can be entered and retained until the computer is switched off; in which event, the data is lost. Data can be retained permanently

when transferred to a storage device. Some memory devices, usually dubbed **flash memory**, retain data when the equipment is switched off.
See Mass storage, Media.

OLAP *Information technology*
Online Analytical Process; applications that allow data to be interrogated.

Operating system *Information technology*
A suite of computer programs for controlling the operation of a computer. It performs such tasks as assigning locations in computer memory to programs, files and data, scheduling jobs and controlling the input/output of the system. MS-DOS and Unix are examples of current operating systems.

Packet switching *Information technology*
An economical way of using a data communications network. Small blocks of data, complete with destination addresses and identifiers, called packets, are independently transmitted from source computer to destination computer. They are reassembled in proper sequence at the destination.

Protocol *Communications, Information technology*
A set of rules governing the flow of information within a communication system.

Sequential access *Data storage, Information technology*
A method of retrieving computer data or instructions, by passing through all locations between the one currently being accessed and the required one. This is typically the case with magnetic tape storage, which stores data in strict sequence from beginning to end. The computer has to go through all the data on the tape from the start, until it gets to the bit you want. Naturally this is very time-consuming, compared with storage on disk or CD ROM.

Syquest *Information technology*
A form of high-volume, portable media storage for computer data. The size of the unit is 5.25 in, in various storage capacities, including 44 Mb, 88 Mb and 200 Mb.

Appendix 4
Print and production terms – still in use but going out of style

Copperplate *Print*

An intaglio printing process (*qv*), which uses copper or steel plates. The printing image is cut into the metal, either by hand or machine, or chemically etched. The sunken image is filled with ink. The paper to be used is first slightly moistened, then applied to the plate with considerable pressure. This draws the ink into the paper, producing a dense, crisp image of very high quality. The surface of the paper ends up slightly embossed on the printed surface, with a slightly dented impression on the back.

Copperplate printing used to be very popular for letterheads, business cards, invitations and share certificates. The advantage was the high quality of the paper and the printed image, and the status it conferred on the sender. Nowadays it is much less used, but still admired when it turns up on a letterhead or card – by those who recognize it.

Today, copper plates are used for short, high quality print runs. They are comparatively expensive to produce, and therefore best used where the budget, and the desired promotional effect, are appropriate. For longer runs, steel or chromium-plated copper plates are used. Also known as steel-die engraving.

See Blind embossing, Die-stamping, Embossing, Thermography.

Cylinder press *Print, Printing processes*

A letterpress printing press in which metal type and illustration blocks are locked up in a flat frame called a **forme** (*qv*). The paper is laid on top of the forme; the cylinder rolls across it, pressing it on to the inked type. In most modern presses of this kind the forme moves along under the cylinder. This delivers sharp, crisp, dense copies (provided, of course, that the inking, make-ready and paper are correctly set up).

See Flatbed, Forme, Letterpress, Make-ready, Plate, Pull.

Electro *Print, Production*
Short for **electrotype**. A duplicate printing plate used in hot-metal letterpress printing. The duplicate, or **dupe**, is produced from the original by electroplating. The printing surface is grown as a thin copper skin, with the body of the plate added in base metal, to bring the printing surface up to type-height. Letterpress is now little used in Europe, the USA and other industrialized countries, having been replaced by litho. However, it may still be in use in some developing countries.

Elite *Printing, Typesetting, Typography*
A unit in the measurement of type size; not used much now, having been largely replaced by scaleable type and a system of **point** sizes.
See Pica.

Flatbed *Print*
A letterpress printing press in which the printing surface is flat. This is a bed called a **forme**, which contains the metal type and illustrations. The forme passes to and fro under an impression cylinder, the paper being compressed between the two. There will not be many flatbed presses in use in the UK today; with the exception of some speciality printers, most print shops use offset litho. You may find some in developing countries.
See Cylinder press, Forme, Letterpress, Plate, Pull.

Flong *Print*
A material used in rotary letterpress printing, comprising sheets of papier mâché material for the production of stereo moulds. A stereotype, or **stereo**, is a copy of a printing forme, or a printing block. The forme is flat, but the metal printing plate required is curved. To produce a curved plate, a dampened flong sheet is positioned over the forme, and heat and pressure applied. This is done to ensure that all the detail in the forme is impressed into the flong. A stereo printing plate is produced from the flong by curving it to the arc of the plate cylinder, and casting hot metal into it. When cooled, the stereo plate is mounted on the press, and made ready in the usual way. The origin of the word is said to be French, *flan*.

Forme *Print*
In letterpress printing, a metal frame containing type, illustrations and furniture. The material within is made up into pages, and locked up solidly in a **chase** – a metal frame – ready for printing.
See Cylinder press, Flatbed, Letterpress, Plate, Pull.

Hypo *Photography. Reprographics*
The abbreviation for **sodium thiosulphate**, a chemical used in fixing the image on photo-sensitive material once it has been exposed and developed. The term is also used for **sodium hyposulphite**, which serves the same purpose in the photographic darkroom.

Letterpress *Printing processes*

A relief printing process similar to **flexography** (*qv.*), but prints from rigid, cast metal printing plates and metal type. As with flexography, ink is applied to a raised surface image and transferred by pressure to the paper or board to be printed.

In the EU and the USA, and most industrialized countries, letterpress is little used, most commercial work now being done by **offset litho**.

Points to note about letterpress

- Print quality depends on the quality of the surface of the material to be printed.
- Type-matter is composed on Monotype or Ludlow mechanical typesetting machines. This is termed hot metal setting.
- Halftones and line illustrations are made into flat plates called blocks. These are produced photographically and etched on copper or zinc.
- There are three types of press: platen, flatbed and rotary.
- Platen presses are usually small and fast, used mostly by jobbing printers for small commercial work.
- Flatbed presses produce larger page sizes, up to broadsheet newspaper dimensions.
- Rotary letterpress is web-fed, prints at high speed and uses curved metal plates.

Advantages of letterpress

- Rotary letterpress prints at high speeds.
- Economical for long runs.
- Good for line and tint work.
- Good for monochrome work and spot colour.
- Machine proofing is easy, using special small letterpress proofing presses.

Disadvantages of letterpress

- Not the ideal method for high-quality, four-colour work.
- Small type and fine-screen images are not easily achieved.
- Printing plates can be expensive.
- Make-ready is complicated, expensive and time-consuming.

Optimum and economical uses of letterpress

- small-run newspapers;
- small-run magazines;
- books and small jobbing work such as stationery.

Line block *Artwork, Plate-making, Print, Production*

A letterpress block for printing line illustrations. It is usually etched in zinc alloy with a flat, unscreened surface.

Matrix *Print, Production*
A mould from which identical duplicate printing letterpress blocks or plates are produced.

Movable type *Composition, Printing, Typesetting*
Printing, in the form practised until recent years, came to Europe in the 14th and 15th centuries. The process was accelerated by the invention of movable type by Johann Gutenberg of Mainz, a small town on the Rhine. He and his partners tried to keep it secret; but it's impossible to publish and not risk being copied.

The secret of Gutenberg's movable type is this: individual type characters of metal are cast in individual moulds. The type is set up for articles and books, which are then printed. The typeset pages are broken up, and the type distributed into alphabets ready to be used again. Before Gutenberg, this was virtually impossible, because the technology was unknown or undeveloped. Gutenberg developed movable type technology, so that books could be produced *in commercial quantities!* A goldmine for those who possessed the secret.

Gutenberg published the Mazarin Bible circa 1450. By 1470, the secret had hit the streets of Europe, with Nicholas Jensen, a Venetian printer, starting to design and cast movable type. By 1475 William Caxton was producing his first books in London, using movable type.

The type characters were of three kinds: capital letters, small letters, and numerals and symbols. In the composing-room, type was kept in chests of drawers, called 'cases'. Capitals were housed in one drawer, small letters and numerals in another. The drawers were organized into compartments. Usually the cases were stacked, the capitals cases on top of the cases containing the small letters. The compositor assembled lines of type by hand, and fast composing needed easy access to capitals and small letters. Following the author's manuscript, the compositor would dip into the upper case for the capitals, and into the lower one for the small letters. Capitals soon came to be known as upper case, small letters lower case.

Quad *Print, Typesetting, Typography*
In hot metal composition, blank spacing material lower than type-high, used for filling out lines of type.

Quarto *Paper, Print*
A paper size obtained by folding a standard sheet twice, then cutting it into four smaller sheets.

Quire *Paper*
A traditional term for a twentieth of a ream. A ream is 480 sheets; a quire, 24 sheets.

Routing *Print, production*
In letterpress plate-making, the physical cutting away of the non-printing areas of a plate. Pronounced as in **rout**.

Shrdlu *Typesetting*
The first six characters of a hot-metal typesetting machine keyboard in pre-computer times. The current keyboard configuration for English language computers and typewriters is **qwerty**.

Stereo *Pre-press, Print, Production*
The short form for **stereotype**. In hot-metal printing, a lead-alloy printing plate, usually a duplicate of a copper or zinc original, cast from a mould of the original. The technique is used in letterpress printing and, like letterpress, not now much used in industrialized countries.

In flexographic printing, a flexible plate on which the relief image of one colour of a design has been produced. Usually made of rubber, neoprene or other super-tough material, these stereos are often termed **plates** or **stamps.**

VDU *Information technology, Computing, Desktop publishing, Word-processing*
Visual display unit. A fancy and somewhat outdated name for a computer monitor and its screen. See my comments on abbreviations under VCR.

Zincography *Print technology*
A technique for engraving on zinc plates, mostly used in letterpress printing. The non-printing areas are etched away with acid.